praise for

SPINNING THE GLOBE

"Green, whose previous books include *Before His Time* and *The Soldier of Fortune Murders,* captures the drama and conflicts of this rags-to-riches-to-rags-to-riches story, and his descriptions of some of the Globetrotter games (against their onetime black archrival, the New York Renaissance, and against college all-star teams) give the reader the sense of being there. . . . Green puts readers on the road with the Trotters, through good times and bad, and draws us into the Magic Circle."

—Ira Berkow, *New York Times Book Review*

"Green has written an ambitious, engaging book on the history of the team."

—*Black Issues Book Review*

"Green's straightforward but respectful approach carries over into a balanced handling of the 'minstrel show' reputation that dogged the Globetrotters almost from the beginning, as well as a brief account of the team's modern revival after being bought by a former player. The overall effect of this vividly rendered history is to make readers wish they could see the Globetrotters it describes in action."

—*Publishers Weekly*

"This book title is the first complete history of the Globetrotters ever assembled under one cover. It describes a team that played for fun and frolic (and still does to this very day), bringing the game of basketball within a fun-filled family setting. . . . Comedian Bill Cosby, an official one-dollar-a-year contract player for the Globetrotters, provided the foreword to this informative book."

—*Accessibly Live Off-Line*

"Green's historical look at the Globetrotters flows naturally and isn't just for sports fans. This historical account eloquently explains the perseverance of the Globetrotters despite all obstacles. Readers will feel like they are riding in the back of owner and coach Abe Saperstein's Model T with the Globetrotters traveling from game to game."

—Scripps Howard

"When you pick up this book, you might think that it's only about the Harlem Globetrotters, but that's not all you'll find inside. Author Ben Green dribbles a lot of history in with the Globetrotters' story, and his descriptions of small-town Depression-era America are so vivid that you almost feel like you were there last week. . . . *Spinning the Globe* is a sure shot."

—Terri Schlichenmeyer, *Bookworm Sez*

"Green's [*Spinning the Globe* is a] definitive, myth-shattering, 414-page biography about the Harlem Globetrotters—the first authorized book about the world-famous basketball team that revolutionized the game."

—*Tallahassee Democrat*

*The Rise, Fall, and
Return to Greatness of the
Harlem Globetrotters*

★

BEN GREEN

★ SPINNING

★★★ *the* ★★★

GLOBE

SPINNING

★★★ *the* ★★★

GLOBE

HARPER

NEW YORK ∙ LONDON ∙ TORONTO ∙ SYDNEY

For Daddy,
always my number-one fan,
whom I still miss every day.
And for Goose Tatum,
the greatest Trotter of them all.

★

"Here Interred Lies the Remains of the Man Sambo," on pp. 348–49, from *Sambo: The Rise and Fall of an American Jester,* by Joseph Boskin, copyright © 1986 by Joseph Boskin. Used by permission of Oxford University Press, Inc.

A hardcover edition of this book was published in 2005 by Amistad, an imprint of HarperCollins Publishers.

HarperCollins books may be purchased for educational, business, or sales promotional use. For information, please e-mail the Special Markets Department at SPsales@harpercollins.com.

First Amistad paperback edition published 2006.

Designed by Renato Stanisic

Library of Congress Cataloging-in-Publication Data

Green, Ben, 1951–
    Spinning the globe: the rise, fall, and return to greatness of the Harlem
Globetrotters / Ben Green.
      p. cm.
    Includes index.
    ISBN-13: 978-0-06-055550-4 (pbk.)
    ISBN-10: 0-06-055550-5 (pbk.)
    1. Harlem Globetrotters—History. I. Title

  GV885.52.H37G74   2006
  796.323'64097471—dc22

               2005055860

---

19 20 21 22 BVG/RRD   20 19 18 17 16 15 14 13 12 11

Contents

★

Foreword
by Bill Cosby

★

I was eleven years old when the Harlem Globetrotters defeated the NBA's Minneapolis Lakers for the first time, in 1948. As a budding basketball fan growing up in Philadelphia, I remember the result being exciting news, yet I could not yet grasp the great cultural ramifications this unexpected victory of an all-black basketball team over an all-white, World Championship team would create in the years that followed. While mainstream, professional sports were still predominantly a foreign land to African Americans in the 1940s, holes were beginning to appear in the dike. The Globetrotters' win over the Lakers, combined with Jackie Robinson's headfirst slide over the color barrier in baseball, gave blacks a solid one-two punch against the cultural restraints that had previously bound them in the sports world. The Globetrotters showed the world that blacks could compete with whites on the basketball court, and do so in a way that entertained as well as inspired. The NBA was paying attention. Soon thereafter, Globetrotter Nat "Sweetwater" Clifton became the first African American to sign an NBA contract, joining the New York Knicks in 1950, with many others soon to follow.

Since that landmark day in 1948, the Globetrotters and I have crossed paths several times. I am very proud to have had a role in breaking another color barrier that had existed in prime-time network television. Despite uneasiness by NBC executives, and threats of boycotts by a few southern affiliates, I was chosen to costar in the weekly television series *I Spy* in 1966. Thanks to the Globetrotters and forward-thinking television producers like *I Spy*'s Sheldon

Leonard, America now had examples in both sports and entertainment that African Americans had a place and could prosper in either realm.

The Globetrotters and I also share a love of entertaining people of all ages, making the decision to join the team on the basketball court a no-brainer. I fancied myself a decent athlete, playing football and running track at Temple. Basketball was never my strongest sport, so I was relieved to be selected to play for the Globetrotters rather than perhaps a more suitable position with the Washington Generals. I signed a lifetime contract with the team in 1972, which allowed me to join the team whenever our respective schedules would allow. My salary at the time—one dollar a year—made me perhaps one of the few athletes in history to be paid what he was actually worth. But following the lead of many contemporary athletes, I held out for the big money in 1986, refusing to play for anything less than $1.05. Reluctantly, but wisely, my demands were met by the Globetrotter organization, paving the way for a beautiful relationship that culminated in July 2004, with my induction as an honorary member of the Naismith Memorial Basketball Hall of Fame in Springfield, Massachusetts. The Globetrotters helped design a commemorative locker for the occasion, complete with my old jersey, photos and other mementos of my Globetrotter career. I have been blessed to win many awards during my career, but to be recognized by my peers in another field that I enjoyed, but was never considered quite as proficient in, was a great feeling.

The Harlem Globetrotters have given millions of people around the world those same good feelings over their seventy-nine-year history. They are a true American success story that embodies everything positive about American culture—a true "rags to riches" example of a team overcoming the racial, economic, and logistical obstacles that stood in their way, solely because of their love of basketball and a desire to make people smile. Even today, after conquering all that stood in their way, the Globetrotters are working harder than ever to play more games, visit more countries, and bring their message of peace, tolerance, and goodwill to more and more people around the world. They capture everything positive that sports *can* be. A Globetrotters game is not a place to boo, curse at the referee, or demean your opponent with taunts and threats, but it is where positive values are demonstrated and taught, where laughter and applause fill the air as the Globetrotters demonstrate that sports are about having fun and enjoying yourself—whether on the court or off.

While the Harlem Globetrotters are legendary performers, known in every corner of the globe as the greatest entertainers in sports, the story of how the team came to be is just as entertaining and important as the way they play the game. In *Spinning the Globe: The Rise, Fall, and Return to Greatness of the Harlem Globetrotters*, author Ben Green takes us on a journey on which few have ever embarked. This book stands as the first definitive tale of the history of the Harlem Globetrotters. From touring the Midwest in Abe Saperstein's Model T in the 1920s to becoming a global phenomenon, to the brink of bankruptcy, to a rebirth under the guidance of Mannie Jackson, Green tells a story through the eyes of those involved that will entertain you, shock you at times, and, of course, make you laugh out loud.

I treasure my relationship with the Harlem Globetrotters and team owner, Mannie Jackson. I am sincerely grateful for all the work they have done for the betterment of people around the world. They have earned their title of Global Ambassadors of Goodwill many times over. This is their story.

CHAPTER 1

The Garden

This story begins with a song.

A pure sound of joy. One person, sotto voce, whistling a simple little melody: twelve notes in all, repeating rhythmically up and down the scale. And behind the whistle, carrying the beat, a lone, mysterious percussionist—it could be fingers snapping or rhythm sticks, but it's actually *bones,* a pair of flat rib bones from a cow or a hog, clacking together, driving the tune.

The song wafts across the arena where we are sitting, waiting eagerly for what we know will come. This scene could be happening in any of a hundred arenas in a hundred different towns, from a high school gym in Sheboygan or the Boilermakers Union hall in Yakima to the Cow Palace in San Francisco, but we are actually in Madison Square Garden—the *old* Garden at Fiftieth Street and Eighth Avenue—in New York City.

It could also be any year of the past seventy-five, but tonight is January 1, 1950. New Year's Day. The beginning of the postwar decade and the halfway point of the century. It's a Sunday night, just before seven P.M. Eighteen hours earlier, 750,000 people thronged Times Square to ring in the New Year, clogging the streets between Forty-second and Forty-seventh Streets with the largest crowd in local memory, attributed partly to the bearably chilly temperatures. The city—indeed, the entire country—is in a celebratory mood, having finally sloughed off the lingering shortages of the war years, and the economy is ramping up toward a decade of unprecedented prosperity. It was a wild, joyous New Year's Eve. Midnight revelers cheered as the white ball on the Times Tower descended down its flagpole, Manhattan nightclubs reported a brisk business, the ever-alert news photographers with their Speed Graphic cameras snapped the duke and duchess of Windsor dancing at the Sherry-Netherland Hotel, and those seeking a more solemn beginning to the year had pilgrimaged to St. Patrick's Cathedral, where Francis Cardinal Spellman led a midnight pontifical Mass.

This evening, the Garden is packed with nearly 19,000 people, the largest crowd ever to watch a professional basketball game in the city. A standing-room-only sellout. Earlier this afternoon, there was a near riot at the box office after the standing-room-only tickets sold out in fifteen minutes and 7,000 disappointed fans were turned away; a special detail of New York's Finest had to be called out to calm the angry crowd.

Fans that come to see the New York Knicks are habitually late, often straggling in halfway through the first quarter, but *this* crowd was here thirty minutes early, knowing that the best part of the evening will happen *before* the game. It's a family crowd: Mom and Dad and the whole nuclear gaggle of kids, and three generations in some cases, with Grandma and Grandpa along for the night, and all of them scrubbed squeaky clean and dressed in their Sunday best. The men are in suits and ties, the women in the calf-length skirts that are the fashion of the day. There's an air of giddy anticipation, much as there was in Times Square last night, and a murmur of excitement ripples through the stands as everyone waits for what they know is coming.

And then it begins—the whistle and the bones.

The lights come up and five tall, graceful men jog out onto the floor, dressed in white silk warm-up jackets that every boy in the arena covets as soon as they see them. The men are led onto the court by the two most acclaimed basketball players in the world: Marques Haynes, who does things with a basketball that no one has ever done, and Goose Tatum, the Clown Prince of Basketball, a talented and temperamental comic genius. The players are introduced one at a time, to thunderous applause, then form a circle around the foul line and start passing a ball, whipping it behind their backs, between their legs, faster and more expertly than these fans have ever seen. They roll it up one arm and down the other, spin it off their fingertips, feint one way and flick it the other, bounce it off their heads, their behinds, their chests. And the song is driving it all, that whistle and the bones.

By now, the spectators can't help themselves, it's physically impossible—their feet are tapping. Entire families tapping in unison. Dad's spit-shined brogans, perhaps almost imperceptibly, but tapping nonetheless; Mom's black pumps, with quiet decorum; and Junior's stinking Converse All-Stars, which should have been thrown out with the trash weeks ago. All tapping. Some in the crowd are humming, too. They have no idea of the words to the song. There may not even *be* any words to this song, except for the only three that matter, and they sing them under their breath at the end of each line:

"Sweeeet Georgia Brown"

This song can mean only one thing: the Harlem Globetrotters★ are in town and we are going to have the time of our lives. The song is like a Rorschach test for American culture. There is no two-headed dog in the picture, no repressed sexual memories, no oedipal urges. There is only one message: the Harlem Globetrotters make people happy.

The crowd is mesmerized, their eyes riveted on the court, as the players weave a spell of enchantment over the Garden. The one person *not* watching the Magic Circle is the team's owner, Abe Saperstein, who is standing in front of the Globetrotters' bench and, by force of habit, scanning the stands, expertly counting the house. It is a skill honed over twenty-five years—a necessity in leaner days as protection against disreputable promoters and vanishing gate receipts, but even now, when he no longer has to worry about the gate, a habit that refuses to die.

Abe Saperstein is the most incongruous figure that one could conjure up to be the owner of this team. He and his players are a juxtaposition of opposites, as different as any human beings could be. It goes far beyond the obvious, that the players are black and Abe is white—a London-born son of Polish Jews who immigrated to

---

★ *A note on spelling: until approximately 1947, Globe Trotters was generally spelled as two words, and I have followed that convention throughout the book.*

America when he was five. Where the players are lithe and tall (most are well over six feet), Abe is embarrassingly short, barely five foot three, and so squat and round that he looks like a bowling ball in a suit. In his youth, Abe was something of an athlete himself, and until the mid-1930s served as the Trotters' lone substitute, wearing a basketball uniform under his suit, but his athletic days are long behind him and no artifacts remain. While his players are the epitome of style and grace, whether in their uniforms or in their off-duty tailored suits and fedoras, Abe is perpetually dressed in high-water pants held up by suspenders *and* a belt, in a rumpled black suit that some players suspect is the only one he owns.

Yet Abe Saperstein has overcome his physical limitations with boundless drive and ambition, a ferocious work ethic, uncanny relationship skills, and an all-encompassing marketing vision constrained only by the boundaries of space and time. His promotional genius is an impregnable force of nature that will not be limited by geography, national borders, riots and revolutions, a Babel of foreign tongues and dialects, monetary exchange rates, rain, wind, blizzards, or acts of God. Whether indoors or out, day or night, in a desert or a deluge, traveling by car, rail, plane, or camel, he will find a way to put on a game. If space travel to the moon were available, Abe Saperstein would have the Harlem Globetrotters on the first ship. He is a complicated, multilayered personality—a pioneering humanist to some (the Abe Lincoln of basketball) and a racist huckster to others, the purveyor of a demeaning minstrel show for whites.

Nonetheless, this much is indisputable: from their humble beginnings in the late 1920s, the Harlem Globetrotters have risen to become the most successful basketball team in America. In the beginning, it was just five black players and a stumpy Jewish guy in a rattletrap Model T, barnstorming across the American heartland, playing obscure whistle-stops and tank towns that no one else would play—Owatonna, Wahpeton, Cut Bank, and Plentywood—where no hotels would house them, no restaurants would feed them, and service stations wouldn't let them use the bathroom or the phone, playing seven nights a week and twice on Sundays, taking on all comers, from the local brake factory team to the smart-aleck college kids, and kicking the white boys' asses—not just beating them, but making fools of them in the process, leaving the crowd laughing in their wake—traveling 40,000 miles a year in the dead of winter, in Montana, Minnesota, and the Dakotas, winning 95 percent of their games and still barely getting by, going hungry on many nights, driving 200 miles to find a black-owned boardinghouse or a family that would take them in. The Harlem Globetrotters were not just a great barnstorming team; they were a sociology class on wheels, bringing black hoops and black culture to a hundred Midwestern towns that had seen neither, and in the process transforming Dr. James Naismith's stodgy, wearisome game—which was still sometimes played in chicken-wire cages by roughneck immigrants with flailing elbows and bloodied skulls, a sport more resembling rugby—into an orchestration of speed, fluidity, motion, dazzling skill, and, most improbably, inspired comedy.

Tonight is a landmark in that slow rise to glory. This is the Globetrotters' first game in Madison Square Garden, the Mecca of American sports. For a decade, Abe has been begging to play the Garden, but has been relegated to smaller venues around the city—the Sixty-ninth Regiment Armory or the Westchester County Center in White Plains. But tonight, as "Sweet Georgia Brown" and the Magic Circle transport the crowd to heights of wonder and delight, Abe Saperstein can bask in the knowledge that he has finally reached the mountaintop, the "Broadway of sports"—the Garden. And after the box office mayhem that occurred this afternoon, the Garden will now be begging *him* to return. What's more, this game marks another milestone: it's being filmed by Paramount News for its weekly newsreel—"The Eyes and Ears of the World"—which will be seen by millions of moviegoers around the country.

It goes without saying that the Globetrotters are the most popular basketball team in the United States; that is the *least* of their accomplishments. No other basketball team at any level, amateur or professional, even comes close. The owners of the fledgling National Basketball Association are constantly pleading with Abe to play doubleheaders with NBA teams, just to draw a crowd. Tonight, in fact, the New York Knicks will play the "feature game" against the Philadelphia Warriors but, as Dick Young will make clear in tomorrow's *Daily News,* "Nineteen thousand fans certainly weren't there to see the Knickerbockers and Warriors."

No, the Globetrotters have transcended basketball; they are now, arguably, the most popular American sports franchise of any kind, rivaled only by the New York Yankees. But it goes deeper than that: "Sweet Georgia Brown," the Magic Circle, Goose Tatum's hook shot, and Marques Haynes's dribbling are embedded in American sports imagery, right alongside Joe DiMaggio's silky swing, Jackie Robinson's stealing home, or Joe Louis dropping Max Schmeling with a stiff right. By tomorrow morning, kids on school-yard courts all over the city will be throwing blind hooks from the foul line, dribbling on one knee, and tossing behind-the-back passes to their friends as they imitate the Trotters' famous weave, inevitably drawing screams of protest from their coaches. In truth, the Globetrotters are more accessible to the average fan than other sports heroes. None of us can hit a fastball like DiMaggio, steal home like Jackie Robinson, or throw a right with the power of Joe Louis, but every kid in America who has ever picked up a basketball has tried to dribble like Marques and shoot Goose's hook. We have *all* been Globetrotters.

But there is more. The Globetrotters are not just the most popular basketball team in America, and certainly the most entertaining; they also may be the best. In the past two years they have staked their claim to that title, beating the NBA's best team, the Minneapolis Lakers, twice in a row in head-to-head showdowns. Prior to the first game, in February 1948, the conventional wisdom among the nation's sportswriters, not to mention the cold cash laid down with America's bookies, was that the Trotters didn't stand a chance. No bunch of "sepia clowns" could stand up to the Lakers' six-foot, ten-inch center, George Mikan, the most dominating big man in the game. But the Globetrotters played the Lakers straight-up, ran them off their feet in the second half, and won on a last-second shot. That win was dismissed as a fluke, but the Trotters did it again the following year, winning by four points, and this time even "put on the show"—beating Mikan and then dancing on his grave. All over America, black families raised up the Trotters as heroes to the race.

When the Magic Circle ends, the Trotters and their opponents, the New York Celtics (descendants of the Original Celtics, a storied franchise), go through a *standard* warm-up, shooting layups and set shots, and then the game begins. After what we've just witnessed, the game itself feels almost anticlimactic, but not for long. This Globetrotter team is more than just Goose and Marques, as Abe Saperstein still has a monopoly on the best African American players in the country. There's Nat "Sweetwater" Clifton, a six-foot-seven giant who snatches opposing shots out of the air with one hand, and whom the Knicks have been coveting for years; Ermer Robinson, a remarkable outside shooter, whose last-second bomb beat the Lakers; player-coach Babe Pressley, the "Blue Ox," a fierce defenseman and rebounder; and behind them fresh young talents like Frank Washington, Vertes Zeigler, Bobby Milton, and Wilbert King. Abe Saperstein is an inveterate salesman who has been telling sportswriters for twenty years that every year's squad is "the best team I've ever had," but this year it may be true.

For the first few minutes, the Trotters play it straight and race out to an early lead. Then it's time for the show, and Goose takes center stage. From his spot "in the hole" he directs the Trotters' weave, kicking the ball out to shooters on the wings or backdoor cutters on their way to the hoop. Despite his Jekyll and Hyde personality, Tatum is a true genius on the court and has originated most of the Trotters' gags, or reams. Lanky, loose-limbed, with an eighty-four-inch wingspan, he can crack up his own teammates just by walking across the floor. He has impeccable timing and an inventive streak that allows him to come up with new gags nearly every night. No one, including his teammates, knows what Goose might do. He hides the ball under his jersey, bounces it off a defender's head, then throws up that hook, without looking, and is already strutting down the court when it drops through the net. There will be other great showmen in the Globetrotters' pantheon, but Goose is the greatest of them all.

Then it's Marques Haynes's turn. Almost single-handedly, he has revolutionized ballhandling and dribbling. Blindingly quick, with an unstoppable running one-handed push shot, Haynes can immobilize an entire opposition team, making star athletes look like saps and fools. Tonight, the other Trotters clear the lane and Haynes takes over, dribbling around and through the entire Celtics team. He bounces the ball as high as his head, then six inches off the floor, then while on his knees, and, impossibly, even lying on the floor. The Celtics players double- and triple-team him, lunging for the ball, but never get close. Marques is a bona fide artist, creating a distinctive style of ballhandling that will inspire generations to come and eventually develop into "Showtime." New York fans are savvy and knowledgeable about the game, not easily impressed, but when Marques finishes they afford him the "greatest ovation ever given to a basketball player in the Garden." An unassuming, gracious man, Marques acknowledges the cheers with a slight nod; then it's back to business.

Tonight's game in the Garden is a watershed not just for Abe Saperstein, but for the players, too. After all the years of playing in backwoods gyms and backwater towns, the long nights and endless bus rides, the cold burgers handed out the back doors of filthy slophouses, they finally have the chance to showcase their talents in the Garden, in New York, and on Paramount News all over the land. To the players, the most important thing about being a Globetrotter is not the gate receipts or the comedy routines or the acclaim of the fans, but the game itself. Goose Tatum is a great clown, but the other Trotters see themselves as *ballplayers.* This is *their* game, and they love it so much that some will do it for almost nothing, taking whatever salary Abe offers, just to have the chance to play.

For young African American ballplayers across the country, the Harlem Globetrotters are still their highest aspiration. It has been three years since Jackie Robinson broke the color line in major league baseball, yet professional basketball is still lily-white. After tonight, a skinny sixteen-year-old in Wilmington, North Carolina, named George Meadow Lemon will view the Paramount newsreel and decide that this is *his* dream, to be a Trotter. And another young black man, Mannie Jackson, in Edwardsville, Illinois, will be inspired by the Globetrotters to meld his brains and athletic skills to carve out his own path in the world.

Although tonight's game is testimony that the Harlem Globetrotters have reached the summit, Abe is far from satisfied. From his vantage on the floor of the Garden, he can see the promised land spread out before him, the welcoming Jordan River and the fertile valleys of Canaan, and he is determined to cross over to the other side.

He has every reason to feel optimistic. The Globetrotters are riding the crest of a wave of national optimism: the war is over, the ghosts of the Great Depression are finally entombed, and the conversion to a peacetime economy has unleashed an economic boom. There are new factories, new consumer products, and millions of new babies who Abe hopes will one day be begging their parents to take them to see the Trotters. Economists are predicting that retail sales in 1950 will surpass the all-time record, set just two years earlier, propelled by the sale of new cars, homes, and television sets (which will double from 3.2 million to 7 million in the next two years). New suburban communities, like Levittown, are being built for the emerging middle class. New gadgets and household appliances are flooding the stores, bringing ready-to-cook and frozen foods to harried American housewives and dripless paint and non-skid stepladders to former GIs turned weekend warriors. Looking out at this crowd tonight, in their Garden finery, Abe knows they have money in their pockets—*discretionary income*—to spend. He remembers when the whole country was flat busted, when Globetrotter tickets went for a dime or a quarter, and gate receipts were less than a hundred bucks. He is no economist, but he is a promoter par excellence and knows that his time has come.

He is already brimming with bold new schemes and grand promotions that, in the next two years, will carry the Globetrotters to an *international* stage—transcending not just basketball but sports altogether, making the Harlem Globetrotters the most successful entertainment franchise of any kind in the world.

The Globetrotters' popularity is skyrocketing so quickly that he has turned down three hundred booking requests this season alone, so he's put a second Globetrotter squad on the road—the western unit, which will play the small-town circuit that got Abe to where he is today—thereby freeing up the "Big Team," the eastern unit, with Goose and Marques, to hit the larger markets. The two units will play a combined 247 games this season and 334 games next season, by which time the Harlem Globetrotters will be a year-round operation. In 1954, he'll add two additional squads—the southern unit and a short-lived northern unit—so that four Globetrotter teams will be simultaneously traversing the globe.

In April, he'll unveil one of his most brilliant ideas: the College All-Star Tour, a three-week transcontinental series matching the Globetrotters against the top college All-Americans, playing a different city every night, setting new world records for attendance, and dwarfing the NCAA or NIT tournaments. In May, before his players have caught their breath following the College All-Star games, they'll be off to Europe, making the first of thirty-three consecutive European tours, and soon to South America, Asia, and Africa, where they'll play before popes and sultans, in bullrings and palaces, spreading the game of basketball around the world, and, at the request of the U.S. State Department, becoming one of America's most effective propaganda weapons in the cold war. As admired as the Trotters are in America, their popularity abroad will far exceed it; in the United States they are celebrities, but overseas they will be treated as kings. This rags-to-riches story is so appealing, so *American,* that Hollywood has come calling, and a movie is already in the works that will bring the Harlem Globetrotters to the silver screen.

So on this night, New Year's Day 1950, Abe Saperstein and the Globetrotters are poised on the brink of becoming a worldwide phenomenon. Yet despite the air of rosy optimism in the Garden, all is not well, either for the country or for Abe. In the past few months, the Western powers have been staggered by a portentous one-two punch from the Communist world: the Soviet Union exploded its first atomic bomb, setting off nightmarish doomsday scenarios of thermonuclear war; and then Mao Tse-tung's Red Army overran mainland China, chasing Chiang Kai-shek into the sea, and Mao declared the world's largest country the "People's Republic of China." Exulting in the triumphs of socialism, New Year's revelers in Moscow's Red Square last night hailed the dawn of a "Century of Communism."

For Abe Saperstein, seismic forces are also at work below the surface, forming imperceptible fissures in the foundation of his empire. At this, his greatest moment, when the entire world seems to be waiting to be conquered, he is even now beginning to lose control, and those seismic forces will eventually push the Globetrotters to the brink of ruin.

Most ominously, in June 1950, the NBA will break the color line by drafting the first black ballplayers in its history, and three of the signees—Chuck Cooper, Sweetwater Clifton, and Earl Lloyd—will all have been in Globetrotter uniforms before the draft. Ironically, the

Globetrotters' two victories over the Lakers may have been the final wedge to break down the Jim Crow barriers in professional ball, yet the one person in America who stands to lose the most from the integration of the NBA is Abe Saperstein. In the next few years, he will lose his best players and his greatest stars, and a whole new generation of young African Americans who have come of age during World War II will demand more money and more respect from "Uncle Abe." The rumblings of the civil rights movement are still faint, barely audible in the distance, but in another four years, in the upsurge of the *Brown* decision and the Montgomery bus boycott, Abe Saperstein and the Harlem Globetrotters will be pulled inexorably into that swirling vortex, will come under stinging attacks, from blacks and whites alike, for being Uncle Toms and Sambos, Stepin Fetchits in short pants.

So tonight's game at the Garden is a watershed moment in many ways. These 19,000 people here tonight are having a glorious time, yet none of them has any idea of the years of struggle that it took the Globetrotters to get here. None of them knows the stories of the great ballplayers from the 1930s, men like Inman Jackson and Runt Pullins, who carried the team through blizzards and hailstorms to reach this summit. All the fans know is what they see before them, but none of them know, and few care, about the history of black America in general or the history of black basketball that these men represent. In another fifty years, another crowd in a new Garden will be cheering for other great African American ballplayers—like Julius Erving and Magic Johnson and Michael Jordan and Shaquille O'Neal—but how many of those people will have ever heard of Goose Tatum or Marques Haynes? All they will know is what they see before them, self-contained and absolute: "This is all there is."

In truth, there is a chain of memory that connects all of those players together. It is a chain that leads back here, to the Garden, and to the story of a team whose history spans eighty years and millions of miles. It is a story with all the elements of great drama: struggle and hardship, triumph and tragedy, decay and rebirth.

And it all begins a long, long way from Harlem. . . .

CHAPTER 2

Chicago

Chicago was a town where nobody could ever forget how the money was made. It was picked up from floors still slippery with blood, and if one did not protest and take a vow of vegetables, one knew at least that life was hard, life was in the flesh and in the massacre of the flesh—one breathed the last agonies of beasts. . . . But in Chicago, they did it straight, they cut the animals right out of their hearts—which is why it was the last of the great American cities, and people had great faces, carnal as blood, greedy, direct, too impatient for hypocrisy, in love with honest plunder.

NORMAN MAILER,
MIAMI AND THE SIEGE OF CHICAGO

It seems more than coincidental that the greatest barnstorming team in the world began in the greatest crossroads city in America. No, not New York. And certainly not Harlem. The Harlem Globetrotters are not from Harlem; they have never been from Harlem; they have nothing to do with Harlem. In truth, if they *were* from Harlem, they might never have become globetrotters. People have always been drawn to New York because of its intrinsic appeal, its magnetism as a commercial and cultural center. They come to New York to stay. But the history of Chicago is a story of transport, of moving through on the way to somewhere else.

Chicago developed as a transit point for people and products. It was not a place where anyone came to live, and those who ended up there never intended to stay. Indeed, Chicago may have had the most inauspicious origin of any city in the world. There was no inherent reason to found a city: no safe harbor, no natural resources, no navigable river or alluring geographic features. It was just a muddy portage between two lethargic rivers: the Chicago and the Des Plaines, which ultimately reached the Mississippi. The Potawatomi Indians named it "stinking onion" and refused to live there. French trappers passed through quickly, their canoes loaded with beaver pelts, on their way to New Orleans. For most of the year, it was a colossal mud hole.

But by the late 1600s, French explorers and missionaries—most notably Joliet, Marquette, and La Salle—recognized its potential. If the portage could somehow be bridged, the two great waterways of North America, the Great Lakes and the Mississippi, would be connected, creating a 3,500-mile link between the West and the East. And Chicago would become, in La Salle's words, "the gate of empire, the seat of commerce" for the entire continent. In the 1830s, resolute Yankee speculators determined to make that happen.

First, the Potawatomis were forced out, after their chiefs, staggeringly drunk, signed a treaty that removed them to western lands "too poor for snakes to live upon." Thousands of Irish immigrants were then recruited to dig the Illinois and Michigan Canal, a 100-mile ditch across a disease-ridden swamp. It was a brutal, Herculean task that killed a thousand workers in 1838 alone. The Irish were reviled as "drunken, dirty, indolent, and riotous," and would have likely moved on when the canal was finished except that many were paid in land, so they had no choice but to stay, creating an Irish enclave on the south bank of the river.

When the canal opened in 1848, Chicago immediately became a way station for pioneers heading west and farm products heading east. That same year witnessed the arrival of the first railroad, telegraph line, steamship, and Cyrus McCormick, who built a factory to produce his mechanical reaper. Ten years later, the city's population had nearly tripled, and Chicago was the largest rail, grain, and lumber center in the world. The opening of the Union Stock Yards in 1865, which at its peak was slaughtering 25,000 hogs per day, turned Chicago into "Porkopolis."

It was still an abominable hellhole. The streets were so thick with mud that horses bogged up to their haunches, the city's garbage collectors were herds of scavenging pigs, the Chicago River ran red with blood and decapitated hogs' heads bobbed in its currents, and plank roads had to be laid over the mud to make the city's streets passable. Yet the hustlers and entrepreneurs who had congregated there refused to tolerate such impediments, whether natural or man-made. If no canal existed, they would dig one. If the Chicago River was too shallow, they would dredge it. If the city was sinking in mud, they would jack it up. If raw sewage was flowing downriver into Lake Michigan, and, ultimately, into the city's water supply, they would reverse the flow of the river. And in their greatest triumph, when the Great Fire of 1871 virtually destroyed the city, they would raise up a new one from the ashes that became a model of urban architecture—the first skyscraper city of the air.

By the late nineteenth century, tens of thousands of new immigrants were arriving each year to work in the Swift and Armour packinghouses, assemble McCormick's reapers, or build elegant Pullman sleeper cars. The first wave brought Germans, Bohemians, Swedes, Italians, Czechs, Slovaks, and Poles. Chicago soon became the most segregated city in the country—by ethnicity, not race—with violent repercussions for those who strayed into the wrong neighborhood. Over 300,000 people were packed into wretched slums, which Upton Sinclair described shockingly in *The Jungle*. An English journalist visiting Chicago in 1896 called it the "cesspool of the world!"

Still, they kept coming.

In 1907, five-year-old Abe Saperstein arrived in the Windy City from London with his mother, Anna, and three younger siblings. His father, Louis, had come a year earlier to get settled and find a job. Louis and Anna Saperstein were from Lomza, Poland, where Louis was an apprentice tailor. Neither had the benefit of much education; Louis could read and write Hebrew and Yiddish, but Anna was illiterate.

When they got married in 1900, Louis was twenty years old, which was prime draft age. Lomza was part of the Russian empire, and Jews could be conscripted into the Russian army and forced to serve for as long as twenty-five years. Draft headhunters routinely kidnapped young Jewish boys from their shtetl and shipped them off to military training in Siberia. The Russian army was so oppressive that Jewish conscripts would sometimes mutilate themselves—cut off a finger or puncture an eardrum—to avoid it. Many others fled. Two million Russian Jews, one of the largest migrations in world history, came to America between 1881 and 1924 to escape the draft and the czar's anti-Jewish pogroms.

With the draft hanging perilously over Louis's head, he and Anna decided to escape Poland while they could. On their honeymoon, they sailed to London, never to return. They settled in the Whitechapel District, the center of London's vibrant Jewish community, in a house near Flower and Dean Streets. Louis found a job in a tailor shop. By October, Anna was pregnant, and in July 1902, their first son was born: Abraham Michael. His birthday had no particular significance in London, or Lomza for that matter, but would have great resonance in his adopted land: he was born on the Fourth of July.

By 1906, there were three Saperstein children and a fourth on the way. After six years in London, Louis and Anna decided to seek greater opportunities for their growing clan. So, leaving Anna and the children behind, Louis set out for the land of opportunity, that beacon of hope to immigrants worldwide: he sailed for America.

He landed in New York, was processed through Ellis Island, and found a job in the garment district. Very quickly, however, he realized that New York was not the land of milk and honey he had imagined. The garment district was an abyss of poorly ventilated, dangerous sweatshops employing thousands of hapless immigrants.* Louis had an aunt in Chicago who wrote to him, suggesting that he move there. She even offered to let him stay with her until he could get established. Louis accepted her offer.

When he arrived in Chicago and made his way from the train station to the Jewish quarter on Maxwell Street, it was the end of a 5,000-mile journey from Lomza, yet Louis must have felt like he

---

* *The festering conditions would lead to a general strike by 20,000 garment workers in 1908. Their union won a small wage increase, but demands for increased fire safety were rejected. Tragically, three years later, a fire at the Triangle shirtwaist factory killed 146 workers, many of them young women.*

was coming home. Fifty-five thousand Eastern European Jews were packed into a teeming shtetl-like environment that looked more like the Old World than the New. There was a huge open-air market, peddlers and pushcarts jammed the streets, kosher meat markets and fish dealers were on every block, and the cries of Yiddish peddlers filled the air.

Louis moved in with his aunt on Jackson Boulevard, just north of the "Poor Jews' Quarter," then began looking for work. Nearly 70 percent of Chicago's tailors were Jewish, so jobs were scarce for new arrivals. Working conditions for those lucky enough to find jobs were appalling, as most worked twelve-hour days for six or seven dollars a week. Eventually, Louis saw a newspaper ad for a tailor on Ravenswood Avenue, on the North Side, in a predominantly German, Irish, and Swedish neighborhood. Ravenswood was eight miles from Jackson Boulevard and a world away from the Jewish ghetto. More dauntingly, the ad specified "No Jews allowed." Louis decided to apply anyway, invoking a technique used by many before him: trying to pass as a Gentile. He applied using the surname Schneider, hoping it sounded more German, and less Jewish, than Saperstein (ironically, *Schneider* means tailor in German and Yiddish). He got the job. And so, each morning Louis Saperstein, the Jewish tailor from Lomza, would leave his aunt's house on the West Side, ride the trolley to Ravenswood, and emerge as Louis Schneider, the *goy* tailor.

Although his English was halting (after six years in London, he could speak passable English, but never learned to write more than his name), he made up for that shortcoming by working hard. And he had an intuitive understanding of his craft. He could measure a customer for a suit, then make his own pattern, cut the cloth, and sew the suit.

The owner liked him. In fact, before the year was out, an astonishing stroke of good fortune befell him. The owner decided to move to California and offered to set up Louis in his own business, furnishing everything he needed for his own shop.

Soon, Louis Schneider's Tailor Shop opened its doors. He was a ladies' tailor, specializing in custom suits, skirts, and coats. In less than a year, he had gone from a raw immigrant to a business owner, an entrepreneur. America was truly the land of opportunity.

Louis sent for Anna and the children, who arrived in 1907. They moved first to a house on Roosevelt Road, four blocks north of Maxwell Street. It was an expensive and time-consuming trolley ride to the North Side, however, so they soon relocated to a house on Ravenswood Avenue, near Louis's shop. The Sapersteins were the only Jewish family in the immediate area, although their neighbors wouldn't have known it, since Louis was still masquerading as Louis Schneider. Soon, however, as his customers and neighbors got to know him, he dropped the façade: Louis Schneider's became Louis Saperstein's.

For young Abe, it was a fresh new world of wonder. He had spent the first five years of his life in London, but there was a rawness and virility to Chicago that made London seem almost bucolic. The city was a swirl of constant motion, and the noise from the streetcars and the trains that rumbled right down the middle of Ravenswood Avenue was deafening. The first automobiles were appearing on the streets, but Chicago was still powered by the horse. Horse-drawn wagons and drays were everywhere. There were watering troughs, blacksmith shops, and livery stables on every block. And young children dropped whatever they were doing to chase after the magnificent red fire engines when they thundered by, bells clanging, drawn by teams of lathered Belgian draft horses.

The Saperstein household was quickly filling up with children. There would be nine altogether: five boys (Abe, Morris, Rockmill [nicknamed Rocky], Jacob, and Harry) and four girls (Leah, Francis, Katherine, and Fay). The family was not destitute like so many of the Polish Jews on Maxwell Street, yet they still lived hand to mouth. Their biggest problem was finding a place to live. Most landlords refused to rent to a tenant with nine kids, so Louis would own up to having only three or four. That ruse would work for a few months, until the landlord caught on—"Wait, those aren't the same boys I saw yesterday"—and soon, an eviction notice would be tacked to the door. This happened over and over again; they were truly the Wandering Jews. The youngest son, Harry, born in 1913, lived in nine houses in his first seven years. "We had a helluva time staying in one place," he recalls today. He was born in a house on Clark Street, but evictions forced them into two different houses on Ravenswood, then to Robey, Giddings, and Lawrence Avenue, among others. Louis moved his tailor shop almost as much as the family, and sometimes even ran the business out of the family living room.

This perpetual movement was the leitmotif of Abe Saperstein's childhood. It was the constant backdrop—the rhythms of packing and unpacking, of pulling up stakes and moving on, of seeing new places and new neighbors. Change permeated his formative years, coursed through his blood and sinew, imprinting that restlessness at the molecular level.

All of this frenetic movement took place in a one-square-mile radius of Ravenswood, an overwhelmingly Catholic neighborhood whose parish priest was Father Bernard Shiel (later a bishop), the founder of the Catholic Youth Organization. German families were most numerous (the Steinbachs, Muellers, Muinchs, and Reinbergers), followed by Swedes and Finns (the Gustafsons, Olsons, Pikkarainens, and Bornosts), and the Irish (the Fitzgeralds, Ryans, McMannoms, and Carrs). It was a solid working-class neighborhood. Arnold Olson was a typesetter, Anthony Reinberger a chauffeur, Felix Pikkarainen a carpenter, and John Bornost was a machinist.

The Sapersteins were the prototypical immigrant family in which the parents clung to the old ways, while the children embraced American customs and values. Anna Saperstein spoke only Yiddish to her children, but they answered back in English. She couldn't read a recipe book, but she was a fabulous cook and filled their table with Old World dishes: beet soup, cabbage soup with raisins and sweet and sour sauce, chicken soup with kreplach. Louis was a domineering father and the absolute ruler of the house. Although they lived miles from the Jewish ghetto, Louis would take the kids to Maxwell Street on Saturdays to do the grocery shopping. At his favorite butcher shop, he would buy enough meat to feed a family of eleven for a week—a goose or a duck, a half-dozen chickens, and various cuts of beef—then top off the Saturday ritual by buying each child a corned beef sandwich. The Sapersteins were Conservative Jews, but seldom attended services except on the High Holidays. Louis did send the children to Hebrew School, but could not afford a bar mitzvah for Harry when he reached age thirteen.

A family photo from this period shows a strong-jawed, imposing father and a demure mother, surrounded by a troop of freshly scrubbed children. On one end, young Abe stands out. He was a teeny little guy, but his vitality fairly explodes from the old sepia-toned print—especially the smile. You can sense the energy radiating from him, and one gets the impression that he had been corralled just long enough to slick back his hair, slap on a tie, take the photo and—boom!—he was gone again.

In 1908, Abe and his sister Leah enrolled in the Ravenswood Elementary School, where they were the only Jews in their class. "We did have problems, especially at the time that we were going to school," says Leah, who is now 100 years old. As an undersized Jew in a Gentile school, Abe was a walking target with a bull's-eye on his back. He and Leah were called "dirty Jews" and "Christ killers," and little Abe had so many fights that he snuck into a boxing gym to pick up some pugilistic pointers.

Eventually, however, he discovered the one safe haven where his size and religion didn't matter: the playing field. Sports would become his refuge for the rest of his life. In 1912, he began playing basketball at the Wilson Avenue YMCA, or he'd walk two miles to Welles Park, to play basketball or baseball. He even played second base for a parochial school, although he was a Jewish kid from the public schools. "Abe was crazy about sports," says his youngest sister, Fay. "He lived for sports." The Saperstein living room became the headquarters for Abe's teammates, whom he would invite home to his mother's dinner table. Often he would go to Louis's tailor shop to practice his dribbling in front of the floor-length mirrors.

For many immigrant children, sports were a ticket to assimilation into America, and this was particularly important for Jews, to refute their prevalent image as physically weak "people of the book." Such stereotypes were espoused by prominent anti-Semites like Henry Ford, who proclaimed, "Jews are not sportsmen . . . whether this is due to their physical lethargy, their dislike of unnecessary physical action or their serious cast of mind. . . . It may be a defect in their character."

In Chicago, local settlement houses (such as Jane Addams's Hull House) and the Chicago Hebrew Institute sponsored athletic teams and "physical culture" programs to speed up the assimilation of immigrant children and prove, in the words of Chicago's *Daily Jewish Courier,* that "while we are proud to emphasize our interests in matters intellectual, we must not brand ourselves as physical weaklings." In no time, young Jewish boys from Maxwell Street were rooting for Shoeless Joe Jackson, just like other Chicago youths.

Baseball was the national pastime and, by far, the most popular sport in America. Boxing was a distant second, followed by football and horse racing, with basketball bringing up the rear. Boys from the North Side like Abe rooted for the pennant-winning Chicago Cubs, who began playing in their new Cubs Park (now Wrigley Field) in 1916. At night, they dreamed of following in the footsteps of Cubs stars like Grover Cleveland Alexander and the legendary triple-play combination of Tinkers to Evers to Chance—and they mourned for weeks when the Cubs lost the 1918 World Series to the Boston Red Sox and their sensational left-handed pitcher, Babe Ruth.

Abe Saperstein was quick on his feet and a good fielder at shortstop and second base, but he was "all field and no hit"—at 110 pounds, dripping wet, he wasn't big enough to pound the ball. Although his love for baseball never waned, he eventually gravitated to basketball, where his quickness made up for his short stature.

The baseball diamond was rooted in America's pastoral ethos, but basketball was a game made for the city, requiring only a ball and a makeshift hoop. By the turn of the century it was thriving in inner-city school yards and settlement houses. Jewish children, in particular, embraced the game so passionately that it became known as "the sport of Jews." Basketball put a premium on "the characteristics inherent in the Jew: mental agility, perception . . . imagination and subtlety," wrote Stanley Frank. "If the Jew had set out deliberately to invent a game which incorporates those traits indigenous in him . . . he could not have had a happier inspiration than basketball."

Abe Saperstein had found his sport.

As he entered adolescence, the outer edges of his personality became clear. What stood out most was his facility with words and his ability to make people like him. The boy could flat out talk. The words poured out of him in a ceaseless, irresistible stream. And people liked him.

When he was about twelve, the Clark Street movie theater sponsored a contest to elect the most popular kid in Ravenswood. Each patron entering the theater would write a child's name on his or her ticket stub and drop it in a ballot box. First prize was a two-week try-out at Chicago's Essanay Studios, a prominent silent movie studio and the onetime home of Gloria Swanson, Wallace Beery, Francis X. Bushman, Ben Turpin, and the up-and-coming Charlie Chaplin. The winner of the contest would have a legitimate shot at a movie career. On the last night, Abe was one of five finalists, each of whom had to make a speech, explaining why he should be chosen. His sister Leah wrote his speech and rehearsed him on it, but when Abe stood up in front of the crowd in the theater he was struck by a paralyzing stage fright. It may have been the only time in his life he had nothing to say. Finally, he recovered and delivered the speech perfectly. Some in the audience may have voted for him because they felt sorry for him, but when the votes were tallied he had won.

This was his chance to break free of the immigrant's shackles and live out the American dream. Who knows, with Abe's personality, he might have become a movie star. The first day of the tryouts, he rode his bike to Essanay, where he caught a glimpse of Gloria Swanson. On the second day, however, as he was crossing the Ravenswood rail-road tracks, he lost control, crashed, and broke his arm. His acting ca-reer was over before it began. Still, he had learned a lesson that would serve him well throughout life: his charm and persuasive powers could open doors to the world.

In 1916, Abe entered Lake View High School, the oldest public high school in Chicago, which was close enough to Ravenswood Av-enue to see it from the street. Here, he continued his love affair with sports, playing intramural basketball and baseball his first three years, then making the varsity in both sports his senior year. In baseball, he still couldn't hit his weight, but he was so small that no pitcher could find the strike zone when he went into his batting crouch. Years later, Abe would joke that he hit .500 for the season—he went one for two, with twenty-three walks.

During basketball season, he never made it off the bench in some early-season games, but eventually became the starting left guard on Lake View's bantamweight team. Chicago high school teams were divided into three weight classes—heavyweight, lightweight, and bantamweight (with a 115-pound limit)—so that boys like Abe didn't have to compete against bruisers twice their size.

Basketball in that era was a very different game—one that today's players and fans would hardly recognize. There was a center jump after every basket, players could dribble with two hands, and there was no rule against goaltending, no ten-second limit to bring the ball across half court, no time limit to shoot, and no three-second rule for offensive players standing in the foul lane. The standard offense consisted of slowly working the ball up the court, with players often bulling their way through the defense, as in a rugby scrum, then playing keep-away, passing the ball for long periods of time, until a teammate came open for an easy shot. If one team got ahead by two or three points, it would often go into a full-court stall to eat up the rest of the clock. Scoring was typically in the teens or low twenties; a "real barn-burner" would be if a team reached thirty points.

In March 1920, Abe's Lake View bantamweights captured the northern division of the Chicago high school league, which put them in the playoffs for the city championship. They made it to the semifinals, but lost 15–10 to the eventual champs, Lane Tech. It was the end of his high school basketball career.

At Lake View, he also got his first taste of business and promoting, as he joined the Junior Chamber of Commerce and the Boosters Club. When he graduated in June 1920, Louis and Anna and the other eight children came to the commencement exercise. The principal asked the audience to hold its applause until all of the graduates had been presented, but when Abe marched across the stage to receive his diploma, people clapped anyway. Of course, he had his own rooting section just with his family. He was the first Saperstein to graduate from high school; now he had to figure out what to do with his life.

The same month Abe graduated, his father bought the first house he had ever owned—and not by choice. The Sapersteins had been living right on Ravenswood Avenue, where rents were cheaper because few people could tolerate the noise from the trains that ran down the middle of the street. But then the inevitable eviction notice appeared on their door, and Louis could find no other place to rent in the area. They were about to be kicked out on the street, when Leah, then sixteen, found a house for sale at 3828 Hermitage Avenue, one block away. The asking price was $4,500, with a $500 down payment, which seemed like an insurmountable obstacle. "Papa had never had $500 to his name," Harry Saperstein recalls. But Louis managed to borrow the money from friends and relatives, and the house was theirs.

After fourteen years of wandering, they finally had their own home. It was also the first time they had electricity, as the house had just been converted from gas. Still, it was hardly a mansion: the house was forty years old and had four tiny bedrooms, some barely bigger than a walk-in closet. Louis and Anna claimed the downstairs bedroom, and eight children shared the three rooms upstairs. Harry, Rocky, and Morris slept together in a full-size bed. "I was the 'middle man,' " Harry recalls, with a laugh, "so I never had to worry about the covers." As for Abe, the eldest son, he ended up with no room and no bed, and was forced to sleep on the living room sofa or the enclosed front porch. For some eighteen-year-olds, not even having a bed would have been reason enough to move away from home, but Abe would live with his parents for at least another ten years.

Now that Abe had his diploma, Louis wanted him to come into the tailor shop with him, but Abe was not interested. "He was not cut out at all to be a tailor," Leah Saperstein says. "He wanted nothing to do with the tailor shop." Instead, he took a job at Schiller's Florist, delivering flower arrangements and trying to save enough money to go to the University of Illinois.★

But his heart was still in sports. That was the one thing that gnawed at him, and his dream was to be involved in sports and somehow make a living at the same time. After work, he played on an amateur basketball team, the Chicago Reds, at Welles Park, and eventually convinced the owner of Schiller's Florist to sponsor a basketball team in the Chicago industrial league, for which Abe served as player-coach. Over the next few years, he changed jobs at least two times—moving from Schiller's Florist to the Victor Adding Machine Company and then to the Chicago and Northwestern Railroad—

★ *Abe would later claim to have attended the University of Illinois for about a year, but the university has no record of his ever enrolling.*

and at each job he used his powers of persuasion to convince the bosses to sponsor basketball or baseball teams. The jobs were just an excuse to keep playing sports. And although the Saperstein family had finally put down roots, Abe seemed to have rambling in his blood, and the call of the road lured him away from home for the first time. He did some tramping around the country, hitchhiking to Washington and Oregon to pick apples and harvest wheat.

By 1926, however, he was back in Chicago, sleeping on the sofa again, and still trying to find himself. In truth, he was floundering. At twenty-four, he still had no real purpose or direction in his life, and hadn't really accomplished anything, considering all his energy and ambition. Then, he was offered a job at Welles Park, his old playground haunt. It was a city job, on the public payroll, that would include coaching the Chicago Reds, the amateur basketball team he had once played on himself. Although his dream of *playing* sports still burned as brightly as ever, by then he must have come to terms with the fact that his playing days were winding down. He had rejected his father's trade, but had no trade of his own. His hopes for going to the University of Illinois were fading fast. Since his birth in London, he had journeyed five thousand miles, had moved a dozen times around the North Side—and was it all for this? To keep beating around in dead-end jobs, playing baseball and basketball in his spare time, but getting nowhere?

He had already done some coaching, and liked it. So he decided to take the city job at Welles Park. Finally, he had settled on a vocation. Now he needed a team.

The city of Chicago began as a way station and rose to greatness on the strength of two massive waves of immigration: the arrival of hundreds of thousands of European immigrants, beginning in the late nineteenth century, and the Great Migration of 200,000 African Americans from the Deep South. The Harlem Globetrotters would be born at the confluence of those two great streams.

In the beginning, Chicago was no welcoming refuge for African Americans; in fact, the 1848 Illinois constitution specifically prohibited "Negro immigration" into the state. Freedmen escaping the

South avoided Chicago, settling farther west. At the turn of the century, African Americans comprised a mere 2 percent of the city's population. The first active recruitment of blacks to Chicago was as strikebreakers, to crush a meatpacking strike in 1904 and teamsters' strike the following year. For black workers, this was their only opportunity to enter the skilled trades, but their importation as scabs fostered deep resentment among other ethnic groups.

By 1910, Robert Abbott, founder of the *Chicago Defender,* the most popular black newspaper in the country, was actively promoting Chicago as the "promised land" for black southerners to escape the poverty, repression, and lynchings in the Deep South. America's entry into World War I, in 1917, fueled a massive expansion of Chicago's industries and, inversely, a terrible shortage of labor, as European immigration was sharply curtailed (from 1,218,480 in 1914 to 110,618 in 1918). If fear of the Ku Klux Klan and the promise of northern jobs weren't reasons enough for blacks to leave the South, the Mexican boll weevil provided another, as it cut a swath of devastation across the Mississippi Delta, forcing thousands of black sharecroppers off the land.

By 1916, the Great Migration was in full swing. Labor agents hired by the railroads and steel mills descended on southern towns, recruiting black workers with promises of guaranteed jobs and free train tickets to Chicago. In May 1917, the *Defender* launched the "Great Northern Drive," sounding the clarion call with banner headlines, photographs, and rhymed verse: "Some are coming on the passenger, / Some are coming on the freight, / Others will be found walking, / For none have time to wait." And the stampede was on. Some southern cites were so alarmed by the mass exodus that they banned sales of the *Defender,* fearing that its exhortations would drain the southern labor force. But nothing could slow the tide. Men often made the journey first, found jobs in the slaughterhouses at fifty cents an hour (more than twice the average wage of a southern farmworker), and sent for their families to join them. In 1910, Chicago had 44,000 black residents; by 1920, the number had swollen to 109,458 (a 146 percent increase), with an estimated 50,000 arriving between 1916 and 1919 alone. By 1930, the number would more than double again, to nearly 234,000.

Into this crucible of opportunity and hope, thousands of young black men, following the tracks of the Great Migration, would rise to manhood on the mean streets and school-yard courts of Chicago's South Side.

On March 7, 1907, Inman Jackson was born in Chicago to sixteen-year-old Sarah Jackson, who had left her home in South Carolina and journeyed north, like so many others, seeking a better life. Three years later, in 1910, another teenager, Rosia Pullins, also sixteen, gave birth to her first son, Albert. Unlike Sarah Jackson, Rosia was still in the South, in New Orleans, but soon she, too, would leave her family and make the long pilgrimage to the South Side. She arrived in 1915 with five-year-old Albert, who was already carrying the nickname that would stick with him throughout his life: Runt.

The two boys, Inman Jackson and Runt Pullins, were as different in size and temperament as any youngsters could be. Inman was tall and reserved, deferential, almost laconic, with an aura of dignified silence that surrounded him throughout his life. Runt was, as his nickname implies, small and as thin as a cornstalk, but he had a dynamic personality that seemed to propel him into the limelight wherever he went, just as surely as Inman Jackson sought the shadows.

Other young boys from the South followed the same migratory route. In 1916, nine-year-old William "Kid" Oliver and his younger brother Napoleon rode the Illinois Central from Bolden, Mississippi, to Chicago to join their father, who was already working as a shoeshine boy at the Morrison Hotel, in the Loop. The Oliver boys had been living with their grandmother and grandfather, an ex-slave, on a farm in Mississippi until their father sent for them. "When we got off the train at the Twelfth Street station, I was amazed at all the tall buildings and the horses pulling fire wagons," recalls Napoleon Oliver, now ninety-three. There were others: Byron "Fat" Long and Roosevelt Hudson came from Alabama; Walter "Toots" Wright from Mississippi; Agis Bray from Louisiana; and Randolph Ramsey and George Easter from Tennessee.

As more African Americans poured into the South Side, the housing situation became critical. During World War I, few new houses were constructed, so the existing structures became overcrowded and dilapidated, and the South Side deteriorated into a "festering slum." When blacks attempted to move beyond the "Black Belt" into surrounding neighborhoods, restrictive covenants were passed, white neighborhoods were "redlined," and, if that didn't stop the influx, roaming gangs of hoodlums attacked black families living on the fringes of white neighborhoods. Between 1917 and 1919, twenty-four firebombs were thrown into the homes of black families or their white landlords.

Resentment toward southern blacks came not just from whites, but from native-born Chicago blacks who feared that the unsophisticated country folk would incite additional prejudice against all African Americans. As one black educator described it: "The southern Negro has pushed the Chicago Negro out of his home, and the Chicago Negro in seeking a new home is opposed by the whites. What is to happen? The whites are prejudiced against the whole Negro group. The Chicago Negro is prejudiced against the southern Negro. Surely it makes a difficult situation for the southern Negro. No wonder he meets a word with a blow."

When they enrolled in school, southern blacks were conspicuous by their shabby clothing and halting grammar, and were often two years below grade in schoolwork. That was not surprising given the deplorable funding of public education for blacks in the South, where African American teachers were paid less than half their white counterparts, and black schools were horribly neglected and often in session only five months of the year. Even the *Defender*, the staunchest champion of the migration, published a cautionary list of "do's and don'ts" for new arrivals, including: "Don't appear on the street with old dust caps, dirty aprons and ragged clothes" and "Go clean up north. . . . In the south a premium was put on filth and uncleanliness. In the north a badge of honor is put on the man or woman who is clean."

Following the pattern established during the earlier Jewish migration, black churches, community organizations, and settlement houses sponsored recreation leagues and athletic events for black youth, hoping that sports would speed up the assimilation process. A men's basketball league was operating on the South Side as early as 1909, a church league followed in 1912, and two years later the

South Side Boy's Club and Wabash Avenue YMCA were sponsoring basketball teams that played white teams all over Chicago.

As the Great Migration continued, however, the racial lines in the city hardened, and the segregation of neighborhoods, schools, playgrounds, and beaches became fixed and irrevocable. The racial divide was less noticeable in elementary schools, as younger children seemed almost oblivious to racial differences. When Kid and Napoleon Oliver arrived from Mississippi, they enrolled in Colman Grammar School, which was about 50 percent black, with most of the white students Italians and Swedes. "I didn't know anything about prejudice," Napoleon Oliver recalls. "We all played together, ate together—all the same. We were all buddies." By high school, however, the racial lines were starkly drawn. In 1922, Wendell Phillips High School was 56 percent black, yet had only one black teacher (the lone black teacher in all of Chicago's high schools) and all school clubs were exclusively white. Sometimes, segregation turned to confrontation, even on the basketball court. In 1913, all-white Evanston High refused to play Lane Tech, whose top player, Virgil Blueitt, was black. And when another school with three black players showed up for a game at the all-white Tilden High, the white team not only refused to play but attacked the black players. "[They] got just about laid out," one of the white players said. "The white fellows weren't hurt any, but the coons got some bricks."

Already one of the most ethnically segregated cities in America, Chicago was becoming a cauldron of racial hatred and distrust, with a fault line running across the South Side. In July 1919, the fault split wide open. A stone-throwing clash between black and white youths at a Lake Michigan beach, during which a black boy drowned, escalated into a full-blown riot that swept over the city. Innocent bystanders of both races were pulled off trolley cars and beaten to death; white gangs rampaged through South Side neighborhoods, beating and shooting blacks indiscriminately; armed blacks retaliated against whites in kind; and houses in black and white neighborhoods were burned to the ground.

"My mother wouldn't let us go outside for four days," recalls Napoleon Oliver, who was nine years old at the time. "We could hear 'em shooting downtown. We'd look out the windows and see guys walking up the street with shotguns—there wasn't no law anywhere. The whites was killing everything black, and the blacks was killing everything white."

After four days of chaos, the riot was finally subdued by the state militia, but not before 38 people were killed (23 blacks and 15 whites) and 537 injured. The rioting ended, but the underlying causes of it—and the resentments toward blacks—did not.

In the wake of the riot, the African American community turned inward, creating a protective wall, almost a parallel universe, that was separate and, if not equal, at least independent of the hostile white community. The South Side created its own identity, and even its own name: they called it Bronzeville. Sports became one of the primary mechanisms for rallying together all segments of the black community—southern and northern, immigrant and native-born—into one cheering throng. On the playing fields and basketball courts, the differences between country boys from Mississippi and city slickers from Prairie Avenue quickly faded. They were all players, were all of "our group," as the *Defender* phrased it, and they were all on the same team.

In the black community, as in the white, baseball and boxing were, by far, the most popular sports. The most acclaimed black athletes in Chicago were Rube Foster, the father of Negro League baseball, and Jack Johnson, former heavyweight boxing champion, who infuriated whites with his flashy lifestyle and consorting with white women. It was on the basketball court, however, that South Side athletes would achieve their greatest triumphs in Chicago sports,

In 1922, the Robert L. Giles American Legion Post sponsored a basketball team, made up of World War I veterans from the "Fighting Eighth," an all-black unit, which compiled a 71–5 record in the Chicago city league. The Wabash YMCA and the South Side Boys' Club also fielded successful teams. But the torch for the South Side was carried most proudly by Wendell Phillips High School, which by the mid-1920s was nearly all black. Named for the famed abolitionist, Wendell Phillips became the magnet for athletic and educational achievement in black Chicago.

In 1922, when the Wendell Phillips heavyweight basketball team made it to the city semifinals, the *Defender* urged the entire South

Side to turn out to support the "red and black machine." Dr. Albert Johnson, the Phillips coach, was building a basketball powerhouse with a cadre of talented players—all of them from the South—who would eventually carry the legacy of Wendell Phillips basketball far beyond Chicago: Tommy Brookins, Randolph Ramsey, Toots Wright, Kid Oliver, Fat Long, Lester Johnson, Runt Pullins, George Easter, Agis Bray, Roosie Hudson, and many more.

In 1924, led by the "hot combination" of Brookins, Wright, and Lester Johnson, the Wendell Phillips heavyweights defeated Englewood High, an all-white team, to claim the South Central Division championship and advance to the finals of the city championship against Lane Tech. By the end of the game, Phillips' rooters were hysterical and the school battle cry—"Fight, Phillips, fight!"—rang out across the gym. On March 8, the night of the championship—which the *Defender* called "the night of all nights"—the Chicago Elevated ran a special train from the South Side to Loyola University, the site of the game. Unhappily, the Phillips heavyweights suffered an ignominious defeat, losing 18–4. Lane Tech was led by Bill Watson, its lone black player, and despite Phillips' defeat, the *Defender* nevertheless took solace in the fact that out of two million people in Chicago, the city championship game was decided by six black boys: "Since we had to battle, we bow out gracefully to Bill Watson."

By then, basketball had become more than a mere sporting event on the South Side; it was a major social affair. For years, the Giles Post American Legion team had been hosting dances after their games at the Eighth Regiment Armory. And in 1925, the *Defender* inaugurated its "Annual Winter Classic," which matched Wendell Phillips against one of the top black teams in the county for the unofficial "national cage title." Described as the "greatest spectacle in the history of our Race in Chicago," 4,500 people showed up for the gala, and another 2,000 were turned away. The Winter Classic drew as much coverage on the *Defender*'s society page as on the sports page, as women arrived in silk gowns and men in tuxedos, and fifty-five box seats were reserved for Bronzeville's elite ("businessmen, doctors, lawyers, society matrons, Debs and near debs"). The Wendell Phillips band entertained before the game, the Booster Orchestra played during halftime, and Joe Jordan's Orchestra played afterward until the wee hours, turning the dance floor into a "surging mass of humanity."

By 1926, basketball on the South Side was at its peak. Tommy Brookins, Randolph Ramsey, and Lester Johnson had already left Wendell Phillips but were still playing for the Wabash Y Squirrels, St. Monica's Catholic Church, and the Giles Post American Legion. The Phillips heavyweights had reloaded with Toots Wright, Fat Long, and Kid Oliver, and sixteen-year-old Runt Pullins was coming up through the ranks, already making his mark for the lightweights.

These young men were battle-tested veterans who had played together for years, had won tough games in hostile arenas, facing the taunts and jeers of white crowds, the blind eye of the referee, even the bricks thrown at the "coons." Once they left the sheltering hallways of Wendell Phillips, they would be entering a world that was foreboding and openly hostile to black men. It didn't take a guidance counselor at Phillips to explain to them what their job opportunities were. All they had to do was look around. On every street corner, on every tenement stoop, they saw in the haunted eyes of their fathers, their older brothers, and their friends the limitations of the American dream. Their chances of entering the skilled trades were almost nil, as the craft unions blatantly discriminated against blacks. A civil service job at the post office, which was the top of the career ladder, was almost impossible to come by without political connections. If they were lucky, they might catch on as an unskilled laborer in the packinghouses, sweeping the steaming guts off the killing-room floor, or as a porter or cook in one of the fancy hotels in the Loop, or as a janitor, dishwasher, messenger boy, or shoeshine boy. In any case, that's all they'd ever be—somebody's "boy," bowing and scraping for the white man's dime. A worse fate, shared by many black men, was to have no job at all.

Like all great athletes, what these Wendell Phillips stars really wanted was to find a way to keep doing what they loved and somehow survive. What they wanted most, then, was to play their game.

CHAPTER 3

Abe

Nineteen hundred and twenty-seven was the greatest year in American sports history. It was the apex of the golden age of sports. This was the year Babe Ruth hit sixty home runs. The year the New York Yankees' "Murderers' Row," still considered the best team in history, won the American League pennant by a record nineteen games, then swept the Pittsburgh Pirates in the World Series. It was the year Ty Cobb became the first player to reach 4,000 hits. It was the year of the infamous "long count" in the heavyweight title rematch between Jack Dempsey and Gene Tunney. Red Grange, the "Galloping Ghost of Illinois" and the first professional football superstar, was running wild on the gridiron. Big Bill Tilden was the master of tennis, "Sir Walter" Hagen won his fourth straight PGA Championship, and Bobby Jones won his second British Open and his third U.S. Amateur.

The golden age was ushered in, partly, by the proliferation of radio, which reached five million homes. Radio turned local sports stars into national idols and created a mass popular culture, bringing play-by-play action into every living room in America.

Beyond the sports world, America in 1927 was still rollicking along in the euphoria of the Roaring Twenties, blithely unaware that it would all come crashing down in another two years. It was the year of the first transatlantic telephone call, the first demonstration of television by Philo T. Farnsworth, and the first talking picture, *The Jazz Singer,* with Al Jolson.

Unquestionably, the greatest news event of the year, and perhaps of the decade, was Charles Lindbergh's solo flight across the Atlantic in *The Spirit of St. Louis* and landing at Le Bourget, near Paris, which set off a six-month-long celebration across the country.

Chicago was the perfect symbol for the Roaring Twenties. Al "Scarface" Capone was at the height of his powers, having built an empire on vice—speakeasies, gambling dens, brothels, nightclubs, and racetracks—that brought in a reputed $100 million a year.

On the North Side, Abe Saperstein was still living at home, sleeping on the living-room sofa, and still coaching the Chicago Reds, a lightweight (135-pounds) boys' basketball team at Welles Park. Working for the city parks department had given him the opportunity to meet other coaches, team managers, and promoters in the Chicago sports scene, thereby expanding his world beyond the confines of Ravenswood.

One of the people he had met was Walter Ball, a legendary pitcher from the early days of the Negro Leagues. Ball, who had cultivated a nasty spitball and a reputation as the "swellest" dresser in black baseball, had played for over twenty years, from 1899 to 1923, including a stint with Rube Foster's Chicago American Giants. By the time Abe met him, Ball's playing days were over, but he was still a mover and shaker in Chicago's African American sports world. He knew everybody in black baseball and basketball.

Ball wanted to send a black baseball team from Chicago on tour, most likely playing a regional schedule in Illinois and southern Wisconsin. This was not a novel idea, as Negro League teams had been barnstorming for years, but Walter Ball needed a booking agent to make the contacts and schedule the games—preferably a white man. It would be much easier for a white agent to book games in small Wisconsin farm towns, against local white teams, than a black man.

Using the same persuasive powers that had earned him the title of most popular kid in Ravenswood, Abe convinced Ball to give him the job. (Typically, a booking agent was paid on straight commission, receiving 10 percent of what the team received.)

This was Abe's big chance. And it was the perfect job for him, blending all of his strengths and skills. He had to meet local promoters, shake their hand, and try to convince them that playing Walter Ball's Negro team would be a great entertainment value for their town. He was *born* to do this job. Once he launched into his spiel, a torrent of words poured out, and some promoters may have signed on just to shut him up. But he had the gift of all great salesmen of being able to make a connection, in a matter of seconds, that made the other person feel special. Abe was so likable, so sincere, you couldn't even tell he was selling. He was your friend, he had something you needed, and he was doing you a favor to give it to you—for a price.

He did such a good job that Walter Ball would recommend him in the future. It was the start of a thirty-year relationship between Abe Saperstein and Negro League baseball. Booking Negro baseball games had just whetted his appetite, however. Now he was looking for more.

★

What should be the most basic and rudimentary question in the history of the Harlem Globe Trotters—when and how did the team begin?—turns out to be an intriguing mystery with all the elements of a Sherlock Holmes case. This fundamental question has been obscured by the passage of time, the deaths of the principal characters, and seventy years of hyperbolic press releases. What is absolutely clear, however, is that the official version of the Globe Trotters' origins, as promoted by Abe Saperstein and reprinted in thousands of newspaper articles, could not possibly be true. There are fatal flaws in that official story, which researchers have uncovered long before this book began.

The conventional story of the birth of the Globe Trotters goes something like this: In 1926, Abe Saperstein was invited by Walter Ball to coach the all-black Giles Post American Legion basketball team, which soon evolved into the Savoy Big Five, when Dick Hudson, the business manager of the Giles Post team, arranged to play games at the Savoy Ballroom on Chicago's South Side. However, disputes over money arose, several players quit the team, and the Savoy management soon replaced basketball with roller-skating. Three disgruntled Savoy players asked Abe to form his own barnstorming team, and the Harlem New York Globe Trotters played their first game on January 7, 1927, in Hinckley, Illinois.

To put it mildly, that is utter nonsense.

There are numerous problems with that story—fundamental, profound, and incontrovertible flaws—that prove this official version to be impossible and absurd. The first, and most elemental, is that the Savoy Ballroom did not even exist in January 1927, so there is no way the Savoy Big Five could have already been playing, much less have had several players quit, by that date. Second, there is no evidence that Abe Saperstein ever coached the Giles Post or Savoy teams, and the actual coaches of those teams are clearly identified in newspaper articles and photos. Third, although several Savoy players did quit the team, the Savoy Big Five did not fold—nor were they replaced by roller-skating—and continued playing for many years. Fourth, one of the original members of the Giles Post and Savoy teams claimed, thirty years ago, that *he* started the Globe Trotters, not Abe (and there is documentation to back up his claim), and that Abe, in effect, stole the team away from him. Fifth, Abe never mentioned anything about a "first game" in Hinckley on January 7, 1927, for at least twenty years, until 1947, when he conveniently proclaimed a return to Hinckley as the Trotters' "twentieth anniversary"—which now appears to have been backdated as a marketing ploy.* And finally, even people in Hinckley, including some of the original players in that "first game," have long denied that it occurred in 1927—and have a box score that may prove it.

Simply put, the Harlem Globe Trotters did not exist in January 1927, and they were not playing in Hinckley, Illinois, or anywhere else. Abe Saperstein was a great salesman and a marketing genius, but he was no historian—and he never let the facts get in the way of selling a good story.

So how did the Harlem Globe Trotters actually begin? The real story is much more fascinating than the official version. The truth usually is.

---

* In an October 26, 1951, interview with Red Smith in the New York Herald-Tribune, Abe Saperstein claimed that "the first place we played" was in Hinckley "against the Hinckley high school team," in front of 400 people. However, Abe's story was contradicted by the original Hinckley players themselves, who said, in a 1959 interview, that it was not the high school team (it was the Hinckley Merchants) and it was not in 1927. In the Red Smith article, Abe hints at what may have been the origin of the "first game" story: he says that in 1947, some people from Hinckley wrote him, asking if the Trotters would come back and play a game, and when they arrived, Hinckley put on a "big old fashioned country barbeque and party." From that point on, he began holding "anniversary" games in Hinckley.

In January 1927, the South Side was jumping. Chicago had an inferiority complex when it came to New York, and would acknowledge that subordinate status in later years by calling itself "Second City." On the South Side, however, black Chicagoans weren't willing to concede anything to New York. "They've got Harlem, but we've got Bronzeville" was a common refrain. And indeed, although the Harlem Renaissance was exploding in New York, bringing unprecedented attention to the works of Langston Hughes, Zora Neale Hurston, Duke Ellington, and Louis Armstrong, the South Side was having its own Chicago Renaissance.

Down around Forty-seventh Street and South Parkway, the central hub of Bronzeville, the nightclubs and cafés were hopping all night long. Ethel Waters was playing at the Café de Paris, Bill "Bojangles" Robinson was being held over at the Palace, and a "Deluxe Vaudeville Show" was packing them in at the Grand. Paul Robeson's latest film, *Body and Soul*," with an "All-Star colored cast," was opening at the Twentieth Century Theater. Jazz lovers were snapping up copies of "Big Butter and Egg Man from the West," Louis Armstrong's latest release on OKeh Race Records. And the Regal Theater was holding "Black Bottom" contests, as the latest dance craze swept the nation. "Those were nothing but good times," recalls Napoleon Oliver. "Chicago didn't sleep back then. You had somewhere to go *all the time*—night and day."

Meanwhile, over at the Eighth Regiment Armory, at Thirty-fifth and Giles, the manager of the Giles Post American Legion basketball team was making big plans. Dick Hudson, a twenty-eight-year-old former professional football player, who had had brief stints with three NFL teams, had assembled an all-star cast of ballplayers for the 1926–27 season. Hudson had signed a quintet of former Wendell Phillips stars, including Tommy Brookins, Randolph Ramsey, Toots Wright, and Lester Johnson. He had also imported Joe Lillard, a granite-bodied football player from Mason City, Iowa.

For years, Giles Post basketball squads had been playing around Chicago, but Dick Hudson, who had played football all over the country, had grander dreams of taking his team on the road. There were several white barnstorming teams that were well known in the Midwest, which Hudson would have certainly known, including Basloe's Globe Trotters and Olson's Terrible Swedes. And the New York Renaissance, the most acclaimed black team in the country, had made a few barnstorming tours. If the Rens could make it on the road, there was hope for other black teams.

Dick Hudson was ready to try his luck. This team was certainly talented enough and his young ballplayers were willing to risk going on the road. Most likely, Hudson sought out the man who knew all the ins and outs of barnstorming, perhaps the most knowledgeable sportsman on the South Side: Walter Ball. Reportedly, Ball told Hudson about a young Jewish fellow from the North Side who had done a good job booking baseball games for him, an energetic young man named Abe Saperstein.

The rest, as they say, was history—only not the "official" history.

On December 21, 1926, the *Appleton* [Wisc.] *Post-Crescent* ran a small four-paragraph story under the headline "Colored Cage Team Plays in Vicinity," which described an upcoming winter tour of Wisconsin by the "famous" Giles Post American Legion team, which was billed as the "national colored champions." Eighteen Wisconsin towns were on the schedule, including Little Chute, Kaukauna, Neenah, Sheboygan, Fond du Lac, and La Crosse. There is no proof that Abe Saperstein booked this tour, but his handiwork is all over it. Most characteristically, the Giles Post players were advertised as former college stars from such prestigious universities as Colgate, Amherst, Dartmouth, the University of Southern California, Creighton, Northwestern, and Iowa—although they were actually Wendell Phillips boys who had never set foot on a college campus, and some hadn't even graduated from high school. For years, Abe would employ the same kind of inflated college credentials for the Harlem Globe Trotters—but whether he learned it from Hudson or invented it himself is uncertain. Also, he would later adopt a Dick Hudson innovation that was inaugurated on this tour: halftime entertainment. Hudson brought along a black orchestra, the Wyonne Creole Serenaders from the Dreamland Night Club in Bronzeville, which played at halftime and after the game.

The Giles Post tour of Wisconsin began the last week of

December 1926. They won their first few games handily, but on January 7, 1927—the same date as the alleged "first game" of the Harlem Globetrotters in Hinckley, Illinois—they were handed a shocking 28–14 defeat by Clintonville. After a brief respite in Chicago, they returned to Wisconsin in mid-January and began summarily taking revenge on the local white teams. On January 25, they overwhelmed Watertown by a score of 50–11, a phenomenal score for that era. They were just getting started, however. Over the next few days, they destroyed the Fisher Body team from Janesville, 41–17; put a second whipping on Watertown, 50–10; and finished off the Reedsburg Flashes by a margin of 56–23.

They returned from Wisconsin in triumph, only to come under a withering attack from an unexpected quarter. *Chicago Defender* sports editor Fay Young wrote a scathing column, entitled "Killing Basketball," in which he accused Hudson of "fraud" for claiming to represent Giles Post without the permission of the Legion commander and for falsely advertising his players as former college stars. Young worried that such deception would hurt future teams with "bona fide" players because white fans wouldn't come out "after having once been buncoed." Hudson was the one who caught the flack for the subterfuge, although Abe Saperstein may have been the one who concocted it; yet his role in booking the Giles Post tour seems to have been hidden deep in the shadows.

In the fall of 1927, the South Side was buzzing with excitement over the most anticipated social event of the year: the grand opening of the Savoy Ballroom, at Forty-seventh and South Parkway. Designed by the builder of its famous namesake in Harlem, the Savoy would have a half-acre dance floor that could accommodate 6,000 people. In the weeks before the Savoy's "inaugural ball" on Thanksgiving eve, the *Defender* was flooded with advertisements predicting that the Savoy would be the "most beautiful and luxurious Ballroom in the country."

The grand opening was a tremendous success, as thousands of people turned out in their most elegant finery for the gala. Still basking in that afterglow, the white owner of the Savoy, I. J. (Jay) Faggen, decided to expand beyond dancing to sports. There was a tradition in the African American community of combining dancing and basketball, particularly in Harlem, where the New York Rens played at the Renaissance Casino, and dancing (before and after their games) was part of the evening's entertainment. When Faggen decided to replicate that model, it was only natural that he turned to Dick Hudson, who already had a successful team and, after his falling out with the Giles Post commander, was in need of a sponsor.

On December 31, 1927, the *Defender* announced that Hudson's Savoy Bear Cats, as they were originally called, would make their debut at the Savoy Ballroom on January 3, 1928, against Howard University—with a dance to follow. The Bear Cats defeated Howard twice that first week of January, although by then "Bear Cats" had been dropped in favor of the name they would carry for posterity: the Savoy Big Five. Their inaugural games, like the Savoy's inaugural ball, were extremely successful, with an estimated 1,200 people turning out for each. It was a propitious beginning for the new team in their new home, especially since the Savoy's dance floor was not conducive to basketball. There were columns in the middle of the floor that blocked the view, the hardwood floor was slippery from wax and buffing, and, most annoyingly, there were no seats for the fans, so they had to stand the entire game, craning to catch a glimpse of the action between the columns.

To make sure fans realized that the Savoy Big Five was Hudson's old Giles Post team, the *Defender* referred to them interchangeably as the Legion Five and the Savoy–Giles Post Big Five. It was the same crew: Hudson was the head coach and team manager, assisted by Bobby Anderson (a two-sport athlete who also played Negro League baseball), and the headline stars were the "old Phillips gang" of Tommy Brookins, who was selected as the team captain, along with Toots Wright, Randolph Ramsey, and Lester Johnson. The early box scores read like a Wendell Phillips class reunion, except for Joe Lillard, the bull from Iowa, and the former Lane Tech star Bill "Ham" Watson.

Only one unfamiliar name appeared in those box scores. It was a name that drew no special accolades or evoked any memories of past glories: Inman Jackson. He played only a backup role, scored a total of two points in both games, and drew no mention in the press. It was the first appearance of a mystery man who would eventually rise to become the most famous player of them all.

Inman Jackson was such a private person that no one *ever* knew much about him. Even today there is little definitive information about his personal life, but this much is known: when he made his debut with the Savoy Big Five, he was nineteen years old, living on the South Side with his mother, Sarah, and working as a painter for a cab company. He reportedly went to high school at Lane Tech, Chicago's noted vocational school, but there is no indication that he ever played basketball there. Of course, Bill Watson, his Savoy teammate, had been a star player at Lane and may have been responsible for getting Inman a tryout with the Savoy Big Five. Clearly, he was the most inexperienced player on the team—a raw, untested neophyte on a team of all-stars. Every other player had years of experience in high school and amateur ball, had played in city championship games and had seen their name—and often their picture—headlined in glory on the pages of the *Chicago Defender*. What Inman had going for him—the *only thing* he had going for him—was his size. He was six foot three—the tallest player on the squad and a giant by the standards of the day. In the Savoy's in-house newsletter, *The Savoyager,* one gets the first hint of the greatness that he will achieve: "The big boy from Lane . . . plays a nice game and it is thought that before long he will make them all sit up and take notice."

While the Savoy Big Five was successfully kicking off its first season, the attention of many South Side basketball fans was on a sensational young ballplayer who was rocketing to stardom: Runt Pullins was leading the Wendell Phillips lightweights on a run for the city championship. In January, the Phillips "ponies" ran off six straight wins, grabbing the lead in the Central Division race, and by early February they had clinched the division title. Runt's face had become a fixture in the *Defender,* and his exploits moved sports editor Fay Young to invoke classical allusions: "Phillips' little fellows can do more with a basketball than Nero could do with his fiddle."

On March 10, Runt Pullins led the Phillips lightweights into the championship game against Harrison High. The *Defender* had predicted that "the entire South Side [will] declare a holiday," and, indeed, thousands of fans, including most of Phillips' two-thousand-member student body, filled a specially reserved cheering section. With Harrison's defense concentrating on stopping Pullins, two of his teammates were open under the basket all night and scored sixteen points between them. Phillips won an overwhelming victory, defeating Harrison in a landslide, 32–10. Even the staid *Chicago Tribune* was effusive in its praise, characterizing Phillips as "easily the best lightweight team the city league has had for several years."

The Phillips players were hailed as conquering heroes when they returned to the South Side, and Runt Pullins above all others. The team was so popular, in fact, that no one wanted them to stop playing, so the following week the team was reconstituted as the "Savoy Flashes," and played a preliminary game before the Savoy Big Five's regular contest.

Runt Pullins's high school career had ended, but his basketball exploits had just begun.

With the high school season over, the Savoy Big Five had the spotlight to itself. The squad had racked up wins against college teams from Wilberforce, Lincoln, and Fisk Universities; the Indianapolis YMCA; a renowned Pittsburgh Loendi club; the Alpha Phi Alpha fraternity from New York; and two local Jewish teams, Irving Cohn Jewelers and the Jewish People's Institute. With only one loss (in a return engagement with Wilberforce), the Big Five was starting to make enough noise in basketball circles that Dick Hudson issued a challenge to the New York Rens, the best black team in America, and one of the two best teams overall (along with the Original Celtics, a white team from New York).

But Hudson was overreaching. The Savoys took a tumble when George Halas's Chicago Bruins, a brawny pro team from uptown, made its first visit to the Savoy Ballroom and "toyed with" the Big Five, running out to an 11–0 lead and coasting to a 29–25 win, in a game that wasn't as close as the score indicated. Hudson's team certainly wasn't ready for the Rens.

The Bruins game also marked the first sign of any internal dissension. A few weeks earlier, Hudson had brought in a veteran ballplayer from Cincinnati, Lawrence "Rock" Anderson, who had beat out Toots Wright for his starting job. In a huff, Wright quit the Savoy and joined the Fort Dearborn Elks, a newly formed black team that had played a few of its games at the Savoy.

By mid-April, the Negro League baseball season was opening, and basketball began to fade into the background. Two Savoy players, Joe Lillard and Rock Anderson, left town to practice with their baseball teams (Minneapolis and Cincinnati, respectively), although they were supposed to return for the final game of the season on April 14, against the Evanston Boosters.

And then, just prior to that game, the Savoy Big Five blew up—and the gory details were splashed across the pages of the *Defender*. The story was that Tommy Brookins, Randolph Ramsey, Bill Watson, and Inman Jackson had quit after objecting to bringing Lillard and Anderson back to Chicago for the final game, and paying them to play, when that money could have been divided among the remaining players. Brookins, the team captain, was apparently the ringleader of the insurgency, which left the Big Five shorthanded for the Evanston game. The Savoy management was able to cobble together a team by pulling in some older South Side stalwarts, and Lillard and Anderson returned in time to crush Evanston, 33–12.

The season ended with the Savoy Big Five in complete disarray. Of the players who had seen action in their first game, barely three months before, only Joe Lillard remained. This dramatic breakup at the end of the first season would have repercussions that would haunt Dick Hudson for years.

For Abe Saperstein, 1928 had to have been a disappointing year. His initial bookings for Hudson's Giles Post tour of Wisconsin, a year earlier, had ended in controversy over the inflated college attributions, and once that tour ended, he was out of the picture.

He may have continued to book some Negro League baseball games for Walter Ball, but his promotional career was apparently floundering so badly that he took a job with the city. A regular job— *not* in sports. He was able to wrangle a patronage job from his local ward boss, working as a forester in Chicago's massive Lincoln Park.

Abe had once hoped to study forestry at the University of Illinois, and this job involved hiring tree surgeons to maintain Lincoln Park's canopy of trees. He even got his younger brother Harry a job with one of the tree surgeons.

Whatever he had going in sports, it wasn't enough to quit his day job.

★

The 1928–29 basketball season brought many changes to the Savoy Big Five, which began preseason workouts in early November. First, Dick Hudson was gone, having been replaced as coach by Al Monroe, who was also a sportswriter for the *Defender*. Then Monroe scored a major coup by luring Specs Moten, a former New York Ren who was one of the best players in the game, to sign with the Savoy. And due to the success of the Big Five's initial season, Savoy owner Faggen had even organized a Savoy girls' team and had invited black college teams to play their home games at the ballroom.

The biggest change of all, however, was that Tommy Brookins and his insurgents had not returned. Apparently, their grievances about money had not been resolved over the summer. In fact, Brookins had gone so far as to form his own team. That announcement was made, with no fanfare, in the November 24, 1928, issue of the *Defender* in a minuscule four-sentence article that was sandwiched between a story about boxer Baby Jo Gans and ads for Kidney Plaster that promised to "End Lame Back!" and eczema medication guaranteed to "Stop the itching in one hour!"

The name of this new team was the Globe Trotters.

The article described how Brookins, Toots Wright, and Randolph Ramsey—the old triumvirate from the 1925 Wendell Phillips heavyweights—along with Inman Jackson, Bill Watson, Willis "Kid" Oliver (another former Phillips player), and Bobby Anderson (the previous assistant coach for the Savoy Big Five) had formed their own team called the Globe Trotters, which would be opening its season on the following Thursday, November 29, against a white team from Milwaukee. Interestingly, they would be playing at the Eighth Regiment Armory, their old stamping ground from the Giles Post days. Although his name was not listed in the article, it is very likely that Dick Hudson also was involved with the new venture, which would explain his departure from the Savoy.

Brookins, who was clearly the leader of the team, also predicted that he had lined up the services of Joe Lillard and Rock Anderson, in effect stealing the heart of the Savoy team. But when the Savoy Big Five opened its season (with a redemptive 29–21 victory over the Chicago Bruins), Brookins's prophecy proved false: Lillard and Anderson were both in the lineup, as were Bill Watson and Inman Jackson, who had apparently had second thoughts about going with Brookins and had returned to the fold. Brookins's defection certainly didn't hurt the Savoy at the box office, as more than two thousand fans, white and black, showed up for this interracial matchup.

The Savoy Big Five had a terrific second season, winning 33 of their 37 regular season games. One of those losses was to the legendary New York Rens, who made their first visit to Chicago in early February. Inman Jackson was getting more playing time this year, but the big fellow was still a second-teamer, a backup player to the Savoy's big guns.

As for Tommy Brookins's Globe Trotters, after that initial announcement in November, they completely disappeared from the pages of the *Defender* for two and a half months. Finally, on February 9, 1929, a lengthy article appeared, accompanied by a photo of Brookins, which previewed two upcoming games against Morgan College of Baltimore, to be held at the Eighth Regiment Armory.

There were two intriguing items at the end of the article. First, before the Globe Trotters took the court against Morgan College, a preliminary game was gong to be played by Runt Pullins's All-Stars. Second, there was news that the Globe Trotters had "recently returned from a trip through southern Illinois, where they made an excellent showing, winning seven games and losing two."

Now the story gets *really* interesting.

Thirty years ago, in the early 1970s, Tommy Brookins was living in St. Martin, in the French Antilles, a speck of an island in the Caribbean that is jointly owned by the French and the Dutch. At that time, Brookins owned an Italian restaurant called Portofino on the island, but in the 1930s and '40s he had been a celebrated singer and vaudevillian, entertaining all over the world. In his heyday, he had performed at the Palace Theater in New York, the Palladium in London, and had owned the Cabin in the Sky nightclub in Chicago with his partner and lover, Ethel Waters. His glory days as a basketball player on the South Side were far behind him.

Walking on the beach one day, he came upon Michael Strauss, a sportswriter for the *New York Times,* who was in his bathing trunks, strolling in the opposite direction. Strauss was there visiting his daughter, who lived on the island. A loquacious and outgoing type, Strauss had a habit of greeting everyone he met.

"How ya doing?" he called out as Brookins approached.

"Fine," Brookins replied. "You new to the island?"

Strauss said he was just visiting.

"What do you do?" Brookins asked.

"I'm a sportswriter."

With that, Brookins stopped walking. "What do you know about the Harlem Globe Trotters?" he asked.

"I've covered them a few times," Strauss replied. He had been at the *Times* since 1930, and in his five decades of reporting had covered the entire gamut of sports, including major league baseball, football, boxing, horse racing, snow skiing, college and professional basketball—and the Harlem Globe Trotters.

For the next few minutes, standing there in the sand with the waves lapping at their ankles, Tommy Brookins told an incredible story to this total stranger on the beach. But Strauss was intrigued by what he heard. In addition to his regular job at the *Times,* he was a prolific freelancer, writing articles for over thirty different magazines. He was always looking for a story—about sports, travel, skiing, anything that caught his fancy. And this story definitely caught his fancy. Strauss had known Abe Saperstein personally (by then Abe was deceased), he knew all about the Globetrotters, and his initial reaction was one of incredulity—that this tale could not possibly be true— but the more he listened, the more intrigued he became.

He arranged to meet Brookins at his restaurant, Portofino, for dinner, to continue their conversation. When he got there, Brookins told him more details about the story and pulled out old photos to make his points. Strauss was convinced enough to write a freelance article, but he knew the story would be controversial—and still had doubts himself—so he didn't offer it to a top-tier magazine, like *Esquire,* but sold it instead to a small Philadelphia-based basketball periodical, where it was published with no notice.

Today, Michael Strauss is ninety-one years old and lives in Palm Beach, Florida. He retired from the *Times* in 1980, when he turned seventy, after an astonishing fifty-three years there, but has yet to retire from sportswriting. He is now the sports editor of the *Palm Beach Daily News* and writes at least five columns a week. He doesn't do it for the money, as he's a millionaire from investments in the stock market. "I do it to keep busy," he explains.

And thirty years after his encounter with Tommy Brookins, he still has vivid recollections of it. "Absolutely," he says. "I can see myself standing right there on the beach at St. Martin, and he was talking to me. And I didn't believe it. It came from left field . . . but he was sincere and well-spoken."

The story Brookins told that day on the beach is just as sensational today. And some of it can now be documented.

"It all began with our schoolboy team," Brookins began. He told Strauss about playing on the great Wendell Phillips team that nearly won the city championship, only to lose to Lane Tech. He told him about Dick Hudson starting the Savoy Big Five, which included Brookins, Randolph Ramsey, Toots Wright, Lester Johnson, and Inman Jackson. He told him about beating George Halas's Chicago Bruins (although the Bruins actually beat the Savoy the first time they played, when Brookins was still on the team). And he told him about how they had changed the name of the team to "Tommy Brookins' Globe Trotters" (and later to the Original Chicago Globe Trotters) and moved their games from the Savoy Ballroom to the Eighth Regiment Armory, after Hudson and I. J. Faggen, the Savoy owner, got into a hassle over money.

And then Brookins started talking about Abe Saperstein. He said that the Globe Trotters were hoping to do some barnstorming in

Michigan and Wisconsin,★ to make extra money, and Dick Hudson told them, "Well, I've got a man who I think can help us. His name is Abe Saperstein." Hudson explained that Abe had booked baseball teams in both those states, and could help the Globe Trotters "because he has a white face."

According to Brookins, Abe was hired strictly as a booking agent. The deal was that he would book ten games, for which he would get a 10 percent booking fee of whatever money they made. In addition, Abe asked for $100 expense money up front so he could "go into the country and find us some places to play." The players voted to accept his deal, chipped in the $100 for travel expenses, and off he went.

After Abe booked the games, the Tommy Brookins's Globe Trotters headed out on the road to play them. "Everything was going great," Brookins told Strauss. But one night, after a game ended, the team was sitting in the locker room when a fan came in to congratulate them.

"I saw you guys the other night in Eau Claire," he said. "You fellows are great!"

"Eau Claire?" Brookins responded, quizzically. "We haven't even played there yet. You must be mistaken."

Randolph Ramsey, who had overheard the conversation, was left to deliver the bad news. He told Brookins that Abe Saperstein was booking a second team, using the name Globe Trotters, in Wisconsin. Apparently, while Brookins's was playing in Michigan, the "second" Globe Trotters team was in Wisconsin.

Brookins was shocked—and livid. "How come you never told me until now?" he demanded.

"I was going to tell you," Ramsey said sheepishly, "but I was waiting until I thought you were in a good mood."

When Brookins asked what players Abe had on the other team, Ramsey said, "All the fellows we didn't want."

As soon as Brookins could, he caught up with Abe and confronted

---

★ *In the original article, Strauss wrote that the team wanted to play in Wisconsin and Minnesota, but he insists today that was a mistake, that Brookins had said Wisconsin and Michigan—which is more likely.*

him. "What's the big idea?" he asked. "They tell me you've started another team and used our name."

Abe freely admitted it, saying, "I thought it would be a good idea to book two teams at once." When Brookins told him he hadn't treated them fairly, Abe shrugged and said, "What can I do now? I've booked the games and they're already playing them."

It might have become a much bigger row, but Brookins was ready to get off the road anyway. He had an offer to sing at the Regal Theater, next door to the Savoy Ballroom, for $75 a week. Plus, as he told Michael Strauss, his mother was sick in Chicago and he wanted to be close to her. So he took the singing job. Brookins told Strauss that he had one final meeting with Abe, at which Abe promised to hire some of the original players from Brookins's Globe Trotters, and they parted on good terms. Later, Abe called him and asked if he had spare uniforms left over, and Brookins sent him three sets that were collecting dust in his closet.

That was the end of Tommy Brookins's Globe Trotters, although Brookins himself would still play some basketball, on and off, including with a new Dick Hudson team called the Chicago Hottentots. Primarily, however, he focused on his singing career. And if he hadn't run into Michael Strauss on the beach in St. Martin, his story would have never been told.

Of course, the obvious question must be raised: is the story true?

There are minor inconsistencies with some names and dates, but the fact is that Brookins's version of how the Globe Trotters began has far *fewer* inconsistencies—and is much easier to document—than Abe's official version. We know, for certain, that Brookins, Ramsey, and Wright formed a team called the Globe Trotters in November 1928, and that that team was referred to in the *Defender* as "Thomas Brookins' Globe Trotters." It was his team.

Further, Abe and Brookins both agreed that Dick Hudson was the liaison who originally hooked up Abe with a group of former Giles Post–Savoy Big Five players to start barnstorming, and that Hudson recommended him because of Abe's experience in booking baseball games. Of course, Brookins added one additional qualification: "because he has a white face."

Ultimately, Brookins's story meshes so closely with the chronology of events that can be documented (as opposed to the multiple contradictions in Abe's chronology) that it seems believable. Michael Strauss certainly thinks so, even though he had his doubts at the time. "Oh, it absolutely all started with this guy," he says. "Abe was a booking agent originally—just came upon it by chance. There's no doubt in my mind that's what happened with Saperstein."

Brookins has another expert in his corner. J Michael Kenyon, an Oregon-based researcher who has been studying the Globetrotters for over thirty years, combing through hundreds of reels of microfilmed newspapers and compiling the most comprehensive archive of Globetrotter box scores, game reports, and chronologies in the world, believes the story as well. "Almost every word of what Brookins says in this piece rings true for me," says Kenyon. His only criticism of Brookins lies in how he came up with the name "Globe Trotters," which he claimed was because all five players did "plenty of trotting." In fact, Kenyon's enormous archive shows that two of the most well-known barnstorming teams in the Midwest in the mid-1920s were Basloe's Globe Trotters and the Minneapolis Globe Trotters. As Kenyon explains, "[The name] Globe Trotters was well established in the basketball lexicon by November of 1928, and was there for the plucking by Brookins."

So when and how did the Harlem Globetrotters begin? The best estimate is in early 1929, as a spin-off (or rip-off) of Tommy Brookins's Globe Trotters. In later years, when Abe claimed that the team started in 1927, he may have backdated it by two years to include his first involvement with the Giles Post tour of Wisconsin.

If Brookins's story is correct and Abe surreptitiously booked a second Globe Trotter unit, then who made up this second team? Ironically, it may have been the Savoy Big Five. It could be mere coincidence, but in March 1929, the same time frame in which Brookins's Globe Trotters would have been touring, the Savoy Big Five, under the direction of Coach Al Monroe, was reported to be on a barnstorming tour of—guess where—Michigan and Wisconsin. Could these have been "all the fellows we didn't want"—the players who had stayed with the Savoy, instead of coming with Brookins?

An even more likely possibility involves Runt Pullins, who seemed to be everywhere in late 1928 and early 1929, as these events were unfolding. He had played a preliminary game for Brookins's Globe Trotters, in February 1929, with his own team (alternately called Runt Pullins's All-Stars or the South Side Boys Club Comets). Abe certainly would have known about him, as he was one of the most famous high school ballplayers in Chicago, as a result of his Wendell Phillips championship in 1928. To field a second team, Abe needed a star. Brookins and Ramsey provided that for their team, but Abe needed a "blue-chipper" who could carry a team on his shoulders. Pullins was that kind of player.

Like everything else connected with the Globe Trotters' origin, there is controversy about who those "original" ballplayers were, but the most accurate roster includes Pullins, Toots Wright, Fat Long, Kid Oliver, and Andy Washington—all from Wendell Phillips. Toots Wright and Kid Oliver had both been listed as members of Tommy Brookins's Globe Trotters when the team first formed, but by early 1929, neither one is showing up in the box scores for Brookins's team. Evidently, they had been cut—perhaps they were the "fellows we didn't want." If Abe was trying to put together a second team, Pullins, Wright, and Oliver were all available.

And in an ironic twist, one of the first documented games that this new Globe Trotter team played was in Hinckley, Illinois. But it was on January 21, 1929.* A surviving box score from the game shows that the Hinckley Merchants beat the Globe Trotters by a score of 43–34. According to Runt Pullins, they netted a grand total of eight dollars, which was split six ways among Abe and the five players. "Each of us got $1.60," said Pullins.

The Harlem Globe Trotters were on their way.

---

* In a 1959 newspaper article, several of the original Hinckley players suggested that their first game against the Globe Trotters was in January 1928, but J Michael Kenyon has uncovered a newspaper account that puts the game on January 21, 1929. A surviving box score from that game supports that. Pullins and Toots Wright are both listed in the box score, but in January 1928 Pullins was in the middle of his senior season at Wendell Phillips and Toots Wright was playing regularly for the Savoy Big Five. Neither was likely to be barnstorming with Abe.

CHAPTER 4

Runt

In October 1929, the collapse of the stock market pitched the United States into the worst depression in the nation's history. With the economy in free fall, hundreds of banks closing, breadlines stretching around the block, plants and businesses shutting their doors, Abe Saperstein and his new Harlem Globe Trotters headed out into the teeth of the storm. He purchased a used Model T Ford from a local funeral parlor and drove out of Chicago. "All the banks were closing," he later said, "so we went where there were no banks."

He had appropriated the name Globe Trotters from Tommy Brookins (or even older namesakes), but he added one variation of his own. Instead of the Chicago Globe Trotters, as Brookins had started calling his team, Abe selected the more exotic "New York Harlem Globe Trotters." It was a sign of his marketing acumen, as he realized that an unheralded team of Negro ballplayers from the South Side might have a hard time drawing a crowd if they showed up in nearby Aurora, only thirty miles from Chicago. But when a "dusky quintet from the wilds of New York," as the *Aurora Beacon* described them, "invaded" the high school gym—now that was a draw. The redundancy of putting New York and Harlem together also was shrewd. Abe may have been trying to capture some of the luster of the New York Rens (who were known interchangeably as the Harlem Rens), but he also wanted opposing teams to understand that they would be playing a black team. Harlem, the capital of black America, flashed that message in neon lights. Abe wanted to avoid any potential trouble if the Globe Trotters came to town and kicked the butts of the local white heroes. Nobody could say afterward that they didn't realize what they were getting into.

Before the fledgling team took to the highways, Abe and the players formed a partnership in which gate receipts would be split among them. The five players each got a share, and Abe got a double share to pay for gas, car maintenance, and his booking expenses.* For Abe, this was a giant step up from the 10 percent booking fee he had been receiving. Now he was getting a third of the total receipts, although he also had to foot the bill for travel.

Abe was a one-man band: team manager, chauffeur, booking agent, publicity director, and the lone substitute player. He was everything but the owner—a critical distinction. This was not *his* team; they were all "equal partners," Pullins would say.

Sometimes, if Abe's car was broken down or the weather was bad, the Globe Trotters had to find other ways to get around. One night, they took the train to play a game in Hinckley, and the Hinckley players drove out and picked them up at the station (which was in nearby Aurora). But the ball game ran late and the Trotters missed the last train back to Chicago, so they ended up spending the night on the floor of a doctor's office. Another time, Abe's car was on the fritz, and Kid Oliver's younger brother, Napoleon, drove the Trotters in his car.

Abe ran the tour out of his hat and his overcoat, which were stuffed with chits listing the names, addresses, and phone numbers of every reporter from every cow-town weekly, every promoter or high school coach along the way—anybody who had a court. The scraps of paper spilled out of the pockets of his coat; it was his own mobile filing system. His only office was the front bedroom of his parents' house on Hermitage Avenue, and his office staff consisted of his fourteen-year-old brother Harry, who was taking a typing class at Lake View High. "I needed the practice," Harry recalls, laughing.

---

* Runt Pullins would later claim that Abe got only a regular share, so gate receipts were split six ways. But Abe said that he got a double share, which seems more likely, given his additional expenses.

"Abe couldn't type at all, so I did his typing for the first two years. He rented a typewriter for three dollars a month and set it up in this very small front bedroom in our home. That was his office."

Harry Saperstein typed all of Abe's press releases and telegrams. "Abe couldn't afford the cost of regular telegrams, so he used Western Union night letters," he recalls. A night letter was delivered overnight and allowed fifty words for about the same price as a ten-word regular telegram. In fact, Harry says, Abe dropped "New York" from the team's name just to save the cost of two additional words. He also typed Abe's so-called contracts with promoters, although the Globe Trotters were generally playing for whatever they could get. "The terms were very meager—maybe a twenty-five-dollar guarantee plus ten percent of the gate," Harry says. "He was lucky to get thirty-five bucks."

Despite Abe's multiple roles with the team, however, there was no doubt about who was the real star of the Harlem Globe Trotters. Runt Pullins was the youngest player on the team, at nineteen, but by far the most celebrated. He was only five foot nine and skinny as a rail, but he was the fastest man on the team and could shoot the ball from any spot on the court. "I am convinced that Pullins was the magnet which pulled them together in the beginning," says J Michael Kenyon. "Without Runt, they were just a bunch of guys named 'Joe' (and Abe)."

Runt was still a teenager, and the other players were not much older. Kid Oliver was twenty-one, and Toots Wright and Fat Long were the "old men" at twenty-two. Despite their youth, however, the Globe Trotters had terrific chemistry on the court, which was not surprising since these men had grown up together and played hundreds of ball games on the dirt courts of the South Side. And Pullins, Wright, and Oliver actually lived right around the block from each other. This familiarity was like a sixth sense on the court, an unspoken language. They knew each other's strengths and weaknesses, their favorite shots and moves, and one quick glance or tiny motion of the head was all it took to signal a break to the hoop before the defense could respond.

"The Globe Trotters knew exactly where each man was on every play, and they passed without even looking," the *Aurora Beacon* reported in 1929. "At times they tossed the ball around in an uncanny manner, and always there was at least one man open, usually under the basket."

In 1929–30, their first full season, the *Defender* reported that they "swept through the West like a tidal wave," racking up over one hundred victories. Of course, these were not world-class teams they were playing. There were no New York Rens or Chicago Bruins on the schedule, no noteworthy college teams. The Globe Trotters mostly feasted on a diet of bush-league quintets from the hinterlands: the Fairbanks Townies, Valley City Clothier, A. J. Busch Grocers, Gibson Painters, Kelowna Famous Players, and the Mayville Teachers College Comets.

That first season, they played primarily in Illinois and Iowa, with a possible excursion into Minnesota at the end of the season. Each year thereafter, Abe would add another state or two, gradually expanding into Wisconsin and Michigan, then North and South Dakota, and Montana. It would be six years before they'd reach the Pacific Coast and play Washington and Oregon.

Out there on the vast prairies, the Globe Trotters were playing in small farming communities that had no African American residents (some have few, if any, today). In some cases, the Globe Trotters were the first black men these people had ever seen. Former Trotters remember youngsters coming up and touching them, curious to see if the skin color would rub off. They were also bringing a different style of basketball to the American heartland. When they chose to, the Trotters could play the conventional ball-control, slow-tempo game with the best of them. "[The Globe Trotters gave] one of the best exhibitions of stalling ever seen here," the *Aurora Beacon* wrote. "[They] used the entire floor, and sometimes they would pass to a player under the basket and he would dribble back to the other end of the floor, thru [*sic*] the entire opposing team, and then the performance would start all over again."

But when they wanted to turn it on, the Globe Trotters displayed a new kind of basketball—the *black* style of ball played on the courts of Bronzeville. It was a game of speed, quick passes, and ball-handling wizardry that mesmerized both their opposition and the fans. "They played such basketball as few Aurora fans ever saw," the *Beacon* enthused. "They dribbled thru [*sic*] and around the local five almost at will, and because of their clever and bullet-like passing it was an almost impossible task to cover them."

Although set comedy routines would not appear until a few years later, from the beginning the Trotters melded basketball with showmanship. "The crowd was in an uproar during the last three quarters at the antics and clowning the Trotters mixed with their stellar playing," one Midwestern scribe wrote. Abe Saperstein did not originate showmanship in the sport, any more than he originated halftime entertainment or the Globe Trotter name. The Original Celtics and New York Rens were renowned for their ball-handling exhibitions and spectacular passing, and the Globe Trotters, at least in the early years, were apparently doing the same kind of routines that the Celtics and Rens had been doing for years. Nonetheless, that combination of basketball expertise and showmanship became a primary feature of the Globe Trotters' identity.

And the fans and sportswriters loved it. In 1929, one Midwestern reporter wrote that the Globe Trotters "handled the ball like a Scotchman handles currency." A reporter from the *Mason City* [Iowa] *Globe-Gazette* gave the Trotters similar raves: "Something new in basketball was displayed last night when the New York Globe Trotters bewildered the local cagers with the best short passing game ever witnessed here. The invading colored boys amazed local fans with a clever handling of the ball . . . passed with dazzling speed and enlivened the program with some antics in handling the ball which demonstrated that the colored players were 'too hot' to handle."

The Globe Trotters were beginning to establish their own identity, although they were buried so deep in the provinces that few people even noticed.

★

On December 5, 1930, one of the first great milestones in Globe Trotters history occurred, one that would shape the team's character for decades to come: Inman Jackson made his first appearance in a

Globe Trotter lineup. The big man had quit the Savoy Big Five, which had been reorganized under Dick Hudson,* and joined the Trotters in time for a trip to Cincinnati to play the DeHart Hubbard Lion Tamers, one of the better teams in the Midwest. It was an inauspicious debut for "Big Jack," as the Lion Tamers defeated the Trotters, 39 to 32.

Clearly, he was no savior. While Runt Pullins had always been a star, and Toots Wright and Fat Long had always been starters, Jackson was a career backup—a three-year second-stringer for the Savoy Big Five—and had always been eclipsed by more famous teammates like Tommy Brookins, Randolph Ramsey, Rock Anderson, Joe Lillard, and Specs Moten. Now, for the first time, he had a chance to start. And not just in the one or two games a week that the Savoy had played, but every day and twice on Sundays. It was his chance to find out what kind of player he could really be. And, little by little, as he adjusted to that grueling schedule, the big man began to come around. Maybe that was all he had needed, just time to unlock the natural talent hidden in that big body.

Inman had played against some of the roughest teams in professional basketball, such as George Halas's Chicago Bruins, who had simply transferred Halas's gridiron techniques to the hardwood, but now he was banging under the boards with corn-fed farm boys from every hick team in the Midwest. The great advantage Inman had was his size and strength, which he began learning how to exploit. At six feet, three inches and 200 pounds, he was an imposing figure for that era and was often described as a "giant" in newspaper accounts. And because the rules required a center jump after every basket, he had the opportunity to assert his dominance over the entire game. During one game in Arcadia, Wisconsin, he controlled every single tip.

With Inman in the lineup, the Globe Trotters had the nucleus of the team that would carry them through the bleakest years of the Great Depression: Jackson, Runt Pullins, Kid Oliver, Toots Wright, and Fat Long. Each man had his role. Inman controlled the lane and

---

* Before returning to the Savoy Big Five for the 1930–31 season, Hudson had started another team, the Chicago Hottentots, which included Tommy Brookins and Randolph Ramsey.

the tipoffs, Runt was the outside shooter, Toots Wright was the backbone of the man-to-man defense and a "veritable jumping jack," and Oliver and Long did yeoman's duty under the boards, using quickness, in Oliver's case, and brawn, in the case of the aptly named Fat Long.

By the end of Inman Jackson's first season, the *Defender* was calling him the "most improved player on the squad" and predicting that the "elongated center [was] still coming and should reach even greater heights, but he is considered to be 'too high' now by all those who have faced him."

The Globe Trotters had found themselves a big man.

Inman Jackson's arrival also heralded the creation of two Globe Trotters icons: the dribbler and the showman. Runt Pullins had been drawing plaudits for his dribbling and ball-handling tricks since the first season of 1929. As one reporter wrote: "[Pullins] might as well have had a marble, so adept was he at concealing the sphere. The old hidden ball trick, formerly confined to football, was introduced for the enjoyment of the fans by the Harlem lad." But now Runt and Jackson began to play off each other, incorporating more formalized showmanship into the games; some of their creations would become Globe Trotter staples.

Pullins developed a dribbling routine in which he'd weave his way through the entire opposition. He invented a trick shot from half court without looking at the basket. Jackson perfected a hook shot that he launched with his back to the basket. And his trademark was to palm the ball (which was almost unheard of in that day, as the ball was larger) then hold it out tantalizingly in front of his opponent and snatch it back. "Jackson, the giant center . . . drew a big laugh when he wrapped his large hand around the ball and offered it to Connolly (a local center), drawing it back before Connolly could grasp it," reported the *Mason City Globe-Gazette.* Finally, when the other team took a shot, he would leap up, poke his arm through the net, and knock the ball away. It was a clear violation of the rules, but it got a laugh.

Many of the Globe Trotters' early comedy routines developed

purely by accident. According to one Trotter legend, they were playing a game in Williamsburg, Iowa, in an old meeting hall with pot-bellied stoves at either end, when Kid Oliver backed into a red-hot stove and ran screaming across the court, smoke trailing from his shorts like a vapor trail. The crowd roared, thinking it was intentional, but Oliver was actually on fire. Kid Oliver's rear end was soon fine, but the message was clear: white fans liked to laugh at the antics of black ballplayers. It was the first sign of a troubling racial aspect of the Globe Trotters' popularity. Many more controversies would follow.

★

By 1931, the Great Depression had taken a stranglehold on the country. Nearly a quarter of the workforce was unemployed and industrial output was one half its 1929 level. Thousands of banks had closed, wiping out the life savings of millions of Americans, and the national banking system was on the verge of collapse. Nearly two million Americans were homeless, hundreds of thousands of farmers in the Dust Bowl had been driven from their land, caravans of desperate Okies were streaming into California, looking for work, and Hoovervilles were springing up under bridges all over America. Yet President Herbert Hoover insisted that "prosperity is right around the corner," refused to support federal relief programs because they would undermine "self-reliance," and offered a veiled condemnation of the unemployed, implying that those who wanted a job could find it.

In the face of the ever-deepening crisis, the Globe Trotters had their best season yet, and their schedule expanded to 150 games. It was a high-volume, low-margin business, as gate receipts from most games were so paltry that the Trotters had to play every night to survive. Sometimes they carried that to absurd lengths. In one stretch that winter they played 61 games on consecutive nights.

Despite the Herculean schedule, there were signs that the Globe Trotters' fortunes were improving. Abe purchased a second Model T (with 79,000 miles on it) to use as a baggage car, which followed behind what he facetiously dubbed the "club car." In March 1931, he told the *Chicago Defender* that the Globe Trotters had "experienced the greatest financial season since their organization and this is something to be proud of in these days of business depression."

One cannot truly appreciate the boldness of this venture, and its improbable chance of success, without pulling out an old highway map and plotting the team's itinerary through these numbing years of the Depression. It is difficult to even locate some of the towns they played: Baraboo, Menomonie, Pardeeville, and Mauston. These were towns that few people had ever heard of, even in nearby states: Zumbrota, Grand Meadow, Lanesboro, Owatonna, Otteson, and Mendota. They were towns on the "blue highways" of old road maps, the two-lane country roads that William Least Heat Moon described so eloquently in his book by the same name.

The Globe Trotters were the kings of the "tank towns," as Runt Pullins described them, so named for the water tanks that were visible from a distance. "In my dictionary, beside the definition of 'tank town' there should be a picture of Mendota," says J Michael Kenyon, the world's foremost authority on the Globetrotters' schedule.

It wasn't just the smallness of the towns; it was the distance between them that made the Trotters' schedule so daunting. Two-hundred-mile hops between games were typical; three or four hundred miles were not out of the question. And those miles cannot be measured by today's standards, with the cruise control set on 75 mph, the heater purring silently, the defroster and rear window defoggers cutting the ice, the cushioned captain's chairs with adjustable lumbar support, the Interstate rest areas mindlessly clicking by, and the fast food joints looming up at every exit. No, the Globe Trotters did it in a Model T Ford with a top speed of 30 mph, which had no heater, no defroster, leaky windows, six-inch-diameter tires, no shocks or I-beam suspension, and there were no rest areas or welcome stations along the way. One must also factor in the debilitating effects of cold weather, as the Trotters were traveling in the dead of winter in a wretchedly intemperate region of the country.

Once they arrived in a town, with their kidneys battered from the jostling, their toes numb from the cold, and their joints stiff and sore from the absurdity of six grown men—five giants and a midget driver—all crammed together in a rattletrap flivver, they had to play a basketball game. They had to run up and down the court for an hour, then take a shower (if they were fortunate), or more likely just towel off and pile back in the car, hopefully with a couple of bucks in their pockets. If they were lucky, they might find a restaurant that would serve blacks, but often they had to "live off the grocery"—buy some crackers and bologna or a couple of doughnuts. If they were *really* lucky, they might find a hotel that would rent them a room, but all too often there were none (good luck finding any kind of hotel in Rugby, North Dakota, or Malta, Montana, much less one that would rent to blacks), so they would drive on through the night to the next stop, or to the home of an African American family that would let them sleep on the floor. Then they did it all over again the next day. Day after day, from late November to early May, 150 games a season.

The fact that the Harlem Globe Trotters did not just survive but prevailed, to paraphrase William Faulkner, was a testament to their courage, determination, talent, and perseverance. It was also, not in small part, a measure of the desperation of the times. Thousands of other Americans were standing in breadlines or selling apples on street corners. Playing basketball, even under these conditions, didn't seem so bad.

A multitude of stories about the hardships of those early years have been passed down over decades, although some may be more folklore than fact. There was the game in Princeton, Minnesota, during a horrendous blizzard, with the temperature well below zero and only fifteen fans in the stands, when Abe discovered that the gym had just been painted and the fumes were making everyone sick. All the doors and windows had to be opened, and players and fans alike nearly froze to death.

There was a night in Waterloo, Iowa, when the temperature was so cold that *nobody* showed up for the game. The Trotters and the Waterloo team played anyway, but when the game was over there were no gate receipts to split. Abe begged the promoter to give him five bucks, just to buy food and rent a place to sleep. When the Trotters piled back in their old Model T, one of the Waterloo players, Dell Raymond, felt sorry for them. "I reached in my pocket and gave them sixty cents," he recalled in a 1968 interview.

And there was the time the Globe Trotters showed up in Wheatland, Iowa, a town of five hundred people, to find that the hayloft of a barn had been converted into a makeshift court, complete with bleachers on either side. Lester Johnson, a former Wendell Phillips and Savoy player who was moonlighting with the Trotters, was driving in for a layup when he got shoved and crashed right through a boarded-up door, falling twenty feet down a flight of stairs. Fearing that he was dead, the team rushed downstairs to find Johnson sprawled in a pile of manure, unhurt but screaming epithets that eastern Iowa might not have heard before. From that day on, Johnson would forever be known as "Luscious Lester."

In the early years, the Globe Trotters carried just five players and Abe. No substitutes. No second team. When a player got hurt or sick or fouled out, there were no backups to take his place. Sometimes it didn't matter. In Marshalltown, Iowa, after one player fouled out in the fourth quarter, the Trotters played on with only four—and eventually three. As the local *Times-Republican* reported: "The last five minutes of the second game were finished with only four Trotters on the floor. . . . As a matter of fact, Pullins got tired in the final minute and went over and sat down, leaving Jackson, Wright and Easter to battle it out. The number did not make any difference. The chances are that trio could have beaten either of the local fives in a regulation ball game if it wanted to turn on the steam."

For the first few years, Abe was the only substitute, and he wore a uniform under his street clothes, just in case. It had been a decade since his brief stint at left guard for the Lake View bantams, and the intervening years had not been kind to his body or his skills. All of the extra weight he put on seemed to settle around his waist, and sometimes the Trotters might have been better off playing on with four, or even three, and leaving Abe on the bench.

In Fargo, North Dakota, they lost by one point when Kid Oliver was unable to play, and the *Fargo Forum* placed some of the blame on Abe: "Apparently handicapped by loss of its regular fifth man, the Harlem quint failed to click effectively. . . . A. M. Saperstein, diminutive manager of the traveling outfit, was the fifth man in the lineup." His statistics in the box score were dismal: no field goals, no free throws, and three personal fouls.

Other sportswriters were openly sarcastic, with Abe the target of their ridicule. "Four clean-limbed young colored men and a squat, bandy-legged chap of Jewish extradition [sic] furnished local basketball devotees some exceptional diversion here Saturday night," wrote the *Arcadia* [Wisc.] *Leader.* "Saperstein was the only man on the team who seemed to be working hard, while the colored fellows seemed just as fresh after the game as at the start." And once, in Montana, after a Trotter starter came down with appendicitis, Abe had to fill in for an entire week, and the team obviously suffered with him in the lineup. "[Saperstein's] shooting and passing was not up to the standard of the other four members of the team," the *Great Falls* [Mont.] *Tribune* reported.

With six men stuffed into one Model T, living and working together in close quarters for months at a time, conflict was inevitable. There were no documented racial incidents between Abe and the players, but a dispute over money did lead to blows. After one game, Fat Long thought that Abe had shorted the players while splitting the gate, and an argument ensued. "Fat ended up punching Abe," says Napoleon Oliver, who heard the story from his brother Kid. "And Fat got so mad that he left the team, but he soon came back."

Other times, however, there were acts of kindness and consideration that transcended the racial distinctions between Abe and the players. After a game in Des Moines, the Globe Trotters couldn't find a hotel that would allow blacks, so Abe rented a room in a white hotel and had the players sneak up the fire escape, climb through the window, and sleep in his room.

They traveled together, played together, lived together, and suffered together through the hardships of the Depression. There were weeks when they had only one or two bookings, and many games where the turnout was so low that their take wasn't enough to buy a hot dog. With admission prices usually a quarter for adults and a dime for children, a crowd of 200 would net the Trotters only around $25 or $30—less than $3 per man. There was one game in the early years when an overly optimistic promoter promised Abe a $25 guarantee or 40 percent of the gate, whichever was more. Total gate receipts that night were $5.95.

"I owe you twenty-five bucks," the promoter said.

"Just give us our $2.40," Abe responded. "Maybe we'll be back this way again sometime and things will be better."

It was typical of Abe's dealings with promoters. He was always thinking ahead, looking toward future games with larger crowds. No town was too small, no gym too cramped or decrepit for Abe to book a game. He was constantly scaring up new bookings on the fly, as the tour progressed. If he managed to get a game in one town, he'd scout out new contacts in the neighboring burgs and book those on the Trotters' return. The Globe Trotters might pass through the same county two or three times a year, hopscotching between towns, mining every quarter or half-dollar to be found.

And once Abe got his hooks in a promoter, he never let go. The Trotters returned to the same towns year after year. The only contract Abe had was a handshake or a ten-word telegram: "Game confirmed for October 12th. 8 PM. Forty percent gate." But that was enough. Promoters knew they could count on him. Indeed, entire towns came to depend on the Globe Trotters' annual appearance. No matter how desolate the winter had been on the prairies, no matter how many blue northers had come howling down from Canada or how many interminable weeks of arctic gloom, the people in those little towns knew that on the appointed night the Globe Trotters would show up at the high school gym and put on a show that made the winter more tolerable. It was the highlight of their year, and farmers would be talking about it for weeks around the feed store, as they warmed their fingers over the stove and waited for the thaw. One of Abe's great strengths was that he never forgot those tank towns that helped him survive the Depression, even years later, when his team had succeeded beyond anyone's expectations. And those tank towns returned that loyalty in kind.

The young boy who had never stopped talking, who was always in perpetual motion, had found the perfect channel for that bubbling spring of energy. Abe Saperstein developed relationships with promoters in hundreds of towns across America—and, later, around the world. He remembered everyone's name—every arena owner or high school coach, every principal or Rotarian with access to a gymnasium, auditorium, National Guard armory, church basement, livery stable, or barn.

Above all others, he had a special passion for sportswriters. Early on, Abe showed a remarkable talent for building rapport with sportswriters. It reaped huge dividends for the Trotters, of course, but this went far beyond good marketing. Abe *loved* sportswriters. He loved hanging out with them, chewing the fat, swapping lies, and, most of all, talking up his team. Sportswriters in that era were a different breed. They were a grizzled, hard-drinking, chain-smoking lot, and a sports editor of a small-town paper had lifetime employment. These guys died in the saddle, strapped in behind their Underwood Noiseless, with a crushed fedora on the back of the chair, dandruff cascading down their coffee-stained coat, and a half-smoked Camel dangling from their lips. Over the next few decades, Abe would build a network of *hundreds* of sportswriters—men whom he had first met in the early 1930s, when they were all full of piss and vinegar—who would become his biggest boosters.

He courted reporters as if he were a heartsick lover. He wrote them, wired them, and called them incessantly. He sent them press releases before the season began, wrote again as the game date approached, then dropped by to see them when he hit town. He kept his brother Harry chained to the rented typewriter in the Sapersteins' front bedroom, pecking out dozens of cheap-rate "book telegrams" (the same text sent to multiple recipients) to sportswriters in every town the Trotters played. Abe was using mass-mailing techniques before they even had a name.

Unfortunately, once he started yakking with a sports editor, he never knew when to shut up. It was as if he couldn't help himself, the hucksterism just poured out of him so profusely that perhaps even he couldn't remember what was true and what was false. He had a chronic tendency to embellish, exaggerate, and sometimes lie. For instance, he repeatedly gave out contradictory, wildly varying, and demonstrably inaccurate figures for the Trotters' win-loss record—always in their favor. In Abe's calculus, the Trotters didn't just improve from year to year, they improved *retroactively*—apparently going back in time and redeeming themselves in games they had already lost. And once Abe made a claim—true or not—he would keep repeating it, apparently believing that if he said it enough or could convince some reporter to write it, that would make it so.

One striking example was the way he made up college credentials for his players, most of whom were lucky if they'd graduated from Wendell Phillips High. His intent was apparently to circumvent the Amateur Athletic Union's (AAU) rule against amateur teams playing professionals, which could have severely curtailed the Globe Trotters' pool of potential opponents. So Abe attempted to make the Globe Trotters seem like all-American college boys out for a lark. This had echoes of the Giles Post tour of Wisconsin in January 1927, when Abe (or Dick Hudson) made up similarly preposterous claims. He claimed that Toots Wright was a former All-American at Crane College, Inman Jackson was a grad of City College of New York, and, subscribing to the principle that if you're going to tell a lie you might as well tell a whopper, he even fabricated Ivy League credits for Kid Oliver and Runt Pullins, who he said had graduated from Brown University.

Abe saved his most elaborate fantasies, however, for his own erstwhile athletic career. The sometime starter at Lake View High started telling reporters that he had played professional basketball. And once he crossed that imaginary line, Abe would alter the story from reporter to reporter and town to town as it suited his fancy. He told some writers that he had played pro ball in Philadelphia, told others about his career in Rochester, and his personal favorite was that he was "still under contract" to the Cleveland Rosenblums, one of the most famous pro teams in the mid-1920s. When he really got wound up, he went so far as to claim that he had been "the leading scorer" in the professional basketball league. In later years, Globe Trotter players would joke about Abe's "little man complex" and call him "Little Caesar" behind his back, and while he was a compulsive embellisher, repeatedly trying to pump up his own image, he was no fool. Abe repeated these fables about his "pro career" only when he was talking to reporters out west, hundreds of miles from Cleveland or Philadelphia or Rochester, so he didn't have to worry about anybody checking him out. In later years, when the Globe Trotters were making regular forays back east, he quietly dropped the pro basketball stories from his résumé.

Throughout 1932, the most ghastly year of the Depression, when national unemployment approached 25 percent, the Globe Trotters kept soldiering on. They already had more requests for games than they could fill in Iowa, Wisconsin, Minnesota, and South Dakota—their familiar stamping grounds—but Abe's dreams were more expansive than the Great Plains or the rolling hills of South Dakota, and so he pushed on into the Rockies, into the uncharted territories of Colorado, North Dakota, and Montana, where no one had ever heard their name. In 1932, they reportedly even crossed the border into Canada, making the first of many forays into British Columbia. The Globe Trotters had been playing the tank town circuit in the Midwest for five years, but as they moved into the mountain states, Abe was booking even smaller, more remote towns, if that were possible. They played Maddock, Crosby, and Wahpeton, North Dakota; Choteau, Roundup, and Crow Agency, Montana.

The logistics of playing in the mountains were more challenging than anything the Globe Trotters had ever faced. Two-hundred-mile hops between games in Iowa or Minnesota were nothing compared with those same distances in the Rocky Mountains, where they were traversing snow-covered passes at six thousand feet. In Montana, the roads sometimes became so impassable that they had to leave their cars and take trains to their next stops. And they were moving into a new dimension of cold weather that was more brutal than anything they had experienced. In the early 1930s, Montana had its warmest winters in history, yet in February the mercury still dropped to twenty below in Poplar and minus eleven in Big Sandy, both towns that the Trotters played.

On the court, there were important changes as well. By 1932, the Globe Trotters were beginning to establish their own identity, which distinguished them from other teams on the barnstorming circuit. With Runt Pullins and Inman Jackson leading the way, they were winning over 90 percent of their games (even allowing for Abe's inflated figures), albeit most of their victories still came against very ordinary competition. The Globe Trotters rolled through the 1931–32 season, playing 146 games and reportedly losing only 10. At least a few of those losses could be blamed on the weather. In March 1932, for instance, they got stuck in a snowdrift on their way to Rochester, Minnesota, and it took two hours to get free. Abe called ahead to delay the starting time, but when the Trotters finally arrived, they lost 29–25. Perhaps showing the lingering effects from that episode, or just worn down by the grueling travel, three nights later they were trounced 71–35 by the Spring Grove Independents, the worst loss in their history, when two Spring Grove players scored 32 and 24 points, respectively.

The Trotters' usual strategy was to try to get an early lead and then go into their full-court stall and ball-handling routines. The crowds loved the showmanship, but it also served a second purpose: to give the Trotters a chance to rest their weary legs. Standing in place, whipping the ball around the court, the players didn't have to run. The fans were so enthralled that they didn't realize that the Trotters were actually catching a breather. Sometimes the strategy backfired, however, as there were games where their goofing off allowed the other team to catch up and, in some cases, actually beat them. And some teams were just better than they were. The Rochester [Minn.] Elks Aces turned the hat trick, beating the Globe Trotters three straight times.

Ultimately, however, it didn't matter. Their margin of victory and even their record of wins and losses were becoming secondary to entertainment. The Trotters still wanted to win but, more important, they wanted to give the crowd such a good show that they would be invited back. And beating the local heroes by a handful of points, rather than in a blowout, was more likely to generate a rematch. The crowd went home laughing, and the opposition players, who had avoided complete humiliation, were hankering for another shot. The Trotters' tactics were obvious to knowledgeable observers; in many newspaper accounts, sportswriters would note that the Trotters passed up easy shots and were content to "have fun" once they got a lead.

For the first time since the arrival of Inman Jackson, there was a shakeup in the Globe Trotters' starting lineup. Kid Oliver, one of the original Trotters, who was a journeyman but never a star, was replaced by sharpshooting George Easter, another former Wendell

Phillips player, who was a familiar face to the other Trotters. He had played with Runt Pullins's All-Stars and lived around the corner from Runt and Fat Long. Another familiar face, Rock Anderson, who had played for the original Savoy Big Five and many other pro teams, also appeared in the Globe Trotters lineup at times, apparently filling in for the injured Fat Long. As for Kid Oliver, he continued playing part-time for the Globe Trotters, but eventually returned to Chicago, got married, and went to work for Argo Corn Starch, where he would spend the next thirty years.

Other changes followed.

By the 1932–33 season, Abe had so many requests for games that he fielded a second Globe Trotter unit (which included Kid Oliver) that stuck close to home, playing a limited schedule in Illinois and Iowa. After five years of barnstorming, Abe had the formula down pat, and so he also organized a white basketball team, the New York Nationals, and sent it out on the same byways as the Globe Trotters, usually a few weeks behind them. His brother Rocky managed the team, which had a tremendous run of victories, but could not draw like the Globe Trotters and eventually folded.

Somehow, in between all of his travel and promoting, Abe found time to begin a courtship of Sylvia Franklin, from Kenosha, Wisconsin, whom he would eventually marry. Her father, perhaps hoping that his daughter would land a bigger catch, advised Abe that he should do more to promote the Saperstein name. So Abe had new lettering sewn on the team's jerseys, reading "Saperstein's Harlem New York." It was a sign of his increasing stature in the sports world and of his growing desire to make the Trotters *his* team. Abe and the players were still splitting the gate receipts, with Abe getting a double share, as they had since their partnership began in 1929. But now Abe was trying to assert control in ways that would lead to the first great crisis in the team's history.

In the early 1930s, the game of basketball itself began to change in ways that would profoundly affect the Harlem Globe Trotters. The National Basketball Committee, which regulated college teams, enacted two new rules that would significantly alter the game. First, a line was painted across half-court (previously there had been none), and teams were required to advance the ball across the line within ten seconds. Second, when an offensive player had possession of the ball in the foul lane, and had his back to the basket, he had three seconds to shoot, pass, or move out of the lane.* Although the new rules were specific to college teams, they were adopted by most professionals, including the Globe Trotters. The full-court stall had been one of the Trotters' favorite tactics, but Abe realized that the Trotters' offense would now have to change. As he announced in a 1933 press release:

> I am making some replacements and developing a new style of play to meet the change in rules. The new men I have are head and shoulders above the men I intend replacing. . . . My new style of play is startlingly different and I am willing to gamble that half the clubs that see it will use it after watching it in action.

In the short term, the new rules propelled the Globe Trotters farther down the path toward showmanship and comedy, as they could no longer use the entire court for their stalling and passing displays. In any case, Abe's "startlingly different" style held up well under the new restraints. As the *Grand Forks* [N.D.] *Herald* reported: "The Trotters have possession of the ball most of the game and the new rules have not affected their play, for they can play just as good a game of keep away in half of the court as they can in the entire floor."

After five years, the Globe Trotters had developed a loyal following in many parts of Minnesota and Wisconsin, and were generally well received by the fans. On the court, however, there were ferocious battles between the Trotters and opposition players that sometimes led to physical confrontations. When that happened, racial prejudices that had been simmering beneath the surface sometimes came pouring out. In Minneapolis, at the end of one particularly

---

*A few years later, the three-second rule was expanded to include any player in the lane, whether he had the ball or not. And the confusing issue of whether his back was to the basket or not was dropped.

rough game (football star Bronko Nagurski was playing for the other team), Inman Jackson got into a shoving match with the rival center and threw a haymaker that broke the white player's nose. A melee ensued, as a "wild rush of spectators and basketballers" charged onto the court. Jackson and the other Trotters made a run for their dressing room, where they were saved from physical harm by the game announcer, who locked them in. Local police were called to disperse the crowd, but it was an hour before the Trotters could leave the gym. And there was such a furor about the near riot in Minneapolis that a local Catholic team threatened to cancel its upcoming game with the Trotters. The Globe Trotters couldn't wait to leave Minnesota.

In their first four years, the Harlem Globe Trotters had managed to carve out their own niche in the Great Plains and in the mountain states—an isolated refuge where they could outlast the Depression. In the meantime, the more famous pro teams in America, which were based in eastern cities, were barely surviving. The New York Rens, for instance, who in 1931 had been playing before 10,000 delirious fans at the Renaissance Casino, averaged only 400 fans for their first five games two years later. The Rens were forced to leave the East and make a long road trip down south, where they played black college teams before crowds of 200 or fewer. And the Savoy Big Five, newly reconstituted under Dick Hudson's management, had also been forced to go on the road, and the *Defender* reported that they were playing in "hick towns and feeling that they were lucky to be able to perform at all."

It was Abe Saperstein's foresight to have anticipated the hard times and have staked out his territory years before the big name teams were forced to join him on the blue highways. He now had a four-year jump on the competition. Sensing his advantage in the Midwest and the Rens' vulnerability, Abe began to challenge the Rens' preeminence as the unofficial "colored world champions." Showing his chronic tendency toward hyperbole, Abe began trying to convince the world—or at least his loyal band of Midwestern sportswriters—that the Trotters were on the same plane as the Rens. "Only the New York Renaissance team can rival this colored club when it comes to playing basketball," the *Breckenridge* [Minn.]

Gazette-Telegram faithfully reported in January 1933, "and Manager Saperstein believes his team could win the world's colored basketball championship could he sign the Renaissance team for a series of games."

Not surprisingly, Rens' owner Bob Douglas completely ignored Abe's boast, which was ludicrous. The Globe Trotters were nowhere near as skilled as the Rens, who had been playing the top pro teams in the country for years. When Douglas refused to dignify Abe's challenge with a response, Abe simply ratcheted up the rhetoric, telling the *Defender* that the Globe Trotters were officially laying claim to "the National cage title," and asserting that the Trotters had "repeatedly challenged the New York Rens, but the Harlem team has avoided meeting the Westerners." In lieu of playing and beating the Rens, Abe was now trying to claim the title by default, which was even more preposterous. In truth, probably the last thing Abe wanted was to actually play the Rens. He had already been ducking the better teams in the Midwest, and had been waxed three times in a row by the Rochester Elks Aces and soundly beaten by the Minneapolis Barnsdalls, who were hardly in the same league with the Rens. But again, Abe's marketing brilliance shone through. He understood that in marketing, if not in reality, *saying* something enough can make it so.

Abe must have realized as well that every team needs a great rivalry, and so he set his sights on the greatest team of all, particularly in the black community. For the next five years, the Trotters and the Rens would be circling each other like two great panthers, drawing close enough to pick up the other's scent, then moving warily away.

CHAPTER 5

Inman

In January 1933, America began to allow itself to hope again, after nearly four years of utter despair, due in large part to the optimism of one man—Franklin Delano Roosevelt. In his inaugural speech, FDR told the country, "The only thing we have to fear is fear itself," and in the First Hundred Days of his administration he rammed through Congress an alphabet soup of new federal programs—including the AAA, CCC, FERA, and NRA—to stop the bleeding.

At first glance, there would seem to be little in common between Franklin Roosevelt, the wealthy Wasp aristocrat from eastern highbrow society, and Abe Saperstein, the immigrant Jew who had grown up living hand to mouth, moving constantly to keep ahead of the eviction notices. Indeed, there is no comparison between the gravity of FDR's responsibilities and those of Abe. But the men shared two fundamental traits: they were incurable optimists and great salesmen. FDR was trying to sell the American people on his New Deal, which gave the federal government an unprecedented role in economic affairs, while Abe, in his own way, was also peddling hope in the face of despair, selling the American public a form of escapist entertainment—a night at the ball game—to survive the turmoil of the Depression, which had already destroyed the dust-blown dreams of millions of Americans.

In November 1933, Abe began the new season with guarded optimism, knowing that his vagabond team had not only survived, but was beginning to flourish on the back roads of America. The core of the team—Runt Pullins, Inman Jackson, Toots Wright, and Fat Long—had been intact for four seasons, giving the Globe Trotters the continuity to one day challenge the vaunted Rens. Little did any of them, including Abe, realize what turmoil awaited them in the next few months, or how a season of such hope would come crashing down, provoking the greatest crisis in the Globe Trotters' early history.

In early November, the Trotter players gathered in Chicago for ten days of intensive preseason practice—a regimen that would become a test by fire for generations of Globe Trotter hopefuls. Abe brought together all of the players from the two Globe Trotter squads, plus the white New York Nationals, and they were scrimmaging against each other two hours a day.

There were only two players whose jobs were secure: Runt Pullins and Inman Jackson, the stars of the team. But all of the other slots were up for grabs, and by the end of training camp William "Razor" Frazier beat out Toots Wright and Rock Anderson for the fifth starting spot (although Frazier and Anderson would rotate throughout the season). Wright was relegated to the second unit along with Kid Oliver.

But Runt and Inman were untouchable. Jackson, now twenty-six, had matured into one of the most dominating centers in professional ball. He was the focal point of the offense, particularly under the new rules that emphasized the half-court game. "Jackson is the key man of the team," reported the *Alexandria* [Minn.] *Echo Press.* "His effective play under the basket is almost unstoppable and when Big Jack makes up his mind to score a few buckets, it's well nigh impossible to stop him."

Pullins, only twenty-three, was one of the greatest outside shooters in the game and consistently led the Trotters in scoring. In fact, Abe was bragging that Runt had set an "American record" by scoring 2,581 points during the 1931–32 season, although that was another of Abe's nebulous claims. (To begin with, no American scoring records were being maintained at that time, so there was no official scoring record to break. And while Pullins often scored in double figures, he would have had to average over 17 points per game for the season, and surviving box scores from that year don't show him even approaching that.)

Runt and Inman were the heart and soul of the team. Oliver, Long, Wright, and Rock Anderson could rotate between the first and second units, but Runt and Inman were always there. Without them, it seemed, there could be no Globe Trotters.

The Trotters opened their 1933–34 season in Pittsburgh, then drove to Detroit for a Thanksgiving Day game at the Central Community Center, later known as the Brewster Center. This was the first game in what would become a season-opening tradition for the Globe Trotters. The Brewster Center was a recreation center in Detroit's African American community that would become legendary as the training ground for Joe Louis and a dozen future Globe Trotters. The season openers between the Trotters and the Brewster Center team would become huge social affairs in east Detroit, with fans dressed to the nines and standing room only in the modest-sized gym.

In this inaugural game, Runt Pullins and Inman Jackson were off their games, scoring only 6 points between them, but George Easter saved the day for the Trotters, hitting for 12 points from long range and leading the Trotters to a 1-point win, 28–27. The most impressive players on the floor that day, however, were two young Brewster players: Harry Rusan and Gus Finney, whose performances made a strong impression on Abe.

After leaving Detroit, the Trotters headed to their familiar haunts in Wisconsin and Minnesota for most of December and January. There, Abe carried his unconsummated rivalry with the New York Rens to new heights of presumptiveness. Since Bob Douglas, the Rens' owner, had never contested Abe's default claim to the "colored world championship," Abe now went even further and claimed it retroactively. He told a Green Bay reporter that the Globe Trotters had owned the "world's colored professional championship for the past several years."

Of course, Abe could spout off all he wanted in Green Bay, but the black press was having none of it. On January 27, 1934, the *Defender* made its position clear, when sports columnist Al Monroe, a former coach of the Savoy Big Five, described the Rens as "undoubtedly the greatest sports attraction in the world." The Rens were coming to Chicago to play the Savoy team, and Monroe predicted that "when you see the Rens perform you'll be watching the nearest thing to sports perfection." And although he may have had a vested interest, Monroe also made it clear which team he thought was in second place: "the nearest approach to the Rens right now is the Savoy Big 5." The Globe Trotters, to Abe's certain consternation, were not mentioned at all. Abe might be able to convince the *Owatonna* [Minn.] *People's Press* or the *Fargo* [N.D.] *Forum* that the Trotters were the world's colored champs, but nobody was buying it in Chicago or New York.

Nonetheless, Abe remained undeterred. In February, the Trotters followed their usual route into the Dakotas and Montana, where Abe kept up the drumbeat about the mythical "world championship." And out there in the boonies, where there were no other black teams, who was going to dispute him? After all, Abe had convinced these same sportswriters that he was "still under contract" to the Cleveland Rosenblums. In fact, he eventually persuaded some of them to join his cheering section. "This team is one that has for several years run the Renaissance to cover in a perpetual challenge for the world's colored basket ball championship, which the Rens cannot see fit to accept," wrote Preston Hinebaugh.

Ironically, at the same time Abe was bragging about the Globe Trotters' straight basketball skills, their showmanship was becoming more overt, as the players were continually inventing new tricks and wrinkles. Inman Jackson developed more elaborate hand tricks, palming the ball and rolling it up and down his arms. Fat Long started spinning the ball on one finger. The Trotters played catch as though the basketball was a baseball. More and more, the Trotters' comedy was getting top billing over the basketball. One newspaper ad described them as "a 5-man circus—you'll laugh yourself sick over their antics between gasps at their skill." And the further the Trotters got ahead of an opponent, the more they clowned. In Winona, Minnesota, they played a game against Babe Didrikson's All-Americans, a team featuring the greatest female athlete in the world, who had won two gold medals at the 1932 Olympics. The Trotters built a 20 to 6 lead in the first half, then "clowned the rest of the way."

By February 1934, the Globe Trotters were heading toward

Montana, in the midst of a terrific season. As a reflection of their success, Abe had even booked the Globe Trotters' first-ever tour of the West Coast, with games scheduled in Spokane, Seattle, and Portland, among other cities. And then, shockingly, it all fell apart—the West Coast tour, the mythic "colored championship," the whole damn team.

In February 1934, Montana was enjoying the most unseasonably warm winter in its history. Average temperatures were nearly ten degrees above normal, and highs reached the seventies in some parts of the state. Snowfall was the lightest ever recorded. The snowcaps had completely disappeared from the lower elevations of the mountains, and ice was melting in the streams and rivers. Livestock were turned out of their barns to feed on the range. Farmers in the southern part of the state were out disking their fields, and some even risked an early planting. On the evening of February 12, a brilliant meteor was observed in the southern sky, which was interpreted as an omen of good luck.

Like the locals, the Harlem Globe Trotters were basking in the unexpected warmth, as they played their way across the state in anticipation of their West Coast tour. Their first game had been in Poplar on February 7, in the northeast corner of the state, only fifty miles from Canada. Poplar was in the Fort Peck Indian Reservation, the home of 6,000 Sioux and Assiniboine Indians. Prior to the game, the neighboring *Wolf Point Herald News* carried an ad that described the Trotters as "the Sensational Darky Champions"—and one can only wonder how that description went over with the Sioux.

From Poplar, the Trotters worked their way across the state's northern rim on U.S. Highway 2, through Malta, Chinook, and Havre to Shelby, where they played an unscheduled doubleheader on the eleventh, after so many people were turned away for the first game. Then the Trotters headed south to Great Falls, and into the Rockies for games in Butte, Helena, Bozeman, and Harlowton, winning every game along the way. At last, the Globe Trotters looped back east, driving to Billings for their last scheduled game on February 17.

It had been a sensational road trip so far, and the unexpected mild weather had made it even sweeter. Runt Pullins, in particular, had played terrifically, scoring 18 points in Great Falls and 15 in Bozeman. In the latter game, the *Bozeman Chronicle* marveled at how he "took the first five tipoffs and dropped them through the hoop for field goals without moving a foot and before the [opponents] had a chance to get their hands on the ball."

And then the Trotters ran into a buzz saw in Billings, losing 38–33 to the Golden Bobcats, a team made up of former Montana State University stars, including three former All-Americans (Frank "Pop" Ward, Cat Thompson, and Keith Ario). Runt Pullins had scored 17 points, more than half of the Trotters' total, but it wasn't enough.

The loss to the Golden Bobcats injected an arctic chill on the otherwise balmy Montana trip, but what occurred in the locker room *after* the game was far more memorable—and numbing. In the five years they'd been together, Abe and the Globe Trotter players had always split the gate receipts seven ways, with the five players each getting one share and Abe getting two, to pay for transportation and promotion. Their entire history—and their recent success—had been built on this egalitarian partnership: they were all co-owners of the team, not employees. In the lean years, driving through the blizzards in Abe's funeral-parlor Model T, nobody had made any money, but now, on a good night with a full house, they could end up with thirty or forty bucks apiece—far more than they could make working a regular job back home in Chicago. As recently as early February, just before the Trotters arrived in Montana, Abe had described their financial arrangement to the *Minot* [N.D.] *Daily News:* "The Trotters play on a percentage basis, which finds each one ready to do or die for that dear old alma mater, Mazuma."

But on this night, in anticipation of their West Coast premiere, Abe announced that he was making some changes in the organization. From now on, he said, there would be no more splitting the gate, no more playing on a percentage, no more do or die for dear old Mazuma. Instead, the players would now be paid $7.50 per game. In effect, the players would now be employees, not co-owners. And the Harlem Globe Trotters would henceforth be Abe Saperstein's team. He would no longer be just the manager and promoter; he would be the owner. The boss.

Whether Abe had been planning this monumental shake-up for a long time is unknown. He may have been influenced by his future father-in-law, Mr. Franklin, who had already convinced him to build up the Saperstein name by putting it on the jerseys. Or the idea may have come as a gradual evolution, as Abe's promotional empire expanded. He was booking two Globe Trotter units, plus the white New York Nationals; had invested in a Negro League baseball franchise; and was promoting another baseball team called the Cleveland All-Nations, which boasted eleven players representing eleven different nationalities. He was becoming a sports magnate, he had professional standing in his field, his name and his face were known to sportswriters in a half dozen states. Why should he still be splitting gate receipts with five Negroes who were lucky to be on his team? And it was *his* team. He was the one doing all the legwork, arranging the bookings, sending out the publicity, massaging the sportswriters, haggling with promoters, collecting the money, and dividing up the receipts. And, not insignificantly, he was the one getting most of the attention in the press—which he liked a lot more than he might admit.

Whatever Abe's motivation, the reaction to his ultimatum was immediate: the team blew up in front of him. Runt Pullins, Fat Long, and George Easter refused to go along with this new edict. Years later, Pullins would claim that the players had been averaging around $40 apiece per game, so $7.50 per game would have meant a drastic reduction in their incomes. "We felt that as long as we had all started as equal partners, we should stay that way," Pullins said.

When Abe refused to back down, the team split right down the middle. Pullins, Easter, and Long quit on the spot, while Inman Jackson and Razor Frazier threw their allegiance to Abe. This appeared to be a mortal blow. Abe might be able to handle the loss of Easter and Fat Long, whose physique was starting to emulate his nickname more each day, but Pullins had been the team's headliner since 1929. Abe had spent five years building up Runt, canonizing him as the holder of the imaginary "American scoring record," and describing him in publicity materials as the "kingpin of the dynamite trio" (Pullins, Jackson, and Toots Wright) and the "sensational midget" with a "natural eye that can find the hoop from the most difficult angles of the floor." At Abe's urging, sportswriters had done their part to enshrine him as well, calling Pullins the "fastest man . . . ever seen on a basketball court" and a "sensational shooter" who "delights his audience by shooting accurately without looking at his basket, backwards, and from ridiculous positions during the game." One scribe accorded him the highest praise of all, for a white sportswriter, knighting Pullins as "the Bronze Nat Holman" (Holman was the star of the Original Celtics).

Now, overnight, Runt was gone. And Long and Easter were gone with him. Abe and the two remaining players, Jackson and Frazier, were stranded in Montana with a full schedule of games but no team to play them. The heralded West Coast tour seemed doomed, and the "colored championship" just a foolish pipe dream. News of the Trotters' breakup soon appeared in the press, with one paper labeling it "an insurrection" and another describing a "disturbance in the front office." With no other choice, Abe suspended the tour and retreated to Chicago, along with his two loyal players, their season in shambles.

This was the first crisis in the Globe Trotters' early history and a crossroads in Abe's management of the team. If he had left well enough alone, the Trotters were on the verge of unprecedented success, with prospects for opening up the entire Pacific Northwest. Now, his actions had destroyed the team and raised fundamental questions that would determine its future: Whose team was it—Abe's or the players'? Who would be at the center of the organization—Abe, as the owner, or Runt Pullins, the star of the team? Finally, who would run the show? Was Abe going to be the boss or the coach, the owner or merely the manager?

If Abe Saperstein anguished over these questions, it certainly wasn't for long, because he acted decisively upon returning to Chicago. He called the Brewster Center in Detroit, got in touch with Gus Finney and Harry Rusan, the two young stars of the Brewster team who had been so impressive in the Thanksgiving Day game, and offered them jobs. "How soon can you get here?" he asked. Then he recalled the venerable Rock Anderson, who at age forty-one had been bouncing around pro teams for two decades, including at least four separate stints with the Trotters. Abe now had a starting five.

Finally, he reached out to the sportswriters whom he had been romancing for five years and claimed that the three rebel players had not quit but had been fired. Long's dismissal, he said, was due to his getting "fat around the middle"; and the loss of Easter and Pullins, his biggest star, was of no concern because they had been replaced by "superior players." And, as they would for nearly forty years, the sportswriters bought his story hook, line, and sinker. "Better Than Ever" was the headline in one paper, whose sports editor repeated Abe's version of the crisis verbatim:

> No one hated to break up his old Harlem Globe Trotter combination any more than did Abe Saperstein. . . . But just like all teams, gradually changes had to be made. First went Oliver, then Long was replaced, but came back a year later; this season went the smiling Wright.
>
> Always it was Pullins and Jackson around whom the Globe Trotters play centered. Then Pullins gradually started causing Saperstein trouble and the break finally came last week when Saperstein realized that if things progressed any further he would merely be the booking manager. Pullins did not think that the mild tempered Abe would ever fire him, but that's just what happened. Now that he's taken the step, Saperstein is glad of it and in a letter to me today he says that the new blood and the set up have given him a classier ball club than ever.

Abe's handling of this split with Runt Pullins would become the template for similar player revolts in decades to come. Abe had crossed his own Rubicon from which he would never look back. From this point on, no player would be indispensable, and the most important member of the Harlem Globe Trotters would be their owner, Abe Saperstein. He was the institution; he was the franchise. Players would be seen as cogs in the machine to be replaced with newer or better parts. Each player would have a designated role—the dribbler, the showman, the wing man—and when one left and a new one arrived, Abe would merely crank out a press release to announce the arrival of a "superior player" who made the Globe Trotters "better than ever." And if Abe said it, the sportswriters would surely write it, and it must be so.

★

Less than three weeks after the breakup in Montana, the new "improved" Harlem Globe Trotters were back on the road, with Gus Finney, Harry Rusan, and Rock Anderson joining Inman Jackson and Razor Frazier in the lineup. In early March, they started playing their way across Minnesota and North Dakota, hoping to salvage the West Coast tour.

In Runt Pullins's spot, Abe inserted Rusan, another small, fast, eagle-eyed guard. Finney took George Easter's place, and Rock Anderson supplied a wide body in the lane, replacing Fat Long. And since Negroes all looked alike to white people, who could tell the difference?

It took Rusan and Finney about a week to hit their stride, but then the Trotters reeled off a string of victories. After beating the Minot (N.D.) Elks by a score of 47–31, the manager of the Minot team was so impressed that he told the *Minot Daily News,* "The Trotters displayed better form than in any of the previous eight encounters with the Elks."

Not everyone agreed. "Without Easter and Pullins, the sensational scoring pair formerly with them, [the Trotters] were not the outfit they were a year ago," wrote the *Minneapolis Star.*

By late March, however, the reinvented Globe Trotters seemed to be, as Abe had predicted, "a classier ball club than ever." Surprisingly, they even garnered their first story in the *Pittsburgh Courier,* the second most popular black newspaper in the country. In a glowing piece, *Courier* columnist Chester Washington compared the Globe Trotters favorably with the Rens:

> [The Globe Trotters are] now sweeping through the Midwest like a relentless tornado. Although not from Harlem, this quintet is a close rival to the mighty Renaissance, now an established by-word in world championship basketball circles. The basket-tossing Trotters, managed by A. M. Saperstein,

combine a great passing game, superlative ball handling, interspersed with a generous amount of odd and unusually comic floor antics.

As for Runt Pullins, within a few weeks he had formed his own team, which he called, after an exhaustive name search, the Harlem Globe Trotters. It was the first of many copycat teams that would crib the Globe Trotters' name. Runt took his team right back to Minnesota and the Dakotas, challenging Abe on his familiar turf. He even managed to steal games out from under Abe's nose. In Rochester, Minnesota, a game was advertised for Abe's Harlem Globe Trotters, but it was actually Runt's team that showed up to play.

By mid-March, the two identically named teams were competing head to head, and Abe was frantically trying to clear up the confusion over which was which. He told the *Fargo Forum* that his team was the "original Harlem Globe Trotters," which had been organized seven years ago in New York by Abe, while the other club was "under the direction of Pullins and Easter, two former players with Saperstein's team who have split with the original club."* Despite Abe's efforts, however, there were now *two* Harlem Globe Trotter teams touring the Midwest, and others would soon be on the way.

The most conspicuous effect of Runt Pullins's departure was that Inman Jackson now became the unquestioned leader of the team, shouldering the load as top scorer, showman, and team captain. This was a huge adjustment for Jackson. "He had been surrounded by the same players for four years, but now he had a completely new team," says J Michael Kenyon. And despite his taciturn nature, "Big Jack" was forced to step into the role of the headliner, carrying the team on his back. And as he did that, the tributes began to roll in. One paper reported: "The leading role in the professional basketball show last night was played by Inman Jackson, towering center of the Harlem five, and with all due credit to other great pivots seen here none compare with tall Inman."

As team captain, he became the leader both on and off the court.

---

* *This statement contains at least two, if not three, factual errors: the Trotters were not from New York, were not seven years old, and were not, most likely, organized by Abe.*

He even began to take on management and marketing responsibilities when Abe was away booking games, as shown in this letter to the editor he sent to the Iron River, Michigan, newspaper:

> To Iron River Basketball fans
>
> We wish to extend our thanks for a very pleasant stay in your town and also say we have never had a more interesting game than we had with your young team. Now it is never our plan to run up a large score on our opponents and our first quarter is always spent keeping an even pace just enough to win nicely. But I must say we surely underestimated the Iron River boys and in the last quarter that game was anybody's game. Of course, we could beat the boys in a return game, but we would surely play it differently.
>
> THE GLOBE TROTTERS
> INMAN JACKSON, CAPT.

He took his leadership role so seriously that not even a severe injury could keep him out of the lineup. In mid-March, he damaged an artery in his left arm so badly that he couldn't use the arm at all, yet he still played every minute of the next few games. "Jackson played the entire game with just one hand and arm to work with and was still the best two men on the floor," the *Helena* [Mont.] *Independent* reported.

In late April, the Trotters made their third venture into Canada, playing a series of games in Winnipeg and other cities. Their opponents included Abe's white New York Nationals and the House of David, an unusual barnstorming team sponsored by a communal religious sect in Benton Harbor, Michigan (the House of David players all wore beards, which was part of the sect's doctrine, although many of the players were not members of the faith).

When the Canadian tour ended, the Globe Trotters turned and headed home to Chicago, having survived the total breakup of the team. Abe would report that gate receipts were "twice as gratifying as last year," which further validated his earlier prediction that the team was "better than ever."

The split with Runt Pullins was not only a demarcation point in Abe's control of the team, it was also a tipping point in the Trotters' progression toward full-fledged clowning. In some ways, the departure of Runt, Toots Wright, Fat Long, and George Easter—all of whom were serious ballplayers—freed up Abe to move into pure showmanship. He no longer had any pressure to fluff up Runt's fictional "American scoring record" or the "colored world championship." Now he could make the Globe Trotters whatever he wanted.

In the 1934–35 season, Abe added two new players, Opal Courtney and Pat McPherson, to go along with Jackson, Frazier, and Rusan. Almost immediately, new comedy routines began to appear. The *Duluth* [Minn.] *News-Tribune* had one of the earliest accounts: "Not content with baffling the Duluthians with straight ball-handling, the Trotters spun the ball dizzily in professional 'wheel' plays, bounced the sphere to make it return to the handler, and rolled it along the floor between the legs of the All-Stars, to the amusement of the crowd."

Opal Courtney was quickly incorporated into the show, spinning the ball on his finger for several minutes at a time and dribbling the ball four or five inches off the floor. Inman Jackson had been doing palming tricks for years, teasing his opponent with the ball, but now he began to openly taunt them, balancing the ball on their heads or rolling it between their legs.

In December 1934, during a game in Iron Mountain, Michigan, a former player from Olson's Terrible Swedes named Tony Wapp began one-upping the Trotters, waving the ball around, windmill style, and bouncing shots off his head. He was showing up the Trotters at their own game, and had the fans in hysterics. Fearing that they were losing the crowd, Inman Jackson felt he had to do something dramatic, so he spontaneously drop-kicked the ball from the free throw line. Amazingly, the shot went it. It was an impromptu reaction to Wapp's showboating, but the crowd went wild, assuming it was part of the act. The reaction was so phenomenal that Inman practiced the dropkick and began attempting it every night. In that same game, Jackson unveiled another gag that would become a Trotter standard for decades. As the game clock was winding down, he hoisted Harry Rusan, the smallest member of the team, onto his shoulders, and Rusan dropped the ball through the basket as time expired.

There was a Pygmalion effect with the trickery. The more the Trotters clowned, the more the crowd demanded it. So the players added comic elements to their traditional ball-handling repertoire, developing routines that were repeated each night. As the Poplar, Montana, paper reported: "They twirled the ball on finger tips. They rolled it between the legs of Great Northern players. They bounced it off arms, elbows and shoulders as the crowd shouted with glee."

A subtle transformation was occurring that only more knowledgeable observers of the game would have noticed. In the past, the showmanship had been secondary to playing ball, and was unveiled only when the Trotters had a safe lead or as a stalling tactic, to give them a rest, but now the showmanship began to take precedence over everything else. They were entertainers first, ballplayers second. In January 1935, the *Aberdeen* [S.D.] *Daily News* wrote:

> [T]he Negroes play primarily to entertain in their own quaint showmanlike manner. You might just as well rip down the bankboards and the baskets once they begin to hit on all eight because they're just in the way. An advertised basketball contest is abruptly turned into a Broadway vaudeville act with the spectators in one continuous round of applause while swaggering in their seats.

More and more, sportswriters began to focus on the Globe Trotters' entertainment value rather than their basketball skills. "Furnishing a laugh with each motion, a chuckle with every dribble," one Montana paper reported, "the Harlem Globe Trotters gave a clever show here tonight." And the *Spokane Spokesman-Review* added this critique: "The [Globe Trotters] make the basketball do everything but talk . . . [and] put on an entertainment that equals vaudeville." To Abe, the results were clear: clowning sold tickets. Barnstorming basketball teams were crawling all over the Midwest, but the Trotters were carving out a unique niche. With the Trotters' popularity on the rise, Abe increased his guarantee to $75 a game, plus a fifty-fifty split of the gate. Yet he still couldn't fill all the requests for games.

The 1934–35 season was rolling along splendidly, with all indications that it would be the Globe Trotters' best season ever, when Abe was suddenly embroiled in another controversy with Runt Pullins, one year after their split. Pullins was still barnstorming in Montana and the Dakotas with his team, now known as the New York Globe Trotters (and soon thereafter as the Broadway Clowns), which included Pullins, George Easter, Fat Long, and Randolph Ramsey. Everywhere Abe went, it seemed, Runt had either been there ahead of him or was right on his tail. An irate Abe started "bombarding" local newspapers with letters and telegrams, attempting to "prove that his club is the original Globe Trotter five and that the other clubs bearing this or similar names are imitators." He told the *Great Falls Tribune:* "While imitation is flattering, it is often confusing to the paying public."

Pullins's wasn't the only Globe Trotter knockoff team on the Midwest circuit, as a plethora of black teams were now descending on Abe's formerly exclusive turf. There were the New York Harlemites, the Negro Ghosts, the Colored House of David, and, most troubling, the Famous Globe Trotters, owned by Bobby Grund from Iowa. This battle with copycat teams would plague the Globe Trotters for sixty years, generating a half dozen lawsuits and millions of dollars in legal fees.

Abe's problems with Pullins were minor, however, compared with the imbroglio that erupted in 1935 between Abe and the Amateur Athletic Union (AAU), which regulated amateur sports. The AAU had an ironclad rule against amateur teams playing professionals, and violators would be banned from further competition. The graybeards who controlled the AAU did not play around: the great Jim Thorpe had been stripped of his two gold medals from the 1912 Olympics after a reporter revealed that he had played semiprofessional baseball, and in 1936, after his triumph at the Munich Olympics, Jesse Owens would be suspended by the AAU for not participating in an AAU-sponsored European tour.

The AAU constitution defined an amateur as "one who engages in athletic competition or exhibition solely for the pleasure and physical, mental or social benefits derived therefrom and to whom the sport . . . is nothing more than an avocation." Furthermore, all players had to have valid AAU membership cards and all teams had to carry an AAU travel permit, which allowed only twenty-one-day barnstorming tours. By any reasonable interpretation, the Globe Trotters were clearly professionals, yet Abe had somehow managed for years to play college and amateur teams in Minnesota, Wisconsin, Montana, and the Dakotas without being challenged. The Trotters depended on those games to fill out their schedule, and purported to have thirty-five college teams scheduled in 1934–35 alone.

When the Trotters arrived in Oregon in February 1935, however, they passed into the jurisdiction of the AAU's Pacific Northwest district, which apparently held the rules in higher regard. Aaron M. Frank, the district president, demanded that Abe produce his AAU travel permit and his players' AAU cards. When Abe couldn't (because he had none), several amateur teams in Oregon and Washington canceled upcoming games against the Trotters. This was a looming disaster that threatened to destroy the entire West Coast tour. A more timid businessman might have been dissuaded by the absurdity of convincing President Frank that the Trotters played solely for pleasure, but not Abe Saperstein. He assured Frank that the Trotters' AAU papers were all in order, but he had inadvertently left them in Chicago and would go home straightaway and fetch them. Of course, there were no such AAU papers in Chicago and Abe had no intention of going home to fetch anything.

What he did, instead, was begin poring over the AAU rulebook like a constitutional lawyer preparing an oral argument before the U.S. Supreme Court, looking for a loophole. And he found one—a hairline crack in the impregnable foundation of the amateur creed that might be exploitable. Although the AAU was adamant that players could not be paid, the rules did allow them to receive up to $8.50 per day for "travel expenses."

This was the opening Abe needed. With the unshakable confidence of a master salesman, he launched a campaign to convince the AAU that five African American men with no other means of support, in the middle of the most devastating economic depression in American history, had been traveling nonstop for five months, driving 30,000 miles in an unheated Model T, playing upwards of 150 games, merely for the pleasure of amateur competition and a pregame hamburger. The proposition was farcical, but Abe had faith in his ability to win over the AAU leadership; and compared with some of the other fables he had invented about his players' Ivy League credentials and his own pro basketball career, this was minor league embellishment.

His initial tactic was to find a more sympathetic audience, since President Frank seemed like a tough nut, so he began working on T. O. "Lefty" Hoagland, an AAU district commissioner in Spokane, where the Trotters were playing. He started wheedling Hoagland with an endless stream of jabberwocky, telling him that the Central AAU, which regulated the Trotters' home state of Illinois, had issued the team's travel permit, and that the Trotters' AAU cards had just expired on February 1 and the new ones hadn't arrived yet. Further, he insisted that the Trotter players received "far less" than the AAU's $8.50 daily expense limit. And finally, he had one of his brothers in Chicago send a telegram to Hoagland claiming that the Central AAU had designated the Globe Trotters as "good-will ambassadors for the National A.A.U."

Incredibly, it worked—at least for the moment. Lefty Hoagland emerged from Abe's impassioned presentation as a born-again Globe Trotter disciple. "The Globe Trotters are amateurs," he proclaimed authoritatively, "competing under the expense limit specified by the A.A.U." But Hoagland went even further, praising the Trotters as *exemplars* of the amateur spirit. "They not only do basketball a great deal of good, with their remarkable displays, but they serve as good-will spreaders of the Amateur Athletic Union," he said.

One might expect that Abe would have been ecstatic, but he wanted more. He wanted the AAU to bring down its wrath on Runt Pullins and Bobby Grund and his other professional competitors, to shut them out of the Pacific Northwest entirely. And Lefty Hoagland gave him just what he wanted, designating the Trotters as the "only officially sanctioned amateur team among all of the barnstorming quintets which have visited the northwest in recent weeks." In effect, Abe was now the *exclusive representative* of the AAU, carrying its official imprimatur, which would completely slam the door on Pullins and the others.

Abe's seduction of Hoagland had been smashingly successful, but it all came crashing down on February 19, when district president Aaron Frank reentered the fray. Obviously suspicious that Abe's only documentation had been a telegram from his brother—*not* from the Central AAU—Frank sent his own telegrams to two AAU officers in Chicago, asking them to authenticate Abe's claims. Their response was brief and direct.

> The Harlem Globe Trotters have played all season without a permit. . . . Under the 21-day rule now in force they cannot qualify as an A.A.U. team, nor do they qualify under Article 17 of our constitution. A permit to travel was denied them.

Employing a Wild West analogy to describe Frank's ruling, *The Oregonian* reported that he had "carved another niche in the handle of the big gun he has been waving" in the faces of Abe and other barnstorming teams that had invaded the Pacific Coast to play "unsuspecting college and A.A.U. basketball teams." If Frank was a gunslinger, then Abe was a dead cowboy dragged out of the saloon and buried on Boot Hill.

The West Coast tour was wrecked, the thirty-five scheduled games against college teams were gone. Yet Abe still wouldn't give up, and a week after Frank's ruling, Abe sat down with the sports editor of the *Mason County* [Wash.] *Journal* to plead his case all over again. He still insisted that his players were paid "considerably" less than the AAU's $8.50 daily limit for expenses, and complained that the AAU's twenty-one-day travel limit was "formulated purely to hamstring such touring attractions as the Globe Trotters." As often happened, once Abe got wound up he couldn't stop himself, and his familiar lies came spilling out again. He repeated his old story that "each of his players was a college graduate," and added several new whoppers about himself, claiming that he had been a "cage star" at the University of Illinois,* had played "several years of professional ball in the East after graduation," and had quit the pros after being "traded to a team he didn't want to play for."

---

* *Today, the University of Illinois has no record of Abe Saperstein having ever been enrolled at any of its campuses.*

All of it did him no good. President Frank wouldn't budge and several amateur teams canceled their games with the Globe Trotters. This was the opening skirmish in a thirty-year war between Abe and the AAU that would only intensify over the decades, as the AAU would adopt an even more restrictive definition of amateurism and even harsher penalties for violators, perhaps motivated, in part, by Abe's attempts to pawn off the Trotters as amateurs. It would get so bad that some amateur teams would take to the court against the Trotters wearing masks and using fake names (the "Masked Marvels," for instance) to hide from the AAU and maintain their amateur status.

In the wake of the AAU fiasco, the Globe Trotters' clowning became even more overt. Much like the earlier crisis with Runt Pullins, Abe's conflict with the AAU propelled the Trotters farther down the road to showtime ball. And although both crises were painful to endure, they were also liberating. The split with Pullins freed Abe from any allegiance to straight basketball, and the AAU controversy freed him from trying to maintain the façade of amateurism. Now he was unleashed to pursue an entirely new form of basketball. And by the end of the 1934–35 season, the Globe Trotters were creating more elaborate—and controversial—comedy routines than ever before. Prior to this, the Trotters had simply expanded upon their standard ball-handling tricks, spinning the ball on their opponents' heads, passing it with such English that the ball came back to them, or rolling it up and down their arms. But now they moved into a realm of comedy that was one of the oldest, and most popular, traditions in America: the minstrel show.

> Here you are, ladies and gentlemen, Sambo,
> The dancing doll. . . .
> He'll keep you entertained. He'll make you weep sweet—
> Tears from laughing.
> Shake him, shake him, you cannot break him
> For he's Sambo, the dancing, Sambo, the prancing,
> Sambo, the entrancing, Sambo Boogie Woogie paper doll.
>
> RALPH ELLISON,
> *INVISIBLE MAN*

White people in America have been laughing at black people since before the nation was born. Comical, stereotypical images of African Americans were prevalent during the colonial period, fueled by white perceptions of blacks as "mirthful by nature." As Joseph Boskin says in his seminal work, *Sambo: The Rise and Demise of an American Jester:* "Presumed to be intrinsically comical, black actions became a vast source of white humor." As early as the 1790s, white actors in blackface were performing parodies of blacks on the stage, and by 1828, when the song "Jim Crow" became a popular hit, a pantheon of comic Negro characters (including Sambo, Tambo, Rastus, Pompey, Caesar, and Uncle Tom) had become institutionalized on the American stage. Minstrel shows became so popular, in both the North and South, that, according to Boskin, at least thirty-nine full-time minstrel companies were performing prior to the Civil War.

Even after Emancipation, the minstrel show survived for nearly a hundred years. In the 1930s, the Federal Theater Project, one of FDR's New Deal programs, staged minstrel shows around the country and distributed minstrel scripts to Boy Scouts, school groups, and youth clubs. During World War II, the USO dispensed hundreds of minstrel songs and skits to military bases around the world. And as late as 1954, Bing Crosby and Danny Kaye performed a minstrel bit in the film *White Christmas.* Strangely enough, black minstrel groups (with black actors wearing burnt cork) were very popular in the African American community, and were still performing well into the 1930s (including at the Savoy Ballroom in Chicago, which even held an annual minstrel ball). The image of the happy-go-lucky, shuffling, lazy, ignorant, chicken-stealing, craps-shooting, dialect-spouting, whiskey-sipping, conniving black man who's always trying to fool Mr. Whitey was promulgated in American popular culture in songs, plays, novels, racist jokes (in the 1920s, *Collier's* and *Reader's Digest* devoted sections to "Negro Humor"), comic books, postcards ("coon cards"), Currier and Ives prints, salt and pepper shakers, Mammy and Sambo figurines, and red-suited yard jockeys. In the twentieth century, that tradition was carried on by radio, movie, and television characters such as Stepin Fetchit, Amos 'n' Andy, Farina, Buckwheat, and Rochester.

The Harlem Globe Trotters, more than any other black team in America, must be understood in the context of that complicated history. It would be a simpler equation if they had remained just another black barnstorming team struggling to make a living in the Depression, but as the comedy routines in their games increased, so too did the scrutiny of what made those routines funny. In other words, what were their white audiences laughing at, and what images of black men were the Globe Trotters portraying? It is not coincidental that the Globe Trotters rose to prominence at the same moment in history when the highest-paid black actor in the country was Stepin Fetchit, and the most popular black radio stars (although they were actually white actors) were Amos 'n' Andy, whose show debuted on Chicago's WGN in 1928, when Tommy Brookins's Globe Trotters were just forming.

By March 1935, Abe Saperstein had begun incorporating gags that played off the traditional stereotypes of African Americans that white Americans had been laughing at for decades. The most conspicuous example was a new "craps-shooting" gag that became part of every game: while two Trotters played keep-away from the opposing team, the other three would lounge on the floor, rolling dice. There seemed to be a deliberate transition from showing off the Trotters' superlative basketball skills, and making fools of their white opponents, to making fun of blacks. Today, in hindsight, Abe's use of such stereotypes to get laughs seems inexcusable, but in the context of that time, it would have been a natural progression for a white owner of a black team, in search of comic inspiration, to draw on the most pervasive tradition of black humor in American popular culture.

Abe's increasing use of stereotypical humor, modeled on the popularity of Stepin Fetchit, was obvious to fans and sportswriters alike. They got the jokes. Indeed, some sportswriters began to mimic the racial overtones, using minstrel dialect. A headline in one British Columbia paper read: "Cullud Gemmen From Noo Yawk Will Show How Hoop Game Should Be Played." And some of the Trotter players were even given minstrel roles and nicknames: "Abe Saperstein's traveling minstrel show featuring End Men Robert 'Stepin Fetchit' Frazier . . . and Harry Russan [sic], a kinky-haired mite with more tricks than you could shake a stick at, arrived at the Viking gym a little late last night."

By the end of the 1934–35 season, the Harlem Globe Trotters had overcome the loss of their top star, the threat of copycat teams, and the embarrassment of being run out of Washington State by the AAU. They had forged their own unique blend of basketball and comedy, some of it overtly racial, that would define their legacy for decades to come. They had proven themselves to be survivors, had taken the worst blows the Depression could offer, yet they were still stuck in the backwaters of the American heartland. Over the next few years, Abe Saperstein would attempt to move the Globe Trotters onto the national stage, to build a national reputation that would open the doors to the gleaming cities back east. And to do that, he knew that he would have to challenge the greatest team of all.

CHAPTER 6

The Rens

In January 1939, Abe Saperstein, the former Lake View bantamweight, was anxious to move up to the heavyweight ranks. And frankly, time was running out. He was thirty-six years old, with a wife and a one-year-old daughter, Eloise, and the signs of middle age were rushing headlong at him at an alarming pace. All his life he had been teased about being short, but now his girth was catching up with his height, and that too was becoming a source of ridicule. The list of unflattering adjectives used by sportswriters to describe him was expanding as fast as his waistline: round little man, rotund, roly-poly, squat and barrel-chested, pudgy, chunky, a bowling ball—the list went on and on.

Moreover, the Globe Trotters had been out on the road for a decade, yet other than an occasional game in Detroit, Chicago, Portland, or Seattle, they were still playing the tank town circuit. If Abe's team was ever going to break into the big time, it would have to come soon. He had paid his dues in the boonies for ten years; now he wanted more.

By most measures, Abe was already a successful businessman. In the past four years, he had developed a stable of black teams, including two Globe Trotter units (east and west) plus the Boston Brownskins, which functioned as a minor league club for the Trotters. He had even branched out beyond black teams, and was promoting ethnic teams of every description. Currently, he was fielding the Hong Wa Kues, a team of Chinese Americans from San Francisco, and the Cleveland All-Nations team. In addition to his own teams, he had a financial interest in several "farm teams" in Detroit and Dayton, Ohio, and had developed a feeder system for new players, as a result of his relationships with black coaches in Cleveland, Cincinnati, and Detroit. And during the spring and summer, he was busier than ever with Negro League baseball, as he now owned the Chicago American Giants and was the publicist for the greatest event in black baseball, the East-West All-Star game in Comiskey Park.

Abe's stature as a businessman and promoter had grown accordingly. He was no longer the young "smiling lad" of 1929 who did it all, as team manager, driver, ticket taker, and substitute player. No, in the eyes of the press, he had become a sports mogul—a full-fledged business magnate with a staff of secretaries in Chicago and a cadre of road managers who oversaw his teams while he was home, booking more games. And although sportswriters may have poked fun at his waistline, their adoration of him bordered on reverential. He had been lauded as a "guiding genius," a "pioneer," the "originator of entertainment basketball," and the "Little Napoleon of the Hardwood" with an "uncanny wizardry of judgment."

The Harlem Globe Trotters were still his flagship team, and they were doing better than ever. Abe had increased their schedule to 160 games per year, yet he was still overwhelmed with requests for games, including from such far-flung places as Hawaii, Mexico, England, France, and Estonia. And despite the lingering Depression, now in its tenth year, gate receipts had increased each year.

The Globe Trotters were still winning over 90 percent of their games, but they had evolved into a full-blown show business extravaganza. When promoters booked a game with A. M. Saperstein Enterprises, they didn't just get a basketball game; they got a traveling vaudeville show. Borrowing from Dick Hudson and the old Giles Post tour of Wisconsin in 1927, Abe now carried his own halftime entertainment, including such acts as Bunny Leavitt, the world's champion free throw shooter (Leavitt set the record by sinking 372 free throws in a row, missed one, then hit 499 in a row). Leavitt also served as the Trotters' road secretary when Abe was away.

On the court, the Globe Trotters' show had become so entertaining that fans sometimes didn't want the games to end. In Vancouver, the referee was booed when he blew his whistle to end the game, and one man yelled out, "If you tell me how much you want for that whistle, I'll buy the dang thing." Sometimes the officials themselves couldn't bear to end the show. As one newspaper reported: "Even the timekeepers and referees were so intrigued they looked on wide-eyed and let the show go an extra four minutes."

The Globe Trotters were drawing more attention than ever from the press. They had been featured in *Ripley's Believe It or Not* comic strip, had been compared to having "dinner with the Marx Bros.," and one enthusiastic writer claimed that they put on a show that "had Ringling Brothers beat forty ways for Sunday." Abe's likeness and those of his players were now recognizable across the Midwest and Pacific Northwest, having been displayed on a series of cartoon posters that he had commissioned by noted Chicago artist Forrest B. Myers.

As the team's popularity had increased, the entire Globe Trotter operation had been upgraded. The days of bouncing around the Dakotas in the old unheated funeral-parlor Model T were finally gone. A near disaster in Montana, in April 1936, might have forced the issue. After the clutch burned out on their car, Abe and the team were stranded in a blizzard and marooned for two days in a sheep-herder's cabin with seventeen people. That winter was so ferocious that they had to travel by train much of the time, yet even their train was trapped in a snowslide for fifteen hours. Now, however, the Trotters were traveling in a specially equipped station wagon, in which they logged over 35,000 miles per year.

Abe had changed, the Globe Trotter operation had changed, and so had the game of basketball. In the past four years, the rules had changed more dramatically than in the previous forty-eight years since Dr. Naismith invented the game. Two fundamental changes had ushered in the modern game of basketball. First, the center jump after every basket was eliminated, and then the three-second rule in the lane was extended to *any* offensive player, with or without the ball. Almost overnight, basketball was transformed from a plodding game in which slow-footed players hunkered under the basket, hog-ging the lane, to one of constant movement. To their credit, the Globe Trotters adapted brilliantly to the new rules. Abe had the foresight to recognize the implications right away, and predicted that the new three-second rule would "eliminate the pivot play or 'Man-in-the-hole' entirely and make a much faster game. . . . I am getting an almost all new team, a bunch of boys who are 'Runners,' for in this new game a player will have to be on the go all the time."

The Trotters were forced to abandon their traditional offense, which featured a "double pivot"—with Inman Jackson planted under the basket and a second pivot man near the free throw line. Now forced to move with the ball, the Trotters developed a figure-eight "weave" revolving around a single post man, which would become their signature for decades.

True to his word, in the wake of the new rules Abe recruited a new crop of players. Almost all of the old-timers were now gone: Kid Oliver, Toots Wright, Fat Long, Opal Courtney, William "Stepin Fetchit" Frazier, and Gus Finney. Only Harry Rusan, the dead-eye shooter from Detroit, and Rock Anderson, who would make his final curtain call with the Trotters that season, were still on the team. And, of course, Inman Jackson—Abe's Rock of Gibraltar.

The new Globe Trotter players were bigger, faster, stronger, and more athletic than their predecessors. Some of them had *true* college experience, as opposed to the faux college pedigrees that Abe had made up. The new players included: Ted Strong, a six-foot-three, 207-pound bruiser from Baltimore with gigantic meat hooks ("the biggest hands in basketball," Abe would say), who was also an All-Star first baseman for Abe's Chicago American Giants; Babe Pressley from Cleveland, a terrific rebounder and defenseman; Bernie Price, a six-four center from Toledo; Zach Clayton, a Philadelphia native with a linebacker's physique; and Bill Ford, from Columbus, Ohio, a smooth outside shooter.

The one constant through all of the changes had been Inman Jackson. He had looked like an old man since his mid-twenties, but now, although only thirty-two, he looked ten years older. The wear and tear of over fifteen hundred basketball games in ten years, play-ing a game a night and twice on Sunday, had eroded his skills and aged him beyond his years.

Abe and Jackson both realized that his playing career was coming to an end, but Abe made it clear that "Big Jack" could have a job with the Globe Trotters for as long as he wanted. In their ten years together, traveling five months out of the year, often rooming together on the road, and sometimes having to share a bed in a bug-infested hotel, the two men had moved beyond employer and employee to build a deep, abiding friendship. It was a tribute to the character of both men that they had transcended the barriers of race to build a bond of respect and affection. In every major crisis that the Globe Trotters had faced, Inman had stood with Abe, side by side. When Runt Pullins quit the team, Inman stayed—and the Trotters would have certainly folded if he had left. When Abe had to rebuild the team from scratch, Inman was the cornerstone upon which he built. When Abe decided to move into comedy basketball, Inman was the showman who invented the hand tricks and palming routines that made it happen.

Like any friendship, the relationship had not always been harmonious. Jackson was stoic and sober-minded, not given to frivolities, and would never use two words when one would do. That reticence would sometimes be misinterpreted as subservience, and some Globe Trotter players would even label Inman an Uncle Tom—a "big yaller Tom," they'd call him, or "Abe's boy"—but Inman Jackson was no Uncle Tom. He stood up to Abe when necessary. They sometimes argued and disagreed, and once got so mad that neither one would speak to the other for three weeks, even though they were still sharing a hotel room at night.

As his business enterprise continued to expand, Abe faced a dilemma that any executive must address: whom could he trust with the business? Clearly, Abe had decided that Inman Jackson was that man. By the 1936 season, they began making plans for Inman's transition after his playing days ended. Inman was grooming Ted Strong as his replacement, teaching the young bull his trademark tricks: juggling three basketballs, palming a ball and waving it around his head windmill style, and his "hocus-pocus" gag of teasing an opponent with the ball, then snatching it back.

Two years earlier, Abe had announced that the 1936–37 season would be Inman's "farewell tour" as a player, and fans across Montana, the Dakotas, and Washington State, whom he had entertained so superbly over the years, gave him a rousing sendoff. As planned, the following season Inman moved to the bench as a coach and team manager in Abe's stead, except for occasional fill-in stints on the court. But in 1938–39, the old warhorse would be called out of retirement to serve as the player-coach of the Trotters' "eastern" unit (considered the second team) while Abe directed the main squad (the western unit).

By 1939, Abe Saperstein was an unqualified success in every respect but one. That exception was huge, however, and gnawed at him constantly. In the black press, he was still relegated to playing second fiddle to the New York Rens. The Globe Trotters were enormously popular out west, but the Rens were the unrivaled rulers of the East and the favorite of both the African American community and the black press. The Rens were the main obstacle in Abe's way, guarding the door to the inner sanctum of basketball glory.

For five years, the Rens had ignored the Trotters completely. No matter how many challenges Abe had thrown down, no matter how many claims he had made to the mythical "colored championship," Rens owner Bob Douglas had resolutely ignored him.

One of Abe's problems was that it was difficult to get the attention of the major black newspapers—the *Chicago Defender, Pittsburgh Courier, Amsterdam News,* and the *Afro-American*—which had been focused almost exclusively on the exploits of Jesse Owens and Joe Louis, the most celebrated black athletes in the country. Owens had been elevated to iconic status after his four-gold-medal performance at the 1936 Munich Olympics; and Louis, who had been briefly sidetracked by his loss to Max Schmeling in 1936, skyrocketed to fame when he beat Schmeling in a rematch and then claimed the heavyweight title from James J. Braddock in November 1937.

With the Rens ignoring him, Abe had managed to track down the other legendary team in professional basketball, the New York Original Celtics, although by 1938, the Celtics were no longer legendary or original. Their three greatest stars, Nat Holman, Joe Lapchick, and

Dutch Dehnert, had retired, and after several internal splits the team was now owned by singer Kate Smith. Still, the Celtics' reputation was formidable, even if their talent was not. In March 1938, the Globe Trotters and Celtics had played in Chicago, with the game ending in a controversial tie. With 1:10 left in the game and the score tied, the Celtics had suddenly left the court, claiming they had a train to catch. But Fay Young, sports editor of the *Defender,* accused the Celtics of bolting to protect their bets, and claimed that some of the players were still in Chicago the next morning.

In any case, the game helped build the Trotters' reputation. If they could play with the Celtics, they could play with the Rens. First, however, they had to catch them. In January 1939, determined to finally get Bob Douglas's attention, Abe ran an announcement in the *Courier*:

Want the Rens

Harlem Globe Trotters, one of the best sepia cage teams, are trying to get a game with the New York Renaissance, Negro professional champions.

Abe had been issuing such challenges out west for five years, primarily in white papers, but this one, on the front page of the *Courier's* sports section, was harder to ignore. A week later, Abe finally got a response—not from Bob Douglas but from his road manager, Eric Illidge, who launched a ferocious counterattack in the *Courier.*

Renaissance Calls Harlem
Globetrotters "Court Clowns"; Will Play
Them 'Winner-Take-All' Game:

Branding the famous Harlem Globe Trotters as the "Clowns of the courts," and also expressing their willingness to answer their challenge to a series "on a winner take all basis," the noted New York Renaissance basketball team answered the singing challenge of the Harlem Globe Trotters Monday. . . . Illidge [said] that not only are the Rens unafraid of Abe Saperstein's Trotters but they would play them at any time, at any place, for nothing. . . . The Renaissance also state that the Globe Trotters are misinforming the basketball public by advertising that they have played and defeated them, when in reality the two teams have never met.

This was hitting Abe in his most vulnerable spot. The question was percolating through the black community: were the Globe Trotters sensational ballplayers or Stepin Fetchit clowns? Clearly, Illidge was speaking for Douglas, who would later make the same criticisms himself. Douglas felt that Abe's brand of showmanship was demeaning to African Americans and the equivalent of a minstrel show in shorts. Douglas didn't like the Trotters' clowning and he apparently didn't like Abe.

In truth, this debate over the Globe Trotters was becoming more polarizing, and not just between Abe and Douglas. By 1939, the Globe Trotters' clowning had become even more stylized, and relied heavily on racial stereotypes. The Trotters were still performing their traditional ball-handling tricks, and had now added a slow-motion football pantomime and a baseball routine, in which one player would pitch the basketball to another, striking him out. These gags were fairly neutral in terms of racial imagery, but their "craps-shooting" gag had palpable racial overtones—which is exactly how audiences and sportswriters interpreted it. "The boys stopped shooting after piling up a 24–0 lead," one reporter wrote. "After that someone produced some dice and the job of playing was left to one man while the other four busied themselves getting some new shoes for junior." Another writer described it this way: "They went through football formations, baseball antics, and finally tossed out a pair of 'bones' and rolled for each other's knee guards."

In addition to the craps shooting, Abe had added another troubling bit to the show: Ted Strong spent the entire game chattering in a high-pitched, childlike, almost unintelligible voice—what one reporter described as "forty minutes of vociferous squealing by big Ted Strong, the gigantic guard, [who] drew gales of laughter with his moans of 'foul, foul.' "

Was this innocent slapstick comedy or an insidious effort to make African American ballplayers look like buffoons? At least one reporter interpreted it as the latter: "This writer has seen the

Harlems in action and—'Fo' goodness sakes, they sho can toss those buckets.' " Even when complimenting the players, sportswriters' own racial stereotypes leaked into the language. "You have seen a cyclone; you have heard a symphony; you have rubbed shoulders with aristocrats," one wrote. "Now step forward and meet the star spangled black rosebuds of Harlem. . . . Anyone who saw Papa Saperstein's dusky darlings last year knows just what can be done with the big brown melon for which those gentlemen of Georgia have such an affinity—and how easy it can be made to look."

In fairness, while some audiences may have been laughing *at* the Trotters, they were usually laughing even harder at the Trotters' white opponents—who were, in most cases, the fans' hometown heroes. During one game in New Westminster, British Columbia, the local team put all nine of its men on the court at the end of the game, trying to stop the Trotters from scoring. As the paper reported: "The Adanacs were really and truly stooges and were so intent on stopping the invaders that they had nine men on the floor for five minutes. It only added to the hilarity."

A decade later, Ralph Ellison would write in *Invisible Man:* "I am invisible, understand, simply because people refuse to see me. . . . When they approach me they see only my surroundings, themselves, or figments of their imagination—indeed, everything and anything but me." The Globe Trotters' white audiences didn't see the humor as demeaning because it was how they *imagined* blacks really were. But Bob Douglas saw it—and didn't like it. And he wasn't the only black businessman who recognized the racial subtext of Abe's humor. In February 1939, the *Courier* ran a cartoon showing five Harlem Globe Trotter players and their team manager (a black man) standing beside the referee. One of the Globe Trotters is barefoot, and the referee is pointing at his feet and warning, "All right, but if he's gonna play like that, he's gotta cut his toenails!"

Ultimately, however, to a marketing virtuoso like Abe, all publicity was good publicity, and despite the Rens' dismissive reaction, Abe had to be thrilled that, after years of futile pursuit, the battle was finally engaged. To Abe, playing the Rens was almost more important than beating them; at least the Trotters would be validated as being in the same league.

Now that the Rens had responded to the challenge, the black press quickly embraced the idea. The *Pittsburgh Courier* began pushing for a showdown: "With such a great court duel brewing, one which the public would surely support, the *Courier* sports department suggests that the rival managers book the teams in a two out of three game series for the sepia court title. The games would be played in three large cities, with each team's share of the proceeds being donated to charity."

Once the Rens put their prestige on the line, they were determined to keep the heat on Abe. The next week, they issued their own challenge in the *Courier,* which was headlined "Globe Trotters Afraid?"

> The Harlem Globe Trotters, claimants to the sepia court title, have failed to answer the challenge tossed at them by the famous New York Renaissance. Cage fans are beginning to wonder if the Trotters are backing down.

Suddenly, after five years of nonstop boasting, Abe fell strangely silent. For the next month, there was not a word from anybody in the Globe Trotters organization about the Rens. The main Trotter unit was playing out west, on a monthlong trek through British Columbia and Washington, which might have partially explained the silence, but it was also a shrewd move on Abe's part to let the Rens dangle.

Eric Illidge now got a taste of what it was like to be ignored, and he didn't like it. The first week of February 1939, he made a special trip to the *Courier's* office, cornered sports editor Wendell Smith, and delivered a vitriolic tirade against the Trotters:

> "I have just dropped in . . . to inform you for the 15th successive season that we have the best basketball team in the world. . . . We have the greatest team in the country . . . and in a three game series will run any of them half ragged."

Smith was a Rens loyalist, but even he felt that Illidge "doth protest too much," and prodded him about the Trotters' challenge:

"There is no doubt about the greatness of the Renaissance. If memory doesn't fail us, they've been winning ball games since the Industrial revolution. But, like it or not, some gentlemen from their own home town have been going around the country of late and telling folks that the only reason they haven't won the cage title from Eric's boys is because they can't get a game with the Rens. The gentleman behind the woodpile answers to the name of the Harlem Globe Trotters."

This was too much for Illidge, who began shouting and gesticulating so wildly that Smith called him "Eric the Red face."

"I brand that story about us not wanting to play them in the same terms that President Roosevelt branded the stories about him getting us entangled with them Europeans," Illidge exclaimed, suddenly elevating the Trotters-Rens rivalry to the looming war in Europe. But Illidge was just warming up. "We will play the Harlem Globe Trotters anytime, anywhere," he said. "They've been going around telling folks how good they are, and how they will beat us, but we issued them a public challenge and they're afraid to answer it."

Obviously relishing his role at the nexus of the controversy, Wendell Smith attempted to broker a game:

So the challenge has been reissued again. The Renaissance are demanding the Globetrotters answer this time, or keep their traps shut forever more. Which, in our way of thinking, is no more than right. It is now the duty of Mr. Abe Saperstein, owner of the Harlemites, to offer some kind of answer. If all this talk about the Globetrotters being able to beat the Renaissance has been issued by "lil" Abe, and we have reason to believe that it has, for publicity purposes, we would suggest that he put a muffler on his ballyhoo. For the last time, Mr. Saperstein should answer this challenge or forever more hold his peace.

Abe remained silent. In truth, he could afford to let the controversy with the Rens simmer because it appeared that it would resolve itself: both teams had been invited to the first World Professional Invitational Basketball Tournament in Chicago, scheduled for late March, where they would likely meet. And Abe didn't need to say a word about the rivalry because Eric Illidge couldn't *stop* talking about it. The Trotters' impudence had so outraged him that he was nearly out of control, and had become the Trotters' best marketing agent. Unwittingly, he was doing what Abe had been unable to do himself: build national interest in the black press about a showdown between the two teams.

★

On March 12, in their final tuneup before the World Professional Tournament, the Globe Trotters staged a rematch in Chicago with Kate Smith's New York Celtics, with whom they had had the controversial tie the previous year. Thanks, no doubt, to Eric Illidge's meltdown a month earlier, the *Pittsburgh Courier,* which had typically ignored the Trotters, did something it had never done before: it sent a reporter to cover a Trotters game.

The Celtics were an aging, over-the-hill quintet, and this time the Trotters left no doubts about their superiority, winning going away, 37–24. The *Courier's* Chester L. Washington Jr. came away impressed, to say the least. He called the Trotters "one of the greatest colored cage combines of all times," and described how they had "swept the Celts off their feet" with their "dazzling" ballhandling. Washington also reported on a postgame "verbal jam session" with some prestigious black coaches and former players, who had been arguing over which team was better, the Trotters or the Rens. The consensus was that the Rens still held a "majority of superiority," but the Trotters might beat them on an "off night."

This was too much for Illidge, who sent two telegrams to Washington, bragging that the Rens had already beaten the Celtics twice, then added a little jab at Abe. "Globe Trotters take notice," he said with a smirk.

"Thanks for the wires, Eric," Washington wrote. "And until something happens to disprove this contention, that [Rens] quintuplet circus deserves the ranking of the top court combination in the country."

When the pairings were announced for the upcoming World Professional Tournament in Chicago, the Trotters and Rens were placed in the same bracket, meaning they would meet in the semifinals (if they won their first two games). The bottom line was that they would have to go through each other to win the world championship. The rivalry was as hot as it could get. The two teams had been dissected, analyzed, and critiqued. The only thing left was to play the game.

★

By the end of March 1939, all hell was breaking loose in the rest of the world, and America was deeply divided about how to respond. On March 15, Adolf Hitler's storm troopers had seized Czechoslovakia and dared Great Britain and France to do anything about it. The next day, in a driving snowstorm, the Reichsführer himself paraded into the ancient capital of Prague, unfurled his personal banner over Hradcany Castle, the presidential palace, and declared the fallen nation a German protectorate. The Nazis immediately dissolved the Czech parliament, banned elections, and launched an anti-Jewish campaign, which set off a panic among Prague's Jews, who jammed the railway stations, attempting to flee.

Hitler had then taken aim on Poland, and threatened that if anti-German protests in that country didn't stop immediately, Germany would be "compelled to take other measures." Six months earlier, at the Munich Conference, Britain's prime minister Neville Chamberlain had conceded large portions of Czechoslovakia to Hitler, then flown home and announced that he had achieved "peace in our time." By March, however, it was clear that Hitler interpreted that agreement to mean a piece of Czechoslovakia, a piece of Poland, and all of Europe. Chamberlain was now frantically trying to cobble together an international stop-Hitler drive.

Hitler wasn't the only one causing problems. Armies were mobilizing across Europe, Asia, and Africa. In Rome, cheered on by throngs of delirious Black Shirts. Benito Mussolini endorsed Hitler's seizure of Czechoslovakia and threatened to move himself against the French colonies of Algeria, Tunisia, and Morocco. In China, Japanese troops were driving deeper into the central provinces, bringing the fighting almost to the doorstep of Shanghai. And in Spain, Generalissimo Francisco Franco had finally crushed Republican insurgents after the three-year Spanish Civil War and was preparing to accept their unconditional surrender.

In the face of this worldwide turmoil, President Roosevelt was pleading with Congress to amend the Neutrality Act to allow him to sell more arms to Britain and France. Isolationist hawks in the Senate were having none of it, however, and attacked Roosevelt for leading the nation toward "entangling alliances" to defend French and British colonialism. "I would send no money to European war chests, no munitions to any nation engaged in war, and above all, no American boy to be sacrificed to the machinations of European imperialism," roared Idaho's senator William E. Borah.

Perhaps the most fervent isolationist and FDR-hater in the country was newspaper mogul William Randolph Hearst, who owned two Chicago papers, the *American* and the *Herald-Examiner*.* The *last* thing Hearst wanted was more attention paid to the saber rattling abroad, and so, coincidentally or not, his Chicago papers had organized a wonderful distraction for the sporting public: the first-ever World Professional Invitational Basketball Tournament, scheduled for the last weekend in March.

Backed by Hearst's money, the *American* and the *Herald-Examiner* put up $10,000 in prize money and promoted the tourney as the "world series" of professional hoops. Co-promoters Harry Hannin and Harry Wilson invited the top twelve professional teams in the country, and predicted the "greatest array of cage talent ever assembled in one place." It didn't quite work out that way, however, as a number of the invitees declined to participate, and the final slots were still being filled four days before the tournament began. Nonetheless, it was an impressive lineup. The best-known teams were the Rens, Globe Trotters, and New York Celtics. Also in the mix were the Sheboygan Redskins and Oshkosh All-Stars, two of the better teams from the fledgling National Basketball League (*not* the NBA, which had yet to be formed); the bearded House of David; Chicago All-American Harmons; Fort Wayne Harvesters; Cleveland White

---

* *The two Hearst papers would merge into the* Chicago Herald-American *later in 1939.*

Horses; New York Yankees; Illinois Grads; and Clarksburg (W.V.) Oilers.

To further legitimize the tournament, Harry Hannin invited George Halas, owner and coach of the Chicago Bears football team and the Chicago Bruins basketball team, to serve as the tournament commissioner, and Nat Holman, legendary star of the Original Celtics, who was now coaching at City College of New York, to be "honorary referee." For the actual game referee, the promoters had hired the most flamboyant official in basketball, Pat Kennedy, who was famous for his histrionic calls. "No-no-no-NO-NO!" he would yell, "You can't DO that!"

Even with the support of the Hearst empire, however, this inaugural tournament had a difficult time getting press coverage. The *Chicago Tribune* and *Chicago Daily News,* for instance, were understandably reluctant to promote an event organized by their biggest competitors and didn't even mention the tournament until the day before it started. In addition, basketball was still lagging in popularity behind baseball, boxing, football, horse racing, and perhaps hockey; and *professional* basketball was the lowest rung on the ladder, below college and high school hoops.

The top sports stories that weekend were about the Chicago Cubs' and White Sox's final spring training games, a Golden Gloves boxing tournament in Chicago, the upcoming Masters golf tournament, and the national *collegiate* basketball championship—the forerunner of today's NCAA "March Madness"—which would be decided in Chicago on Monday night, when Ohio State and Oregon battled for the national crown. Indeed, the promoters could not have selected a worse weekend for the tournament, given the competition.

There was a deeper reason why the *Chicago Tribune* and the *Chicago Daily News* ignored the tournament: two black teams were playing. And one of them—the New York Rens—was the favorite to win. The rivalry between the Trotters and Rens might have been a hot story in the black press, but the white papers treated it like so many other issues in the African American community: they ignored it completely. Even when the *Chicago Tribune* got around to mentioning the pro tournament, the *Trib's* sports editors couldn't bring themselves to face the race issue head-on. They reported that the "lone Chicago representative" in the tournament was the Chicago Harmons, completely ignoring the fact that the Globe Trotters were from Chicago, too. The Trotters had been in business for over a decade, yet through either ignorance or intent, the *Tribune* still couldn't accept them as a hometown team.

Despite the poor timing for the tournament, at least the weather had cooperated. It had been a glorious week in Chicago, as a warm front brought an early hint of spring. Friday's temperature had reached nearly eighty degrees, and Lincoln Park had been filled with young couples in love and with mothers pushing "freshly starched" babies in strollers. Thousands of office workers in the Loop had taken a half-day holiday, and there was a run on gasoline to fill up for drives in the country. By Sunday afternoon, however, winter was settling back in: a Canadian front was pushing in from the north, bringing showers and colder temperatures. By Monday morning, it would be freezing again.

Teams had begun arriving for the tournament on Saturday, March 25. The Rens checked into the Hotel Grand on South Parkway, where they always stayed in Chicago. "We could look out our windows and see people riding horses up and down the median of South Parkway," recalls John Isaacs, now ninety years old and the lone surviving member of that Rens' squad.

Naturally, the players, coaches, and owners of every team wanted to win. The $1,000 top prize would be insulting by today's standards, but it was decent money in Depression dollars. The real prize, however, was the title—"world professional champions"—which would be worth ten times more than the prize money in future bookings.

Of all the people involved in the tournament, however, the person who had the most at stake was Abe Saperstein. He had spent the past five years promoting the Globe Trotters as the equal of the Rens, with all of his bravado about being the "colored world champions," and now he had to back it up. Publicity and marketing could go only so far; the Trotters had to prove themselves on the court.

With the world championship at stake, Abe went looking for some additional firepower. The Globe Trotters had three solid veterans—Harry Rusan, Ted Strong, and Bill Ford—and three up-and-coming stars—rookies Babe Pressley, Bernie Price, and Hilary Brown, a six-foot-three defensive specialist. And there was Inman Jackson, of course, but he could be counted on for only a few minutes at a time. So, like George Steinbrenner trading for a fireballing closer to help the New York Yankees in their September stretch run, Abe went looking for a closer. Not surprisingly, he looked to Detroit, his most reliable pipeline for new talent (more Globe Trotters have come from Detroit than any other city), and ended up signing Larry Bleach, the best basketball player in the city. A former two-sport star at the University of Detroit and the first black captain of its basketball team, Bleach was a prolific scorer. He signed with Abe just before the tournament and arrived in Chicago in time for the first game.

Sunday's opening round was scheduled at the Madison Street Armory, with a tripleheader in the afternoon and another tripleheader that night. The semifinals for each bracket would be played Monday night, and the championship game was set for Tuesday. The Celtics and Rens, as the presumptive favorites, had been given byes in the opening round, so they would have to win only one game to make it to the semifinals. But the Globe Trotters would have to win twice on Sunday to even have a shot at the Rens.

The Trotters opened their run for the world title in the second game of the afternoon tripleheader, in front of 2,500 fans. Their opponent was the Fort Wayne Harvesters, a team of former Indiana, Butler, and Purdue University players. Three minutes into the game, the score was tied at 7 all, but then Larry Bleach paid his first dividend, hitting a "long looping shot" to start a 6–0 run. The Trotters' switching man-to-man defense completely "bewildered" the Harvesters, who were held scoreless for four and half minutes. At halftime, the Trotters went into the dressing room with a 21–15 lead.

In the second half, the Globe Trotters completely dominated the Harvesters. They opened up a comfortable lead in the final quarter and then, to the delight of their fans, put on the show. The game ended with the Trotters leading 41–33 and the crowd "screaming for more." This may have been the world series of professional basketball, but the Trotters were still going to put on the show if they got the chance.

One down, one to go.

That evening, the Trotters were scheduled to play the nightcap at 10:30 P.M., so they had a chance to watch the Rens' opening game against the New York Yankees. The Trotters had been hearing about the Rens for years, but they were even more formidable in person. This was a team with no weaknesses. There was a cadre of gifted veterans, led by team captain "Fat" Jenkins, known as the "Babe Ruth of basketball," who in his prime was regarded as the quickest player in the game; Eyre Saitch, a long-range gunner who moonlighted as the second-ranked tennis player in the country; Zach Clayton, a former Globe Trotter who had gone over to the Rens this season; and the Rens' twin big men, Tarzan Cooper, a six-foot-four low-post specialist, and "Wee Willie" Smith, a six-foot-five behemoth who could play outside as well as underneath, and could shoot the ball like a guard. If the veterans weren't scary enough, the Rens had a trio of "young bloods" who would have been marquee stars on any other team: John Isaacs, a star point guard from Textile High in New York and the first player Bob Douglas had ever recruited out of high school; Pop Gates, a six-foot-two former all-city pick from Ben Franklin High in New York, who would eventually be elected to the Basketball Hall of Fame; and Puggy Bell, a twenty-three-year-old star from the Harlem YMCA.

The Yankees were not expected to give the Rens much trouble, but they did have one ace in the hole: future Hall of Famer John "Honey" Russell, their player-coach. In his day, Russell had been the best defensive player in basketball, leading the Cleveland Rosenblums to three American Basketball League titles, but he was now thirty-seven and past his prime. "Oh, but Honey Russell could still play," John Isaacs says, admiringly. "Like most of those fellows from that time, they played with their head."

Honey Russell, who would later coach Seton Hall and the Boston Celtics, knew that his team couldn't compete with the Rens' speed or talent, so his game plan was to employ a ball-control offense and a physical defense to keep the Rens out of their rhythm. To everyone's surprise, it worked. The Yankees took an early lead and then sat on the ball, stalling time off the clock. On the rare occasion when the Rens got the ball, the Yankees' suffocating defense kept them from getting "a peek at the basket." The Yankees were challenging every shot and fouling often, but the Rens were missing badly at the free-throw line. Pop Gates alone missed six free throws, and the team missed a total of twelve. At halftime, the Rens were behind 11–7, and the fans were sensing an upset.

Rens manager Eric Illidge felt he had to gamble to get back in the game, so he pulled two of his aging veterans, Eyre Saitch and Fat Jenkins, and inserted two of his younger stars, John Isaacs and Puggy Bell. With fresh legs in the game, the Rens started forcing the tempo, and the momentum began to swing. In the end, it was the "young bloods" who saved the day. The Rens had scored only 7 points in the entire first half, but they outscored the Yankees 23–10 in the second, and came from behind to win 30–21.

The Rens were in the semifinals. Now it was up to the Trotters to do their part.

Their opponent in the nightcap, the Chicago Harmons, was expected to provide more of a test. They had three former DePaul University stars who had played on the 1936 Olympic team, and their owner, Frankie Harmon, had brought in his own closer: Mike Novak, a six-foot-nine All-American center from Loyola University. Novak had just completed his college career Wednesday night in Madison Square Garden, where Loyola lost to Long Island University in the finals of the Basketball Writers Association tournament (now known as the NIT). Immediately after that game, a bidding war for Novak had erupted among the Harmons, Kate Smith's Celtics, and the New York Yankees, but he ended up signing with the hometown Harmons just in time to suit up for the tournament. His specialty was goaltending, which was legal at the time, and Novak had perfected the technique of leaping up and swatting an opponent's shot away just before it hit the rim—a tactic that so infuriated some coaches that they were advocating a goaltending rule, which would eventually be passed. Given that the Trotters' tallest men were six-foot-three (Ted Strong and Hilary Brown), the towering Novak could be an intimidating presence in the lane.

And that's exactly how the game began. Novak batted away a number of the Trotters' shots and, on the offensive end, scored 9 points. But the Globe Trotters shut down the rest of his teammates, who tallied only three baskets among them. The Trotters built a

22–13 halftime lead and won 31–25. Again, Abe's Detroit investment paid dividends, as Larry Bleach led the scoring with 11 points.

At long last, the much anticipated showdown between the Rens and Trotters was going to happen. They would play Monday night in the semifinals of the World Professional Tournament, on the largest stage that professional basketball had ever seen. Whether Abe had really wanted to play the Rens or had just been challenging them as a publicity stunt, he was going to get a chance to make his greatest boast come true. And if the Trotters could, in fact, beat the Rens, then maybe all of his other blarney would be accepted as well. Perhaps the wandering Jew, the boy who slept on the living room couch until he was thirty, would at last find a home. The young man who couldn't figure out what to do with his life would be at the top of his profession—an unqualified success.

If Abe had a lot riding on this game, so did his players, particularly Inman Jackson. One game could not wipe away all the memories from ten years of hard traveling—the two-hundred-mile hops between games and the frigid nights sleeping in a Model T, the stale doughnuts and inedible hamburgers, or the indignities and insults from white people who thought themselves too good to let these tired and hungry men sleep in their flea-ridden motels or eat their greasy slophouse food. One game could not make up for the thousands of hostile glances from Midwestern farmers who had never seen a black face in their town or the bug-eyed stares of their children, who reached out to touch the players' skin to see if the black would rub off.

No, not even a win over the Rens could erase those memories, but it might consign them forever to the past and lead to a brighter future of playing in big towns and big arenas, sleeping in respectable hotels and eating in decent restaurants, creating a life unlike any they had imagined before. A victory could ensure them a future of playing the game they loved and not destroying themselves in the process.

Monday dawned cloudy and gray, with rain showers in the forecast. The balmy springlike temperatures still lingered, but Old Man Winter would be making a return visit that evening, with the mercury dropping back into the thirties. Rens owner Bob Douglas, who seldom traveled with his team, had arrived in Chicago for the big game. In anticipation of larger crowds, the semifinals and finals had been moved from the Madison Street Armory to the more spacious Coliseum. By this point, even the white press had picked up on the importance of the Trotters-Rens showdown and was finally giving the teams their due. "If the pro tournament doesn't do anything else, it at least has finally brought together two teams that fans have been waiting for years to see clash—the New York Renaissance and the Harlem Globe Trotters," columnist Leo Fisher wrote in the *Chicago American*. "These two great Negro quintets are the most adept ball-handlers who have ever stepped on a floor, as far as we're concerned, and when they start their intricate maneuvers against each other at the Coliseum tonight it will be something wonderful to behold."

By 7 P.M., the afternoon showers had stopped, and the crowd began filing into the Coliseum for the evening's tripleheader. The Celtics and Sheboygan Redskins were playing an elimination game in the other bracket at 8 P.M., followed by the Rens and Trotters at 9 P.M., and the Oshkosh All-Stars would face the winner of the Celtics-Redskins game at 10 P.M. By tip-off of the first game, the Coliseum was packed with 8,000 fans, many of them African Americans. A contingent of well-known college coaches, in town for their annual convention, also were in attendance, including Nat Holman of CCNY, Adolph Rupp of Kentucky, and Branch McCracken of Indiana.

After Sheboygan dispatched the Celtics in the first game, it was time for the Trotters and Rens. Even though the Rens' young Turks—John Isaacs and Puggy Bell—had sparked their come-from-behind win against the New York Yankees, Bob Douglas and Eric Illidge started their veteran guards, Fat Jenkins and Eyre Saitch, along with Pop Gates and Tarzan Cooper at forward, and Wee Willie Smith in the pivot. The Trotters countered with Harry Rusan, Babe Pressley, Ted Strong, Hilary Brown, and their hired gun, Larry Bleach. Inman Jackson had played briefly in the first two games, but against the Rens he would never leave the bench.

By the time the warm-ups were concluded, the crowd was already in a frenzy. The excitement in the Coliseum was palpable as tip-off approached. For Abe and the Trotters, all of their dreams were right in front of them. The Rens had more experience in such big games, but even they were feeling the tension. Bob Douglas was so nervous that he could not sit down, and paced up and down in front of the bench.

Pat Kennedy, the theatrical referee, motioned both teams to center court for the opening tip. The players shook hands and wished their opponents a good game. Despite the rivalry, there was mutual respect among the players, although the same could not be said for the owners, as the contest had become a blood feud between Abe and Eric Illidge. The players jockeyed for position around the circle. Ted Strong and Willie Smith, the opposing centers, crouched down to make their leap. Kennedy tossed up the ball, and the game was on.

And then, amazingly, as suddenly as it began, it appeared to be over. The Rens raced out to an 8–1 lead before the fans had settled into their seats. Their big men, Cooper and Smith, were manhandling the smaller Trotter players inside, and Fat Jenkins was hitting from the perimeter. The Trotters seemed to be in a daze, moving in slow motion compared with the Rens. Harry Rusan, the smallest man on the court at five-nine, was completely neutralized by the Rens' larger, faster guards; Larry Bleach and Babe Pressley were clanging shots off the rim; and Ted Strong and Hilary Brown could do nothing against Cooper and Smith.

It got worse. The Rens hit another bucket and a foul shot to make it 11–2. Under the old rules of basketball, the game would have been effectively over. Even under the new rules, it might well be. There was no twenty-four-second shot clock, no time limit on holding the ball, and the Rens and Trotters had each won *hundreds* of games by getting a 4- or 5-point lead and then stalling the rest of the game. The Rens didn't do comedy routines like the Trotters, but they were the most renowned ball handlers in the world and experts at eating up clock time. A 5-point lead was the Trotters' safe margin, at which point they would put on the show—but this was a 9-point lead, a blowout by the standards of the day.

But the Trotters were playing so poorly, the Rens didn't need to stall. Even when the Trotters had the ball, they couldn't score. They went fifteen minutes in the first half without scoring a single point, despite numerous open shots at the basket. They were stone cold. Frozen. They were choking in the biggest game of their lives.

It was Abe's worst nightmare. After all his puffery and boasting, when the Trotters finally got a chance to show the world what they could do, they were embarrassing themselves. The Trotters didn't look like contenders for the crown, but pretenders. They were playing like one of the hick teams they'd been feasting on for years—the Wahpeton Science Wildcats or Buck Bailey's Angels or the Wenatchee Men's Store. Few people had actually expected the Trotters to win, but if they didn't at least make a game of it they would lose all credibility. Instead, they were playing like rank amateurs, not even in the same class with the Rens.

With the clock winding down in the first half, the Trotters finally hit a couple of baskets and whittled the lead to five points, and the half ended with the Rens up 15–10. Five points wasn't an insurmountable lead, but the way the Rens handled the ball, it was close to one. There is no record of what Abe or Inman Jackson said to their disheartened players in the locker room, but it hardly mattered. Everyone in the room knew that unless they started hitting some buckets, the game was over. The Rens were even better at playing keep-away than the Trotters, and so they would have to make the most of their few possessions.

As expected, the Rens came out in the second half and went into their stall. The Trotters seldom got the ball, and even when they did, they were still missing their shots. The few times they managed to score, the Rens responded in kind. The third quarter ended with the Rens still ahead by 5. No matter what the Trotters did, the lead held. The Rens weren't even having to extend themselves.

In the fourth quarter the same pattern continued, with the seemingly impregnable 5-point lead still holding. With four minutes left in the game, the Rens increased the lead to 8, and the game seemed hopelessly out of reach. The clock wound down to two minutes. Time was running out. And then, out of the blue, Babe Pressley hit a long set shot, his first basket all night. Larry Bleach followed with another bomb, and the lead was down to four. It was the closest the Trotters had been since the game began. The crowd stirred back to life. Abe was exhorting his team from the bench. Bob Douglas, who had been pacing the sidelines all night, had chewed his half-smoked cigar down to a stub.

On the Rens' next trip down the court, the Trotters defense stiffened. The Rens missed a shot, and the Trotters got the rebound. They worked the ball upcourt and passed it inside to Ted Strong, who had been smothered all night by Wee Willie Smith and held to only 2 points. This time, however, the big man responded, laying in a basket that cut the lead to two points: 25–23.

There were forty-eight seconds left. Miraculously, the Trotters had come back. They had a chance to win. The fans were screaming. The noise in the Coliseum was deafening. The Rens dribbled the ball up the court slowly, taking their time. With no twenty-four-second clock, once they got the ball across the half-court line, they didn't need to shoot. If the Trotters couldn't somehow get the ball, the game was over. The Rens passed the ball around the key, playing keep-away. The clock was ticking down. Thirty seconds. The Trotters had to foul or steal the ball. Frantically, they were trying to press whichever Ren player had the ball, doubling up on him, trying to force a mistake. Twenty seconds. Suddenly, with the Trotters all sagging on the ball, big Tarzan Cooper saw an opening underneath and broke down the center of the lane, catching his defender unaware. The Rens' ball handler saw him break, whipped a pass to him, and Cooper laid it in. There were fifteen seconds left. The lead was back to 4. A two-possession game.

It was over. The Rens won 27–23. When the gun sounded, their fans rushed onto the court, mobbing the Rens players. Although most of the fans were from Chicago, many were still Rens loyalists in their hearts. Bob Douglas was surrounded by well-wishers. The Globe Trotters straggled off the court, unnoticed by the cheering fans. They were numb and crestfallen, heartsick with the weight of the loss. All the years of building toward this golden opportunity, and now it was gone.

★

The next night, in a game that was clearly anticlimactic, the Rens faced the Oshkosh All-Stars for the world championship. Oshkosh had cut a swath through the other bracket, eliminating the Clarksburg

Oilers and Sheboygan Redskins to earn a spot in the finals. The All-Stars were led by Leroy "Cowboy" Edwards, a former All-American from Kentucky and three-time National Basketball League (NBL) scoring leader, who had already set a tournament scoring record with 18 points in the win over Clarksburg. "Edwards was a horse," says John Isaacs. "And he could take it to the rack, too. . . . If somebody got in front of Leroy, he'd run over them like a Mack truck."

Only 3,000 fans, fewer than half the number that had watched the Rens and Trotters, turned out to see the game. Most of those were rooting for Oshkosh. The two teams had played twice earlier in the year, splitting the two games, and the championship game started out dead even, with the score knotted at 6–6 after seven minutes of play, and 9–9 after eleven. It was a "rough and tumble affair," the *Defender* reported, with both teams fouling often. "That Oshkosh team was massive," Isaacs recalls. "All they wanted to do was beat you up— leg whip you, just lay you out." The big men for both teams—Tarzan Cooper and Wee Willie Smith for the Rens, and Leroy Edwards for Oshkosh—were shutting down the lane, forcing everything to the outside.

Then, halfway through the second period, the Rens exploded. Isaacs, Cooper, and Pop Gates hit five straight baskets, initiating an 11–0 run that blew the game open. The Rens outscored the All-Stars 15–2 before halftime, and went to the dressing room with a 24–11 lead. In the second half, both of the Rens' big men, Tarzan Cooper and Willie Smith, fouled out, and Leroy Edwards was able to rally the All-Stars to within 5 points, but the Rens responded and coasted to a 34–25 victory. They had won the world championship and the $1,000 first prize.

In the consolation game, the Globe Trotters rebounded from their devastating loss to defeat the Sheboygan Redskins, 36–33, in what the *Chicago American* called "easily the best game of the night." Sheboygan led through most of the first half, but the Trotters pulled within one point, 20–19, at the break. Early in the third quarter, Larry Bleach hit two quick baskets to put the Trotters ahead, and the lead seesawed throughout the rest of the game, with the Trotters finally pulling out a thrilling 36–33 victory.

That win earned the Globe Trotters third place and a $400

check. Babe Pressley was selected to the all-tournament team, along with Leroy Edwards and the Rens' Zach Clayton and Puggy Bell (who was chosen as the Most Valuable Player). But third place wasn't something Abe was going to brag about on his publicity posters. Winning the tournament could have opened doors to the biggest venues in the country, but losing to the Rens doomed the Trotters to a purgatory of more rotgut food, filthy hotels, and thirty-dollar purses in Polson, Montana, and Chelan, Washington.

Even more galling, the Rens had stolen the championship trophy in the Trotters' backyard, so they had to sit and watch as the South Side embraced the Rens as conquering heroes. Bob Douglas hosted a big party at the Hotel Grand, and toasts were being raised all night long in Bronzeville's clubs and bars. The next morning, the *Defender* took a photo of the Rens at the Chicago train station as they were about to head home to New York. The players were dressed in suits and topcoats and were doffing their hats in a victory salute. The *Defender* splashed the photo across the top page with the caption "Happy World Champions Off for Home."

While the Rens were celebrating, the African American community expressed pride—and even some aggravation—at how well the two premier black teams had done in the world tournament. Wendell Smith of the *Courier* even leveled an oblique charge of racism against the promoters for seeding the Trotters and Rens in the same bracket. "If they hadn't been paired in the same bracket with the flawless Rens, we might have two sepia teams playing for the title," he wrote. "But, of course, they just couldn't let that happen, could they?"

Despite their loss, the Globe Trotters were praised for their all-around play. "The Globe Trotters have the nucleus of a fine, promising young club," Chester Washington wrote. "They, too, should go places." And the Trotters could find some solace in their courageous comeback at the end of the Rens game, when they cut the lead to 2 points. They had not embarrassed themselves, after all, and had proven they could play with the Rens. But there was no way to soften the blow of losing the most important game in their history. The Trotters were relegated, once again, to playing second fiddle to the Rens. Only now there were no doubts about it. Previously, Abe might have been able to get some takers for his boasts, but now the proof was in: the Rens were the champs, the Trotters were third-place chumps.

It might have been easier to handle if they could have gone back on the road and played their way through the pain. That might have taken their minds off the loss. But the season was over, so they had to listen to the recriminations all summer and fall, answering the same question over and over, like an interrogation that would never end: "Why didn't you beat the Rens?"

Truthfully, there was only one answer to that question: the better team had won. Whether the Globe Trotters would ever get another shot at the Rens, no one knew.

CHAPTER 7

Sonny

It took only one game for Abe Saperstein to realize that his new Harlem Globe Trotters team was different. On November 26, 1939, in one of the first games of the 1939–40 season, the Globe Trotters took on the bearded House of David at the White City arena in Chicago. The Trotters had played the "Bearded Aces" many times before, and they had always been tough opponents. Although the Davids had been eliminated in the first round of the World Pro Tournament by Honey Russell's New York Yankees, they were still a hard-nosed professional squad that could hold its own against anybody.

Yet in this game, the Trotters had completely outclassed the House of David, coasting to a 31–19 win that was more lopsided than the score indicated. Abe played every player who had dressed out—nine altogether—yet the Davids were never in the game. It was the first inkling that this team might be special.

Abe Saperstein was not a man who wallowed in self-pity or gnashed his teeth about the misfortunes that life had bestowed upon him. In his father's Yiddish vernacular, he did not *kvetch*. Nor was he the reflective type who anguished over past mistakes or how he might have gone wrong. He was a man of big ideas and big dreams, and the crushing defeat by the New York Rens in the 1939 World Tournament had not deterred those dreams for an instant. He had moved on, with the same resolute determination he had shown in 1934, after the tumultuous split with Runt Pullins.

Truthfully, he was too busy to mope. His summers were more and more occupied with Negro League baseball, promoting the East-West All-Star game at Comiskey Park (which regularly outdrew the major leagues' All-Star game), along with managing Satchel Paige. He was also booking upcoming basketball games for the Trotters, the all-Chinese Hong Wa Kues, and another of his quirky promotions, a team of professional football players playing basketball (on the premise that fans who would pay to see these big lugs beat each other up on the gridiron would pay to see the same mayhem on the basketball court.)

So Abe had plenty to keep him busy over the summer. But the loss to the Rens still stuck in his craw. And being a man of action, Abe decided to do something about it. Something dramatic. It had been obvious to anyone who knew basketball that the Globe Trotters had been manhandled by the Rens, who were too big, too strong, and too fast. Yes, the Trotters had come back in the last few minutes to make a game of it, but the Rens had been coasting since the second quarter, sitting on their lead. If they had tried to run up the score, the results could have been ugly. So Abe decided to completely remake his team—to transform the Globe Trotters into a club that could match up with the Rens. In other words, he wanted to clone the Rens.

The first way he tried, in typical Saperstein fashion, was to buy the Rens players outright. "Abe Saperstein wanted the Rens to leave Bob Douglas en masse and come to play for him," says John Isaacs. "When that didn't work, he decided to go individually—and he wanted me. He even had Harry Rusan contact me and try to get me to come play. I told him, 'Okay, but first put my money in escrow, then I'll consider it.' Rusan looked at me like I was crazy. I decided, I'm not gonna get caught up in this."

When Abe's attempt to raid the Rens failed, his only option was a wholesale housecleaning of the Trotters. Since the beginning of the team, the Globe Trotters had always had a little guy as one of their stars. First it was Runt Pullins, then Harry Rusan and Gus Finney, who were all five-nine, or smaller. It may have been a subconscious link to Abe's own playing days at Lake View High, but the little guys were always the featured performer in the show. They were the fancy dribblers and trick-shot artists. For over a decade, those little guys had been entertaining fans in Montana, Minnesota, and Washington, but on the front lines of the World Pro Tournament in Chicago, the

Globe Trotters' little guys had been completely overmatched. With monster centers like Mike Novak and Tarzan Cooper swatting balls above the rim, and six-foot-two athletes like Pop Gates and John Isaacs playing guard, the little guy was an anachronism, a fossil from basketball's Stone Age. In the Rens game, little Harry Rusan had been shut down completely by the bigger Rens guards.

What the loss to the Rens showed most clearly was how much the game had changed. Five years earlier, Inman Jackson, at six-foot-three, had been considered a giant on the Iron Range, but now every team had taller and more agile players—guys like Wee Willie Smith and Leroy "Cowboy" Edwards, and the Trotters' Hilary Brown and Bernie Price.

So Abe went looking for players who fit the new prototype. Sadly, that meant the end of the road for some of his most loyal players, including: Rock "Pops" Anderson, whose career stretched all the way back to the Savoy Big Five; Bill Ford, who had been out with the team since 1935 (although he would make another brief appearance a few years later); and, most significantly, it meant cutting Harry Rusan, the quintessential little guy, who had bailed out Abe in the aftermath of the Runt Pullins insurrection.

By the start of training camp in early November, they were all gone. The only holdovers from the previous year's team were Ted Strong, Hilary Brown, Bernie Price, and Babe Pressley. And of course Inman Jackson, who was doing more of the hands-on coaching, but would still be pulled out of mothballs from time to time.

To find new players, Abe once again turned to the network of black coaches and farm teams that he had developed across the Midwest. The Rens had de facto territorial rights to the best players in the East, so Abe staked his claim to the Midwest and South. And even if the Globe Trotters had not attained the same heights as the Rens, they were successful enough for Abe to attract the best black players in those regions. When training camp opened, he had brought in five new players: Sonny Boswell, Roscoe "Duke" Cumberland, Marvin Freeman, Everett "Ziggy" Marcell, and Chuck Bowen. These signings indicated how much Abe was expanding his recruiting territory: Boswell and Cumberland were from Toledo, Freeman was from Memphis, and Marcell from Houston.

The cream of the crop were Cumberland and Boswell. They had both played at Toledo's Scott High, where Boswell had set the school scoring record, then played pro ball with Jesse Owens's Olympians. In the 1938–39 season, Boswell had starred for the Dayton entry in the Midwest Independent League.

Cumberland was six foot three and 175 pounds (he would eventually fill out to 210) and a rugged inside player who could also shoot from the perimeter. Boswell was an unimposing physical specimen: he was a wiry six-foot-two, 165-pounder with skinny legs who seemed too frail to hold up in the brutish world of pro ball. But the scrawny kid may have been the best pure shooter in all of basketball. He was a selfish gunner and a shameless ball hog who would take a shot whether he was ten feet out or thirty, even with two defenders draped all over him and a wide-open teammate standing under the hoop. But when Sonny Boswell got on a roll, he was unstoppable.

In the game against the House of David, the Trotters started Boswell, Cumberland, Ted Strong, Babe Pressley, and Hilary Brown—none of them under six-foot-two. Abe had his new prototypes. After the White City game against the Davids, the Trotters set off on their regular pilgrimage through Minnesota, North Dakota, Montana, Oregon, and Washington, then northward into Canada. Almost immediately, Sonny Boswell starting showing signs of being the most prolific scorer the Trotters had ever had. By the time they made it to Washington, in early January, he was lighting up scoreboards nearly every night. He scored 16 against the Yakima YMCA All-Stars, 26 points against the Olympia Sta-Dry Ducks (out of the Trotters' 42 total points), 20 against the Port Townsend All-Stars, 17 against the Grandview Town Team, and 24 against the Seattle Select Stars. After just two months on the pro circuit, the *Bellevue* [Wash.] *Journal* proclaimed him "American's best long shot man." When the Trotters crossed into Montana, he kept up his terrific pace. He hit for 20 against the Helena All-Stars, and reportedly even scored 48 points in one game—an incredible feat in that era.

What made these accomplishments so remarkable was that almost all of his points came from outside. He was not scoring off fast breaks or driving to the basket, but on two-hand set shots from long range. He may have been the best shooter in the world, but he was a one-dimensional player with glaring weaknesses in the rest of his game. Most notably, he wouldn't, or couldn't, play a lick of defense. "Sonny couldn't guard anybody," Jim "Nugie" Watkins says emphatically. Watkins, now eighty-four, played with the Trotters, and Boswell, in the early 1940s. "But he could *really* shoot. He would step back and shoot that ball so high that when it came through the net it wouldn't even move." Some of the other players resented his ball-hogging, until they started seeing the results. "When the guys realized that Sonny could shoot them to a championship, they protected him on defense—doubling up on his man," says Watkins. Another ballplayer might have been insulted by his teammates' covering for him on defense, but Boswell never protested. "Sonny was a pimp," says Watkins, chuckling. "He let them do it. He never did say, 'You don't need to guard my man.' No, he'd say, 'I can't guard that good, but I can shoot.' "

And could he ever. When Abe and Inman realized what kind of cold-blooded killer they had in Boswell, they oriented the entire offense around him. "Abe always protected his shooters," Watkins recalls. Fortunately, Sonny Boswell wasn't the only dangerous weapon in the Trotters arsenal. Babe Pressley, Hilary Brown, Duke Cumberland, and Bernie Price could all put up big numbers, and Ted Strong could still score when needed. On nights when Boswell's shots weren't falling, one of the other players would fill the void. There were games when three or four Trotters would score in double figures.

With Boswell leading the way, the Trotters were scoring more points than ever before. Instead of the low-scoring affairs of the past, with point totals in the 20s or 30s, they were consistently scoring over 50 points a game. And their margins of victory were increasing as well. The Trotters had traditionally held down the score, not wanting to embarrass their local hosts, but with Boswell raining baskets from all over the court, they were overpowering opponents, thrashing them by 20 points or more, sometimes doubling the other team's score, even though the Trotters still spent most of the fourth quarter putting on the show. The scores were outrageous: 51–25, 44–22, 55–40, 54–29. Even the *Courier*'s Chester Washington, a longtime Rens man, couldn't help but notice when the Trotters rattled off 56 wins in their first 57 games. "Out in the great northwest . . . the Globe Trotters are going like 'Gang Busters,' " he wrote. "Along with the Rens, the Trotters rank with not only the best sepia quints in America but with the best fives in basketball, regardless of color."

It wasn't how many games the Trotters were winning, but *how* they were winning them that was so striking. In the past, Abe would have reined them in, because beating teams this badly was bad for business. They were annihilating local teams that he had been playing for a decade, humiliating them in front of their own fans. But Abe didn't call off his players, even at the risk of creating ill will with long-time promoters. It might have been the first time in his life that he did something that was completely counterproductive for his business.

There can be only one explanation: he wanted to beat the Rens. As usual, Abe was looking down the road, already steering toward the biggest landmark ahead: the 1940 World Professional Invitational Tournament, which was scheduled for late March. Abe made his intentions very clear to sportswriter Alex Shults of the *Seattle Times,* when he sat down with him in January 1940. In his typically loquacious style, Abe started bragging about the Trotters. "[We are] tops of all the touring pros," he began. "We play on an average 155 games per season, draw the biggest crowds and get the most publicity." When the loss to the Rens came up, as it always did, Abe insisted that the Rens' victory had been a lucky fluke, and that the Trotters had lost only because "a shot went into the basket and 'Englished' out again." Of course, this bit of revisionist history was contradicted by the fact that the Trotters had lost by four points, not two, and that the Rens had never seriously been threatened until the final seconds.

The Globe Trotters may have built their reputation on clowning, but Abe Saperstein was deadly serious when it came to winning. And the entire 1939–40 season was pointing toward a hopeful rematch with the Rens in the World Pro Tournament. The Trotters had improved themselves in every facet of the game. They were bigger, stronger, faster, and now had the most dangerous shooter in basketball. If a few hick teams had to be sacrificed as warm-ups for the tournament, so be it. Abe had lost once to the Rens—had been humiliated and manhandled, his "Englished out" blarney notwithstanding—but if he got a second chance at them, he intended to be ready.

★

In March 1940, the world situation was even bleaker and more threatening than the year before. Britain and France had officially declared war on the Axis powers; German U-boats were prowling the North Atlantic, sinking British merchant ships almost at will; and the Luftwaffe was bombing British naval anchorages (although England's cities had as yet been spared), inducing the first civilian casualties.

Yet there was a different tone to the news stories in Chicago's papers from the previous year. In 1939, there had been a naive outrage about Hitler's seizure of Czechoslovakia, but such incursions had become so commonplace that there was now a sense of resignation and revulsion toward it all. In the intervening months, Hitler had overrun Austria and Poland, Mussolini had invaded Ethiopia, and Joseph Stalin, who was preparing to sign a nonaggression pact with Hitler, had occupied parts of Finland. Yet the hostilities were thousands of miles away, across a vast "ocean fortress," and it was still possible for Americans to wall themselves off from the whole bloody mess. The true horrors were yet to come.

Indeed, America had its own problems to worry about. The Depression still had a death grip on the economy, and a weary public was looking more and more to the entertainment industry to escape the bad news at home and abroad. Hollywood was having a banner year. People were lining up at Chicago's movie houses to see Walt Disney's long-awaited *Pinocchio;* Bing Crosby and Bob Hope in *Road to Singapore;* Spencer Tracy and Robert Young in *Northwest Passage;* and a bright young star, Henry Fonda, in *The Grapes of Wrath.* Chicago's Apollo Theater was featuring *Sidewalks of London* with Vivien Leigh and Charles Laughton, but fans were arriving early to see a short entitled *Life of Seabiscuit,* about the knock-kneed racehorse who had just returned from a career-threatening injury to win the Santa Anita Hundred Grander.

In the weeks leading up to the Second Annual World Pro Tournament, the Hearst newspapers had pulled out all the stops to promote it. William Randolph Hearst himself was in financial straits, having been forced to declare bankruptcy and sell off or consolidate many of his twenty-eight newspapers. In Chicago, for instance, his flagship evening paper, the *Chicago American,* had merged with the less popular morning tabloid, the *Herald-Examiner.* Still, the new

Herald-American spared no efforts to promote the World Pro Tournament, which it was now officially sponsoring. Everything about this second year was on a larger scale. The prize money had been increased to $15,000. The number of teams had been expanded from twelve to fourteen. And whereas in 1939 some of the invited teams had declined to participate, this year over twenty teams were clamoring to get in. Weeks in advance, the *Herald-American* started cranking out stories about the tournament, and the resulting demand for tickets was so great that the box office had to be kept open at night and every game was expected to sell out.

Half of the fourteen teams were returnees, including the Globe Trotters and Rens, Oshkosh All-Stars, Sheboygan Redskins, Fort Wayne Harvesters, House of David, and Clarksburg Oilers. The seven new entrants included George Halas's Chicago Bruins, the Kenosha (Wisc.) Badgers, Washington (D.C.) Brewers, and two teams each from Ohio (the Waterloo Wonders and Canton Bulldogs) and New York (the Rochester Seagrams and Syracuse Reds).

There were also many familiar faces among the players. Big Mike Novak, the six-foot-nine All-American from Loyola, was playing this year for George Halas, as was his former college teammate Wibs Kautz, a first-team All-Star selection for the National Basketball League. The Oshkosh All-Stars were led, once again, by Leroy "Cowboy" Edwards, former All-American from Kentucky, who had claimed his third consecutive NBL scoring title. As in the previous year, several team owners had beefed up their lineups by signing former college stars, with the most celebrated being Wilmeth Sidat-Singh, a Hindu star for Syracuse University, whom the *Rochester Chronicle* had called "the greatest cage player of all time."

Abe Saperstein had also attempted to add additional firepower to the Trotters' lineup, but had been stymied repeatedly. Last year's high scorer, Larry Bleach, was now a Detroit police detective and couldn't get off work. At the last minute, Abe had tried to sign Agis Bray, a former Wendell Phillips star, but the tournament committee ruled that Bray was ineligible because Abe had missed the deadline for finalizing team rosters. Making matters worse, the committee also ruled that Hilary Brown, who had been rotating between the Trotters and the Chicago Collegians, was ineligible for the same reason.

This was a catastrophic blow. It was bad enough losing the scoring potential of Bleach and Bray, but the six-foot-three Brown was a defensive specialist who would have been one of the Trotters' primary bulwarks against the Rens' big men, Tarzan Cooper and Wee Willie Smith, who had wreaked havoc the previous year.

Abe finally managed to sign one player, Al Fawks, formerly of Western Reserve University in Cleveland. And he asked Leon Wheeler, the coach of Detroit's Brewster Center, to assist him on the bench. Otherwise, the Globe Trotters would rely on the six players who had carried the team to 98 wins against only 3 losses: Sonny Boswell, Bernie Price, Babe Pressley, Ted Strong, Duke Cumberland, and "Old Ironsides" himself, Inman Jackson.

A year before, the Trotters and Rens had been placed in the same bracket, which ensured that two black teams could not possibly meet in the finals. But this year they were placed in the same *sub*bracket, so they would meet in the second round, if they both won their first game. Once again, the tournament promoters had eliminated the possibility of two black teams playing for the championship.

The Trotters' first game was on Sunday afternoon, March 17, against the Kenosha Badgers, a team led by three former Creighton University stars. It was no contest. The Trotters annihilated the Badgers in the same fashion they had ninety-eight other teams that year. They jumped out to a 33–20 lead at halftime, then blew the game open in the second half, limiting the Badgers to only 3 points and running away with a 50–26 win. Bernie Price and Sonny Boswell scored 14 and 12 points, respectively, and the Trotters toyed with Kenosha throughout the game. The Globe Trotters had given notice, right off the bat, that they were a team to be reckoned with.

The Rens must have got the message, because they also crushed their first-round opponent, the Canton Bulldogs, by the lopsided score of 42–21, with Puggy Bell leading the way with 13 points.

The long-awaited rematch was at hand.

★

Over 5,000 fans were jammed into the Madison Street Armory on Monday night to witness the main event. The betting line was 2–1 in favor of the Rens, which was not surprising given their relatively easy handling of the Trotters the year before. The Rens put the same team on the floor as in 1939, except for Fat Jenkins, who had retired. Tarzan Cooper, Wee Willie Smith, John Isaacs, Pop Gates, Zach Clayton, Eiyre Saitch, and Puggy Bell were no less formidable than in the previous year, but at least they were *familiar*. The Trotters knew exactly what they could do. The Rens still had a height advantage with Cooper and Smith, but the Trotters were stronger inside with the addition of Duke Cumberland. Still, the loss of Hilary Brown, their best defensive center, could prove fatal. The Trotters did have the element of surprise in their favor, as the Rens had never faced Sonny Boswell.

Referee Pat Kennedy, the master of histrionics, once again called the teams to center court for the opening tip, and the game was on. In 1939, the Rens had bolted to an 11–2 lead, but the Trotters were determined to send a message that this was a different year and a different team. Not surprisingly, the Trotters' primary messenger was Sonny Boswell, who hit a couple of early bombs that showed the Rens why he had been tearing up teams all season long. But the Rens were too good and too experienced to be intimidated by Boswell or anybody else, and they came right back, matching the Trotters basket for basket.

The opening quarter ended with the Rens up by only one point, 12–11. The second quarter turned into a defensive struggle, with the two teams battling like heavyweight fighters slugging it out in the center of the ring. The lead seesawed back and forth, and the half ended with the Rens ahead 18–16.

After one half, two things were clear: the teams were much more evenly matched than they had been the previous year, and Sonny Boswell held the fate of the Trotters in his hands. If he was on in the second half, no one, including the fabled New York Rens, could stop him. If he was off, the Rens would win.

The third quarter was played in an adrenaline-induced fury, with both teams nearly doubling their first-half points in that quarter alone. Boswell was hitting from every angle and the Rens resorted to fouling him, in a desperate effort to stop the onslaught, but he was making them pay from the free throw line. Puggy Bell and Pop Gates were keeping the Rens in the game, however, and despite the frenetic pace, neither team could pull away. They were matching each other basket for basket, and the quarter ended with the Rens still ahead by one, 31–30.

After three quarters, the game was dead even. The lead would change hands fourteen times during the game, with neither team able to build a comfortable margin. It had come down to a test of which team would crack.

And then, perhaps as a result of the pressure, both teams went cold in the final period. No one could hit a basket. On both ends of the court, the defenses were challenging every pass, every drive to the lane, every shot. The scoring frenzy of the third quarter had been a harbinger of the up-tempo style of basketball that would appear in the 1940s and '50s, but in the fourth quarter, with the game on the line, the Trotters and Rens reverted back to the roots of the game, to the deliberate, ball-control style from the 1920s and '30s. Both teams were playing conservatively, afraid to make a mistake that would cost them the game. Minutes went by without either team scoring. With two minutes left in the game, each team had scored only 4 points in the quarter, and the Rens were still up by one, 35–34.

As the clock wound down, the tension in the Armory was becoming unbearable. Each possession was critical; any errant pass or shot could determine the outcome of the game. Fans for both teams were up out of their seats. It was almost too excruciating to even watch. The big hand on the scoreboard clock on the wall seemed to be moving in slow motion as it dialed toward zero.

With a minute and forty-five seconds left, the Rens' Zach Clayton was fouled, and the former Trotter hit one free throw to make it a 2-point Rens lead, 36–34. Now the Trotters had the ball for what could be their final possession. If they missed a shot and the Rens got the ball, they could run out the clock. The Trotters brought the ball across half court. No one in the Armory had any doubts about who would get the ball. Sonny Boswell had carried the Globe Trotters all night, scoring 18 of their 34 points—more than the rest of the team combined.

But the Rens were collapsing their entire defense on Boswell, intent on denying him the ball. The Rens were determined not to let him beat them. The clock was down to one minute. The Trotters were frantic. Boswell was double-teamed. Someone else would have to step up. Then a pass went in to Babe Pressley in the corner. "The Blue Ox" was a terror on the boards but was not known for his offense. Tonight, in fact, he had yet to score a point. Worse, he had caught the ball in an awkward position, with a difficult angle to the rim, but he threw up a shot anyway and, miraculously, it went in. The score was tied.

The Rens called time-out with less than a minute to play. Bob Douglas substituted Eiyre Saitch, one of his best outside shooters, for John Isaacs. The Rens brought the ball across half court and looked for an open shot. With about thirty seconds left, a Ren player took a shot, but the ball caromed off the rim and the Trotters grabbed the rebound. They would have the last shot to win the game. Again, everyone was looking for Sonny Boswell. If it came down to one shot, there was no question who was going to take it. And this time, despite the Rens' best efforts, Boswell got the ball. With time running out, the best long-range shooter in all of basketball had one final chance to put the Rens away. This is why Abe had revamped the entire team, why he had brought in Boswell in the first place—to have it all come down to this last shot.

And then, unexpectedly, the Rens did something stupid: Boswell was fouled before he could shoot. It was a boneheaded play. A coach's worst nightmare. You *never* foul at the end of the game and give the other team a free throw to win. Make them hit a basket, and by all means don't give them a freebie at the line. But one can almost forgive the Rens for their mistake. Boswell had been killing them from outside all night, and the Rens didn't want to let him beat them from out there in his comfort zone. They would rather force him to the free throw line, where perhaps, under the scrutiny and pressure of the moment, he would choke.

But Sonny Boswell was an assassin. He hit the shot.

The Trotters were ahead by one, with only seconds left to play. After Boswell's free throw, the Rens had to bring in the ball from under the Trotters' basket. There was not enough time to work the ball up the court and run a play. They had to do something desperate. And they did: Puggy Bell turned and sprinted down the court as fast as he could, catching the Trotters off guard. He was streaking down the sideline like a football wideout on a "Hail Mary" route. And his teammate who was in-bounding the ball saw him break free and heaved the ball as far as he could. Bell ran under it and caught it in full stride. He was all by himself, going in for a breakaway layup to win the game.

There was only one Globe Trotter anywhere near him, and that was Inman Jackson. But there was no way the "old man" of the Trotters could hope to catch the speedy Bell. Inman shouldn't have been in the game in the first place. He was a relic of the ancien régime, yet Abe still insisted on playing him out of loyalty. But Inman had been completely ineffective, scoring no baskets and no free throws. A younger player could have made a run at Bell and perhaps cut him off, or at least fouled him before he could shoot, but all Inman could do was lumber down the court behind Bell as he went in for a game-winning shot.

Then a wondrously strange thing happened. All Bell had to do was run in for an uncontested layup, the easiest shot in basketball, which he had made thousands of times before. But just before he reached the basket, he heard footsteps, glanced back over his shoulder, and saw Inman rumbling down the court toward him. In that split second of hesitation, when Puggy Bell looked back, what he must have seen was not a thirty-seven-year-old broken-down has-been who had stayed out way too long, four years past his "farewell tour," but the ghost of what Big Jack had once been, the most feared player on the Iron Range and the Pacific Coast, a man who had controlled every tip and intimidated every center he faced. Somehow, on that futile chase downcourt, trying to run down a young blood he could never hope to catch, Inman Jackson had summoned up the last faint aura of his former greatness. And when Puggy Bell looked back and saw him coming, he lost his concentration for just an instant. He lost track of where he was on the court, overran the basket, and when he looked up to shoot the layup he was *under* the backboard. He had gone too far. Realizing his mistake, he compounded it by stopping his dribble. Now he was stuck. All he could do was lean back as far as he could and throw up a clumsy shot off the backboard, trying to bank it in. Incredibly, he missed. The ball hit the rim and bounced straight back. There was still a second or two left, enough time for

Bell to retrieve his rebound and put it back in. He leaped for the ball, but someone beat him to it.

It was Inman Jackson.

The old man had been too slow to catch Bell, but he had kept running anyway, even when it appeared to be hopeless. With the game seemingly a lost cause, Inman had kept coming. No one in that arena, not even Abe Saperstein, understood the importance of that last shot more than Inman Jackson. No one had paid the dues that he had, in wear and tear on his body, in sweat and blood, playing sick and injured and in pain. And so he kept on running, and when the youngster Puggy Bell made the worst mistake of his career, it was the old pro who was there to snag the ball. He held it in a death grip in his big paws. Tarzan Cooper came running up and wrapped his arms around Inman, trying to snatch it away. But no one—not even the entire Rens team—could have pried that ball free. The final buzzer sounded with Cooper draped all over Inman Jackson, trying to wrest the ball away.

The game was over. The Trotters had won by 1 point, 37–36.

The next day, Sonny Boswell, who had scored 19 of the Trotters' 37 points, was acclaimed as the star of the game, and rightfully so. "If the Rens could have tied Sonny Boswell's hands behind him, the 1939 world champs might have repeated," the *Defender* wrote. No sportswriter even mentioned Puggy Bell's miscue or Inman Jackson's game-saving rebound, or how he had run the entire length of the floor to snare it. But today, sixty-five years later, that is the one play, and the only play, that the Rens' John Isaacs, the sole survivor from that game, still remembers. "If Puggy had hit that shot, we would have won by one point," he says ruefully. "But Inman Jackson got the rebound, and the horn sounded."

Undoubtedly, it was Sonny Boswell, the Trotters' sensational young star, who had won the game, but it was their oldest player, the grand old warhorse, who had preserved it. In the history of basketball, there have been a number of legendary plays that have proved decisive in championship games. Some of the most memorable include the Boston Celtics' John Havlicek stealing the ball to seal Game 7 of the 1965 Eastern Conference finals against the Philadelphia 76ers; Christian Laettner's buzzer-beater in overtime against

Kentucky in 1992 to give Duke the NCAA East Region championship; and Michael Jordan's twenty-foot jump shot in 1998 to bury the Utah Jazz and clinch the Chicago Bulls' sixth NBA championship. In the storied history of the Harlem Globe Trotters, Inman Jackson's final rebound against the Rens may be the most decisive play of all.

*

By all rights, the Globe Trotters' victory over the Rens should have given them the world championship, but they actually had two more games to play. After the exultation of finally beating the Rens, one could have almost predicted a letdown in their next game. Tuesday night, in their semifinal game against the Syracuse Reds, Sonny Boswell was completely off his game, scoring only 6 points. Fortunately, as they had all year, other players picked up the slack. Babe Pressley and Duke Cumberland chipped in 8 points apiece, and Bernie Price added 7 more. More important, the Trotters' defense allowed only three Syracuse players to score any field goals, which sealed their 34–24 win.

That victory put the Trotters in the championship game on Wednesday night against George Halas's Chicago Bruins. The game should have been billed as an all-Chicago final, but the *Chicago Tribune* still hadn't figured out, or accepted, that the Trotters were even from Chicago. "The Chicago Bruins and the Harlem Globe Trotters, a Negro team from Seattle, Wash., will battle for the championship," the *Trib* inexplicably wrote.

The Bruins had been the obvious favorites of Chicago's white press and had garnered the lion's share of copy during the tournament. They were led by big Mike Novak and his former Loyola teammate Wibs Kautz, who had gone wild in the tournament, scoring 24 points in each of his last two games. In their semifinal win over the Washington Brewers, however, Novak had sprained his ankle and been forced to leave the game; his status for the championship game was questionable.

Despite Novak's injury, the bookies had made the Bruins a 3–1 or 4–1 favorite over the Trotters, as the conventional wisdom was that Ted Strong could not possibly contain Novak, even if he wasn't

100 percent. With the Trotters' best defensive big man, Hilary Brown, disqualified by the tournament committee, the Trotters were so shorthanded that they dressed out only seven men for the game.

Sixty-five hundred fans turned out for the championship game on a chilly Wednesday evening. The crowd was mostly white and mostly rooting for the Bruins, although the Trotters did have one special contingent of cheerleaders: the New York Rens, who, despite their rivalry, knew that their ultimate loyalties lay with their race.

Early on, it appeared that the bookies might be right. With Novak hurting, Wibs Kautz took up the slack, hitting two straight buckets in the first thirty seconds to give the Bruins a 4–0 lead. But the Trotters then clamped down on Kautz, who would score only one more point the entire night. A few minutes later, a Sonny Boswell free throw tied the game at 4 apiece.

It was a sluggish first quarter, with both teams overanxious and unable to score. It was going to be an old-style brawl, with rough play under the boards, free-swinging elbows, and every shot contested. Referee Pat Kennedy was constantly bellowing out fouls, but neither team could hit from the line (the Bruins hit just 9 of 23 free throws all night, and the Trotters made only 5 of 16). In the first quarter alone, there were six lead changes, the score was tied five times, and the Trotters led 7–6 at the end of the period.

The scoring picked up in the second quarter, as the Bruins ran off 4 straight points, but Boswell, Strong, Price, and Cumberland all scored to give the Trotters their own 4-point advantage. Boswell was starting to heat up, which was bad news for the Bruins, and he gave the Trotters a 7-point lead. With a minute and a half left in the second quarter, still up by 7, the Trotters went into their half-court stall, and took what appeared to be a commanding 20–13 lead into halftime.

Globe Trotter fans were giddy, anticipating a world title, and the Trotter players might have gotten caught up in the delirium, because they came out lackadaisically after halftime and promptly let the Bruins right back in the game. The Bruins scored 7 straight points to tie the score, then took the lead outright. Despite his gimpy ankle, Mike Novak was beginning to wear down Ted Strong, and midway through the third quarter Strong picked up his fifth foul. The disqualification of Hilary Brown once more came back to haunt the Trotters, as Abe had to call on Inman Jackson to defend the Bruins' center. Inman had saved the game against the Rens, but this was asking too much of him, even with his great heart and courage. Inman was giving up six inches and forty pounds to Novak, and all he could do was foul to keep the bigger man at bay.

The third quarter was a disaster for the Trotters. They went from being ahead by 7 to being behind by one, 21–20, as the Bruins held them to one point in the entire period. It appeared that the emotional win over the Rens had taken too much out of them. So much had been riding on that game—perhaps they had been pointing to it *too much*—and the Globe Trotters appeared to have nothing left in the championship game.

The fourth quarter was more of the same, as the Bruins built an 8-point lead with only five and a half minutes to play. The Trotters had dug themselves into what appeared to be an insurmountable hole, and the players seemed "paralyzed," according to the *Defender*.

But then, with their dreams of a world championship slipping away, the Trotters' resolve stiffened. Babe Pressley hit a free throw, and Duke Cumberland connected on a long shot from outside. At the urging of assistant coach Leon Wheeler, Abe finally pulled Inman Jackson, who had drawn three personal fouls in his futile attempt to guard Novak, and replaced him with the only other player in uniform: Al Fawks, the former Western Reserve player from Cleveland, who had seen only limited action in one earlier game. Ten seconds after entering the game, Fawks hit a long set shot, and the Bruins' lead was down to two, 29–27. Now it was the Bruins' turn to go cold, as they hadn't scored a point in nearly four minutes. Babe Pressley made a basket, and the score was tied.

Apparently doomed a few minutes earlier, the Trotters had fought their way back. Their fans came back to life. "The packed house was in a frenzy," the *Defender* reported. Even the usually restrained *Herald-American* described the 6,500 fans as "on the verge of hysteria."

There was a minute left in the game. The Trotters got the ball back and Bernie Price dribbled to center court, then, surprisingly, pulled up to take a shot. He was impossibly far out—*too* far out to be taking any kind of shot, particularly with the game on the line—but he let fly anyway with a two-hand set shot. The fans watched the ball's slow descent toward the hoop, then let out a collective gasp as it went through the net with a soft *swish*. The Trotters were ahead by 2, their first lead since early in the third quarter.

In the closing seconds of the game, three Bruin players missed free throws (indeed, the outcome of the game could have been different if *either* team had been able to connect from the free throw stripe). When the final gun sounded, there was bedlam on the court, as the Trotters' players and fans rejoiced over their win. In the Globe Trotter locker room, players hugged each other, and Abe, Leon Wheeler, and trainer Dr. Powell Johnson held a triumphant "powwow." On the other side, in the gloom of the Bruins' locker room, owner George Halas "had little to say." The Globe Trotters collected the $1,000 first prize, and Abe gave each player a $100 bonus. To no one's surprise, Sonny Boswell was named the tournament's Most Valuable Player.

The next day, Leo Fischer of the *Herald-American* praised the Trotters for their courageous comeback and called the game "as brilliant a contest as has ever been staged in these parts," although he did throw a little cold water on their victory, attributing the Bruins' loss, at least partly, to Novak being "crippled." Fay Young of the *Chicago Defender* had no such reservations about the Trotters' win, and even added a racial commentary to their triumph. "I have come to the conclusion that basketball is not a white man's game," he wrote. "The pale faces just don't know how to play it."

For the second year in a row, the South Side was celebrating a world championship. The unofficial mayor of Bronzeville hosted a party for the Trotters and the Rens at his Club DeLuxe, and even invited the Bruins, although none of the white players showed up. Nonetheless, the celebration lasted long into the evening. The Harlem Globe Trotters were champions of the world.

Eight months after capturing the world pro championship, the Globe Trotters got an unexpected bonus that might have been more valuable than the title itself. On the night of November 29, 1940, they hosted the inaugural All-Star Classic in Chicago Stadium, in front of the largest crowd ever assembled to watch a basketball game.

The All-Star Classic was another promotion dreamed up by the *Chicago Herald-American,* in hopes of capitalizing on the success of the 1940 pro tournament. The idea was to match the world professional champs against a team of the best college players in America, as chosen by a panel of thirty-six sports editors. The Globe Trotters just happened to be in the right place at the right time, having won the pro tournament the same year that the All-Star Classic debuted. It would prove to be the single most publicized game in their early history.

Abe recognized the marketing potential of this game early on, and began drumming up publicity weeks in advance. He told the press that the Trotters would be reporting to training camp a week early to prepare for the All-Stars. And instead of training on the South Side, as usual, they would be training in Sheboygan, Wisconsin, where they would scrimmage daily against the Sheboygan Redskins. This was one of many innovations that Abe would contribute to the sport, as the Trotters were one of the first professional teams to hold out-of-town training camps.

Abe's own efforts to publicize the All-Star game were augmented by the *Herald-American,* which promoted the game with self-serving zeal. And the black press applauded the *Herald-American's* willingness to showcase the game, even with a black team playing. As Wendell Smith wrote in the *Courier:* "Sports editor Ed Cochrane might have waited until the Trotters had fallen off the pedestal of cage supremacy and then put on his big game with a white quintet. . . . Sepia cage fans, I am sure, will repay his broadness and liberal attitude by jamming the portals of the Chicago Stadium on November 29!"

The College All-Stars, who were coached by Northwestern's Dutch Lonborg, included Ralph Vaughn of USC, Bob Carpenter of Texas Tech, Ed Sadowski of Seton Hall, and Rex Ellis of Notre Dame.* The *Herald-American* ran lengthy stories on every aspect of the All-Star game. They had photos of the college boys arriving in Chicago, and daily practice reports. Their entire focus, however, was

---

* *Two of the selected players, Ralph Giannini of Santa Clara and Jim McNatt of Oklahoma State, decided not to play after the AAU's gray eminences, who were still haunting Abe Saperstein, warned that the college players would lose their amateur status if they played the Globe Trotters.*

on the *white* All-Stars; almost no mention was made of the Globe Trotters, who seemed to be incidental to the whole affair.

Nonetheless, the results of this marketing onslaught exceeded anyone's expectations: 20,583 fans filled the cavernous Chicago Stadium. Abe would proudly claim it as a world record (until the Trotters broke it many times over). More impressive, it was a racially mixed crowd, perhaps the largest mixed gathering in U.S. sports history.

The pregame ceremonies reinforced the racial harmony, as the honorary "mascots" for each team, Miss All-Star and Miss Bronze America, were introduced at midcourt. The teams were introduced, then opera star John Pane-Gasser sang "The Star-Spangled Banner," and the inimitable Pat Kennedy led the teams to center court for the opening tip-off.

With so much pregame publicity, the contest itself could have easily been a letdown, but it more than lived up to the hype. The All-Stars led for most of the first period, and took a 13–11 lead into the second quarter. They extended their lead to 18–12 midway through the second period, but Sonny Boswell, Babe Pressley, and Bernie Price got the Trotters back in the game, tying the score 20–20 at half-time. The score was tied again at the end of three quarters, 30–30, and during the final period the lead changed hands repeatedly. With two minutes to play, the Trotters held a 37–35 lead and, perhaps too cockily, started putting on the show, attempting to run out the clock. But the All-Stars intercepted a pass and scored, and then, with just seconds remaining, Ralph Vaughn of USC hit an apparent game-winning basket to give the All-Stars a 39–37 lead.

For all intents and purposes, the game was over. The Trotters had to bring the ball in under the All-Stars' basket and go the length of the court, but there was not enough time. So they did the only thing they could do: they got the ball to Sonny Boswell. When you have the deadliest gunner in the game, why would you do anything else? Boswell barely had time to get to half court, then heaved a desperation shot as the buzzer sounded. The ball went straight in.

Sonny Boswell had done it again. They were going to overtime.

The lead seesawed back and forth during the five-minute overtime period, with numerous lead changes. All 20,000 fans were on their feet, "screaming themselves hoarse," as the two teams carried the fight up and down the court. With a minute left, the All-Stars were ahead by 2, but Babe Pressley hit a basket to tie the score at 42-all. Then the All-Stars' cocaptain, Stan Szukala of DePaul, took a pass on the right wing, cut toward the basket, and hit a shot to win the game, 44–42.

When the final buzzer sounded, the most amazing spectacle of the entire evening occurred. As Wendell Smith described it: "In one of the wildest demonstrations we have ever witnessed, 22,000 fans rose as one after the battle was over and gave both teams an ovation that shook the lofty rafters of this mammoth stadium."

If the pregame publicity had been a tad hyperbolic, the postgame descriptions went beyond superlative. "Wow! What a game and what a finish," was the lead in the *Chicago Defender,* which predicted that the Trotters, even in defeat, had "lost not one bit of their reputation." Most eloquent of all was Wendell Smith, who had been a Rens loyalist for many years, but with this game would become the Trotters' biggest fan. He described the contest as "basketball's first real dream game" and ended by saying: "Sometime, somewhere a greater basketball game may be played . . . but until that happens the one I saw here tonight will go down as the greatest." But Abe Saperstein might have summed it up best of all, saying: "It was the night we came into our own."

The one-two combination of the world championship and the All-Star Classic was the greatest publicity bonanza in the history of the Harlem Globe Trotters, and it catapulted them to a new level of fame and respect. For over a decade, Abe had been promoting his team with very little to go on, except for his own creativity (which sometimes strayed into the world of make-believe), but now he had two sensational hooks—and he sold the hell out of them. Give a natural-born marketing wizard a championship title *and* the All-Star Classic, and just see what he can do.

The most immediate effect was that "world's basketball champions" became the lead to every news article, press release, and marketing letter about the Trotters—and Abe would continue using it for years, long after the Trotters had ceded that title to other teams. New team stationery and envelopes were printed up with the phrase stamped across the bottom in forty-eight-point type, along with a logo of Inman Jackson holding three balls, superimposed on top of a globe.

There were other improvements. Abe hired a traveling secretary, Chuck Jones, from Vancouver, to manage the team in his absence, and a full-time publicity man, Bill Margolis, a former newspaper reporter. He rented a two-room "suite" at 192 Clark Street, although it was just a tiny two-room cubicle about the size of the bedrooms in the Saperstein house. Most significant, for his players, he bought a used army "carry-all"—a cross between a station wagon and a panel truck—and emblazoned "1940 World Professional Champions" on the sides. The new vehicle gave the players more room to stretch out, and they passed the long drives between towns napping, playing endless games of bid whist, or singing. The carry-all was a definite improvement from the old days in Abe's Model T, but it was still just a glorified truck. It had no heater, and in the dead of winter icicles would form on its uninsulated roof and hang down like daggers above the players' heads. One player had to always stay awake to break off the icy stalactites so they didn't spear them in the head when the carry-all hit a bump. The players wrapped their legs with blankets, like mummies, and put lit kerosene railroad lanterns on the floorboards to keep warm.

Pro basketball, in general, and the Globe Trotters, in particular, were starting to draw increased media attention. Abe boasted that noted sportswriters Bill Corum and Grantland Rice, the dean of American sportswriters, had "made us their pets." And *Esquire* and *Collier's* both ran glowing pieces on the team.

As a result of this coverage, attendance swelled. In early 1941, Abe told a sportswriter, "We're drawing more basketball customers than we ever dreamed of before . . . by 200, or perhaps even 300 percent. Perhaps basketball interest is booming, but of course we're world champions now and getting publicity such as no basketball team ever got before." Not content to merely ride this crest of publicity, Abe redoubled his marketing efforts, reaching out to new towns and venues. In December 1940, for instance, he sent a blind marketing letter to Delford T. Precht, manager of the New Ulm Brick and Tile team in New Ulm, Minnesota:

> The original Harlem Globe Trotters, nationally famous colored basketeers . . . and one of the most popular groups of touring cagers . . . in the history of the sport (if newspaper comments and attendance marks are any criterion) are now in the first phases of their fourteenth annual tour of the United States and Canada.
>
> The 'Trotters, who turned out the world's record breaking basketball attendance of 22,000 in Chicago's huge Stadium, November 29th, playing last season's College All-American basketball squad . . . can be developed into the sports spectacle of the year for your city.

Abe told Precht that he still had three open dates in January, and laid out the terms of a contract (the Trotters would get the first $20 in receipts, then the remainder would be split 50-50). Abe was relentless once he had a promoter in his sights, so he sent a follow-up letter to Precht a week later. By then, he had brand-new stationery with the *Herald-American*'s story about the Trotters' championship game wrapped around the left margin.

Abe's sports empire was also expanding. He added two new teams to his ever-increasing stable: the Chicago Brown Bombers, which played mostly on weekends in the Chicago vicinity, and the newly resurrected Savoy Big Five, which became a farm team for the Globe Trotters, and sometimes even played as a Globe Trotter second unit.

The most striking indication of how the Trotters' status had changed, however, was that the Rens were now chasing them, instead of the other way around. Eric Illidge admitted to Wendell Smith that the Rens' "sole wish"—even more important than winning their other games—was to atone for their loss to the Trotters. Nine months after the game, Illidge was still moaning and making excuses about the loss. "They caught us on an off night," he whined. "We couldn't get going. It was the worst game any Renaissance team has played in years. At that, they only beat us by one basket." The Rens would remain a formidable team for another nine years (until Abe actually bought them), but from 1940 on, the Harlem Globe Trotters would be the preeminent black team in America.

Immediately after the All-Star Classic, the Trotters headed west, playing their way to Washington, Oregon, and then into Canada. They still had the championship squad intact: Sonny Boswell, Babe Pressley, Bernie Price, Duke Cumberland, and Ted Strong, but they were strengthened by the full-time addition of Hilary Brown, along with Agis Bray and Roosevelt Hudson, two more former Wendell Phillips stars; veteran guard Bill Ford, who returned after a one-year absence; Al Johnson, a former player for the Savoy Big Five and the New York Rens; Tony Peyton, another Toledo player; and Roscoe Julien. And Inman Jackson, now five years removed from his "farewell tour," was still playing a few minutes in most games.

The abundance of talent allowed Abe to put two units on the road full-time. Jackson was the coach and road manager for the first unit (with Boswell, Strong, Price, Pressley, Hilary Brown, and Agis Bray), and Abe hired Winfield S. Welch, the longtime baseball manager of the Birmingham Black Barons, as the road manager of the second unit, which played alternately as the Globe Trotters or the Savoy Big Five.

Despite the increased attendance and publicity, however, the logistics of keeping the Trotters on the road were still formidable. It was a grind, whether they were world champions or not. The only internal communiqué from this period that still survives, a December 26, 1940, letter from Abe to Inman Jackson, provides a revealing behind-the-scenes look at the challenges that even a successful barnstorming team faced. It also gives an intriguing view of Abe's hands-on management style and of the relationship between the two men. As road manager for the first unit, Inman was required to send daily reports, by either wire or mail, itemizing the gate receipts, travel expenses, and giving a summary of the team's performance. Inman's unit had spent Christmas playing in the Spokane area, and this letter from Abe (with his characteristic use of ellipses, in the style of Walter Winchell) was his response to one such report:

Jack:

Received your wire from Spokane as well as package of mail with reports . . . from Missoula. Pleased to hear that the team is shaping up somewhat better . . . and hope that this is a reality . . . rather than something to make me feel good . . . over the Christmas period.

Taking care of the car every thousand miles . . . is an excellent idea . . . as transportation has proven that it is the life blood of any traveling team. . . . Gee, transportation means everything. Welch is having no end of trouble with the Buick. The bearings and rods burned out . . . carburetor shot . . . and every day something else. They are playing real good ball although Detroit beat them last night 41–38 . . . after leading by five points in the last four minutes . . . with Ford going out with a torn-up knee . . . the same knee that has caused him lots of trouble. Cumberland's ankle is also messed up.

Thank everyone for the pleasant Christmas wishes . . . and tell "Sonny" that his pleasant card home was much appreciated, as I know the sincerity behind it.

Regarding monies advanced . . . everything okay so far. Brown and Strong have drawn considerably . . . so would welcome your taking care of the other boys with some advances following the Spokane game . . . and again following the Ellensburg game. . . . Tell Burns and Strong . . . that money orders for $15.00 each were sent to Mrs. Boyd and Mrs. Strong just before Christmas.

I haven't heard from you on the Palouse game, as I write this . . . but am looking for something before the day is out . . . Keep in touch with me daily as instructed . . . My next mail will be in care of Gonzaga University where you are at Sunday night. . . . Look for it.

"ABE" SAPERSTEIN

Sonny Boswell, so sensational in his rookie season and during the World Professional Tournament, was even more phenomenal his second season. He was hitting in double figures most nights and scoring over 20 points on a regular basis. One night, in Port Angeles, Washington, he tried a dropkick from seventy-five feet, nearly the length of the court, that went through the net "so cleanly that half the crowd sat dumb for a moment, not realizing what had happened." Boswell was no longer just a scoring machine; he was becoming a great showman. He could spin the ball on his finger for forty-five seconds, and during games would sometimes steal the referee's whistle and run around blowing it, halting play.

All over the country, sportswriters were effusive in their praise of Boswell. A Salt Lake City sportswriter testified that no other player he had ever seen in twenty years "could hold a candle to the present star of stars, Sonny Boswell." Another scribe even coined a name for one of Boswell's moves, which he called the "Boswell Glide." And Wendell Smith devoted an entire column to him, predicting that Boswell was "destined to go down in basketball's book of all-time greats." Abe Saperstein had the greatest player on the greatest team in America.

Perhaps the most indiscernible, and insidious, change that occurred after the Trotters' 1940 triumphs was in Abe Saperstein himself. Invigorated by the Globe Trotters' spectacular achievements, Abe became even more self-assured in his dealings with sportswriters and promoters—and more full of himself. And as his stature and prestige increased, he began to separate himself from his players, creating a distinct racial barrier that kept them apart. In the early years, he had sometimes shared a bed in a flea-bitten hotel with his ballplayers or slept crammed together in the back of his old Model T, but those days were gone. He was now a successful entrepreneur—a *white* owner of a thriving sports enterprise—and gradually he distanced himself from his ballplayers. He began to hold himself above them, not just in terms of income and lifestyle but in his attitudes as well.

It showed up first with sportswriters. Clearly, one of Abe Saperstein's greatest pleasures was talking to sportswriters. It may have been the place where he was most comfortable. For him, hanging out with the fourth estate was the equivalent of joining an exclusive men's club, such as the Reynold's Club in Chicago, which would not accept him because he was a Jew. But Abe suffered from a flaw shared by many compulsive talkers: he never knew when to stop. And sometimes, enthralled by the sound of his own voice, he would lapse into reflective discourses on the intelligence, constitution, and habits of African Americans. With hindsight, he might have preferred that his comments had never seen print.

One of Abe's confidants was Alex Shults of the *Seattle Times,* and in December 1940, Abe was regaling Shults with a recitation of the Trotters' wins and losses, when he suddenly veered off into a history lesson on the Globe Trotters' evolution from straight basketball to clowning. "When we first coached this team to start its clowning and trick ball handling they didn't like it," Abe explained. "They wanted to be serious about every game. Then they tried the trick stuff in public and when the fans laughed and applauded the boys thought it was grand. A Negro is a natural entertainer and it wasn't long until we had to watch the team to keep them playing basketball until victory was safe before clowning too much."

On another occasion, Hal Straight of the *Vancouver* [B.C.] *Sun* asked Abe, "What is there about a Negro that makes him such a great athlete?" Flashing a smile, Abe replied, "I can answer this one by heart." He suggested that white athletes were too soft, because of their pampered upbringing. "But the Negro is the son of a hard worker," Abe said. "Take Joe Louis. Dumb as all get out. . . . Even today he can't think for himself. But he had a beautiful body . . . developed . . . built up . . . and could do anything he was asked . . . and he had to be asked." Within five years, Abe predicted, "the Negro will dominate sport in North America. Then after that he'll flatten out to the same level as the white man." After delivering this lesson in cultural anthropology, Abe turned to employee relations. Hal Straight asked if Negroes were hard to manage. "They are temperamental," Abe replied. "You have to watch yourself. . . . But with a Negro you either have to be boss or nothing and I'm boss and we get along swell."

Abe's condescending attitude toward his players crept into other conversations. In January 1941, he was giving one Seattle sportswriter a detailed breakdown of the Trotters' expenses, and explained that he paid for transportation, but the players paid for their meals. "This, as you might imagine, isn't very popular with the boys," Abe said. "They'd be tempted to scrimp if it wasn't for the tonic I make 'em take." He claimed that his mystery tonic, combined with daily doses of haliver oil and viosterol, prevented the players from catching colds, but added, "that tonic gives them such an appetite they sort of forget they're spending their own money and eat everything they can lay their hands on."

He was even more patronizing in front of a Canadian writer, to whom Abe complained that although modern basketball called for "intricate plays and systems," the Trotters had none. Abe's explanation was that "Negroes are anything but bright so he can't teach them plays. They depend entirely on ball handling, which they do better than anybody else because of their enormous paws."

Most damning of all, he once allowed sportswriter Pete Sallaway, from Victoria, British Columbia, to visit the Trotters' dressing room at halftime while Abe was chewing out the players for sloppy play. "What's the matter with you fellows out there?" Abe barked. When the Globe Trotter players returned to the floor, Abe turned to Sallaway and asked, "Pete, why is it such fine athletes are so dumb? They just can't think for themselves. I wonder just how far they would get if they didn't have me around to figure out such situations. It was the same in the Chicago tournament. I'm certainly not boasting but I can truthfully say that is one championship that was won from the bench."

If Abe believed that his players were too dumb to learn plays, think for themselves, or realize that they were spending their own meal money, and so temperamental that he either had to be "boss or nothing," he was certainly not alone. In fact, the racial stereotyping of the Globe Trotters seemed to become more explicit as they became more popular. In January 1941, for instance, the *Lynden* [Wash.] *Tribune* carried an ad for an upcoming Trotters game with the headline: "Hi, Rastus!" Below the caption, the Globe Trotters were described as "those side-splitting rascals and championship basketball clowns."

In fairness, Abe Saperstein would have been considered enlightened on the race question compared with many whites at that time. Indeed, he thought of himself as a champion for black ballplayers. And there were times when he defended the Globe Trotters' courage and character. In a 1941 *Collier's* article, he told writer Stanley Frank:

"[This] team is my baby because it's helping to disprove a lie everybody believes about a persecuted race. I come from a persecuted race myself. I know what it means. Negro athletes are supposed to be strictly front runners. You know, great when they're ahead but inclined to fold up when the white boys put the pressure on them. In other words, they haven't guts. The Globe Trotters have done as much as Joe Louis to show that idea is cockeyed."

Abe described to Frank how the Trotters had fought back from an 8-point deficit against the Chicago Bruins to win the world title. "If they were going to quit like dogs, that was the time," he said. "But they won the title. . . . On the whole, colored boys are just as loyal and courageous as white players. Basketball ain't seen nothing yet."

Still, Abe was a product of his environment and carried some of the same prejudices—whether implicit or explicit—that permeated American society. He was certainly not an overt racist like Senator Theodore Bilbo of Mississippi or a demagogue like Father Coughlin, and he would have never called his players "niggers." But by his paternalistic, patronizing, and contemptuous remarks to his cronies in the press, he made it plain that the Globe Trotter players were not his equal. After the 1934 split with Runt Pullins, the Harlem Globe Trotters had crossed a first great threshold, and now they were crossing a second. Abe had made it clear in 1934 that he was the owner and the players were employees, not partners; and now he was making it equally clear that he was not just their boss but their superior.

★

One thing that winning the world championship did *not* change, at least in the short term, was the Trotters' schedule. Abe had already booked most of the games for the 1940–41 season, so the team was still playing such remote hamlets as Sedro-Woolley, Mossyrock, Hoquiam, Enumclaw, Ilwaco, and Wenatchee (all in the state of Washington). To his credit, Abe went out of his way to reassure his faithful promoters that the Trotters would not forget them. "Now that we're world champions we're not going to pass up our annual visits to those places where we feel we are at home," he said.

Abe understood that the foundation of the Trotters' success lay in the great heartland of America—not in the big cities—and he did not intend to abandon the tank town circuit that had sustained them through the hard times. As he told Stanley Frank of *Collier's* magazine:

> "World champions, my eye. . . . The world is not one tour-nament held in Chicago. We're crossroads champions, that's what. We won that title by playing in every whistle stop in the country and showing people how this basketball game should really be played. The Globe Trotters are the most widely traveled team in America and they're known more intimately in the deep bush that any sports organization in circulation. Sure, they've heard about the Yankees and the Cubs and the Green Bay Packers in the provinces and on the prairies, but the fans off the beaten track have seen the Globe Trotters. It makes a big difference."

While he would not abandon the heartland, Abe was already envi-sioning the biggest prize of all: New York City. "Give us a crack at . . . Madison Square Garden and we'll really jam the joint," he pleaded in January 1941. It would be almost another decade before he would get his wish, but as the Trotters' fame spread, they began to receive booking requests from larger cities. In 1941, they made their first ex-tensive probe into California, then initiated their first major eastern swing, looping through Ohio, Rochester, Pittsburgh, Washington, D.C.; Baltimore, Charleston, West Virginia, Richmond, and finally circled back to New York City (although not to the Garden), where they played the New York Jewels in the Royal Windsor Palace (also known as St. Nick's).

By late March, as they worked their way back to Chicago to de-fend their title in the 1941 World Pro Tournament, the Globe Trotters were on top of the world, and more popular than any professional bas-ketball team in the country. It seemed like nothing could go wrong.

And then it all came crashing down.

After winning their first game in the tournament against the Newark Elks, the Trotters were upset by the Detroit Eagles, 37–36.

The Trotters played listlessly, particularly in the fourth quarter when the game was on the line, and the *Defender* blasted the Trotters for having "disappointed many of their followers by their poor performance." The paper blamed the loss on late-night partying by some Globe Trotter players, who were seen at Bronzeville night spots "until the rays of the morning sun were breaking over Lake Michigan." The Detroit Eagles went on to defeat the Rens and win the title, but that didn't soften the blow of the Trotters' defeat. It would be the Eagles who would meet the College All-Stars in November. The Trotters' reign as world champs was over.

And then it got worse. On Easter Sunday, the Globe Trotters were scheduled to meet the Midwestern All-Stars in a benefit for Chicago's Provident Hospital. But just before the game, Sonny Boswell, Duke Cumberland, and Hilary Brown got in a dispute with Abe over money and quit the team. Boswell and Cumberland walked out before the game, and Brown quit immediately after.

That was the final game of the season, so there was plenty of time to resolve the differences between Abe and the players, but, instead, the grievances festered all summer long. Rumors circulated through Bronzeville that Boswell was going to form his own team, just like Runt Pullins. In October, the story hit the papers, and the *Courier* reported that the three players were "severing relations" with Abe Saperstein and that many South Side fans, including some prominent businessmen, were siding with the players. According to Nugie Watkins, the players even tried to convince Inman Jackson to join the uprising. "They wanted Inman to quit Abe and come with them," says Watkins. "And when he wouldn't, the guys called him an Uncle Tom and 'Abe's nigger' and all that kind of stuff. But Inman stayed with Abe all the way."

As it turned out, Boswell and the other "outlaws," as the *Defender* labeled them, didn't start their own team but did something far worse: they signed with the Rens. And Bob Douglas, being no fool, welcomed them with open arms. What a disaster! The Trotters' top players had quit Abe and gone over to the enemy. It was 1934 all over again. The Trotters' headliner, Sonny Boswell, had left and taken two of the team's best players with him. And, once again, it was all about money.

But Abe had been through this once before, and he handled this crisis in exactly the same way he had in 1934. He invited a new crop of players to training camp and announced smugly, despite all evidence to the contrary, that the Trotters would be "better than ever." By now, he believed that the Globe Trotters were bigger than any player, even Sonny Boswell. That belief was sustained by the knowledge that hundreds of black players around the country were clamoring to play pro ball, and since Abe had a virtual monopoly on the market (except for the Rens), he knew that they would be thrilled to play for whatever money he offered. "Abe could always find guys who would play for nothing," recalls Vertes Zeigler, a Trotter in the mid-1940s. "Hell, what other choice did they have?"

Among the rookies who reported to camp in November 1941, by far the *least* promising of the lot was a rawboned country boy from El Dorado, Arkansas, named Goose Tatum. He talked slow, walked funny, and looked like a circus freak, with arms so long that they nearly reached his knees. This was the man who was supposed to replace Sonny Boswell, the smoothest ballplayer in the game? The idea was laughable.

The Trotters broke training camp in Sheboygan (it was their second annual visit), then promptly lost eight games in the first month. This makeshift "replacement" team was shaping up as a disaster. Still, Abe kept telling reporters confidently that the Trotters would start clicking and soon be on their way to even greater fame and renown. Unbeknownst to Abe, six thousand miles from Chicago, Japanese dive-bomber pilots were completing their final practice runs, preparing for a rendezvous with destiny.

CHAPTER 8

Goose

Reece "Goose" Tatum did not look like an athlete. His body seemed all out of proportion, with arms so long (he had an eighty-four-inch wingspan) that, while standing up straight, he could touch his kneecaps. His arms actually got in his way; they were like twin anchors weighing him down. He was six foot three, but until his frame filled out he was all arms and legs—a graceless, gawky man-child. And he was pure country—a "handkerchief head," the Bronzeville hipsters called him—whose Arkansas drawl oozed like red clay. He walked with a loping shuffle, those ridiculous arms flapping in front of him, and his big feet splayed out to either side.

As soon as he showed up in training camp, the other Trotter players started laughing at him. They laughed just watching him walk across the court. They laughed when he talked. And they laughed most of all when he tried to play ball—he was a *baseball player*, for Chrissakes, a first baseman for the Birmingham Black Barons in the Negro Leagues, who Abe somehow thought could be turned into a basketball player. But he was so unpolished, so lacking in basketball fundamentals, that the players couldn't help themselves—they had to laugh. And once they started laughing, they never stopped.

This was his gift: Goose Tatum could make people laugh. They laughed at him when he wasn't even trying, and once he figured out how to merge his physical attributes with an intuitive sense of comic timing, no one could stop. Hidden beneath the awkward, gangly frame was a creative spark waiting to emerge, and it was to Abe

Saperstein's credit that he recognized that spark and provided the stage on which Goose would light up the world.

Goose Tatum was symbolic of a new generation of Harlem Globe Trotters. In the early years, the team had been made up of the first generation of the Great Migration, the sons of sharecroppers who had left the Deep South searching for the promised land on the South Side of Chicago. But Goose's family had never left the South. And in the wake of the Sonny Boswell–led revolt, Abe would begin looking more and more to rural areas for his players, recruiting country boys, like Goose, who lacked the sophistication of their big-city cousins. "Chicago boys were pretty slick," says Nugie Watkins, a Chicago native himself. "But after that group quit Abe, he never recruited many city boys after that. Most of the guys came from little rural towns—like Goose."

Indeed, Goose Tatum brought with him the naiveté of the country, but he also had an authenticity that had not been dulled by years in the North. He was raw, unrefined, and totally original. At first, some called him a rube. Soon, they would call him a genius.

Until the day he died, Goose Tatum was elusive about his age, and, like his contemporary Satchel Paige, his actual birth date was always shrouded in mystery. The most commonly accepted date has been May 3, 1921—which is even listed on his death certificate—but the 1920 U.S. Census shows him as a nineteen-month-old toddler, which would put his actual date of birth in 1918.

He was born in Bradley County, Arkansas, about a hundred miles from Little Rock, near the Louisiana and Texas borders. Prior to the Civil War, Bradley County had been part of the cotton belt, and although King Cotton had been deposed by the boll weevil and the big plantations were gone, this was still very much the Old South. A majority of Bradley County's 15,000 residents were African Americans, many of them descendants of slaves, and the blacks and poor whites were still tied irrevocably to the land. Prior to World War I, the virgin pine flats and hardwood hammocks had been discovered by northern lumber companies, such as Weyerhaeuser, and were now being decimated as ruthlessly as the weevil had annihilated the cotton crop (in 1928, for instance, the Arkansas Lumber Company clear-cut its entire holdings of 85,000 acres in Bradley County, then went out of business). Most black families were either farming or working in the local sawmills and logging camps.

The Tatum family had been living in Bradley County for at least a hundred years. Goose's great-grandfather Adam Tatum, born in slavery in 1818, had farmed a small parcel of land just a few miles from where Goose was born. In 1920, the Tatums were living near Sumpter township, which was too tiny to even be listed on maps of the day. It was just a crossroads, with fewer than 500 people scattered through the piney woods. Goose's father, Benjamin Franklin Tatum (called Frank), was a farmer and an African Methodist Episcopal (AME) preacher. Goose was the fifth of seven children born to Mary Alice Tatum (although she would lose her eldest son in a drowning).

When Goose was about five, the Tatums moved twenty miles south to Calion, in adjoining Union County, where his father and older brother, Booker T., found jobs in a sawmill. But Calion was flooded by the Ouachita River, so the Tatums moved again, to Norphlet, eight miles farther west, where Goose and his siblings enrolled in the Burnt Mill Negro School. There were no organized sports teams for blacks, but Goose played sandlot baseball and rigged up his own makeshift basketball hoop, nailing a rusty barrel hoop to a tree and using a Pet milk can for a ball.

The Burnt Mill Negro School only went through the ninth grade, so most black children had no choice but to quit school and take their place in the fields or logging camps. But Frank and Mary Tatum wanted more for their children, so they made one final move, to the county seat of El Dorado, twelve miles away. Theirs was not a triumphant entry into El Dorado: the Tatums arrived in a mule-drawn wagon, with Frank, Mary, six children, and all of their belongings. Elvie Walker, now eighty-six, was there to witness their arrival. "They had some good-looking ol' mules," recalls Walker.

El Dorado was named after the fabled Spanish city of gold, and the name proved to be prescient, as "black gold" was discovered in 1921, when a gusher spouted one hundred feet in the air. The discovery of oil set off a frenzy that turned the sleepy town into a tent-city boomtown overnight. Over 460 wells were drilled in the first ten months; the population multiplied sixfold, from 4,000 to 25,000; and local residents erected food stands in their front yards to feed the treasure-seekers. El Dorado became the hub of Arkansas' most productive oil and gas field, and oil money funded the construction of new hotels, opulent homes, a Gothic-inspired courthouse, and a half dozen banks. Most of that money bypassed the black community, but oil fever did attract many African Americans to El Dorado, including doctors, dentists, barbers, and businessmen.

By the mid-1930s, however, when the Tatums arrived, the boom had long since faded, and the Great Depression was pummeling El Dorado as harshly as any place in the country. Inevitably, the black community suffered most of all. A few black men still worked for the Lion Oil refinery, but many more had been forced onto the relief rolls. The lucky ones hooked on with the WPA or CCC, or found jobs as porters, cooks, or dishwashers in El Dorado's hotels. Black women were relegated to domestic work or taking in laundry. In the fall, flatbed trucks would arrive from Mississippi and recruit young black men to work the cotton harvest in the Delta.

The Tatums moved into a house on Arkansas Street, in the heart of El Dorado's most thriving, and infamous, neighborhood, which was known as "St. Louis" because of the nightclubs, juke joints, pool rooms, barber shops, barbeque joints, and even a few houses of ill repute that lined Liberty Street. On Saturday nights, African Americans from every town in a fifty-mile radius would pour into St. Louis for dances at the Plaza and the St. Louis Inn. They would come from the logging camps in Magnolia, Mount Holly, and Three Creeks; the oil fields in Mackover; and even from Bernice and Junction City, Louisiana. By ten P.M., Liberty Street would be impassable, as zoot-suited men and women in their Saturday night finery clogged the street.

This was the world that young Goose Tatum was thrust into, after spending his entire life in the sticks of Sumpter, Calion, and Norphlet. He was extremely shy and a loner, the kind of boy who would barely speak, even when spoken to. Surrounded by the cacophony of Liberty Street, he was more inclined to hang out by himself, or with one close friend, rather than in the crowd. In El Dorado, that one friend became John Willie Banks, nicknamed "Dean," and the two boys made an odd couple. Tatum was tall and gangly and hardly said a word, while Dean was barely five feet and a nonstop talker. Inevitably, their friends in St. Louis nicknamed them "Mutt and Jeff."

The origin of Goose Tatum's famous nickname is as mysterious as his age. There are three contradictory stories, each with its advocates: his sister Thelma, who passed away in 2003, always insisted that it was because goose liver was his favorite food; Elvie Walker claims that his best friend, Dean, hung the moniker on him because he "strutted around like an old goose" on the baseball diamond; and Tatum himself told reporters, in later years, that he got the name after leaping to catch a football, and somebody said he looked like a goose. In any case, he would be Goose forevermore.

That fall, the Tatum children entered Booker T. Washington High School, which actually included grades one through twelve.* Goose performed well in school when he put his mind to it, but that was not very often. As he would later say, "School was not for me." None of his classmates would have ever predicted that he would become a world-renowned comedian, as he barely spoke, responding only when teachers called on him, and was reticent even around his peers. He showed only a passing interest in girls, avoided the temptations of Liberty Street, cared nothing about fishing or hunting, and had an aversion to physical labor. "I never knew Goose to work at all," says Walker. In fact, Tatum and Dean—Mutt and Jeff—came up with an ingenious scheme to make money: before daylight, they would steal milk bottles off people's front stoops and redeem them for the ten-cent deposit. Tatum was especially adept at this gambit. "Goose always had a great big old black coat on, so he could hide those bottles," Walker recalls. "He'd grab a bottle and be gone."

One thing was clear: he did not envision his future in the logging camps or oil fields. The only thing he really loved to do was play ball. Baseball was his first love. He would play sandlot games with other boys from St. Louis—and sometimes, despite Jim Crow covenants against it, they would even face off against local white

---

* Before the oil boom in 1921, El Dorado had no black high school, so children had to go to Little Rock or Pine Bluff to get a high school education. But in 1923, Washington began expanding to include the upper grades and graduated its first class in 1927.

boys. The ball field was the one place where all of the restrictions and institutionalized inequalities fell away. It was just two teams going at each other, and may the best one win. Seven decades later, Elvie Walker still remembers those fierce battles. "Them was some ball games," he says. "Just get out there and play."

When it was too cold for baseball, Goose and his friends switched to basketball, although they lacked both a court and a ball. Instead, they played in the living room of an old abandoned house on North West Avenue with ten-foot ceilings and hardwood floors. The boys nailed an empty lard can to the wall and, using a tennis ball, played for hours.

Playing sports was the one place in which this shy, awkward boy came alive. By the time he was in high school, Goose would hitch-hike twenty or thirty miles away—to Damascus, Magnolia, or Stevenson—to play in a baseball game. He went alone, usually, or with his friend Dean. "If there was going to be a game, Goose would somehow find a way to get there," says Walker. Once, Goose and Dean hitchhiked all the way to Louisiana for a game, and didn't return home for many days. Their families began to worry about their safety, but the boys finally straggled back to El Dorado, their clothes torn and dirty. Dean told a harrowing tale about a white farmer who had captured them and forced them to work on his sweet potato farm. They finally escaped in the middle of the night, running through the swamps with sweet potatoes stuffed in their shirts for sustenance on the journey home. "We were enslaved down there," Dean said. Years later, Goose would repeat the story to his young son Reece III.

One fall, Tatum tried out for the Washington High football team, which was quarterbacked by Elvie Walker, but he didn't like the contact and quit. When basketball season rolled around, however, he made the varsity squad. Washington High didn't have a gym, so home games were played on the dance floor of the Plaza, a club in St. Louis.

By 1936, Goose had grown tired of school and dropped out of Washington High after only two years. That summer, he made his first money as an athlete. El Dorado had a white minor league base-ball team, the El Dorado Lions, sponsored by Lion Oil Company. It was a Cincinnati Reds farm team in the Class D Cotton States

League. Inspired by the white Lions, Goose, Dean, Elvie Walker, and other players organized a black equivalent, the El Dorado Black Lions (although they received no funding from Lion Oil). Their first season, they stayed close to home, playing black teams in nearby towns. The white Lions let them use their ballpark, Rowland Field, for home games, and they traveled to away games in Walker's Model A Ford. The two teams would split the gate receipts "after the nut" (after paying expenses for gas, food, baseballs, umpire, and rent for the ballpark), with 60 percent to the winners and 40 percent to the losers. A player's share might only be fifty cents or a dollar, but Goose was just happy to be paid for playing ball. He was now a professional.

The next season, some local black businessmen sponsored the team, and the Black Lions began traveling as far as Little Rock, Pine Bluff, and Shreveport, Louisiana. They played Saturday night games under the lights at Rowland Field, and their ball games became a popular prelude to the dances at the Plaza and the St. Louis Inn. "It was a hot time in the old town," recalls Newt Ellis, ninety, who was the team's player-manager. Even the white players from the El Dorado Lions came out to watch their games, and the black players reciprocated (they were admitted free to the white games). The players' shares of the gate receipts grew to $15 or $20—good money for a two-hour game in the Depression.

Tatum was a decent hitter, spraying the ball to all fields, but he was struggling in the field. He played outfield, but his long arms seemed to interfere with his fielding and coordination. He was not particularly fast, and he was so gangly that it took him a while to get up to speed chasing down fly balls. Then, inspiration struck. Newt Ellis, the Black Lions' player-manager, who was a college student at Arkansas A and M, decided to try Tatum at first base. "Goose couldn't get around too well in the outfield, because of his build," recalls Ellis. "But with his long arms and long legs, he made a hell of a first baseman."

The move to first base did something else for Goose—it gave him a chance to entertain the crowd. When he caught a ball on a put-out, he'd whip his glove across his body or windmill it around his head, turning a routine out into a little show. Or when he stretched out those freakish appendages to snare a one-hop throw in the dirt, he'd jump up and do a little dance around the bag, waving his glove to display the ball. When the crowd responded, he added more flourishes and capers. He was such a funny-looking guy anyway, it didn't take much to get the crowd laughing, and when he *tried* to be funny, people loved it.

Off the field, such clowning would have been totally out of character for him. But this was a revelatory experience that would forever change his life: Goose realized that he could make people laugh. This bashful, taciturn young man, a loner in every other area, had found a way to connect with people. What was difficult for him one-on-one seemed easier at a distance, in front of a crowd. And, perhaps for the first time, his oddly shaped body was working in his favor.

At the end of that season, the Black Lions went their separate ways. Newt Ellis returned to Pine Bluff for his senior year at Arkansas A and M, and the local players oiled their gloves with Neetsfoot oil and packed them away, then returned to their jobs at the shoeshine stands and hotel kitchens. But Goose was not ready to quit. He knew that he wanted to make his living playing ball, but he could never do that in El Dorado. So he said good-bye to his family and friends, hopped a freight train heading north, and hoboed to Louisville, Kentucky, six hundred miles away. He had reportedly read an article in the *Pittsburgh Courier* saying that the Louisville Black Colonels were looking for ballplayers. When he arrived, he looked up the owner of the Black Colonels, Leonard Mitchell, and convinced him to give him a tryout. Mitchell was impressed enough to put him on the team, and he also gave him a place to sleep and a job cleaning apartments (Mitchell had the maintenance contract at a white apartment complex). Goose cleaned apartments and did yard work during the week, and played with the Black Colonels on the weekends.

The Black Colonels were in the Negro Southern League, which was several steps above the competition Goose had faced with the Black Lions. They played teams like the Atlanta Black Crackers, Memphis Red Sox, St. Louis Stars, and Birmingham Black Barons. Goose played first base or right field. At first base, he continued to expand his repertoire of showboating tricks. "He was a marvelous first baseman," recalls Jimmie Armstead, eighty-six, one of his teammates. "He had such flash, and would do all kinds of tricks with the ball."

As in El Dorado, the teams split the gate receipts after the nut, but in this league the players could make as much as thirty dollars a game. "We weren't getting rich off it," Armstead says, "but that was almost as much as a week's pay for a regular job." Combined with his wages at the apartment complex, Goose was making more money than he'd ever had in his life. But he certainly wasn't spending it on the high life. Many of the Black Colonel veterans were heavy drinkers, but Goose seldom went to bars or socialized with his team-mates. "He didn't hang with anybody, really," says Armstead. "He was by himself most of the time; a loner." Even during the ball games, Goose maintained his distance. "He'd usually be sitting at the end of the bench by himself, just studying the game," says Armstead. Part of his reticence was due to his extreme shyness, but he was also younger than most of the players, and more immature. "He was very childish," Armstead remembers.

When he wasn't working or playing ball, Goose's primary enter-tainment was going to movies by himself or, in the off-season, to basketball games at Louisville Central High, Louisville Municipal College, or black recreation centers. Curiously, he'd watch the games for hours, but would never play. He'd scrutinize the players, watching their moves and shots, absorbing the strategies of the game. In his own contemplative fashion, he was learning the intricacies of the game. "It was like he was preparing for something," says Armstead.

Indeed, he was.

Goose Tatum spent a couple of years in Louisville, playing alternately for the Black Colonels and the Zulu Cannibal Giants, the most con-troversial team in the history of Negro League baseball. The Zulus took the field wearing grass skirts, fake wigs and beards, and some-times in whiteface. They played mostly for white audiences against white teams. After relocating from Miami to Louisville, the Zulus' owner arranged to share players with the Black Colonels—including Jimmie Armstead and Goose Tatum. "We'd play as Zulus one week-end and Black Colonels the next," Armstead recalls. Although the notion of black athletes wearing grass skirts and fake beards seems in-conceivable by today's mores, Armstead judges it in the context of the times. "I was glad to have an opportunity to play ball," he says. "I really enjoyed it."

Goose ended up leaving Louisville because of an altercation with the Black Colonels' owner, Leonard Mitchell. According to Armstead, Mitchell had been drinking heavily one night, took offense at something Goose said, and started cursing him and punching him. To defend himself, Goose put a headlock on Mitchell, enveloping him in his long tentacles. Always courteous, Goose pleaded with the older man, "Please, Mr. Mitchell, don't hit me." But Mitchell kept trying to get at him, so Goose squeezed harder. Mitchell turned pale and started to faint. "To tell you the truth," Jimmie Armstead recalls, "Goose was about to kill him." It took the two biggest players on the team to pry Goose off, as he was deceptively strong. The fight, such as it was, was over, but Goose was so upset about Mitchell's attack that he bought a bus ticket to Chicago and never returned.

Over the next two years, he played with other Negro League teams, eventually ending up with the Birmingham Black Barons, whose manager, Winfield S. Welch, had started working for Abe Saperstein as a Globe Trotter road manager in the off-season. There are conflicting accounts about how Goose ended up with the Trotters, but his version was that Welch saw him fooling around with a basketball one day in Fort Benning, Georgia, after their baseball game was rained out, and invited him to the Globe Trotters' training camp.

When he arrived in November 1941, he had far less basketball experience than any of the other hopefuls, but Abe recognized Goose's flair for showmanship. Inman Jackson worked with him, as he did with all the rookies, to teach him the ball-handling tricks that he had been doing for a dozen years. But Goose had an aptitude for improvisation. He didn't just repeat the tricks, he expanded on them, adding his own variations, spinning off new gags from the old standards. Inman Jackson had been a great *showman* and ball handler, but he was no clown; he was too dignified for that. But clowning seemed to come naturally to Goose, and despite his inexperience on the basketball court, his potential as a showman seemed limitless.

Goose was so raw, however, that he would play sparingly, if at all, for the Globe Trotters that first season, and likely spent the bulk of it with one of Abe's farm teams. When the basketball season ended, he would play first base for the Ethiopian Clowns,* which were owned by Abe's friend Syd Pollack. The Clowns were nearly as controversial as the Zulu Cannibal Giants, as they intentionally parodied black stereotypes, painting their faces white and putting on a pregame show—"shadow ball"—for mostly white audiences. In the *Courier*, Wendell Smith labeled them a "minstrel show" and urged black fans to boycott them. Nevertheless, Tatum would become a star first baseman for the Clowns and continue to expand his showmanship and trickery.

As the 1941–42 season unfolded, Abe was feeling so confident about the future of his team, even after losing Sonny Boswell, that he predicted that professional basketball would have its greatest year ever. He told the *Courier*, "People don't realize how fast professional basketball is growing. Why the whole country is basketball conscious." Abe and the Globe Trotters were looking forward to an upcoming grudge match against the Detroit Eagles, who had knocked them out of the 1941 World Pro Tournament and then gone on to claim their crown. It was the Globe Trotters' chance for revenge. The game was set for December 7, 1941.

The Japanese attack on Pearl Harbor caught the U.S. Navy by surprise, killing some twenty-four hundred Americans, sinking or crippling sixteen warships, and disabling much of the Pacific Fleet. The next day, President Roosevelt addressed a joint session of Congress, where he called December 7 "a date which will live in infamy" and asked for a declaration of war. The nation was reeling, still struggling to come to grips with the enormity of what lay ahead. But in the immediate days after Pearl Harbor, Americans lived in a limbo state between war and peace, between mobilizing for world war and continuing their normal lives. The Harlem Globe Trotters, for instance, played a regularly scheduled game in Decatur, Illinois, on December 9, although it was moved from the local armory to the high school gym after Governor Dwight Green canceled all nonmilitary use of state armories. During halftime, the public address system

---

* *That year, the Clowns were based in Cincinnati, but would soon move to Indianapolis.*

piped in President Roosevelt's speech to the nation. Yet the game went on.

A few days later, as planned, the Trotters left on their usual West Coast tour, although fourteen games had already been canceled because of the war. Soon, however, as the nation mobilized to fight the bloodiest war in history, and thousands of American men and women lined up to volunteer for the military, the war effort took precedence over everything else. The federal government imposed rationing on all war-related products, including rubber and gasoline. For an organization that depended entirely on travel, the Globe Trotters could have been devastated. Indeed, some barnstorming teams, including the Rens, would be homebound for the duration of the war, and others suspended operations because so many of their players were in the military.

But Abe Saperstein decided to keep playing as long as he could. And once again, his marketing brilliance shone through. He devised an ingenious method for keeping the Trotters on the road, by offering to play games at military bases, often for charity. In effect, the Globe Trotters became part of the war effort. This strategy had a huge secondary benefit, as the Globe Trotters could fill their gas tanks at military pumps and buy a new set of tires, if needed. For the duration of the war, Abe scheduled every third or fourth game at some kind of military installation, including navy bases, civilian shipyards, the Presidio of Monterey, army air corps bases, and innumerable army posts. He offered free admission to base personnel and raised thousands of dollars for military hospitals, recreation facilities, the Navy Mothers club, and dozens of other war-related causes. Although the Trotters made less money, these benefits served a larger purpose: to allow them to stay on the road, where they could also play their regular dates.

By the start of the 1942–43 season, many of Abe's best players were either in the military or working in war production jobs. All eligible men, from ages eighteen to thirty-eight, were required to register for the military draft, but names of draftees were drawn by lottery, so not all men who were fit for service were necessarily drafted—or not right away. And a job in a war-related industry qualified one for a deferment. Bernie Price, Roosevelt Hudson, Ted Strong, and Babe Pressley all went to work at the Studebaker aircraft plant in Chicago, as did former Trotters Sonny Boswell, Hilary Brown, and Duke Cumberland. All of them (except Strong) played basketball for the Chicago Studebakers, which was sponsored by the United Auto Workers local union, and was one of the first integrated professional teams in the country.

Without his top players, Abe told reporters that he was "uncertain" about whether to even field a team, but was "left no choice" because of the "avalanche of requests for games to stimulate the morale of war industry workers and help raise funds for various war fund efforts." There are no doubts about Abe's patriotism, as evidenced by the many benefit games he played, but he also was a savvy businessman who had found a way to keep his business afloat. And by March 1943, Abe would claim that the Globe Trotters were the only pro team still playing every day.

Although he'd lost much of his team, Abe was able to cobble together two Trotter units, using his remaining veterans and a motley crew of newcomers, including Al Singleton, Bob Powell, Wilbert King (another Detroiter from the Brewster Center), Troy Logan, Davage Minor, Vic Kraft, and Buzz Matthews. Once again, Inman Jackson was forced to reprise his role as the lead showman on the first unit (Inman would celebrate his three-thousandth game that season, with "Inman Jackson Day" in Seattle). And Abe even convinced Runt Pullins to come back to the Trotters, seven years after his "insurrection" (Pullins played a few games early in the season, then disappeared from the box scores). One Trotter unit played primarily in the Chicago area, so that players could still work their factory jobs during the day. The traveling unit, under Inman Jackson's direction, was made up of players with military deferments, which Abe would later refer to as the "Psycho Five."

The season was a constant struggle. Players had to be shuffled in and out, juggling the Trotters' games with their war production jobs. Abe could never keep the same lineup on the court for any length of time, and the lack of continuity showed. Even Abe, the eternal optimist, would later admit that the 1942–43 team was the "weakest" in the Trotters' history. Fortunately, the competition was equally inept, as many of the games were against makeshift teams from military installations.

Even with the nation at war and the Trotters doing their patriotic duty to raise morale, racial prejudice did not miraculously disappear from American society. For instance, gas rationing forced Abe to sometimes use public transportation, but the director of the U.S. Office of Defense Transportation threatened to "not allow Negro ball teams to ride buses"—a potential calamity that Abe circumvented by promising to play service teams almost exclusively. And several Trotter games in Missouri were canceled because of fears of a racial incident, after Paul Robeson publicly criticized the Jim Crow seating of blacks and whites during a performance in Kansas City, which prompted most of the whites in the auditorium to walk out. Even during wartime, Americans did not suspend their racial bias.

The emergence of Goose Tatum was the most promising development of an otherwise turbulent 1942–43 season. As his draft number had not yet been called, Goose would play full-time for the Trotters that year. He had started the year as a reserve, coming off the bench, and was still a work in progress on the court. But as the season progressed, he began to come into his own. He scored in double figures in several games, including a 20-point effort in Vancouver. In March, the Trotters were eliminated from the Third Annual World Pro Tournament by the Dayton Bombers, but Goose led the scoring with 17 points in a losing cause.★

It was Goose's leaping ability that first caught the attention of the press. "It can safely be said . . . that Abe Saperstein has found someone who is destined to comet to fame," one writer predicted. "[Tatum] can jump like a kangaroo and is as deadly as a bren gun in the key. He gets up about 11 feet and easily blocks balls dropping into the hoop." In fact, Abe offered to cover all bets that Tatum could

---

★ *That year's world title was captured by the Washington Bears, composed almost entirely of former Rens, including Johnny Isaacs, Pop Gates, Tarzan Cooper, Dolly King, and Sonny Woods.*

jump higher than any basketball player in the country. But it was his freakish wingspan that made him a celebrity. Abe capitalized on the marketing potential of Goose's incredible arms, boasting that they were "the longest in the world" and arranging numerous photo opportunities—often with Abe in the picture, comparing wingspans.

Goose had started the season playing guard, but as he grew more comfortable on the court he began showing off the clowning talents he had honed on the baseball diamond, and soon took on a featured role in the Trotters' show. Inman Jackson, who had recognized Goose's potential right away (he called Goose "one of the finest players" he had ever seen), taught the younger man his signature trick of jumping up and knocking an opponent's shot out of the basket. But Goose added his own spectacular variation: he would leap above the rim and grab the ball in midair with one hand. He took over other of Inman's tricks, such as hiding the ball under his shirt or perching it on the head of a bewildered opponent, and was awarded the coveted role of the "batter" in the Globe Trotters' baseball routine. By late season, he was being described as a "phenom" and the Trotters' "newest sensation," and reporters were gushing over his "screwball antics."

What set Goose apart from Inman Jackson, Ted Strong, Bernie Price, or other previous Trotter showmen was his improvisational ability. No one—including Abe, Inman, or the Trotter players—quite knew what Goose might pull on any given night. Traditionally, the Trotters' show was a well-rehearsed act that had stayed pretty much the same for years. It was always the same, which was part of its appeal—the fans knew what was coming yet it still cracked them up. But Goose did something different every night.

"I should have paid myself to get in," said teammate Ziggy Marcell, marveling at Goose's act. As one reporter said: "He is liable to surprise his teammates any time. Last night he pulled stunts that his pals had never seen before, and that is where Saperstein starts tearing his hair. The players forget all about the game and get as much enjoyment as the fans from watching the Goose." If Abe was already "tearing his hair" over Goose's spontaneity in his first year as showman, he had no idea of what a wild ride it was going to be.

In March 1943, Goose hit the big time, when *Time* ran a story on the Trotters that focused primarily on his showmanship. Again, it was his physical appearance that drew most of the attention, and *Time*'s description strayed close to the line of racial stereotyping:

> The Trotters have produced many a freakish player. None has been more bizarre than their latest find: Reece ("The Goose") Tatum, a 22 year old Arkansan who stands 6 ft. 3, has a reach (from left to right) of 7 ft. 3 in. . . . Tatum deliberately capers around the court in a rocking chimpanzee gait, his long arms swinging, his teeth bared. Going for the ball, he often flaps his arms goose like; when he jumps, he can reach 11 ft. into the air to block opponents' shots.

But just as Goose was becoming a superstar, drawing press notices in every city the Trotters visited, he received a notice of a different kind: "Greetings from the President of the United States." The Goose had been drafted.

He joined the U.S. Army Air Corps, and would spend the next three years stationed at Lincoln Air Field in Lincoln, Nebraska, and MacDill Field in Tampa, Florida. In Nebraska, he played center on the base's Negro team, the Lincoln Wings, which competed in the Negro Servicemen's League (segregation was maintained in the military, even in sporting events). Also stationed at Lincoln was Jake Ahearn, a veteran white player from the Detroit Eagles and House of David, who became Goose's mentor, tutoring him on the basketball fundamentals he had never learned. Goose worked on his basketball skills and also spent hours practicing his clowning. The combination was deadly: he became a prolific scorer in the service league, averaging 15.8 points per game, and was sometimes invited to tournaments, even if his team wasn't playing, just to perform his ball-handling and comedy routines.

Goose would improve so much as a ballplayer during his years in the service that he even defeated the Trotters, which could not have sat well with Abe. In December 1944, he would score 18 points to lead the Lincoln Army Air Field Wings to a 41–39 win over the Globe Trotters, in front of 8,000 screaming fans in the University of Nebraska gym.

And despite his isolation in the cornfields of eastern Nebraska, he would still garner national attention, when Robert Ripley, of *Ripley's Believe It or Not,* featured him in his cartoon, declaring that "Pfc. Reece [*sic*]" can "reach eleven feet and drop the ball down into the basket." In his three years away from the Trotters, the legend of the golden Goose would continue to grow.

★

The departure of Goose Tatum was nearly a death knell to an already crippled Globe Trotters team. More and more of Abe's players had enlisted or had been drafted. Ted Strong was a Navy Seabee in the South Pacific, Hilary Brown was stationed in England, and other former Trotters were serving on the front lines in France and Italy. Abe was so short-handed that he was down to six players, and was forced to do something truly unprecedented: he hired a white ballplayer to take Goose's place. Bob Karstens, a rugged six-foot-three center from Davenport, Iowa, who had been playing pro ball since he was seventeen, signed on with the Trotters in 1943.* Karstens had spent the previous three seasons playing with the House of David, so he had often tangled with the Trotters.

Karstens was no stooge merely filling in for Tatum. He was a gifted ball handler in his own right and is credited with introducing many of the ball-handling tricks that evolved into the "Magic Circle." He would twirl the ball on his fingers, roll it up one arm and down the other arm, or toss it up between his legs and catch it on the back of his neck. Karstens also invented the "wobbly ball"—a basketball with a weight inside that would wobble crazily when it was rolled or thrown. "I was a trickster to start with," Karstens says with a laugh. At ninety, he is the oldest surviving Globe Trotter and still practices his ball-handling tricks for school groups and civic clubs.

---

* Karstens passed away in January 2005. Other than Abe, Karstens is usually credited with being the only other white Globe Trotter, but there have been at least four others. Bunny Leavitt, the world-record free-throw shooter, apparently played a few games in the mid-1930s; Ritchie Nichol, a white ballplayer from Nainamo, British Columbia, played one game for the Trotters in 1944, as a substitute for the injured Babe Pressley; and in December 1944, after three Trotters missed a train to Winona, Minnesota, two white assistant coaches from St. Mary's College played for the Trotters.

After Karstens joined the team, sports reporters began referring to him as the Trotters' "white hope" and raved about his ball-handling. "Karstens, only white member of the team, nearly made the old casaba do a 'Charlie McCarthy' and talk," one wrote. "Seeing is believing and Karstens had fans talking to themselves as he handled the basketball with the ease and grace of a sensational juggler." He also played a leading role in the Trotters' show. If a questionable foul was called on him, Karstens would draw an eye chart on his jersey and hand the referee a pair of glasses, or he'd pull a horn out of his waistband and blow a "Bronx cheer" in the ref's face. At halftime, he would invite several young boys out of the stands for a game of "Twenty-one." And at the end of every game, he launched his "signature shot"—a blind, over-the-head heave from the free throw line with his back to the basket—which usually went in. "That was my best shot," he says. Today, reflecting on his experience as the "only" white Globe Trotter, Karstens recalls it as surprisingly uneventful. "We were all sportsmen," he says. "It was no big deal."

With Goose Tatum plying his trade in the army air corps and with increasingly restrictive gasoline rationing limiting their travel (their mileage dropped from 35,000 to 20,000 per year), the Globe Trotters limped through the next two seasons with a makeshift crew of players. Some of the veterans were able to rejoin the team sporadically, if they could get off from their defense jobs. Babe Pressley, Roosevelt Hudson, and Duke Cumberland, for instance, played some of the 1943–44 season, and even the great Sonny Boswell and Zack Clayton returned to the Trotters for portions of that season.*

Despite the wartime restrictions, however, the Globe Trotters still managed to achieve several new milestones. In 1943 and '44, they made two extended tours of Mexico, and captured the Mexico City Invitational tournament both years. The most startling impact of the Mexico trips was on the Trotter players themselves, who, for the first

---

* In fact, during the 1944 World Pro Tournament, Boswell, Cumberland, and Clayton all played for the Trotters, who were eliminated in the semifinals by the Brooklyn Eagles. The Trotters rebounded from that loss to defeat the New York Rens and earn third place in the tourney. It would be the final game between the two great rivals, with the Trotters holding a two games to one advantage.

time in their lives, were not aware of being black. The Mexican fans greeted them as heroes, without any apparent racial prejudice. It was a phenomenon that would be repeated many times in other countries, where the Trotters would receive better treatment than in their homeland. Wendell Smith, who traveled with the team at Abe's invitation and filed accounts in the *Courier,* wrote: "The Harlem Globe Trotters . . . are getting their first real taste of democracy . . . the Mexicans have adopted the sepia court wizards from the states as their very own. . . . and the treatment they have been accorded since their arrival has never been equaled in the states. These Americano basketeers are idols to the personable, gracious and unprejudiced Mexicans."

If the Mexican tours gave the players a glimpse of life without race discrimination, the Trotters' first venture into the Deep South showed just the opposite. In December 1943, Abe scheduled a series of games in Nashville, Atlanta, Birmingham, and New Orleans, but Jim Crow laws prohibited black and white teams from playing each other, so the Trotters had to play black college teams. In Alabama, segregation was so extreme that black and white fans were not even permitted to attend the same game, so the Trotters had to play one game for whites, then empty the auditorium and play a second for blacks.

In addition to Mexico and the Deep South, during the war years Abe was able to expand the Trotters' U.S. tour to some of the larger cities in the country. In California, for instance, he opened up huge new markets in San Francisco, Oakland, San Jose, San Diego, Long Beach, and Los Angeles.

The Trotters continued to play nearly half of their games against military teams, sometimes playing double- or tripleheaders on the same day. Many of those games were benefits for hospitals, base recreation funds, the Infantile Paralysis Fund, or the March of Dimes. During a two-month stretch on the West Coast, Abe contributed over $10,000 to various charities and service funds, which earned plaudits for him in many circles. Wendell Smith, who had become a Saperstein devotee, anointed the Trotters as "the greatest Negro professional basketball team in the world," and said that the Globe Trotters had "gone farther out of their way to put a little 'umph' in morale in army camps than other cage companies from the ranks of professionals. . . . This is a record no team in the nation can manage."

Not everyone was so impressed with the Globe Trotters' contribution to the war effort, however. In early 1945, James F. Byrnes, FDR's director of the Office of War Mobilization (whom Harry Truman would soon appoint as secretary of state after FDR's death), complained publicly that men who were fit enough to play professional sports were fit enough to serve on the front lines. Abe protested (perhaps too much), insisting that all of his players were 4-F and that he was "only carrying on" with the Trotters' schedule because of his two brothers, Harry and Rocky, who were stationed overseas and had convinced him that sports were essential to keep up morale. "*They* believe in sports," he said, somewhat melodramatically, "and therefore so do I."

Abe's pleadings may have convinced Wendell Smith, but there were some critics who did not believe that Abe's motives were purely patriotic or humanitarian. In January 1944, Harry Borba, sports editor of the *San Francisco Herald-Examiner,* ripped Abe after one of his so-called benefit games at the Alameda Coast Guard station, at which Abe made a grand gesture of donating $876 to the Service Athletic Fund. However, Borba claimed that donation was less than half of Abe's share of gate receipts and that he had walked away with nearly $2,000 in profits. "The Globe Trotters maintain that they build up basketball," Borba said caustically. "They have yet to prove it around here."

The truth was, benefits notwithstanding, the Trotters were raking in big bucks during the war years, and Abe's attempts to portray himself as a self-sacrificing patriot were often negated by his compulsive braggadocio about the money he was making. Around his legions of fawning sportswriters, he simply could not control the urge to impress them with his success. As one reporter for the *Rochester Democrat Chronicle* wrote: "Round as a basketball and high as celery stalk, Abe is known as the Billy Rose of basketball, and not without good reason, for by his own admission he has made more money out of basketball and baseball 'Than I know what to do with.'"

The Trotters were making record profits, and Abe was pulling in even more from Negro League baseball. By 1944, he owned two teams, had a piece of several others, and was still promoting the hugely popular East-West All-Star game (although he was temporarily fired in 1941). "Colored baseball has done so well this summer, has made so much money, that it scares me," he told a Vancouver sportswriter in 1944. "The colored man, coming from cotton picking and menial tasks in the south to work in defense plants, now has money. All he knows is baseball, and he can afford the best seats."

★

On May 8, 1945, the war ended in Europe, with Germany's surrender. Three more savage months of fighting still lay ahead in the Pacific, but an Allied victory was now assured. World War II had fundamentally changed the balance of power in the world, with the old guard in Europe—England, France, and Germany—giving way to two emerging superpowers, the United States and the USSR.

The war years had also changed the face of professional basketball in America. Gas rationing, military enlistments, and the draft had forced some teams to disband completely (including the Cleveland Buckeyes, Chicago Stags, and Detroit Eagles) and had restricted many others (such as the New York Rens) to playing limited schedules on their home turf. Undoubtedly, the war had also hindered the Harlem Globe Trotters, slowing the momentum they had built after the 1940 world championship and the College All-Star game. Yet Abe's determination to keep them on the road, even with a makeshift crew, had allowed the Trotters to emerge from the war relatively unscathed. They had entered the 1940s still playing in the backwoods shadows of the New York Rens, but by 1945 they had emerged into the bright sunlight of postwar America as the most dominant team in the land. In the process, Abe Saperstein had become a successful sports mogul and a wealthy man.

CHAPTER 9

Marques

On March 6, 1946, the finest all-around basketball player in the history of the Harlem Globe Trotters, and the most influential on the sport, was revealed in the person of Marques Haynes, a college senior from tiny Langston University in Oklahoma, who led his college teammates to a 74–70 victory over the Globe Trotters in Oklahoma City. Haynes didn't just beat the Trotters, which was surprising enough, he destroyed them, scoring 26 points—the second greatest performance by an opposition player in Globe Trotter history.[*] None of the great players from the New York Rens had ever scored that many points against them—not Pop Gates, Tarzan Cooper, John Isaacs, or Wee Willie Smith. None of the former college All-Americans in the World Pro Tournament had ever had a game like that—not Cowboy Edwards, Mike Novak, or Wibs Kautz. No player on any team in the "modern era" (since the elimination of the center jump) had ever done that kind of damage to the proud Globe Trotter defense.

So who was this formidable giant-killer who had wreaked such havoc? He was a twenty-one-year-old college boy who appeared too young to shave, and although he was listed at five-foot-eleven and 160 pounds, he was small-boned and so slight that he looked as if he might break in half from a Ted Strong elbow or a hard pick from Bernie Price.

---

[*] *In March 1932, a player for the Spring Grove Independents scored 32 points against the Trotters.*

This remarkable performance occurred during a monumental week in American history. Two days earlier, Jack Roosevelt Robinson had reported to spring training with the Montreal Royals, the International League AAA farm club of the Brooklyn Dodgers, after Dodger owner Branch Rickey had shown the courage to sign him to a Dodger contract. Robinson's breaking the color line in major league baseball was symptomatic of changes that were slowly coming in America. The war had been over for six months, and the one million African Americans who had served in the United States military came home with high expectations that their sacrifices on the fields of battle would be rewarded at home. The world had been transformed, and they expected America to follow suit.

As it had so often before, however, America let them down. Only five weeks after V-J Day, Jesse James Payne, a thirty-year-old black sharecropper in Madison, Florida, was lynched by a mob of angry whites, who snatched him out of the county jail in the middle of the night (with a convenient assist from the local sheriff, who left the keys in his unlocked car), hauled him to a lonely stretch of highway, and riddled his body with bullets. Payne's only crime was that he had allegedly threatened to report the owner of the land that he farmed for overplanting his federal tobacco allotment, and the white man then accused him of raping his daughter. Despite the efforts of Thurgood Marshall and Florida NAACP leader Harry T. Moore, the murder of Jesse James Payne was never solved. The Payne killing exploded in the national press, serving as a stark reminder that race hatred in America was as deep-seated as ever. And despite the contributions of black veterans in the war, they returned to find that discrimination in housing, employment, education, and even in the U.S. military had not been eradicated. Still, African Americans were thankful for small signs of progress, including Jackie Robinson's signing with the Dodgers.

The basketball game between Langston University and the Globe Trotters was not supposed to happen. The Trotters were scheduled to play a team called the Professional All-Stars, who canceled at the last minute. In desperation, Abe telegrammed Langston coach Zip Gayles and begged him to substitute for the no-show All-Stars. Gayles, a legendary figure who coached football and basketball at

Langston for thirty-one years, obliged. If Abe had known what the Trotters were in for, he might never have sent that wire.

Abe had no idea how good Marques Haynes and the Langston Lions were, but some of the Trotter players might have had an inkling. The previous year, Langston had played on a twin bill with the Trotters in Oklahoma City, where they had upset Satchel Paige's Kansas City Stars, one of Abe's farm teams. That night, Marques had been virtually unstoppable, scoring 23 points on what the *Daily Oklahoman* called a "barrage" of "cross country shots."

But that had been a farm team, and this was the Trotters' first unit, the big team, which was nearly back to full strength after the war. Ted Strong had returned from the Seabees and was reunited with veterans Duke Cumberland, Bernie Price, Zach Clayton, Roosevelt Hudson, Ziggy Marcel, and Tony Peyton. Only Goose Tatum was still in the service, but he would be rejoining the team in a few days.

Over 4,000 fans were packed into the Oklahoma City Auditorium for the big game, including many high school basketball players, who were in town for the state prep championships. The auditorium wasn't designed for basketball, but a full-size court had been laid out on the stage, and fans filled the regular auditorium seats and portable bleachers erected on the stage.

During pregame warm-ups, Duke Cumberland, the Trotter captain, moseyed over to Zip Gayles and said jovially, "You want us to take it easy on your boys, Coach? We don't want to show 'em up."

"Hell, no!" barked Gayles, who was a fierce disciplinarian. "Go ahead and play us like you would anybody else. My boys know how to play the game."

That was an understatement. During Marques Haynes's four years at Langston, the Lions had won 112 of 115 games—a .974 winning percentage that was better than that of any team in the country, including the Globe Trotters'. They went two and half years without losing a game, ran off one 54-game win streak, and came into the Trotters game having won 76 of their last 77. Furthermore, Zip Gayles knew full well what Marques was capable of, whether the Trotters remembered him or not.

Gayles was an early pioneer of the fast-break offense, which he described as getting to the basket "first and most." The Lions went full out the entire game, pushing the ball up the court on every possession, in what the *Oklahoman* called their "hell-for-leather 2-points-a-minute style." The Lions' front line of Frank Luster, Lee Blair, and future Globe Trotter Willie Malone was somewhat undersized (Luster was the tallest at six-foot-one), but they were excellent rebounders who whipped outlet passes to a streaking Marques Haynes or the Cudjoe twins, Lawrence and Lance, an identical pair of five-foot-four speed demons. On defense, Gayles mounted a full-court press, with a switching man-to-man defense that yielded turnovers and easy baskets by the dozens. Coming into the game, Marques was averaging over 16 points per game, and Lawrence Cudjoe was right behind him, with a 12-point average.

It took the Globe Trotters only about three minutes to realize that they were in a fight for their lives. Langston came out running, jumping out to a 9–1 lead, and the Lions' swarming defense held the Trotters without a field goal until nearly five minutes had elapsed. Zip Gayles's entire system was built on speed, and although the Globe Trotters were renowned for their speed—indeed, they were known as the "lightning-quick casaba cagers"—they had never encountered any team as fast as Langston. Younger Globe Trotters like Cumberland and Hudson could still get up and down the court, but some of the veterans, especially Ted Strong and Zach Clayton, were starting to show their age. Langston had a bench full of college boys with young legs, and when one got tired, Gayles would send in another. None of the Trotters could stay with Marques Haynes, yet he wasn't even the fastest player on the Langston team. That honor belonged to the Cudjoe twins, who were like angry wasps swarming around the Trotters' legs.

The Globe Trotters had a huge height advantage, however, and they started feeding the ball inside to Cumberland, Strong, and Price, who got the Trotters back in the game. Cumberland, who ended up scoring 22 points, started the comeback with a dunk in the low pivot, and the Trotters muscled their way to a 19–18 lead at the end of the first period. They extended their lead in the second period, and even put on the show a little before halftime, hoping to catch a breather. Since the early 1930s, the Globe Trotters had always relied on the show to rest their weary legs, but every time they tried one of their trick plays against the college boys, Zip Gayles had two Langston players in their face, slapping at the ball. The Globe Trotters weren't used to playing full-out for an entire game, especially at Langston's hell-for-leather pace.

At halftime, the Trotters still managed to hold a 4-point lead, 37–33, but they knew they were in trouble. They were out of breath and feeling their age. Meanwhile, in the Langston dressing room, the college boys weren't even winded, and Zip Gayles was urging on his troops. "This is the last game of the year," he told them. "Let's open it up. If you've got an outside shot, take it." He instructed his charges to turn up the pressure on both ends, knowing that their "firebrand style" would eventually take its toll on the Trotters, like a heavyweight fighter in the tenth round whose legs have gone rubbery. But he also devised a strategy to counter the Trotters' height advantage. "You're faster than they are," he told them. "Beat them into position and box them out."

Langston came roaring out after halftime, going on a 15–7 run to take a 48–44 lead. Marques Haynes was on fire, hitting three straight buckets in the space of fifty seconds. He was pouring in shots from all over the court, stealing passes and converting them into easy layups, fearlessly driving the lane and challenging Ted Strong and Bernie Price, scoring right over them. He and the Cudjoes seemed to be playing at a different speed from anybody else. The Cudjoes were faster than Marques in a footrace, but *nobody* was quicker. He could take one step and be past his defender—and gone! When Marques wasn't flying past the Trotters for layups, he was launching running one-hand shots from the top of the key—"fling shots" he called them, that were impossible to block. He was in perpetual motion, pausing just long enough to aim a two-hand set shot from the corner.

In the second half, the score was deadlocked twelve times, and there were eight lead changes. The Trotters had no choice but to play at Langston's pace, trying to keep up, and the third quarter became a scoring fest. In the first four minutes, the two teams scored 28 points between them. Duke Cumberland, who was keeping the Trotters in the game, fouled out midway through the period, but Bernie Price picked up the slack, scoring 8 points to give the Trotters a slim 58–56 lead at the end of the third quarter.

In the final period, the score was tied at 60 and again at 68, but with two minutes left, Langston started to pull away. The Trotters fought gamely, using their experience and court savvy to keep the Lions from running away, but they were out of gas. With a minute left, Lawrence Cudjoe stole the ball from an exhausted Zach Clayton and went in for a clinching layup. When the final gun sounded, Langston had a 74–70 victory. It was the highest-scoring game ever played, to that point, in the Oklahoma City Auditorium.

Marques had scored his phenomenal 26 points, and Lawrence Cudjoe, whom the *Oklahoman* called "the fly in the Trotters' soup all night," added 21. The most telling statistic, perhaps, was that Langston had managed to outrebound the taller Trotters.

The most humiliating part of the loss for the Trotters was that Langston seemed to take the victory for granted. Marques Haynes, in particular, took it all in stride. "We had the better team," he recalls matter-of-factly. It was just another win. He had such confidence in himself, he believed that every time he stepped on the court he was the best player on the floor. And he expected to win.

After the game, Winfield Welch, the Trotters' traveling secretary, sought out Marques in the Langston dressing room. Welch had apparently called Abe and told him about this remarkable player, because he offered Marques a job on the spot. "You can leave with us tonight," Welch said. "We're going to Dallas."

Any other African American ballplayer in the country would have leaped at the chance to play with the Trotters, but Marques turned him down cold. He would be graduating from Langston in May—the first person in his family to earn a college degree. "My mother would kill me if I quit school," he said. Welch told him he had a standing invitation to join the team after graduation or, if he preferred, to come to training camp in Chicago in the fall. Marques thanked him for the offer and said he would consider it.

That encounter in the dressing room was symbolic of Marques Haynes's entire history with the Globe Trotters. While other players would have done anything to be a Harlem Globe Trotter—accept any salary, put up with any indignities—Marques always kept his options open. "I think I was the first college graduate who ever played for Abe," he says today. "I always knew I could do something else besides play basketball."

He went back to Langston, finished his degree, and spent the summer weighing his options. He had been offered teaching and coaching jobs in Arkansas, Texas, Kansas, Missouri, and Oklahoma, and seriously entertained one offer from Enid, Oklahoma, to teach history and industrial education and to coach basketball. Trying to make a living playing professional basketball seemed like an insecure future, especially compared to teaching. Basketball was still the fourth, or even fifth, most popular sport in America. "I almost took the job in Enid," he recalls.

Eventually, he decided to give the Globe Trotters a chance. He thought traveling around the United States playing ball might be enjoyable. He would give it a year or two and see how it went. Forty-six years, 4 million miles, and over 12,000 games later, he would still be playing ball.

Marques Haynes was born in Sand Springs, Oklahoma, outside of Tulsa, around October 1924 (in the tradition of Goose Tatum and Satchel Paige, he is secretive about his exact age, saying only, "I've been holding at thirty-seven and a half for a long time"). Sand Springs had originally been settled by Cherokee Indians at the end of the Trail of Tears, but by the time Marques was born, the town had 6,000 residents and was one of the leading industrial cities in Oklahoma. There were oil and gas refineries; glass, lamp, chimney, dog food, and box factories; and it was famous for the Sand Springs Home for Widows and Orphans, the Salvation Army Maternity Home, and a school for the deaf.

Although Oklahoma was not a southern state, it might as well have been when it came to race relations. Segregation in Sand Springs was rigid and unquestioned. The African American community was confined to a four-square-block area that was separated from the white section of town by the Sand Springs Railway tracks. Blacks were able to find jobs in the glass, chimney, and dog food factories, but not at the Standard Oil refinery or the Commander textile mill. The two local movie theaters refused to sell tickets to blacks, even to let them sit in the balcony, so African American families had to go into Tulsa to watch a movie.

Marques Haynes was the youngest of four children (he had two brothers and a sister). When he was three, his father abandoned the family and moved to Kansas and, eventually, to Texas; Marques would never know the man until he was grown. His mother supported the family by taking in laundry and working as a domestic in white people's homes. They lived in a house with no running water or electricity, and with a dirt yard that Marques swept with a broom. They nailed cardboard boxes inside the stud walls for insulation and papered the walls with copies of the *Tulsa World*.

What the family lacked in modern conveniences, they made up for in closeness. As the baby, Marques was favored by his mother and his siblings, and that nurturing helped him develop a rock-solid identity and a self-confidence that would sustain him throughout his life. He was outgoing, respectful, and dependable. He had a quick smile and a hello for everyone he met, and the next time he saw them he would remember their name, greeting them with a genuineness and warmth that made people feel at ease. He could have been a wonderful politician or salesman, as he had a way of drawing people in, of making them feel special. *Everyone* liked Marques Haynes.

His lifelong infatuation with basketball began when he was five years old. His sister, Cecil, played on the girls' team at Booker T. Washington High School, and since their mother worked late, Cecil would babysit Marques in the afternoons. She would carry him with her to basketball practice, put him in the corner of the gym to keep him from getting trampled, and hand him a ball. He entertained himself the only way he could: bouncing the ball until Cecil was through.

That bouncing ball would become the primary metaphor for Marques Haynes's life.

When he got older, Marques and two friends invented a game in which they would bounce a tennis ball as they walked the railroad tracks that divided Sand Springs' black and white neighborhoods. The winner was the one who could keep the ball bouncing the longest on the narrow steel rails. It was nearly impossible, at first, but they kept practicing until they could bounce it a dozen times, then twenty, then for five minutes at a stretch. It was just a boyhood game to pass the time, but Marques was developing a heightened sense of touch and feel for controlling a bouncing ball, no matter what size.

Growing up, basketball was all around him. His sister Cecil and his brother Wendell, both of whom played for Booker T. Washington, taught him to shoot on a homemade basket they had constructed by nailing an economy-size food can to the outhouse wall, with a gunnysack for a net and a ball made of rolled-up rags. Marques would sit and watch Wendell and the older boys in the neighborhood play pickup games on a dirt court. If one team built a comfortable lead, the players would start showboating, dribbling between their legs and whipping behind-the-back passes, showing up the other team. Marques studied Wendell's moves and practiced them by himself. He started by mimicking his brother's moves but eventually developed his own dribbling tricks, which he unveiled in pickup games with his peers.

In 1938, he entered Booker T. Washington High School, where he played clarinet in the marching band and tried out for the basketball team. He was the eleventh player chosen, barely making the cut. Booker T. Washington was a basketball powerhouse, and the skinny freshman was riding the bench. When the band director moved band practice to the same time as basketball, Marques had to make a choice. "He made it easy for me," Marques says, laughing. He quit the band to concentrate on basketball, but he was still warming the bench. The fancy dribbling he had practiced for so many hours did him no good at all, as the high school coach was a stickler for fundamentals and would not permit any hint of showboating.

In 1941, his junior year, Washington High qualified for the national Negro high school championship tournament in Tuskegee, Alabama. "We had some terrific ballplayers," Marques recalls. "I wasn't the best player on the team—by far." In fact, the coaches could fit only eight players in the two cars that would make the trip to Tuskegee, and Marques was not chosen. On the morning of the trip, however, one of the eight players got sick, so the coach woke Marques up at home and told him to get ready. In the national tournament, Washington High rolled through its bracket, reaching the finals. Because of the missing player, Marques got his first significant playing time, and he performed magnificently, particularly as a defensive stopper. In the championship game, Washington was matched against the team from Seminole, Oklahoma (it was the first time two teams from the same state had ever played in the finals), which was led, ironically, by Lawrence and Lance Cudjoe. In a low-scoring, defensive game, Sand Springs prevailed, 38–24, giving them the Negro national championship. And Marques Haynes, who wasn't even supposed to make the trip, was named a second-team All-American. He had come into his own in the biggest games of his life.

The next year, his senior season, he finally broke into the starting lineup and made the all-conference team. After graduation, his mother was insistent on his going to college. There was only one option. Langston University was, and still is, the only historically black college or university in Oklahoma. His church took up a collection, raising $25 to help with his tuition. In September 1942, he hitchhiked to Langston, ninety miles away. Wartime gas rationing was keeping many people off the road, so it took him sixteen rides to make the trip, and he rode the last few miles with an old white farmer in a mule-drawn wagon.

Langston, located forty-three miles northeast of Oklahoma City, was a dusty village with no paved streets and only 514 residents, which included the entire student body of Langston University, 300-strong. Founded in 1887, Langston's original mission—inspired by Booker T. Washington—was to train teachers in agriculture and mechanical or industrial arts; in the 1920s, however, the curriculum had been expanded to include the arts and sciences.

When Marques Haynes arrived in 1942, the war had taken away many of Langston's male students. He played quarterback on the football team and won a starting job on the basketball team. Just as in Sand Springs, his natural warmth drew people to him. "Everybody was crazy about him," recalled Frank Luster, a teammate who became a lifelong friend. Under Zip Gayles's strict tutelage, Marques's basketball skills flourished. He was the team's MVP and leading scorer four years in a row, the MVP of the Southwestern Conference three years in a row, and led the Langston Lions to two straight Southwestern Conference titles.

And yet, in his first three years at Langston, as in his previous four years at Booker T. Washington High, he never once revealed the kind of fancy dribbling he had been practicing since childhood. Zip Gayles was a pioneer of fast-break basketball, but he was strictly "old school" when it came to basketball fundamentals. One behind-the-back pass or between-the-legs dribble was enough to bring down the wrath of Coach Gayles, and he only had to get on a player one time to impress the point. He would have been apoplectic if Marques had unveiled any of the tricks he had developed on his own. Thus, at the end of three years of a celebrated college career, no one still had any idea what Marques could do with a ball.

They might never have known if not for an insult.

In February 1945, Langston traveled to Baton Rouge, Louisiana, to defend its title in the Southwestern Conference tournament. During an early-round game, Marques watched from the stands as Southern University, the host team, demolished an outmatched squad from Samuel Huston College by a score of 55–21. Samuel Huston College, a tiny United Methodist school in Austin, Texas (not to be confused with Sam Houston State University in Huntsville), had only one claim to fame: its coach that year was Jackie Robinson, who had taken the job after being discharged from the army. Robinson had not yet signed with the Brooklyn Dodgers, but he was still one of the most famous black athletes in the country, from his college days at UCLA.

Marques got to meet Robinson before the Southern game, and was rooting for his team. But the lowly Samuel Huston Dragons never had a chance. Southern ran away with the game, more than doubling Samuel Huston's point total, and in the last quarter began rubbing it in: they were throwing behind-the-back passes, running a weave at the top of the key, and generally lording it over the Samuel Huston players. Marques felt sorry for Robinson and his players, who were being humiliated by Southern's antics. "They made fools out of them," he recalls. Marques felt it was poor sportsmanship, to the point of being disrespectful, and vowed that if Langston and Southern met in the championship game, he would give Southern a taste of its own medicine.

Langston roared through the first two rounds, drubbing Arkansas State 66–31 and Prairie View 70–50. Southern was their opponent in the semifinals, and they destroyed the Jaguar Cats by a score of 55–27, beating them almost as badly as Southern had defeated Samuel Huston. It was a double elimination tournament, however, so Southern could still make it to the championship game through the loser's bracket. Marques bided his time; he did not want to provoke Zip Gayles until the last game.

The scenario unfolded just as he had hoped. Southern defeated Wiley University by one point, setting up a rematch with Langston in the title game on Saturday night, February 17. Marques told none of his teammates what he was planning, and certainly didn't mention it to Coach Gayles. At halftime, Langston had only a 4-point lead, but in the second half Southern "wilted under the scorching pace and superior marksmanship of the Oklahomans," the *Chicago Defender* reported. Led by Marques's scoring, Langston built an insurmountable 19-point lead.

As the clock wound down, Marques began plotting his revenge. He was going to unveil a phenomenon that no one had ever seen, to that point, but that millions of fans in 106 countries, on seven continents, would witness over the next six decades.

And so, with less than three minutes left, he started doing his fancy dribbling. He dribbled behind his back and between his legs, dribbled the ball two inches off the floor and higher than his head. Two Southern players chased him, but he dribbled right through them. He circled around the key in one direction, then back the other way, weaving in and out of the Southern players. Just when they seemed to have him boxed in, he would feint in one direction and slam on the brakes so suddenly that they'd slide right past him, falling over themselves. The fans rose to their feet and began cheering. Marques kept making circles around the key, juking the Southern players off their feet. He slid down on one knee, hopped back up, and kept dribbling, never missing a beat.

Out of the corner of his eye, Marques saw the one person in the gym who was not pleased with his exhibition. "Haynes, what in the hell are you doing?!" Zip Gayles bellowed. Marques ignored his coach and kept dribbling.

There was a minute left in the game, and by now the whole Southern team was chasing him. The crowd was going wild. Twenty-five hundred people were hollering and stamping their feet on the wooden bleachers, making a deafening racket. But that wasn't enough. People felt they had to do something more to show their appreciation for the improvisational artistry being displayed before their eyes. They started tossing programs on the floor, then coins—pennies, dimes, and nickels—showering the court in tribute. They threw their hats, and even their shirts. No one had ever seen anything like this before on a basketball court. And, in truth, there had never been anything like this on any basketball court. Not on any court, anywhere, since Dr. Naismith had invented the game. What Marques Haynes was doing with a ball had never been done.

Marques kept dribbling. This was the payoff for all the hours he had spent in the corner of the Booker T. Washington gym, a five-year-old kid bouncing a ball to entertain himself, and for all the steamy afternoons he'd spent walking the railroad tracks, bouncing a tennis ball on the rails.

The more exuberant the fans got, however, the madder Zip Gayles became. "Zip, he had a fit," Clarence Hawkins, a Langston teammate, would later recall. Gayles jumped off the bench and chased Marques down the sidelines, hollering at him to stop. Marques kept dribbling, but with fifteen seconds left, a Langston teammate yelled, "Marques, here comes Zip!" The old coach had completely lost his composure and, violating one of the sacred rules of the game, rushed onto the court and started chasing Marques, right along with the Southern players.

Marques faked out his coach with the same deftness he had used on the Southern players and streaked for the Langston goal. Just before the gun sounded, he tossed in a layup and kept right on running for the dressing room, with Zip Gayles on his tail. "You'll never play another game at Langston University!" Gayles bellowed in the dressing room. Marques politely reminded him that it was the last game of the season. A few hours later, after Gayles calmed down, they both had a big laugh about it, and the next year Marques was back on the team.

He did no more fancy dribbling at Langston, however. Zip Gayles made it clear that he would not tolerate it. And Marques stuck to that deal when Langston defeated the Globe Trotters in Oklahoma

City. "I didn't want to take any chances," he says today, and the listener is uncertain whether he is referring to losing the game or setting off Zip Gayles again.

So, when Winfield Welch offered him a Globe Trotter contract in the locker room after the game, he had no idea of Marques's dribbling skills. All he knew was that this college kid had decimated the best pro team in the country. It would be another year before anyone in the Globe Trotter organization had a clue.

★

When Marques Haynes arrived in Chicago for the Globe Trotters' 1946 training camp, Inman Jackson took him downtown to meet his future boss. They got off the El and walked to the offices of A. M. Saperstein Enterprises, located in Suite 504 at 192 North Clark Street. This was the headquarters of perhaps the most successful sports entrepreneur in the country, who either owned or booked a half dozen basketball teams, a handful of Negro League baseball teams (including a Harlem Globe Trotters *baseball* team), prizefighters, even a lounge singer.*

What Marques saw when he walked in was shocking. The so-called Suite 504 consisted of two cubbyholes, which, taken together, would have made a good-sized bedroom. Abe was crammed into the tiny front room, perched behind a desk that was stacked high with publicity photos, road maps, and press releases. Adjoining his "executive office" was an even smaller cubicle where two secretaries and a bookkeeper were sitting almost on top of each other, surrounded by file cabinets. Their desks were backed up to the windows, with barely enough room to walk, much less turn around, in the slot between the file cabinets and the desks. It looked like an office designed for Lilliputians—or by a five-foot, three-inch man who had lived his life on a miniature scale. The most successful sports promoter in the country was working out of a closet. But for Abe, who had slept on a couch in his parents' house or in the back of a Model T Ford for much of his life, it was all he needed.

---

* In January 1946, Abe had even attempted to launch his own baseball league, the West Coast Negro Baseball League, but it did not survive its first season.

A. M. Saperstein Enterprises compensated for its spartan accommodations with hard work and efficiency. Abe had a knack for hiring smart, talented people who were as committed to the organization as he was. And he never asked anyone to work harder than he did. After twenty years in the business, he was still as driven and energetic as ever. No one could keep up with him; that was a given.

Shortly after the war, he had hired a number of key people who would stay with him for decades. These included Marian Polito, his bookkeeper; Phil Brownstein, a longtime coach at Hyde Park High School who became his chief scout; and Wyonella Smith, a young African American secretary who was married to Wendell Smith.★ Abe's brothers Morry and Rocky also began working for him, with Morry helping out in the front office with scheduling and Rocky working as a business manager for one of the Trotter units.

But the most important new hire—indeed, the most significant hire of his entire business career—was Marie Linehan, who began working in December 1945 as Abe's executive secretary. She would spend the next forty-four years with the Globe Trotters—more years than even Abe himself—and would ultimately have a greater influence on the organization than any other person, including Abe.

Marie Linehan (née Grass) was born in Chicago in 1910, the only child of an Irish mother and German American father, and was raised in a strong Irish-Catholic clan. Her mother died when she was a teenager, and she and her father barely scraped by, living with relatives. Marie was extremely bright but had to quit high school to work and help support the family. When she was in her early twenties, she began having lung problems and was sent to a tuberculosis sanatorium. There, she fell in love with another patient, Bart Edward Linehan. After they were released from the sanatorium, they got married, despite her father's opposition. In 1936, Marie gave birth to a baby boy, Tom, but within a year her happy life was shattered when her husband had a relapse of TB and was forced to return to the sanatorium. He never recovered, and died in the sanatorium when

---

★ *Wendell Smith, the longtime sports editor of the* Pittsburgh Courier, *and the most influential black sportswriter in the country, had moved to Chicago to become a columnist for the* Herald-American.

Marie's baby was barely a year old. She was on her own, a grieving young widow with an infant son, lacking even a high school degree. What she did have, however, was a supportive network of Irish cousins, her sustaining Catholic faith, and a fierce determination to make something of herself.

In 1941, she took a job as a clerk at Kelwyn Park High School and worked there for the next three years. Phil Brownstein, a mutual acquaintance, told Abe about her. "I think she could really help you out in the office," Brownstein suggested.

Lord knows, Abe needed it. He may have been a marketing genius and world-class promoter, but he was still running the organization out of his hat and desperately needed someone to organize the front office. Marie began working for him on weekends, but he soon offered her a full-time job. Like Marques Haynes, she was skeptical about the security of a traveling basketball team, and only agreed to take a one-year leave of absence from her school job. After that first year, she was hooked. She would be working for the Globe Trotters, in one capacity or another, almost until the day she died.

Marie's effect on the Globe Trotter front office was immediate and profound. She had a computer-like mind for details, a photographic memory, and enough organizational skills to have planned the Normandy invasion. She established a filing system, in which onionskin copies of Abe's massive correspondence were neatly preserved; she emptied his coat pockets—figuratively, and perhaps literally—converting the scraps of paper with names and phone numbers into an alphabetized contact list.

Abe and Marie were a perfect fit. He was the idea man with the grand vision and charismatic personality to put those ideas into action, while she was the nuts-and-bolts administrator who handled the logistics, made sure the paychecks were cut, the press releases were mailed, and the train tickets were waiting at the station. Marie's thoroughness and dependability freed up Abe to do what he did best—working the hustings, pressing the flesh with sportswriters and promoters, and expanding the tour ever farther, to Mexico, Alaska, and Hawaii—knowing that Marie could run the office in his absence. They talked daily on the phone when he was gone, she wrote many of his letters, perfectly capturing his style and language, and they combined their talents to turn the Globe Trotter organization into a model of industrial efficiency. The front office may have been working out of a hovel, but Abe and Marie created a professional spirit and élan among the staff.

Abe had finally found someone who worked as hard as he did. Marie had no real social life outside of the office. She was an intelligent, attractive woman, yet she never dated after her husband's death, which led to rumors among some of the players that she was a lesbian, and suspicions among others (and even among Abe's family, allegedly) that she and Abe were having an affair. The truth was, she admired Abe, even revered him, and they had tremendous mutual respect for each other, but there is no indication they ever had a romantic relationship. Marie's life was as triangulated as the Holy Trinity: she went to work, she went home to her son, and she went to Mass. Her social network consisted of her close-knit Irish cousins, with whom she played cards and visited on holidays. In her spare time, she worked at making herself into a refined, educated woman. She loved classical music and jazz, kept meticulous lists of new vocabulary words, bought season tickets to the Chicago Symphony, visited van Gogh and Rembrandt exhibits, attended performances of *South Pacific* and other favorite Broadway shows, and taught her son to appreciate the finer aspects of culture and learning. When she got home late from the office, as she often did, she would relax with a Scotch on ice, put on a favorite Virgil Fox or Erroll Garner album, and curl up with a Raymond Chandler or P. D. James novel. Mostly, however, the Globe Trotters were her life.

Marie Linehan had arrived just in time. The organization was growing so fast that Abe had to have a right-hand person to keep it moving. In the 1946–47 season, in addition to the main unit of the Trotters, Abe was fielding the Kansas City Stars, who often played doubleheaders on the same card as the Trotters, but on other nights would don Trotter uniforms and play *as* the Trotters, usually in smaller towns. (This team was sometimes listed as Satchel Paige's All-Stars, if Paige was traveling with them, or as Jesse Owens's Kansas City Stars.) Abe was also keeping three opposition teams in business: the House of David (led by Bob Karstens), the San Francisco All-Nations (made up mainly of Bay Area players), and the All-Hawaii Stars.

This was also the season that Abe initiated a ritual that would become a Globe Trotter tradition: a vaudeville-like halftime show, with Ping-Pong champions, hula dancers, unicyclists, jugglers, and entertainers of every ilk. He had been booking halftime entertainment since the early 1930s, such as Bunny Leavitt shooting free throws, but now the halftime show took on a life of its own. "I remain convinced that what saved Abe more than anything was his addition of the halftime vaudeville shows," says J Michael Kenyon. "On the 1946 Hawaii tour, when he saw the Hawaiian dancing girls and the 'little grass shack' routines, it wasn't long before he was signing up his own halftime entertainers."

When basketball season ended, Abe's baseball promotions were just gearing up; and by the time baseball ended, the Trotters were reporting to training camp. A. M. Saperstein Enterprises had become a year-round operation.

In October 1946, Marques Haynes was one of approximately two dozen ballplayers who reported to the Globe Trotters' training camp at St. Anselm's gym on the South Side. Among them was Boid Buie, an amazing one-armed player who had lost his left arm in an auto accident, yet somehow compensated well enough to have been a star at Tennessee State; and Ermer Robinson, a smooth, skinny-legged army vet from San Diego with a deadly one-hand push shot. Inman Jackson and Babe Pressley, the Trotters' captain, ran the training camp and did most of the coaching; by this time, Abe was only peripherally involved on the court.

Marques, Buie, and Robinson were among the few rookies to make the final cut. Abe told Marques that he would eventually bring him up to the Trotters' main unit—with Goose Tatum, Ted Strong, Babe Pressley, Duke Cumberland, and Ducky Moore—but wanted him to start off with the Kansas City Stars, who needed a dribbler. Ironically, no one in the Globe Trotter organization had yet seen what kind of dribbler Marques was.

Marques was thrilled to be joining the Stars, because they were scheduled to tour Mexico right after training camp. For the second year in a row, Jesse Owens had been employed by Abe as the traveling secretary of the Stars. He handled the gate receipts, served as a backup announcer, and was the emcee for the halftime show, but his primary value was his name. The four-time Olympic gold medalist was still one of the most popular athletes in the world, although it had been a decade since his triumphs at the 1936 Munich Olympics.

At halftime of the Stars' games, Owens would often give exhibitions of sprinting, hurdling, and broad jumping, then make a brief talk about "problems facing the country today." Abe's relationship with Owens, like most racial questions involving Abe, was a complicated matter. On one hand, Owens needed money and Abe provided an opportunity for him to make an honest living off his fame; on the other hand, Abe was criticized by some, particularly in the black press, for demeaning Owens by staging spectacles in which he raced against a horse and, once, against heavyweight champion Joe Louis (Louis ran backward and Owens on his hands and knees).

Marques Haynes, who drew the honor of rooming with Owens on the road, leans toward the latter view. "Jesse was one of the classiest people I ever knew," he says. "He was very intelligent, very personable, and a good speaker. . . . [But] I thought it would have been better if Jesse just made his speech about his experience at the Olympics and how he won those medals. I really didn't think it was necessary for him to be out there running—because that was about ten years after Munich."

When the Kansas City Stars got to Mexico, it didn't take Marques Haynes very long to show what kind of exceptional player he was. The Stars carried only six players on the trip, including Marques, Vertes Zeigler, Sam Wheeler, John Scott, Greene Farmer, and Bob Karstens, the white "trickster" who had returned from the House of David. When they got to Mexico City, they discovered that their opponents, the Chihuahua State Teachers College, had pulled in the best players from the region, from Chihuahua to Guadalajara, and had nearly twenty players dressed out. Once the game began, the Chihuahua coach started substituting five new players at a time, always keeping fresh legs in the game. Adding to the Stars' woes, Mexico City sits at seventy-four hundred feet, and the high altitude was taking a toll on their stamina. "In that rarefied air, we couldn't breathe," Vertes Zeigler recalls. At the start of the fourth quarter, they were clinging to a one-point lead but were completely exhausted. Even worse, two of their six players had fouled out, leaving only four players on the floor. It was only a matter of time before the fresh Chihuahua players overwhelmed them.

That's when Marques took over.

"Some of us wanted to take a time-out," Zeigler recalls, "but Marques said, 'Give me the ball; y'all take a rest.' "

Then, while the players and fans watched in amazement, Marques went into his dribbling routine. The Chihuahua players gave chase, but no one could catch him. He dribbled half-circles around the key, slid down on one knee, actually sat on the floor—and the ball never stopped. He bounced it so low (only two or three inches off the floor) and so fast that the ball sounded like a machine gun. And whether he was running, standing still, kneeling, or lying flat, no one could take the ball. It wasn't just how fast he was dribbling that made it so remarkable, it was how fast he was *moving*. He would start and stop, change directions, fake one way and go the other, as if his knee joints were made of rubber, instead of tendon and cartilage. When he had pulled this routine on Southern University, he had done it only for the last three minutes of the game, but now he just kept dribbling—five, six, seven minutes. He was still going.

"The rest of us was just laying on the floor, pretending we were shooting dice," says Zeigler. "And the Chihuahua players was all trying to catch Marques, but they couldn't. So then we got up and started acting like *we* were gonna chase him, diving at the ball . . . all nine of us now. But you couldn't stop Marques from dribbling that ball."

The Chihuahua players couldn't call time-out without possession of the ball, so the clock kept ticking. Unbelievably, Marques dribbled out the entire fourth quarter. Then, as he had done against Southern, he raced in for a layup just as time expired, giving the Stars a 3-point victory.

It was such an astonishing exhibition that the players who witnessed it would still be marveling at it over half a century later. It is a safe assumption that no other player in the history of basketball has ever done it, before or since. "That was the first and last time I ever did that," Marques recalls, laughing. "The whole damn quarter; I wouldn't advise it."

From Mexico City, the word was sent back to Abe that this Haynes kid was something special. By January 1947, Marques had incorporated his dribbling into the Stars' regular routine, and when the Stars played on a doubleheader bill with the Trotters in San Francisco, it was Marques who was singled out by the *Herald-Examiner:* "Marques Haynes, K.C. guard, staged a side-splitting show of his own in the final minute of the first game, dribbling up and down the court, through the opposition's defense and out again, as the Hawaiians tried desperately to break up the play."

Abe realized what a gold mine he had and brought Marques up to the big team for the end of the California tour, which put Goose Tatum and Marques Haynes in the same lineup for the first time. By mid-February, this new tandem was ready to be showcased. The Globetrotters, Kansas City Stars, House of David, and Hawaiians had been playing doubleheaders in California; then they slowly worked their way to El Paso, Texas. As elsewhere in the South, El Paso's Jim Crow covenants prohibited black and white teams from playing each other, so the Trotters and K.C. Stars hooked up in the first game of a doubleheader. Goose poured in 28 points, and Marques bewildered his former teammates, who now had to chase him instead of admiring his handiwork. "Number one dribbler Marques Haynes, who moves the ball from every angle, had the Stars trying madly to corner him to regain possession," the El Paso paper reported.

Goose was already being billed as the "Nation's Best Known Basketball Player," and Marques had a dribbling act like none in the Trotters' twenty-year history. Abe now had two extraordinarily gifted stars who would go on to become the most celebrated ballplayers in the world.

In late February, Abe had arranged for the Trotters, Stars, and House of David to go to Havana, Cuba, for the first Cuban Invitational Tournament. Following a game in Cincinnati, the three teams boarded a private Pullman car that Abe had rented, which would carry them to Miami, where they were to catch their flight to Havana. The Trotters had been the toast of every city they had played on their triumphant West Coast swing, including Los Angeles, San Francisco, and Seattle; and in Cincinnati they had played before the largest crowd in the city's history.

But once their private Pullman crossed the Mason–Dixon line, there were jarring reminders that they were now just another bunch of uppity niggers. When the train left the Cincinnati station, their Pullman porter warned them, "Once we cross that Dixon line, y'all got to keep these window shades down. If them peckerwoods see you riding in this car [with the House of David players] they're liable to shoot." The white players on the House of David were allowed to eat in the dining car, but the Trotters and Stars had to stay put and wait for the porters to bring food back to them. But several of the Trotters from northern cities decided to test the limits of southern hospitality. When the train stopped in Corbin, Kentucky, in the foothills of the Appalachians, Sam Wheeler and Vertes Zeigler noticed an ice-cream parlor about fifty yards from the train station. They walked over to check it out. When they walked in, some local teenagers who were playing the jukebox looked up and gave them a hard stare. Wheeler approached the waitress behind the counter.

"I'd like an ice-cream cone, please," he said. The young woman was so stunned she didn't respond. "I'd like one, too," Zeigler added.

Finally, the waitress found her voice. "What flavor you want?"

"Well, I want a strawberry and a vanilla—a double dip," Wheeler replied politely.

The waitress said, "Sorry, but I can't give you strawberry and vanilla."

"Well, what flavors you got?" Zeigler asked.

"Ain't got nothing but chocolate for y'all," the waitress said, with a smirk.

Zeigler, who had a quick temper, told her where she could stick that chocolate, then turned and bolted out the door, with Wheeler right behind him. The local boys took off after them, hollering threats and racing them to the train. The Trotters' Pullman porter was standing on the platform, but when he heard the commotion he snatched up his little stepstool, threw it on the train, and jumped aboard himself. Wheeler and Zeigler had to leap onto the train.

"Those peckerwoods were dead behind us," Zeigler recalls, laughing. "Man, we jumped in that car and slammed that door. They was throwing bricks and rocks as we pulled away."

The train pulled out of the station before the situation worsened, but traveling secretary Winfield Welch was furious with the two players. "You damn fools, you wanna get everybody killed!?" he yelled. "We got these House of Davids in this car—what you think they'd do if they found out?"

"You tell Abe that's his fault," Zeigler said defiantly. "I ain't gonna be living like that."

When they arrived in Havana, the Trotters rolled undefeated through the Cuban Invitational Tournament, then followed that up with their second successful tour of Hawaii. Their fame was spreading beyond the boundaries of the continental United States, and they were at last living up to their name.

★

By the 1947–48 season, all of the elements were in place for the Harlem Globetrotters to explode into a national phenomenon. After World War II ended, there had been fears that the economy might slip back into a depression, but the conversion to a peacetime economy had jump-started the greatest economic boom in the nation's history. For the first time in twenty years, the American public had money to spend on sports and entertainment—the two realms that the Globetrotters straddled better than anyone. They were packing in the crowds wherever they went: 20,000-plus fans showed up at Chicago Stadium to see a *regular season* game, not some special exhibition against the College All-Stars. They were now playing the biggest cities in the United States, they were immensely popular in Canada, and they had made successful tours of Mexico, Cuba, and Hawaii.

Internally, Abe Saperstein now had a front office staff, headed by Marie Linehan, which could handle the demands of a worldwide sports enterprise. In terms of publicity, the Trotters had hit the biggest jackpot of all in December 1946, when *Life* magazine, the most popular periodical in the country, ran a feature story on the team. If there had been any remaining doubts that the Trotters had hit the big time, the *Life* story now made it official.

One indication of the Globetrotters' maturation was that they published their first "yearbook" (in effect, an elaborate game program), with photos and bios of Abe and the players. The yearbook contained the reprinted columns of a dozen sportswriters from across the country, each one praising the Trotters to the heavens.

Finally, Abe had the most talented African American players in the country. His yearly refrain that the Trotters were fielding the "best aggregation in team history" had finally come true. There was a cadre of battle-tested veterans, led by player-coach Babe Pressley, Ted Strong, Ermer Robinson, Ducky Moore, Vertes Zeigler, and Sam Wheeler, which was bolstered by an infusion of new talent: Lawrence and Lance Cudjoe (Marques Haynes's former teammates at Langston); Frank Washington, a lanky forward from Philadelphia who had played with the Washington Bears and Detroit Gems; and Wilbert King and Boudreau King, two more Detroiters from the Brewster Center pipeline.

And then there were Marques Haynes and Goose Tatum. Goose was already famous nationwide, and had created his own persona as the "Clown Prince of Basketball," melding the Globetrotters' old standards with his own creativity to invent a new genre of comedy basketball. Goose was naturally funny, but he worked hard to perfect his craft. He studied the great comedians and clowns, like Charlie Chaplin and Emmett Kelly, learning new techniques. Like them, he could make people laugh *and* cry, although in Goose's case they were usually laughing *until* they cried.

He had a standard repertoire of gags for every game, but he was brilliant at tailoring those gags—or "reams," the players called them—to a particular audience, improvising new twists and subtle nuances on the fly. He was like a great jazz soloist, such as Charlie Parker or Dizzy Gillespie, who at that very time were shaping their own new art form—bebop—from the musical streams of swing, blues, and big band.

To catalog all of the funny things that Goose did on the court would be impossible, because he did new things nearly every night. When the Trotters played in Hawaii, he donned a grass skirt and did his own crazy hula in the pivot. "People were laughing so hard they were crying," Marques Haynes recalls. He would snatch a camera away from a fan and take a picture of himself, voguing wildly for the camera. Or he would steal a woman's purse and rifle through it, loudly announcing its contents to the crowd.

At halftime of a game in Wichita, Kansas, as the Trotters and their opponents started making their way to the dressing rooms, Goose lingered behind. "What the fuck is he doing now?" one of his teammates asked. The players stopped to watch as Goose went up in the stands and found a young boy, then brought him out to center court. "Oh, shit, he's gonna get us lynched," the player muttered. By now, the entire crowd was watching. People on their way to the concession stand had stopped and were asking the same thing as his teammates, "What the hell is he doing?" He took the little boy down to one basket and showed him how to shoot a hook, but no matter how hard he tried, the boy couldn't make it. So finally Goose picked him up, put him on his shoulder, and the boy dropped the ball in the hoop. The crowd cheered wildly. But Goose wasn't finished. He led the boy over to the Globetrotters' bench and sat him down, then grabbed one of the Trotters, took *him* up in the stands and sat him down beside the boy's parents. The crowd was in hysterics.

One of his classics was a pantomime fishing skit in which Goose would amble out with a cane pole and a straw hat. He'd carefully step into his imaginary boat, row out to center court, toss out his line, and wait for a bite. When he hooked a big one, he'd start reeling it in but end up capsizing the boat and floundering around like a drowning man. Some of the other Trotters would "swim out" to rescue him, drag him to shore, pump his chest to expel the water, and end up reviving him by taking off his sneaker and putting it under his nose. Goose would leap straight up, a saved man! It was Charlie Chaplin, Buster Keaton, and Marcel Marceau on a basketball court.

Many of the reams that Goose created would be imitated by Globetrotter showmen for decades to come. He designed a "stringball," for instance, which had a long rubber band attached to it and would spring back to him when he shot a foul. Or he'd hide behind the Trotters' basket while the opposition team had the ball, then catch a full-court pass and, instead of dropping in an easy layup, kneel down and calmly tie his shoes. As the opposition players came thundering downcourt toward him, he would calmly stand up, put on a couple of extraordinary fakes, and toss in his soft hook. During a time-out, he would sneak up behind the opposing team's huddle, pretend to be eavesdropping on their strategy, then tiptoe back to the Trotters' bench and whisper the "big secret" to his teammates. Sometimes, he would go sit in the stands, or in a woman's lap, while the action was going on at the other end of the court, then swipe a floppy hat off some guy and race out on the court, waving and hollering for the ball.

With all of this talent at his disposal, Abe had completely overshadowed his competition. The New York Rens were still around, but Bob Douglas could no longer seriously compete with Abe for the best African American players, and could not even come close in ticket sales. The white pro leagues were no competition either. The more-established National Basketball League (NBL), which had been around since 1937, was limited to small and medium-sized cities, such as Sheboygan, Oshkosh, Rochester, and Youngstown. And the fledgling Basketball Association of America (BAA), formed in November 1946, had seen four of its original eleven teams go bankrupt the first season, and the surviving clubs were hemorrhaging red ink. The BAA was staying afloat partly because Abe had agreed to play doubleheaders in BAA cities, in the hope that the crowds that turned out to see the Trotters would hang around to see the white pros.

In the seven years since their world championship of 1940, the Harlem Globetrotters had achieved far more than Abe could have envisioned a decade earlier, but he was already dreaming of even greater challenges and mightier rivals to vanquish.

CHAPTER 10

The Lakers

In 1948, George Mikan, the six-foot-ten center of the Minneapolis Lakers, was dominating the sport like no other big man ever had. When Mikan had first arrived at DePaul University in 1942, he was a clumsy, slow-footed freshman who was so blind (with 20/300 vision) that, even wearing Mr. Magoo glasses, he had to ask teammates to read the game clock. But first-year DePaul coach Ray Meyer recognized the youngster's fierce competitiveness and put him through a rigorous, unorthodox training program: he made him shoot thousands of hook shots with either hand, hired a female dance instructor to improve his footwork, and engaged a boxing coach to help him develop better hand-eye coordination. Once Mikan mastered the hook shot, he was unstoppable. The foul lane was only six feet wide at the time, so he could camp out within easy range for his hook. During his college career, he led DePaul to an 81–17 record, was a three-time All-American, twice led the nation in scoring, and was selected as the National Player of the Year in 1946. His senior year, he carried DePaul to the NIT championship, averaging 40 points a game in the tournament, including a record 53 points in the semifinal game, in which he outscored the entire Rhode Island team. He was the charter member of an exclusive club (which later included Elgin Baylor, Wilt Chamberlain, and Julius Erving) of ballplayers who single-handedly changed the sport. Mikan blocked so many shots that the NCAA instituted its first goaltending rule, and in 1951, the NBA widened its foul lane to twelve feet to neutralize his hook.

After graduating from DePaul, he played one year with the Chicago American Gears, then signed with the Minneapolis Lakers of the National Basketball League (NBL) in November 1947. The Lakers had recently signed another college All-American (and future NBA Hall of Famer), Jim Pollard, a six-foot-five slasher from Stanford University who, on any other team, would have been the franchise. Pollard was a more complete player than Mikan, as he could score inside or outside, had great improvisational skills, and was one of the first pros to play "above the rim," as reflected in his nickname, the "Kangaroo Kid" (he once injured his elbow by hitting it on the backboard). Over the next seven years, Mikan and Pollard would carry the Lakers to six league titles (one in the NBL, one in the BAA, and four in the newly merged National Basketball Association) and establish the NBA's first dynasty. In 1950, Mikan would be voted the Greatest Player in the First Half Century by the Associated Press.

In early 1948, however, all of that glory was in front of them. The Laker team was less than a year old and was looking to establish its credibility in the pro ranks. When Arch Ward, venerable sports editor of the *Chicago Tribune,* wrote that the Harlem Globetrotters were the best basketball team in the world, Max Winter, the general manager of the Lakers, took it as a personal affront. He called up Abe, who was a friend, and challenged him to a game.

Abe quickly agreed. He and Winter both recognized that a Lakers-Trotters matchup would be a sure moneymaker. Whatever symbolic questions of racial superiority might be settled, the game was certain to reap huge profits. They scheduled a one-game showdown at Chicago Stadium for February 19, 1948. As Winter would recall years later, "Little did Abe, or I, or anyone else connected with it, realize that it would turn out to be one of the most memorable basketball games of all time."

On the surface, it should have been just another big game. After all, the Globetrotters had been playing white pro teams for years, including other members of the National Basketball League. They had waged fierce battles with the Oshkosh All-Stars and other NBL teams in the World Pro Tournament in Chicago, had held preseason training camps with the Sheboygan Redskins, and had taken on the best white team in the East, the Philadelphia Sphas. Further, the NBL had already integrated in 1942–43, when the Chicago Studebakers played that season with current and former Globetrotters Sonny Boswell, Duke Cumberland, Hilary Brown, Bernie Price, and Roosevelt Hudson. In the 1946–47 season, four additional black players had played in the league, including Pop Gates and Willie King, who also played for the Globetrotters. And the New York Rens would actually join the league during the 1948–49 season, playing under the name of the Dayton Rens, thereby becoming the first black team in a white pro league.

What made this game special was George Mikan. He was the first dominating big man of the modern era in basketball—a center who could take over a game, scoring at will and controlling the defensive end of the court. And the fact that he was a local boy, raised in nearby Joliet and graduated from DePaul, made a Lakers-Trotters showdown in Chicago even more sensational.

Although the racial dimension of the game was never explicitly mentioned in the white press, it was an all too obvious subtext: the best white team in the country versus the best black team. The fact that Jackie Robinson had just completed his first season with the Brooklyn Dodgers in October added extra traction to the racial issue. Labeling George Mikan a "Great White Hope" would depreciate his impact on the game, as he was reshaping modern basketball on the basis of his size and skills, not his color, but he undoubtedly carried the weight of white assumptions of superiority on his shoulders. Indeed, the game was being characterized in the press as a "private duel" between Mikan and Goose Tatum, each of whom was revolutionizing the game in his own unique way. Simply put, there was no one else like Goose *or* Mikan—and now they would be going head to head. The *Chicago Sun-Times* predicted it would be the "toughest test of Mikan's brilliant career."

More broadly, the game would represent a showdown between two contrasting styles of play—the white style, of which the Lakers were the ultimate prototype, and the black style of hoops played by the Trotters. Conventional wisdom among white sportswriters was that the machinelike efficiency of the Lakers' half-court offense and their structured man-to-man defense would triumph over the "undisciplined" school-yard style of the Trotters.

As game day approached, the bookies made the Lakers an 8-point favorite. The pregame hype for the contest was building not just in Chicago but in Minneapolis, where the *Minneapolis Morning Tribune* called it pro basketball's "dream" and the "Game of the Year."

Oddly enough, the players on both teams might have been paying less attention to the hype than anyone else, as they were playing a full schedule leading up to the game. The Globetrotters arrived in Chicago only the night before the game, after a three-week tour of California. They came to town riding a 103-game winning streak. The Lakers arrived with an 8-game winning streak but, more impressive, a 9½-game lead in the NBL's Western Division over the Tri-City Blackhawks, whom they had defeated two nights before the game against the Trotters.

George Mikan was eager to establish bragging rights in his hometown, and Marques Haynes was anxious to disprove the perception of the Lakers' superiority, but not all the players on either team were looking forward to the game. Ermer Robinson, the Trotters' sharpshooter from San Diego, couldn't understand why Abe had scheduled a game against such a formidable opponent; and some of the Lakers felt they had nothing to gain and everything to lose by playing the Trotters. Years later, Jim Pollard would complain that the game was "for the owners, not the players. I didn't take it seriously . . . it was a pain in the neck." And the Lakers' coach, Johnny Kundla, who had played against the Trotters in the early 1930s, didn't consider the Trotters a serious threat, but merely a show team.

Few sportswriters gave the Trotters a chance, and even Abe was having doubts. In public, he maintained his usual breezy optimism, but he admitted to his family that he was worried about the Lakers' height advantage. The tallest Trotter was Goose Tatum, at six-foot-three-and-a-half, but Mikan was six-foot-ten, and Pollard was six-foot-five. In an effort to shore up his bench, Abe brought in the best players from the second unit, including center Sam Wheeler, Vertes Zeigler, and the diminutive shooter Wilbert King.

Even though the game was held on a bitterly cold Thursday night, 17,823 fans showed up at Chicago Stadium. The crowd included more whites than blacks, but not many. "The whole South Side of Chicago came out for that ball game," recalls Marques

Haynes. The Lakers and Trotters matchup was actually the first game of a doubleheader, with the BAA's Chicago Stags and New York Knicks playing the nightcap, but there was no doubt which game the fans had come to see. In addition to those watching in the stadium, thousands more were listening on radio, as the game was being broadcast back to Minneapolis.

In the Trotters' locker room before the game, Abe gave a brief pep talk, then turned the floor over to player-coach Babe Pressley, who laid out the game plan. The Globetrotters realized that there was no way Goose could handle Mikan one-on-one, as he was giving up seven inches and fifty pounds, so other players were going to have to sag on the Lakers' center, double-teaming him whenever he got the ball. Additionally, Pressley told them not to hesitate to foul Mikan hard and often. There was no "one-and-one" rule at that time, so a nonshooting foul drew only one shot.

The game plan, which had sounded plausible in the dressing room, fell apart completely when the game began. Mikan was stronger and quicker than the Trotters had expected, and he was simply overwhelming Goose, who had never been noted for his defensive prowess, even with an opponent his own size. The Lakers jumped out to a 9–2 lead, and were threatening to run away with the game. Pressley, known as the "Blue Ox" because of his great strength ("He'd make Muhammad Ali look like a little boy," teammate Sam Wheeler would say years later), was the Trotters' best defender, so he began switching off his man to help Goose, trying to deny Mikan the ball. But then Pollard started hitting from the baseline, and the Trotters fell further behind.

At halftime, the Lakers held a 32–23 lead, and it would have been worse if Marques Haynes and Ermer Robinson had not been scoring from outside. Mikan had put on an awesome display, racking up 18 points and completely embarrassing Goose, who had yet to score.

In the locker room at halftime, the Globetrotters realized that their game plan had failed miserably and they would have to come up with a new strategy, or they were doomed. One problem in the first half was that Abe had insisted that they run their trademark Globetrotters offense, with three players running a weave out front and working the ball into Goose. But Mikan was smothering Goose in the pivot, and even when Goose managed to get off a shot, he was ice cold. Babe Pressley and Marques Haynes spoke up, insisting that the Trotters abandon their standard offense and start pushing the ball, to take advantage of their speed, and shooting from outside, instead of trying to work inside against the taller Lakers. "We had a lot of good outside shooters," Marques recalls, "particularly Ermer Robinson, Wilbert King, and myself."

They made one other halftime adjustment. For the rest of the game, they were going to hammer George Mikan every time he touched the ball. It was a risky tactic, as Mikan was a 78 percent lifetime free-throw shooter, but the Trotters gambled that he couldn't hurt them any more at the foul line than he was from the field.

Both strategies worked. The Trotters started fast-breaking every time they got the chance, and when fast-break opportunities weren't there, Wilbert King, Ermer Robinson, and Marques Haynes started connecting from the outside. The Globetrotters began the third quarter with a 10–2 run, cutting the Lakers' lead to 34–32.

On defense, the hack attack against Mikan was taking its toll. "We were doing *everything*," Sam Wheeler recalled in a 1987 interview. "If we'd had hatchets in our hands, he would have had scars on him—they would have taken 100 stitches." Once, Mikan got so frustrated with Goose's pushing and shoving that he lost his temper. His old college coach, Ray Meyer, could see the explosion coming. "I was sitting at the scorer's table and Goose was really roughing up Mikan," he remembers. "I saw Mikan's face get real white and I thought, 'Omigod, here it comes,' and Mikan leveled Tatum with a vicious elbow."

The flagrant foul earned Mikan a technical, and the Trotters, sensing that they were getting to him, kept up the pressure. "When we fouled him, we fouled him *hard*," recalls Vertes Zeigler, who played a reserve role. "We said, 'If they're gonna call a foul, be sure to make him bleed.' And that's what we did. We went to beating on him and slapping them glasses off him." Ultimately, the Trotters rattled Mikan, and the usually reliable free throw shooter missed seven of eleven attempts from the line.

At the same time, Goose finally started having success against Mikan on offense, hitting for 9 points in the second half and helping the Trotters take their first lead, 38–36. But their strategy of fouling Mikan was starting to cost them dearly, as Goose, Babe Pressley, and Ducky Moore were all in foul trouble.

Shortly before the end of the quarter, there was a frightening moment in the game. Mikan and Marques Haynes went up together for a rebound, and as they wrestled for the ball in midair, Marques's hands slipped off and he fell hard to the floor, landing flat on his back. He was able to continue playing, but a few minutes later the exact same thing happened again. This time, Marques hit the floor with a sickening thud, and Mikan landed on top of him. The two men lay sprawled in a heap on the floor. As Marques lay motionless on his back, not moving, the crowd fell silent, fearing a serious injury. Eventually, Marques was able to struggle to his feet and, despite being in obvious pain, refused to come out of the game.

The fourth quarter was a seesaw affair, with the lead repeatedly changing hands. The fans were on their feet for nearly the entire period, too excited to sit down. Marie Linehan, who was sitting at courtside, would say later, "I couldn't talk for a week, I screamed so hard."

With seven minutes to go, the Trotters led 50–48, but then Babe Pressley fouled out and was replaced by the old veteran Ted Strong, who was past his prime and too slow to contain Mikan. The Lakers surged back into the lead, 56–55, when Mikan hit another field goal, his twenty-third point of the night. Then, Wilbert King and Marques Haynes made consecutive baskets to send the Trotters back on top, 59–56. All night long, the outside shooting of Marques and Ermer Robinson, with 15 points apiece, and King, with 12, had kept the Trotters in the game.

There were two minutes left. Now, with the game on the line, the Lakers' two stars responded. Pollard hit a bucket to make it a one-point game, 59–58. The next time down the court, Mikan went up for one of his patented hook shots and Goose hacked him; the shot was good, which would have given the Lakers the lead, but referee Bill Downes ruled that Goose had fouled Mikan *before* the shot. Fortunately, the big man's woes continued at the foul line, as he missed the free throw, and the Trotters' fragile one-point lead still stood.

That was Goose's fifth foul, however, so he and Pressley were both out of the game, and now it was up to Sam Wheeler and Ted Strong to defend Mikan. Realizing they had a mismatch, the Lakers went right back to Mikan the next time they had the ball, and Wheeler had no choice but to foul him. This time, Mikan hit the free throw to tie the game.

Now there was a minute left. There was complete bedlam in the stadium, as fans for both teams were standing and screaming. The Trotters brought the ball up the court. Some of their fans began yelling "Freeze the ball!"—preferring to run out the clock and go to overtime rather than possibly missing a shot and giving the Lakers another chance to win. But with Goose and Babe Pressley already on the bench, the Trotters did not want to risk an overtime. They were going to play to win.

The clock ticked down to thirty seconds, then twenty-five, twenty, fifteen . . .

In wartime, they say the first casualty in any battle is the truth, as the fog of war obscures what really happened. Today, fifty-seven years after this momentous battle in Chicago Stadium, there are at least three contradictory accounts of what transpired in the last few seconds. Not surprisingly, as the game has grown in significance over the years, some of the participants have placed themselves at the center of the action, and others now remember it differently than they once did.

In a 1987 interview, for instance, Sam Wheeler, who is now deceased, claimed that he had rebounded a missed shot, then passed the ball to Ermer Robinson, who "took two little pumps and let it go." Vertes Zeigler, who also played in the game, claims today that *he* snared the final rebound and passed the ball the Robinson, who "wound up and turned it loose." Big George Mikan has given two different accounts of the final play in two separate autobiographies. Even Marques Haynes, whose memory has proven remarkably accurate in many instances, has recounted slightly different versions of the last seconds. Today, his best recollection is that the final play began with him inbounding the ball on an out-of-bounds play under the Trotters' basket. "I passed it in to Wilbert King, and he passed it back to me," he says, "I dribbled around [the key], and Robbie [Ermer Robinson] and I made eye contact. I was going toward him and he was coming toward me, and I passed it to him, then set a fake screen on [Jim Pollard], who was defending him. And Robbie, as soon as he got the ball—Wham!—he let it go."

The only point that all accounts agree on is that the ball ended up in the hands of Ermer Robinson, the slender forward who was known as "Shaky" because of his nervous chain-smoking habit and morbid fear of airplanes. Robinson was a finesse player who disliked rough play under the boards, preferring to launch rainbow shots from outside. He had the purest outside shot of any Globetrotter since another skinny-legged shooter named Sonny Boswell, whom he slightly resembled.

Accounts differ about how far out Robinson was, but he was at least twenty feet, and perhaps as far as the NBA three-point line. He barely had time to set his feet and then let fly with a one-hand push shot—a transition between the traditional two-hand set and the new jump shot that was beginning to come into vogue. Abe Saperstein had never liked Robinson's one-hander, as Abe was a traditionalist who wanted his players to shoot the two-hand set he had grown up with. But now, in the last second of the most important game in the Trotters' history, it all came down to Robbie's one-hand push.

Robinson shot the ball on an incredibly high arc; it was a rain-maker that was still in the air when the final gun sounded. As the reverberation echoed through the stadium, there was a sense that time was standing still, as if the moment had been frozen by a photo strobe. Seventeen thousand people watched, their mouths agape, as the ball slowly descended out of the spotlights, spinning on its axis, and slipped silently through the net.

Some Laker players and coaches thought the shot was no good, that Robinson had released it after the buzzer, but the referee raised his arms, signaling that it was good. The Trotters had won, 61–59.

For a brief moment, there was a hush in the arena, as if people could not really believe that the Globetrotters had won. Then, as the *Herald-American* described it, the place "went mildly insane." People hugged complete strangers. The Trotters lifted Robinson onto their shoulders, carrying him off the court in triumph. "No story book game could have had any better finish," the *Chicago Defender* reported.

Most basketball insiders were surprised by the outcome. "I was shocked, even though I knew the Trotters were a very good team," says Ray Meyer. "I think the Lakers took them as a joke. Then they found out that they could play, and they took them serious [from then on]." The Lakers were stunned. "Our players couldn't believe what had happened," Max Winter later recalled. "They were devastated."

In the Trotters' locker room, there was jubilation and profound relief. The players hoisted a beaming Abe into the air, and he showed his delight with the win by handing out cash bonuses.* George Mikan showed his class by stopping by to congratulate the victors. "One hell of a game guys," he said.

Most of the Trotters were going out to celebrate, but Marques Haynes was in such pain from his two horrendous falls that he went back to the Trotters' rooming house and went to bed. The next morning, he could barely move and decided to go to the hospital, where X-rays confirmed that he had fractured the fourth lumbar vertebra. Amazingly, he had played the second half with a broken back. The doctors put him in a full body cast and he walked out of the hospital, but he was through for the season. He went home to Sand Springs, Oklahoma, to recuperate.

That night, the celebration continued until the wee hours on the South Side. The Trotters were the guests of honor at a party in the Persian Hotel, where they ate lobster and listened to Lionel Hampton and his band. Timuel Black, a respected educator and author from Chicago, was at the game that night and recalls the reaction in Bronzeville. "It was an event of great pleasure for those of us who had grown up on the South Side . . . to see this all-black team playing this all-white team and winning," he says. "It was a great evening. We went back to our various bars or taverns and talked about it. It was more than just a victory of the Trotters; it was also a victory of the black community over the hostile white community. It was not as big, or as universal, as when Joe Louis defeated Max

---

* According to Vertes Zeigler, Abe gave most players $100, but gave $150 to Ermer Robinson and $200 to Goose. In 1987, Sam Wheeler claimed that each player got a $1,000 bill.

Schmeling, but there was a feeling of elation that gave us a sense of achievement and pride."

There had been other important games in the Globetrotters' history, including the 1940 world championship and the first College All-Star Classic, but this victory over the Minneapolis Lakers eclipsed them all. The Trotters' earlier triumphs had established them as a legitimate basketball team and had cracked open the doors to big arenas in big cities, but the 1948 victory over the Lakers pushed the Trotters onto the national stage and blew open the doors to the biggest arenas in the biggest cities in the land. From this point on, there would be no stopping them. The Harlem Globetrotters could legitimately claim to be the best team in the world.

Not surprisingly, some basketball experts believed that the Trotters' win over the Lakers was a fluke—due either to the Lakers taking the Trotters too lightly or to poor officiating, or both. Even forty years later, in a 1987 interview, Lakers' coach Johnny Kundla would still be complaining about the referees, who he claimed were Abe Saperstein's employees and had favored the Trotters. "We should have won if we got any breaks at all in the officiating," he said. "It really was unfair." Yet his complaints about favoritism seem unfounded, as the refs had called nineteen fouls against the Trotters, versus only fifteen against the Lakers.

Almost as soon as the game ended, the Lakers started clamoring for a rematch. "Our players wanted a rematch as soon as possible," said Max Winter. For their part, the Trotters were equally anxious to show the world that the win was legitimate. Very quickly, Abe and Winter agreed to a series of games (they would play a total of eight), both in Chicago and Minneapolis.

Still, the players and fans had to wait a year for the next game, which was scheduled for February 28, 1949, in Chicago Stadium. In the intervening year, the Trotters had improved themselves considerably, as Abe had signed Nathaniel "Sweetwater" Clifton, an agile six-foot-seven former Chicago high school phenom who was one of the most coveted players in the country.

The Savoy Big 5, the forerunners to the Harlem Globetrotters, in 1928. (Left to right) Assistant Coach Bobby Anderson, Randolph Ramsey, Inman Jackson, Bill Watson, Tommy Brookins, Joe Lillard, William Grant, Toots Wright, Lester Johnson, and coach Dick Hudson.

Earliest surviving photo of New York Harlem Globe Trotters, from the 1930–31 season. This squad played together for five seasons. (Left to right) *Abe Saperstein, Toots Wright, Runt Pullins* (seated), *Fat Long, Inman Jackson, and Kid Oliver.*

Harlem Globe Trotters in 1933. (Standing, left to right) *Inman Jackson, Rock Anderson, Toots Wright, George Easter, Runt Pullins, and Abe Saperstein.*

Inman Jackson, the first Globetrotter showman, circa 1935.

Runt Pullins, the star of the early Globe Trotters, who broke away from Abe Saperstein in 1934 and formed his own team.

"It was the night we came into our own," Abe Saperstein said of the November 1940 match-up between the world champion Harlem Globe Trotters and a team of College All-Stars, which set a world record for attendance with 22,000 people.

The Harlem Globetrotter
squad that won the World
Pro Championship in
1940. (Left to right)
Traveling secretary Chuck
Jones, Babe Pressley, Sonny
Boswell, Hillary Brown,
Inman Jackson, Ted Strong,
and Bernie Price.

Sonny Boswell, one of the greatest outside
shooters in Globetrotter history, who led them
to the World Championship in 1940.

Bob Karstens, the first full-time white ballplayer to play with the Trotters, who filled in during the 1942–43 season, when Goose Tatum was in the military. Karstens is credited with developing many of the ball-handling tricks that became part of the Magic Circle.

Legendary Globetrotter Goose Tatum, the most inspired and original showman who ever wore the uniform, shooting one of his deadly hook shots in early 1950s.

The fabulous Goose Tatum.

Harlem Globetrotters battle the Minneapolis Lakers in February 1949 at Chicago Stadium, in the Trotters' second (and last) victory over the Lakers. Globetrotter players are (left to right) Ermer Robinson, Babe Pressley, Sweetwater Clifton, Marques Haynes, and Goose Tatum. Laker great George Mikan is second from the left.

The great Ermer Robinson launches a two-hand push shot over the outstretched arms of George Mikan during one of the Globetrotters-Lakers games. Robinson hit the winning shot at the buzzer to beat the Lakers in February 1948.

Marques Haynes, the greatest dribbler in Globetrotter history, who inspired generations of ballplayers with his talents.

Marques Haynes performs his dribbling routine in Nancy, France, despite a pouring rain, during the Globetrotters' first European tour in 1950.

The Globetrotters set a world record for attendance when 75,000 people turned out in Berlin's Olympic Stadium in August 1951, to welcome Jesse Owens back to the scene of his four–Gold Medal triumph in the 1936 Olympics.

Abe Saperstein, circa 1958.

Marie Linehan and Abe Saperstein in the Harlem Globetrotters office in the mid-1950s.

Globetrotter showman Bob "Showboat" Hall (right) drives to the basket against College All-Star player Jerry Bird (left) in the 1956 World Series of Basketball.

Pope Pius XII grants the Harlem Globetrotters a private audience during their around-the-world tour in 1952.

Publicity posters for The Harlem Globetrotters (above), *released in 1951, and Go, Man, Go!, starring Dane Clark and Sidney Poitier, the second full-length Hollywood picture on the Globetrotters, which was released in 1954.*

Soviet premier Nikita Khrushchev (right) greets the Harlem Globetrotters in Moscow's Red Square in August 1959. Members of the Globetrotters' party include Abe Saperstein (to Khruschchev's left) and Tex Harrison (behind Abe).

Harlem Globetrotters perform in a bullring in Pamplona, Spain, in 1962.

The Harlem Globetrotters make one of their many appearances on The Ed Sullivan Show. *This show, in the mid-1960s, featured* (from left to right) *Leon Hillard, Meadowlark Lemon, Curly Neal, Showboat Hall, and Geese Ausbie.*

(Opposite) *Wilt Chamberlain, who performed one full season with the Globetrotters (in 1958–59) before going to the NBA, and returned for thirteen summers to play with the Trotters on their summer European tours.*

One of the last photos taken of Abe Saperstein, in summer of 1965, in Greece with (left to right) *Meadowlark Lemon, Geese Ausbie, and Curly Neal. Abe was in declining health, and would die less than a year later, in March 1966.*

Curly Neal (left) and Meadowlark Lemon (right), the two most famous Globetrotters in the 1960s and 1970s, perform the Trotters' classic baseball skit.

Lynette Woodard, the first female Harlem Globetrotter, who signed with the Trotters in 1985.

Globetrotter showman Geese Ausbie shoots a free throw with the "string ball," one of the Globetrotters' most famous gags, in the 1980s.

Globetrotter players Tex Harrison (left) and Mannie Jackson (right) in Belgium in the early 1960s. Harrison is now the Globetrotters' coach and Jackson owns the team.

Mannie Jackson, current owner of the Harlem Globetrotters, who became the first African American to own a major sports franchise when he purchased the team in 1993.

South African president Nelson Mandela (left) welcomes Harlem Globetrotter owner, Mannie Jackson, and Trotter players in June 1996. The Trotters would return to South Africa the next year to perform for Mandela's seventy-ninth birthday.

Curley "Boo" Johnson, veteran Globetrotter dribbling specialist, helps a young fan spin the ball on her finger in a 2002 game.

Michael "Wild Thing" Wilson soars for a sensational dunk. Wilson is in The Guinness Book of World Records *with a record twelve-foot dunk.*

In the meantime, the Lakers had gone on to win the 1947–48 NBL championship, then bolted to the upstart BAA in 1949. They were on their way to winning that league's championship as well (the two leagues would merge into the NBA by the 1949–50 season).

If the buildup to the first game was intense, the hype for the rematch was even more so. "The Trotters-Lakers game has again gripped the imagination of the entire sports world," the *Pittsburgh Courier* proclaimed. "With the Trotters again sweeping everything before them in their jaunts here, there, and everywhere; and the Lakers apparently headed for professional league domination once more, it seems certain that the contest will decide for the second year in succession which is the greatest basketball team in the world." Again, most sportswriters were picking the Lakers to win the rematch, even though their starting forwards, Jim Pollard and Don "Swede" Carlson, could not play because of sprained ankles.

Despite being played on a Monday night, the second game drew an even larger crowd than the first one, with 20,046 people filling Chicago Stadium to capacity. It was the second largest crowd in the stadium's history, topped only by the 20,583 who had seen the Trotters play the College All-Star Classic in 1940. In another sign of the game's importance, Movietone News was there with a film crew, documenting the game for its weekly newsreel. No matter which team won, millions of people in theaters around the country would be watching the highlights.

This time around, the Globetrotters had a completely different game plan, because of the addition of Sweetwater Clifton. They now had a man who could cover Mikan one-on-one, at least as much as anyone could handle him. Plus, they were much more familiar with Mikan, as he had played three games against them the previous year (when the Trotters made their third tour of Hawaii, Mikan had flown over and played for the Trotters' opposition team, the New York Celtics, leading them to two wins out of three games he played).

The game began with Mikan controlling the opening tip to Lakers' guard Jack Dwan, who pulled up and hit a long-range bomb to give the Lakers a 2–0 lead. Then, for the next few minutes, both teams were ice-cold, missing badly from outside. The Trotters were particularly inept, repeatedly clanging set shots off the rim.

Goose had started off trying to cover Mikan, but then the big man banked in a hook and got another easy basket off a tap-in, so Clifton switched with Goose. The Trotters still weren't hitting, however, and the Lakers led 8–1 after the first five minutes. The Globetrotters were even cold at the free throw line, missing nine of their first eleven attempts. On the defensive end, the strategy of fouling Mikan, which had worked so well in the first game, was backfiring; Mikan was red-hot all night from the line, hitting eleven of twelve free throws.

The Trotters finally came to life in the second period. Marques Haynes sank a long two-hander, then Clifton went right over the top of Mikan to steal a rebound, made a beautiful spin move, and dropped in a soft hook. At halftime, however, the Lakers still held a 24–18 lead.

At the beginning of the third quarter, Laker point guard Herm Schaefer hit a basket to extend the lead to 26–18. Then, without any warning, Marques Haynes exploded. He hit four consecutive shots to ignite a 12–0 run, and the Trotters took their first lead. After a Laker free throw, the Trotters went on another 6–0 run. Realizing that Mikan was tiring and getting back slowly on defense, the Trotters started fast-breaking every time they got a rebound, and netted several easy layups. In the third period, the Trotters outscored the Lakers 23–6, to take a 41–32 lead into the final quarter.

It was more of the same in the fourth quarter. Clifton was bottling up Mikan, the Trotters were snaring rebounds and breaking up the court, and Goose hit a sweeping hook in the lane that gave the Trotters a 12-point lead with six minutes to play.

Then something remarkable happened. Against the best white team in the country, the Harlem Globetrotters started putting on the show. The crowd went into a frenzy. In the early years, the show had developed as a way *not* to humiliate their opponents, but to hold down the score against outmanned opponents. Against the Lakers, however, it became a symbolic act of triumph. For a proud Lakers team, this was the ultimate humiliation. As their hometown paper, the *Minneapolis Star,* described it: "Things got so bad for the Minneapolis Lakers here Monday night that old Globetrotter fans started hollering for 'baseball.'"

Marques Haynes began the festivities. Holding the ball on the wing, he wound up like he was going to throw the ball cross court, then spun around in a complete circle and caught the ball behind him. The crowd roared. A moment later, he launched into his full-blown dribbling routine. First, while strutting around like a banty rooster, he dribbled the ball higher than his head, then ran in place, dribbling no higher than his shoelaces; then he raced a few paces to his right, slid down on one knee, actually crawled on his hands and knees, leaped up and ran three feet the other way, stopped, reversed direction, backed up, lurched forward, repeated that twice more, almost too quickly to see, then spun around in a circle and ran all the way across the court. At first, Laker guard Tony Jaros refused to take the bait, but when Marques went down on one knee, taunting him, Jaros couldn't help himself: he came after the ball. Marques jumped back up and started double-clutching, going back and forth, changing directions every other step. A second Laker, Don Forman, drifted over to double-team him. Marques toyed with both players for a few more seconds, then reared up and passed the ball to a teammate.

Then Goose got into the act. He took a pass down low in the pivot and, with Mikan hovering over him, faked as if he was going to shoot his hook, then stuffed the ball under his jersey and started walking away. Mikan looked to the ref for help, while Goose calmly stood near the foul line, his jersey bulging. The ref called a jump ball, which Mikan easily controlled, but who cared? The crowd was having a ball. A few minutes later, Goose again got the ball and started flailing his arms and waving the ball around. The crowd was really getting into it, and Mikan started enjoying the show himself. He let down his guard for an instant, and Goose whipped a pass right past his ear to Ermer Robinson, who went in for an easy layup.

By then, as the *Minneapolis Star* sadly noted, thousands of Globetrotter fans were chanting—"Baseball! Baseball!"—exhorting the Trotters to perform their classic skit. They never did, as that would have been rubbing it in a little too much. While the Trotters were busy putting on the show, the Lakers scored the last 9 points of the game, but the outcome was never in doubt. The final score was 49–45, and even white sportswriters agreed that the Trotters could have won by more. Once again, the Trotters had done the impossible, defeating the mighty Lakers, the most formidable team in professional ball.

In the end, it was Sweetwater Clifton's ability to neutralize Mikan that made the difference. Big George had scored two early field goals against Goose, but once Clifton started covering him, he made only two buckets the rest of the game. The Trotters also had a balanced attack, led by Goose with 14 points, Marques and Clifton with 11 each, Babe Pressley with 7, and Ermer Robinson with 6. For the Lakers, Mikan ended up with 19, but no other player had more than 7. Clearly, the absence of Jim Pollard and Swede Carlson was a major hindrance to the Lakers' chances.

The first victory over the Lakers may have been more shocking, and certainly had a more spectacular ending, with Robinson's last-second shot, but to some of the Trotters' fans, the second win was more satisfying. They had not just beaten Whitey; they had sealed their victory by putting on the show. As Timuel Black recalled his reaction, and that of his friends, "We wanted to see a Trotter victory—*and the show.* We were waiting for the show, which made the victory that much sweeter."

Ultimately, the second win had a much greater impact on the Globetrotters' fortunes because of the coverage of the game on Movietone News. For twenty years, Abe had depended on his network of grizzled, stogie-chewing sportswriters to spread the Globetrotters' fame across the land, in stories pounded out on Underwood or Royal typewriters, set in hot lead, and read by individual readers over their morning coffee. But the second Lakers game was Abe's introduction to an entirely different medium—a *visual* medium—that could bring that game to millions of Americans in every town and neighborhood. Through the Movietone newsreel, those people would *experience* the victory over the Lakers as if they had been there in person. They would marvel at Marques Haynes's dribbling and laugh at Goose Tatum stuffing the ball under his jersey, and know in their hearts—because the silver screen never lied—that the Harlem

Globetrotters were the most entertaining sports spectacle in the country.*

Ever since he was a kid, Abe Saperstein had loved the movies. He had even come close to being *in* the movies himself, when he won the popularity contest at the Ravenswood Theater. His infatuation with Hollywood was still just as strong. On stifling days in the summer, when the electric fans in the Globetrotters' office couldn't keep up with Chicago's climbing mercury, Abe would say, "Let's get out of here!" and take the whole staff to lunch, and then to the movies on Randolph Street, where they'd sit in air-conditioned comfort and catch a weekday matinee. His all-time favorite movie was *The Al Jolson Story,* the saga of the little Jewish boy who makes it big, which he would watch over and over again. Now, for the first time in their history, the Harlem Globetrotters were *in* the movie theaters. It was just a fifty-second Movietone newsreel, but it was a harbinger of a new age that was dawning in America—and for the Globetrotters— in which *electronic* communication, via television tubes and transistors, would soon be mainlining the Harlem Globetrotters directly into every home in America.

---

* *The effect at the box office was immediate: four days after the Trotters' win, the Trotters played before 13,000 in Boston Garden, the largest crowd ever to watch a basketball game in Boston.*

CHAPTER 11

All-Stars

On April 2, 1950, in Chicago Stadium, the site of so many decisive moments in Globetrotter history, the inaugural game of the most audacious promotion in American sports history, the World Series of Basketball, was played between the Harlem Globetrotters and the College All-Stars. It was the first of eighteen games on a three-week, 9,000-mile transcontinental tour of America, played in seventeen major cities before 181,000 fans.

Over the next twelve years, the World Series of Basketball would be witnessed by over *two million* fans and, at its peak, in the mid-1950s, would be the most popular basketball event in America, over-shadowing the NCAA and NIT tournaments and the NBA finals. Its impact would still be reflected over fifty years later, in September 2002, when Larry Brown, coach of the 2004 world champion Detroit Pistons, was being inducted into the Basketball Hall of Fame in Springfield, Massachusetts—the highest honor in the sport. In his acceptance speech, Brown said, "The greatest day I ever spent in basketball was when I was growing up in New York and my father took me to Madison Square Garden to see the Harlem Globetrotters play the College All-Stars."

Only the mind of an Abe Saperstein could have conceived it. And only the front office staff he had assembled, led by Marie Linehan, could have pulled it off. It was the culmination of twenty years of promoting games in byways and whistle-stops across the land, now magnified on a grand scale to the largest cites and arenas in America.

The College All-Star tour was daring, and perhaps insane, on many levels. First, the idea of a transcontinental tour—by *airplane*—was in itself a bold undertaking. Commercial air travel was still fairly uncommon, and many of the players, on both teams, had never flown in their lives. The expenses for such a tour were far beyond anything Abe and Marie had ever incurred. Airfare alone to fly a party of forty people (two teams, coaches, staff, technicians, orchestra, and halftime entertainers), in two chartered DC-3s, to seventeen different cities, one each day, from New York to Los Angeles, cost an estimated $25,000. That was more than the Globetrotters' gross receipts for an entire season a few years earlier. Once they landed in a city, there were additional costs for ground transportation, hotels, salaries, state and federal taxes, liability insurance, publicity (newspaper ads, billboards, posters), stadium rentals (usually 30–40 percent of the gate, after expenses), lights, microphones, and union electricians. Multiply those headaches times seventeen straight days in seventeen different cities—it was enough to make any other sports promoter blanch. But not Abe.

And the logistics of moving that entourage from one end of the country to the other, and back again, all the while rotating players and coaches in and out, were staggering. That's where Marie Linehan's organizational skills came in. She sent each participant a detailed letter listing departure times for the United charter from Chicago to New York, baggage limitations, reservations at the Victoria Hotel on Fifty-first Street, and a reminder not to miss the dress rehearsal in Madison Square Garden.

Somehow, they pulled it off, and did it so successfully that it would become a template for even grander and more audacious tours. If it could be done across America, why not across Europe? South America? Asia? Hell, why not around the world?

The concept of professionals playing a team of college all-stars did not originate with Abe Saperstein but, as with many of his other successes, he recognized a great idea and capitalized on it. College all-star games had been played in various cities for decades, with assorted combinations of collegiate players. The Globetrotters had played many such games, including the most publicized one, the first annual All-Star Classic in 1940.

The vision of a College All-Star *tour* arose in March 1949. Just three weeks after their second victory over the Lakers, the Trotters returned to Chicago Stadium to face the Midwest All-Stars, an amalgamation of players from DePaul, Notre Dame, Marquette, and Loyola. That game happened because the Chicago Stags, the local BAA franchise, were drawing poorly and asked Abe to headline a doubleheader, to help draw a crowd. Abe called Ray Meyer, the DePaul coach, and asked him to cobble together an "all-star" team. "It was really just a lark," Meyer recalls. "The Stags were losing money and asked Abe to play a doubleheader. They paid us twenty-five dollars apiece for the game."

In the aftermath of the Trotters' great triumph over the Lakers, however, 14,451 people showed up for the game. The Trotters, who were without Sweetwater Clifton (he was out with a fever), played listlessly, and lost 51–50, on a last-second shot. Afterward, the *Defender* lambasted the Trotters for being out of condition, and claimed they had "lost some prestige" by letting a pickup team of college boys beat them.

To Abe, however, the game was an epiphany. "Abe saw that it was a gold mine," says Ray Meyer. The idea developed to have the Globetrotters play the top college seniors in the country on a cross-country tour. It would begin in early April, after the NCAA tournament (so the players' college eligibility was already used up) and during spring break for most colleges. Abe adapted a similar model to the one that the *Chicago Herald-American* had been using for a decade with its All-Star Classic, by having a panel of college coaches nominate the players. In fact, Abe hired Harry Hannin, the promoter of the Classic (and the World Pro Tournament), to direct the College All-Star tour; and he hired Ray Meyer to coach the team. Together, Abe and Hannin came up with the high-minded title—"The World Series of Basketball"—which echoed baseball's fall classic.

It was the perfect convergence of all their skills. Hannin and Meyer already had contacts with the top college coaches in the country, who would nominate the players, while Abe had the contacts with the promoters and arena managers to book the games, and with his army of sportswriters to promote them.

Some two dozen players were chosen for the All-American squad, although only about half suited up for any game. In another ingenious move, Abe and Hannin decided to rotate some of the players during the tour—ostensibly to keep players from missing class when their spring break ended—but more important to ensure that local college stars were playing the games in their own geographic areas, to guarantee a turnout of the home fans. And they did the same thing with coaches: Meyer was the head coach for the entire tour, assisted by Clair Bee of Long Island University, but they also had "honorary coaches" from every region (in many cases, the coaches of the top All-Stars), who were rotated in for a few games. Using this method, they brought in some of the most well-known coaches in the country, including Frank McGuire, Honey Russell, Branch McCracken, Ed Jucker, and John Wooden. It was an irresistible combination—the top players in the country *and* their coaches, playing in front of hometown fans, against the most celebrated pro team in the nation. And it proved to be astoundingly successful.

The first year, the tour began in Chicago, ended in Washington, D.C., and included stops in Cleveland, Kansas City, Salt Lake City, Los Angeles, San Francisco, Denver, St. Louis, Detroit, Boston, and Philadelphia, among others. In later years, the series typically began with a doubleheader in Madison Square Garden, worked its way across the country to Los Angeles, then back east to Boston Garden for the finale.

The World Series was a sensation from the start. Thirteen of the eighteen games were sellouts, and all-time attendance records were set in six cities. But the tour grew even bigger as time went on. In 1951, a world attendance record for a basketball game was set, when 31,648 people came out on a wet night in the Rose Bowl.* By 1952, all but two games were played before standing-room-only audiences, including 35,548 fans for a doubleheader at Madison Square Garden. In 1953, the tour was expanded to twenty-one games in

---

* *The Rose Bowl game would make the* Guinness Book of World Records, *but the record lasted for only five months, until the Trotters set a new world record in Berlin. It was probably the least competitive game in the entire history of the Series, as a portable floor was laid directly over the football field, and the combination of falling dew and condensation caused water to puddle on the floor. The players were slipping and sliding so badly (the referee even fell on his behind when he walked out for the opening tip) that Ray Meyer told his All-Americans, "Don't hurt yourself; just let the Trotters put on the show."*

nineteen days, total attendance for the series peaked at 308,451, and new records were set in fifteen cities, including a new American record of 36,256 at the Los Angeles Coliseum.

The World Series of Basketball included more than just great basketball; it was a show business extravaganza. At halftime of every game, Abe would bring out several vaudeville acts, including jugglers, Ping-Pong champs, baton twirlers, accordionists, hand balancers, even Cab Calloway.

Over the years, the College All-American teams included some of the greatest college players of the era, many of whom went on to illustrious pro careers: Paul Arizin, Bob Cousy, Bill Sharman, Bill Garrett, Frank Ramsey, Cliff Hagan, Gene Shue, Larry Costello, Tom Gola, Jack Twyman, Chet Forte, Guy Rodgers, Connie Dierking, K. C. Jones, Walt Bellamy, Bill Bridges, and Tom Heinsohn. In 1954, Abe was applauded for selecting the first two African American players to the All-American team (at the suggestion of the *Pittsburgh Courier*), both of whom, Willie Thomas and Tex Harrison, went on to play with the Trotters (Harrison is still with the organization, as the Trotters' longtime coach).

The pace of the tour was punishing. The college boys were used to playing a game or two a week, but now they were playing every night. "It was a grind—twenty-one games in a row," Ray Meyer says. "The Globetrotters had such an advantage, because they were used to that. They could relax better than anybody I've ever seen. They would get on the plane and before the engines started up they were asleep, and they'd sleep until we'd get off. But we could not sleep, so my guys got pretty worn down. We would play well the first week or so, but after that we were through."

The All-Stars had another disadvantage, which was having no practice time before the tour began. "I'd meet the players the night before the first game and we'd talk about what we were going to do," says Meyers. He had no time to install an offensive system, other than a few basic give-and-go and pick-and-roll plays. "But we had great players," he says. "I've never had that kind of talent before."

And great talent can overcome many disadvantages. The Globetrotters had their hands full with the college boys almost every game—it was like the Trotters and Lakers every night—and seldom got a big enough lead to put on the show. The first year, the Trotters won eleven games but lost seven—the worst winning percentage in their history, by far. In 1954, Frank Ramsey and Cliff Hagan, who had carried Kentucky to a 25–0 record, led the All-Stars to three straight wins and a 6–15 record. The next year, Tom Gola, of LaSalle, established a World Series scoring record of 348 points, and the All-Stars won ten and lost fourteen. And in 1956, the All-Stars won seven of the last ten games, and the Trotters barely won the series with an 11–10 record.

After twenty years of winning over 90 percent of their games, Abe did not take gracefully to losing. "Abe was a madman," Meyer says, laughing. "He had never experienced losing before, and he would go crazy." In fact, Abe would get so mad when the All-Stars won that Meyer would avoid him by walking back to the hotel, rather than riding on the team bus. If the All-Stars won several games in a row, tour director Harry Hannin would warn Meyer, "If you guys beat them any more, Abe will send everybody home." And one year in Boston, on the final night of the tour, the All-Stars started putting on the Trotters' show, with one guy doing a dribbling routine and the others jumping in the lane on free-throw attempts. The crowd was howling, but when Meyer sneaked a peek at the Trotters' bench, he didn't like what he saw. "Abe was turning green," he says, laughing. Without hesitating, Meyer got up and left the building. "I didn't even see the end of the game," he says.

"It was the only time in my career that it paid to lose," Meyer says. "When the Trotters won, Abe would be in a good mood and take us out to dinner, or give the players some extra money." Still, Meyer is proud of the fact that he won more games against the Trotters than any other coach in history.

Abe was so obsessed with winning that he wasn't above planting a stooge or two on the All-American team to give the Trotters an advantage. A panel of college coaches *nominated* the college players, but Abe had the final decision, and he would send out his chief scout, Phil Brownstein, to check out the nominees. In 1955, Brownstein's scouting report on one All-American center read: "Very weak defensively—easy to go around . . . Bulls his way in, not much of [a] ball handler—no fakes around basket—looked bad both nites [sic]." Based on that critique, you might think the player would be scratched from the list, but Brownstein recommended just the opposite: "Use on All Star college squad—tell man playing against him, he's easy to fake & get around." This player did, in fact, play ten games on the tour, averaging 3.5 points per game.

The two teams played hard on the court, but they traveled together* for nearly three weeks on a chartered United DC-6, and friendships inevitably developed. There were long-running poker games in the back of the plane that carried over from city to city. For many of the players on *both* teams, it was the first time in their lives that they had experienced a racially mixed environment. In fact, that United DC-6 may have been the most integrated place in America in the early 1950s.

The only ugly incident that Ray Meyer recalled in ten years of such tours was when a new All-American player unsuspectingly sat in Goose Tatum's "reserved" seat on the plane. "I thought Goose was gonna kill him," Meyer says. But Goose was notoriously moody and unpredictable, and would sometimes "go off" on his own teammates, so that explosion was not necessarily racially motivated.

However, not all racial differences melted away. In later years, both teams stayed in the same hotels, but in the early 1950s the white players were often housed in first-class hotels, while the Trotters were relegated to "colored" hotels in black neighborhoods. This was true even in some of the bigger cities, including San Francisco, Los Angeles, and Philadelphia. And today, some former Globetrotters still resent how much money Abe paid the white players, compared with what they were making. The first year, when the tour arrived in Louisville for the fourth game of the Series (by which point Abe realized it was going to be a smashing success), he told the All-Stars, "Tear up your contracts—they've just been doubled." According to Ray Meyer, from then on Abe paid the All-Stars $2,500 apiece for the full tour, plus $7.50 per diem for meals. Those players who only rotated in for some of the tour got approximately $100 per game (in

---

* The two teams flew on separate DC-3s the first year, but after that flew together on a chartered United DC-6.

1955, for example, one player received $1,250 for twelve games). In addition, the All-Stars were given an assortment of gifts and mementos, including a specially engraved Elgin "All-American" wristwatch, a diamond-studded basketball charm and cuff links, an RCA portable radio, and a Coca-Cola Achievement plaque.

In contrast, in the early years of the tour the Globetrotter players received only their regular monthly salaries (although by 1961, they were getting paid time and a half for the three-week tour). They got no extra money for playing on the tour; to the contrary, there was fierce competition among all of the Trotter units and farm teams to be selected to the team. Abe's attitude seemed to be that they were lucky to be chosen for the tour, so they shouldn't complain about the money. At that time, rookies were typically starting at $300 a month, and many veterans—including Marques Haynes—were drawing only slightly more. So white All-Stars making $2,500 for the full three-week tour, and even those making $100 per game for a partial tour, were making much more money than the typical Globetrotter. Plus, Abe reportedly paid the Trotters less per diem (only $5 per day) than the All-Stars. When one Globetrotter, Josh Grider, complained about that inequity, Abe's response was, "A Negro doesn't need as much money as a white man." His rationale, apparently, was that the white players were eating in higher-priced restaurants than the black players, either because they weren't allowed in, or because the black players preferred "soul food" joints. In either case, it deeply offended Grider and other Trotters who heard the story.

By the end of the first All-American tour, in April 1950, it was the most acclaimed road show in American sports. And beyond the attendance records and gate receipts, it was an unprecedented public relations triumph. Until then, Globetrotter games had been *local* news, covered by the local press in the cities where they played. The College All-American tour, however, was a *national* news story covered by the United Press and put out on the national wire. With this stroke of genius, Abe had devised a way to splash the Trotters across the sports pages of newspapers all across America—from the *New York Times* to the *Berkshire County Eagle*—for three straight weeks! Baseball's World Series might last ten days, at most, if it went to seven games. The NFL championship was over in three hours. Even the Olympics lasted only two weeks. But the World Series of Basketball went on for twenty-one days!

Having conquered America, Abe next set out to conquer the world. The Globetrotters had already been to Mexico, Cuba, Canada, Alaska, and Hawaii, but now they would at last become true globe-trotters. On May 3, 1950, one week after the College All-Star tour, Abe and ten players took off from Idlewild Airport in New York bound for Lisbon, Portugal. In many ways, it was like turning back the clock twenty years. They were traveling in a Pan American Clipper instead of an old Model T, and they were on their way to Europe instead of Cut Bank, Montana, but, as in the old days, they were heading into the wilderness as complete unknowns. For that matter, their sport was also unknown, as basketball was in its infancy in much of Europe. The Globetrotters left the United States at their peak of popularity but arrived in Lisbon wondering if anyone would even notice.

Once again, however, Abe had worked his public relations magic. He had sent Harry Hannin over as an advance man, to work the local press, and so the team was met at the airport by the directors of the Sporting Club of Portugal and a host of reporters and photographers. The Globetrotters' arrival turned into an hour-long photo shoot. That night, the Trotters played their first European game in an open-air stadium in Coimbra with seats for five thousand. Seven thousand people showed up.*

In Coimbra, the Trotters were facing two challenges: the fans' ignorance about basketball and a daunting language barrier. Neither one mattered. The Portuguese laughed just as hard at Goose Tatum's clowning as the crowds had in Madison Square Garden. Indeed, it might have made Goose a better showman, because he had to find ways to get his comedy across without words. The Trotters, it was clear, spoke the universal language of joy.

The Trotters had brought along their own opposition team, the Stars of America (with Bob Karstens on the roster), and their own referee, Elliott Hasan, whose diary provided most of the details of this tour.

After the game, the fans mobbed the players, asking for autographs, reaching out to touch them, not wanting them to leave. Each player was given a bottle of champagne, and the Trotters had to have a police escort to get out of the arena.

It was the same everywhere they went. In Oporto, police were stationed outside the Hotel Imperio to disperse the crowds that clogged the street, waiting for a player sighting. It was as if the Trotters were movie stars or international celebrities—which, by the time they left Europe, they were. Before the tour, Abe had shipped over the official Globetrotter bus, with "Harlem Globetrotters—Magicians of Basketball" emblazoned across the side, and as they drove the big school bus through towns and villages in Portugal's countryside, crowds gathered wherever they went. In Oporto, they played three sold-out games, then flew back to Lisbon, the capital, and played two sellouts there, with top government officials in attendance. The fans were so enamored of the Globetrotters that 4,000 people showed up for an unannounced practice.

From Lisbon, they went to Paris, where they held a giant press conference and ball-handling exhibition for 200 news reporters and every newsreel company in Europe. Then it was on to Geneva, Switzerland, for three more sellouts.

Next up was London, where basketball, which was known as "net ball," was considered a "sissy sport" played only by girls. After their superstar treatment in Portugal, France, and Switzerland, the Globetrotter players were surprised to find that one American tradition had followed them to London: racial prejudice. The Globetrotters were not allowed to stay in the city proper, but had to stay in a small hotel on the outskirts of London.

Their first game was played at the Empire Pool and Sports Arena, adjoining Wembley Stadium, in front of 8,000 specially invited guests and a throng of movie, TV, and newspaper reporters. Abe was so concerned about the British public's lack of understanding of basketball that he hired a British announcer to give a detailed explanation of the game as it went along. He need not have worried. "We were a hit from the beginning," recalls former Trotter Frank Washington. It helped that the game was broadcast nationally on British television, and was the *only* show on the air during that time slot. After that first game, Abe's worries were over. The Trotters played five straight sell-outs in London, and the British promoters begged Abe to add another game to accommodate the demand, "No, Aunt Agatha," one British newsman enthused, "this isn't anything like the netball at your girls' school. In fact, it isn't like anything you've ever seen." As for the British announcer, the crowds actually started booing him, feeling that his long-winded explanations were interfering with the action, and his services were dispensed with quickly.

From England, they flew to Belgium, for games in Antwerp, Brussels, and Liège. Then they returned by train to Paris, where they spent a week playing to sellout crowds at night and sightseeing during the day. Six more games were scheduled in the south of France, including one in Nancy, a night game in an outdoor stadium, which was rained out. Or so they thought. A downpour began in the afternoon and continued right up until game time. The Trotters were already packing their bags to catch an early train to Nice when the local promoter called, in a dither, to ask where they were. Ten thousand people were sitting in the rain, waiting patiently. The Trotters changed into their uniforms and played in the rain. Goose Tatum showed up wearing a derby hat and an old-fashioned striped bathing suit from the 1920s, and Marques Haynes did his dribbling act holding an umbrella in one hand. The crowd stayed until the very end.

The Harlem Globetrotters had taken Europe by storm. The crowds embraced the players as if they were royalty, and, other than the one regrettable experience with the London hotel, the Trotters saw no signs of racial prejudice. In fact, they were treated much better in Europe than in the United States. "Absolutely—we were treated like kings," says Frank Washington. "I had to look in the mirror to see that I was black. People opened up their arms to us. We were down with ambassadors, kings, and queens."

It wasn't just the fans who welcomed them. Unknowingly, the Harlem Globetrotters also had become a propaganda weapon in the cold war. In Oporto, Portugal, the United States vice consul, Leland C. Altaffer, sent a detailed report on their visit to the State Department, saying: "It is believed that [the Globetrotters] made an unusually wide and deep impression of open friendliness both inter-racially and internationally."

After one game, the U.S. consul told the players, "Thank God for you guys, you're the best thing that's ever happened here. We've gotten more cooperation out of these people [the Portuguese government] since you've played here than we've ever gotten." In Geneva, the U.S. consul and other foreign diplomats were honored as special guests at one game. And after witnessing the fanatical response toward the Trotters wherever they went, the U.S. State Department would begin a deliberate campaign to use the Trotters to counteract Soviet propaganda about the oppression of blacks in America.

After their blitzkrieg across Europe, the Trotters boarded an Air France flight to Morocco. In Casablanca, the Trotters played before the sultan and his court. They continued across North Africa, to Algiers, where they toured the famed Casbah, which turned out to be a filthy slum, with narrow alleys, open sewers, and hordes of beggars. Most of the players were frightened or repulsed by it, but Goose Tatum found something soothing about the mysterious place and would disappear into the Casbah for hours. One day, he invited Frank Washington to join him. "Come on, Wash," he said, "let's go to the Casbah." Thinking it was an exotic nightclub, Washington agreed. "Hell, it was a den of thieves," he says, laughing. "I was glad to get the hell out."

From Algiers, the Trotters flew back across the Mediterranean in a Douglass Skymaster to Milan, Italy, where they played before 21,000 people in a stadium erected by Mussolini. They played in Milan, Genoa, and Bologna, spent two days sightseeing in Rome, then crossed the border into West Germany, where they played Munich, West Berlin, Strasbourg, and Metz. The tour ended with five glorious days of sightseeing in Paris, before they came home on the ocean liner *Caronia,* arriving back in New York in early August.

They had been gone for three months, had played seventy-three games, winning all but one, before half a million fans. They had visited fourteen countries, had played in nine, and had won millions of new fans. The Harlem Globetrotters were the kings of the sports world.

★

For Abe Saperstein, it had been the headiest twelve months of his life, with one extraordinary triumph after another. There was the second victory over the Lakers, the debut in Madison Square Garden, the

Movietone and Paramount newsreels, the College All-Stars series, the first European tour, and a record 1.5 million fans who had seen them that season. The Globetrotters' headquarters in Chicago finally looked the part of a world-class organization, as Abe had moved into a modern suite of offices on North Dearborn Street, in the heart of the Loop. Plus, he had opened a New York office on the seventy-sixth floor of the Empire State Building, staffed by his sister Fay and publicity director Walter Kennedy (later NBA commissioner).

It was a story that a Hollywood screenwriter could have written: a rags-to-riches tale of the immigrant Jewish boy and five black ballplayers, traveling across America in a leaky Model T, who were now the toast of three continents. In fact, a Hollywood screenwriter *was* writing it. Alfred Palca, a publicist for Twentieth Century-Fox, had made a movie deal with Abe and had sold a script to Columbia Pictures, which had scheduled filming of *The Harlem Globetrotters* to begin in October 1950.

It had been a magnificent year.

However, even as Abe was basking in the glory of those accomplishments, profound changes were occurring in the American basketball universe that would shake the foundations of his empire. Like a Greek tragedy, at his greatest moment of glory, with his chest swollen with pride, the seeds of his downfall were already being sown. The seeds would lie dormant for many years, during which, to all outward appearances, the Harlem Globetrotters would grow ever more popular and successful. Eventually, however, the seeds would germinate and, like a lowly weed that forces its way through a concrete slab, send out wiry tendrils that would crack through the walls of Abe's business empire and bring down all that he had built.

The first symptom of trouble in Abe's world occurred on April 25, 1950, as the Trotters were packing for Europe, when Charles Cooper, of Duquesne University, was drafted by the Boston Celtics, becoming the first African American to be chosen by the NBA. Allegedly, when Celtics' owner Walter Brown announced his selection of Cooper in the second round, a hush fell over the hotel room where the NBA owners were gathered.

"Walter, don't you know he's a colored boy?" another owner asked.

"I don't give a damn if he's striped, plaid, or polka-dot!" Brown replied. "Boston takes Chuck Cooper of Duquesne!"

Once the Celtics broke the color line, the Washington Capitols selected two black players: Earl Lloyd, a six-foot-six center from West Virginia State, in the ninth round; and Harold Hunter, from North Carolina Central, in the tenth.

For Abe, the drafting of Cooper and Lloyd was disastrous—not for what it meant to the NBA, but for what it meant to the Trotters. Just a few weeks earlier, on April 1, Cooper had signed a contract with the Trotters and had played in all eighteen games against the College All-Stars. Earl Lloyd had also donned a Globetrotter uniform in early April, for a one-week tour, after which Abe told the press that he planned to offer Lloyd a contract after he graduated from college. Instead, two of the top black players in the country, whom Abe would have certainly signed a year earlier, were lost to the NBA.

For three years, Abe had kept the faltering league afloat by playing doubleheaders on NBA cards. Originally, the Trotters would play the first game and two NBA teams would play the "feature" game, but so many fans would leave after the Trotters' game that the NBA had started scheduling the Trotters in the nightcap. Now, the league was showing its gratitude by stealing two of "his" ballplayers. He didn't react to that prospect any better than he had taken to losing seven games to the College All-Stars. According to several published accounts (including Wilt Chamberlain's autobiography), Abe "went crazy" when he heard the news. Two days after the draft, he reportedly threatened the NBA owners, saying that the Globetrotters would never play in Boston or Washington again. Celtic owner Walter Brown, whose team was drowning in debt, nonetheless refused to back down. "As far as I'm concerned," he reportedly said, "Abe Saperstein is out of the Boston Garden right now."

In 1950, the NBA was already lagging far behind major league baseball and the National Football League in integrating. Jackie Robinson was starting his fourth season with the Brooklyn Dodgers, and Marion Motley, Kenny Washington, and Woody Strode were starring in the National Football League. In his 2002 book *They Cleared the Lane,* author Ron Thomas argues persuasively that the number one stumbling block to integrating the NBA was Abe

Saperstein, as team owners "feared the wrath" of Abe and were afraid they would lose their Globetrotter doubleheaders. Given the NBA's financial woes and its dependence on those games, that could have been a death knell for the league. The integration of the NBA had been forced by Ned Irish, owner of the New York Knicks, who had been openly coveting Sweetwater Clifton for over a year, to fill the Knicks' dire need for a center. In an owners' meeting prior to the 1950 NBA draft, Irish reportedly pounded the table and threatened to quit the league if the other owners did not support his efforts to sign Clifton. The owners eventually agreed to integrate, and the Celtics moved first on Cooper.

The drafting of Cooper, Lloyd, and Hunter did nothing to help Irish sign Sweetwater Clifton, however. But ten days after the draft, Abe and the Knicks held a secret meeting to talk about Clifton. Abe may have been angry about losing Cooper and Lloyd, but he was smart enough to realize that his world had just changed, and he was better off bargaining over Clifton from a position of strength. As Ron Thomas has documented, on May 3, 1950, the same day the Trotters left for Portugal, Abe had lunch with NBA commissioner Maurice Podoloff and Knicks' business agent Freddie Podestra. They met in a restaurant in the Empire State Building, where the offices of the Globetrotters and the NBA were only two floors apart.

Clifton was increasingly dissatisfied playing with the Trotters. He was tired of the constant travel and upset because he had learned that Abe was paying the College All-Stars more money than the Trotters. He had another year on his contract, but had already told Abe that he wasn't coming back in the fall of 1950. As Clifton was notorious for "jumping contracts" (in the course of one season, 1947–48, he had jumped to at least four different teams, earning a reputation as the "Satchel Paige of basketball"), Abe apparently decided to get what he could for him right away.

Over lunch, a deal was struck, and a memorandum agreement was drafted and signed that day by Abe and Podestra, with Podoloff as a witness. Clifton's remaining one-year contract was assigned to the Knicks for $12,500, with Clifton to receive the same $1,250 salary per month he had been receiving from the Trotters. Abe told Podestra that he planned to give Clifton $4,000 of the purchase price (even though he had no obligation to do so). They agreed to keep the deal a secret until a mutually agreed-upon time—hopefully, to generate the most publicity. Sweetwater Clifton had just become an NBA player, although he didn't know it at the time.

Abe left that day for Lisbon, and the secret deal was leaked to the press three weeks later. When Clifton heard about it, he gave an interview to the *New York Post,* in which he questioned Abe's right to sell him to the Knicks without his permission, and asked for a fifty-fifty split of the purchase price. "I don't think he had the right to deal me off like that," he complained. "I've been trying to go with the Knickerbockers for two years. He wouldn't sell me . . . I didn't cost him much. I think I should get a split." Typically, no owner of any pro team who sells a player to another team splits the purchase price with the player; that money is compensation for the team that's giving up the player. Abe had told Podestra that he was going to give Clifton $4,000, but after Clifton's complaints appeared in the *Post,* Abe reportedly gave him only $2,500.

In any case, Sweetwater Clifton was now officially a New York Knick. On May 23, Abe received a check from the Knicks for $12,500, as agreed. Clifton, who was already popular in New York because of being a Trotter, went on to have a solid career in the NBA, playing seven years with the Knicks and one with the Detroit Pistons. Chuck Cooper, the first black player drafted, played six years in the NBA; Earl Lloyd, the first African American to actually play in an NBA game (the Washington Capitols opened their season on October 31, 1950—one day before Cooper's Celtics), played nine seasons in the league. Harold Hunter, who was actually the first black player to sign an NBA contract (on April 26, 1950), was cut by the Washington Capitols in training camp.

Abe Saperstein's role in ending, or impeding, the integration of the NBA—like most racial issues involving him—is a complex question that has been written about, and debated, for years. Some have argued that Abe's threatened boycott of Boston and Washington was racially motivated (to maintain his stranglehold on black talent), but one could just as readily assert that it was all about business. He had a signed contract with Chuck Cooper, and the Celtics were raiding his player. If NBA owners were going to draft players under contract to him, he would use the main weapon at his disposal: the double-headers. Abe's angry outburst, two days after the draft, was typical. He would often blow his top, threaten to fire a coach or player—and sometimes do it—only to turn around and hire them back the next week, after he had calmed down. That appears to be exactly what happened with the NBA. There is no evidence that he boycotted the Boston or Washington clubs. To the contrary, the next season the Trotters played a doubleheader with the Celtics in Boston Garden on March 1, 1951; then played Washington's Uline Arena on March 16, 1951; and returned to the Garden with the College All-Stars on April 19, 1951. The Trotters would continue to keep the NBA afloat for another five or six years, until the emergence of Bill Russell and the Boston Celtics' dynasty.

To fully understand Abe's reaction to the NBA's drafting of black players, one must also consider an additional factor. For years, he had been coveting an NBA franchise, and in April 1950, when the draft occurred, he was close to finally getting one. The Chicago Stags were losing so much money they were about to collapse, and the NBA had loaned them $40,000, with a stipulation that by June 1 the club post a $15,000 performance bond. When the Stags were unable to post the bond, the NBA sold the franchise to Abe for $40,000—including $20,000 cash up front. Throughout the summer, he was dickering over player contracts and pursuing possible trades with other teams, but in September, he backed out of the deal, accusing the NBA of "total failure . . . to deliver the franchise and the players in accordance with the promises made by its representatives when I offered to purchase."

However upset Abe may have been about the NBA's drafting of Cooper and Lloyd, and the Knicks' signing of Clifton, he was extremely cordial and supportive toward the players themselves. On May 4, 1950, he sent a congratulatory telegram to Cooper and released him from his Trotter contract, saying: "Considered carefully circumstances surrounding draft considering opportunity initial colored performer NBA. Agreed if satisfactory to you to relinquish my claims your services to Boston Celtics. . . . To me you were you are and you always will be a Harlem Globetrotter. Cordially, Abe Saperstein." As for Clifton, Abe would later tell Wendell Smith, "Frankly, I didn't want to let him go. He was one of our key men. But I let him [go]. After all, the New York team had never used a Negro player. Clifton thought he'd like to be the first, so I told him to go ahead. I agreed with him, it would be a good thing for everyone concerned."

Abe still maintained good relations with Clifton and Cooper after they went to the NBA. Cooper returned to the Trotters in subsequent years, after the NBA season had ended, to play against the College All-Americans, and Clifton would come back for years to make both the All-American and European tours.*

When the glorious 1950 season finally ended, Sweetwater Clifton was gone and the best starting five in Globetrotter history was no more. There have been many great ballplayers on the Trotters, before and after, but the greatest team of all time was the 1948–50 combination of Marques Haynes, Sweetwater Clifton, Ermer Robinson, Babe Pressley, and Goose Tatum.

The Trotters had lost their best big man, and the effects were apparent right away. After their first two landmark wins against the Minneapolis Lakers, the Trotters would never beat them again. By 1950, the Lakers had added six-foot-seven Vern Mikkelsen to complement George Mikan and Jim Pollard, giving them the tallest front line in basketball, and against the much shorter Trotters it was like playing volleyball on one side of the net. The Lakers dominated the remainder of the series, winning five straight games between 1949 and 1952 (including two when Clifton was still with the Trotters), and a final game in 1958, when the series ended.†

The Harlem Globetrotters were unquestionably the most popular basketball team in the world, but by 1951, they were no longer the best.

---

* *Clifton finished his playing career in 1962 with the Chicago Majors, in Abe's failed American Basketball League. Clifton (whose legal name was actually Clifton Nathaniel) then bought a cab and drove that until his death, in 1990, at age sixty-two.*

† *After a six-year hiatus, Abe and the Lakers agreed to restart the series in 1958, but the deal fell apart after one game, due to a dispute over the selection of referees and the use of NBA rules (such as the twenty-four-second clock).*

CHAPTER 12

Ambassadors

I n October 1951, filming began in Hollywood on the *The Harlem Globetrotters,* a full-length feature produced by Columbia Pictures. The film was the brainchild of Alfred Palca, a New York publicist for Twentieth Century-Fox who made his living writing flack for other people's movies but had never written a script himself. In January 1950, he was sitting in a screening room with other publicists when Paramount News' "The Eyes and Ears of the World" came on, featuring the Globetrotters' debut at Madison Square Garden. He and his fellow publicists started laughing, spontaneously, at the Trotters' antics, and a lightbulb went on in Palca's head. To find out if regular audiences would react the same way, he made the rounds of four different movie theaters where the newsreel was showing: the Roxy, Radio City Music Hall, the Paramount, and the Capitol. Everywhere he went, audiences were howling.

Palca moved quickly, contacting Abe and sewing up the movie rights to the Trotters' story (the arrangement called for Abe to get 10 percent of any movie receipts). Working nights, weekends, and on his vacations, Palca crafted his first screenplay and pitched it to five Hollywood studios. Columbia Pictures bought it and budgeted $250,000 to shoot the film.

Palca's storyline revolved around a fictional player, Billy Townsend, a talented but egotistical college star who signs to play with the Trotters, then gets taken down a few notches by his own hubris, before Abe and the Trotters and his long-suffering girlfriend bring him back to his senses—just in time for the inevitable happy ending. The leading role was played by an actual Globetrotter, Bill "Rookie" Brown, a handsome, articulate player from Philadelphia. Abe's role was played by Thomas Gomez, a longtime Broadway and Hollywood character actor who had appeared in *Key Largo* with Humphrey Bogart and Lauren Bacall, and had been nominated for an Oscar, in 1947, for his role in *Ride the Pink Horse*. Gomez had the portly build for the part, and captured Abe's gravelly voiced, "Now hear this, boys"—which in real life, as in the movie, began nearly every speech. Billy Townsend's girlfriend was played by the beautiful Dorothy Dandridge, in one of her first screen roles (Abe reportedly tried to entice Chuck Cooper to stay with the Trotters, instead of signing with the Boston Celtics, by offering him the lead in the movie opposite Dandridge).

The true stars of the movie, however, were the Harlem Globe-trotters, ten of whom played themselves in the film: Goose Tatum, Marques Haynes, Frank Washington, Ermer Robinson, Duke Cumberland, Pop Gates, Babe Pressley, Clarence Wilson, Ted Strong, and Inman Jackson. The studio scenes in the film were shot in a record ten days; then a film crew went on the road with the Trotters in late October, shooting game footage for the next three weeks. It would take a year to cut and edit the film, which Columbia sched-uled for release in the fall of 1951, when the Trotters opened their season.

In 1951, the Trotters would set three world records for attendance at a basketball game, successively breaking their own mark each time. During the second World Series of Basketball, 31,684 people filled the Rose Bowl in Pasadena, including 200 movie stars, producers, di-rectors, and film industry executives. Three weeks later, in Rio de Janeiro's Maracana Estadia, official attendance at a Trotters' game was listed as 50,041, although former Trotter Frank Washington believes there were many more. Maracana had been built to host the 1950 World Cup soccer championship and, with seating for 200,000, was the largest stadium in the world. "I know there were at least 125,000 people in Rio," Washington insists today. That August, in Berlin, the Trotters would set a third world record with 75,000 in Berlin's Olympic Stadium—a mark that lasted until 2004.

In the summer of 1951, the east unit, with Goose and Marques, made a second pilgrimage to Europe, playing fifty-seven games in forty-seven cities, while the west unit made the Trotters' first tour of South America, playing forty-six games in eight countries. By the time those tours were over, it was evident that no matter how popular the Trotters were in America, they were even more so abroad.

In many countries, the Globetrotters introduced basketball for the first time. There were times when they would arrive to play a local team, only to find that the locals had no court and, in some cases, no basketballs, but were using soccer balls instead. On several occasions Abe had to have basketballs shipped over from the States, and usable courts were so scarce that he had three portable floors constructed, which he shipped all over the world, as needed. Even in countries where basketball was played, the players' skills were so rudimentary that the Trotters would often put on exhibitions and clinics for national teams. Ironically, fifty years later, some of those same national teams, which learned to play ball by watching the Harlem Globetrotters, would be defeating the U.S. Olympic "Dream Team" at the 2004 Olympics.

South American fans were so fanatical about the Globetrotters that they were willing to go to extreme lengths to see them, sometimes even resorting to violence. In Ecuador, the army had to escort the Trotters into and out of the arena because crowds had blocked the exits, and soldiers on horseback fired tear gas bombs to prevent a mob from tearing down the walls to get in. In Caracas, Venezuela, the Trotters played in a driving rainstorm. In Brazil, a torrential downpour flooded the arena, but the promoter drilled holes in the floor to drain the water, and 14,000 fans stayed to watch.

The South American tours were epic adventures filled with mystery and political intrigue. In Lima, Peru, the Trotters played in the Plaza de Toros bullring, where the players ran out through the tunnels used by the bulls, and 30,000 people turned out—more than for any bullfight. Before going to Argentina, in 1951, the American embassy warned of civil unrest against President Juan Perón, and said it could not guarantee the Trotters' safety. The Trotters went anyway, and Perón and his wife, Eva, showed up at one game. Perón invited the team to his palace the next morning, where he told them,

"America is a land of many laws that don't mean anything. Here, I don't have many laws, but they *mean something*. I want you to enjoy yourself—go where you want and do what you want to do—and if anybody gives you any trouble, you come back to this office and I will deal with it." Perón gave the players autographed photos of Eva and himself, then sent them on their way. "We had a ball in Argentina," Frank Washington recalls. The Trotters put on two clinics for the Argentine national basketball team, and Eva Perón was so impressed she decreed that "Sweet Georgia Brown" would be played at all Argentine international basketball games.

One year in La Paz, Bolivia, the local promoter absconded with the gate receipts, and the Trotters were thrown in jail, their plane was impounded, and Abe had to get the State Department to bail them out.

Wherever they went, the Globetrotters seemed to have a calming effect on political or labor strife. In Paris, the city's transit system was shut down by a general strike, so 8,200 people walked to see the Trotters play. During a 1956 visit to Argentina, after Perón had been overthrown by a military junta, the country was embroiled in a bloody civil war, yet both sides declared a moratorium to let the Globetrotters play in Buenos Aires. In Honduras, rioting students suspended their demonstrations while the Trotters were in town. In Lima, Peru, the city was paralyzed by a transit strike, with buses and streetcars being burned, yet the unions called off the strike for three days, until the Trotters left town.

By the early 1950s, Globetrotter games had become a magnet for American celebrities vacationing abroad. Art Buchwald and Issac Stern were guest scorekeepers in Paris and Spain, respectively; Clare Boothe Luce, U.S. ambassador to Italy, tossed up the ball for the opening tip in Rome, and Danny Thomas did the honors in London; Walt Disney and celebrity columnist Earl Wilson sat courtside in Rome; and Sugar Ray Robinson donned a Globetrotters' uniform in Paris to warm up with the team.

In many countries, the Globetrotters' arrival was handled like an official state visit. In Japan, they were welcomed at the airport like foreign dignitaries, and an estimated 2 million people lined the motorcade route to their hotel, where a four-story-high poster of Goose

Tatum greeted them. Over the years, the Trotters played before numerous heads of state. In Brazil, they gave a command performance for President Getúlio Vargas. In Monte Carlo, Prince Rainier III presented medallions to Abe and the players. In Athens, twelve-year-old Crown Prince Constantine of Greece tossed up the opening tip and sat on the Trotters' bench. In Cairo, Abe had a two-hour conference with Egyptian president Mohammed Naguib.

The Globetrotters' most celebrated visit with any dignitary, however, was with Pope Pius XII, who granted the team a private audience in 1951. To everyone's surprise, the pope received them again the following year, this time at his summer home, Castel Gandolfo. After the pope blessed them, Abe presented him with an autographed basketball. Curious about the game, which he had never seen, the pontiff asked for a demonstration. In the history of the Roman Catholic Church, it is safe to say that what happened next has never been repeated: the Trotters performed the Magic Circle for an audience of one. No record player was available, so Abe and the rest of the entourage whistled and clapped out "Sweet Georgia Brown," while the pope watched in amazement. Beneath his white cassock, his feet were seen tapping to the music. "My, how clever these men are," the pontiff exclaimed when it was over. "If I had not seen this with my own eyes, I would not have believed it could be done."

In more than seventy-five years of Harlem Globetrotter history, there have been so many memorable events that it is difficult to single out one that stands above all the others. Yet there is one such event, for those who witnessed it, that stands alone. Abe Saperstein and Marques Haynes, for instance, would say that what occurred in Berlin, Germany, in August 1951, was the most electrifying moment in their lives.

On their second tour of Europe, in the summer of 1951, the Globetrotters were not scheduled to play in Berlin—and for good reason. In June, a riot had occurred in Berlin during a boxing match between middleweight champ Sugar Ray Robinson and German challenger Gerhard Hecht. After Robinson was disqualified for a kidney punch,★ the German fans became so angry that they pelted the ring with beer bottles, forcing Robinson to seek cover under the ring, and a phalanx of West German police had to "battle their way out of the angry throng to deliver Robinson to his dressing room." The melee took on ugly racial overtones when Robinson's wife was kicked by one German spectator, while others confronted some black American soldiers who were present, and the crowd began chanting, "Just like Schmeling!"—a reference to Max Schmeling's claim that Joe Louis had fouled him in their second fight. In the aftermath of the riot, the German press decried both the rowdyism of the fans (it was the second riot in a week at a sporting event) and Robinson's foul punches; nonetheless, former heavyweight champ Joe Louis promptly canceled a scheduled August 8 fight in Berlin.

Berlin had been a cauldron of cold war hostilities since its partition into East and West sectors at the end of World War II, but in the summer of 1951, it was heating up even more. And without realizing it, the Harlem Globetrotters were about to be pulled down into the fire.

The first week of August, the Communist-sponsored Third World Festival of Youth and Students was scheduled to begin in East Berlin, and as many as 2 million young people from fifty countries, including 300 Americans, were expected to descend on East Berlin. The two-week-long festival, with the theme of "For Peace and Friendship—against Nuclear Weapons," would include daily concerts, dance performances, art exhibits, and sporting events, mostly featuring Soviet bloc performers. There would also be a major dose of rhetoric condemning Western rearmament, the Marshall Plan, NATO, and "imperialist warmongers." In preparation for the festival, East Berlin was bedecked with flags of many countries and with posters of Uncle Sam, depicted as an old man dripping with blood.

★ *The next day, the West Berlin Boxing Commission reversed the referee's disqualification of Robinson and ruled the bout a "no-decision," although two members of the commission resigned in protest. The referee was later suspended for failing to complete a ten-count after Robinson knocked Hecht down in the first round and for giving Hecht extra time between the first and second rounds to recover.*

West Berlin was mounting its own counterfestival, of sorts, to attract the tens of thousands of Youth Festival delegates who were expected to wander across the demarcation line into West Berlin. There were planned educational activities, music, films, television programs, and hundreds of thousands of specially printed brochures—all designed to counter the poisonous anti-Western propaganda from the other side. To the West Berlin authorities and the U.S. State Department, the Harlem Globetrotters, who were already playing in Europe, seemed like the perfect antidote.

On July 18, the U.S. embassy in Berlin sent a confidential wire to Secretary of State Dean Acheson, asking his assistance in "securing Harlem Globetrotters for Berlin" during the Youth Festival. The request was supported by the West Berlin Senate and sports council "in belief Globetrotters excellent antidote to unfavorable reactions recent Robinson-Hecht fight." Acheson was urged to use his "fullest and immediate best efforts" to arrange the game.

Dean Acheson immediately wired the U.S. high commissioner for Germany, John McCloy, who was located in Frankfurt, saying that the department "endorses recommendation on Globetrotters for this occasion." Serendipitously, the Trotters were playing in Frankfurt on August 15, so McCloy attended the game and made his pitch to Abe. Acheson and McCloy could have looked far and wide before finding anyone more patriotic, and anti-Communist, than Abe Saperstein, but he was reluctant to go to Berlin. As in previous years, Jesse Owens was traveling with the Trotters and performing at halftime, and Abe was apprehensive about taking Owens to Berlin in the wake of the Sugar Ray Robinson debacle. Fearing that Owens would be subjected to similar abuse, Abe at first refused. But McCloy argued persuasively that "this was a job for all free peoples and Americans particularly," and, eventually, Abe agreed to play.

The only remaining problem was how to get the Trotters to Berlin. Their last game in Germany was scheduled for Hamburg on Tuesday night, August 21, and they had to play in Paris two days later, before flying home to the States. That left Wednesday, August 22, as the only possible date for a game in Berlin. But it seemed impossible for the Trotters to finish playing in Hamburg late Tuesday night and get themselves, the Boston Whirlwinds (their opposition team), and, most challenging of all, their portable basketball floor to Berlin, 175 miles away, in time for an afternoon game.

The United States Air Force came to the rescue. Commissioner McCloy arranged for three C-119 "Flying Boxcars" to airlift the two teams and their floor to Berlin on Wednesday morning, where they would have a few hours to set up before the game.

On August 20, McCloy put out a press release, announcing that the Trotters would play a special exhibition in Berlin's Olympic Stadium and that Jesse Owens would be accompanying them, returning for the first time to the site where he had won four gold medals fifteen years earlier. Originally, Abe had been worried about taking Owens into the racially charged atmosphere of Berlin, but McCloy's announcement made Owens the centerpiece of the entire event. As an added incentive, McCloy announced that Abe was offering free admission to the game and was inviting "each and every resident of the Berlin area, particularly the youth of that outpost city."

The World Youth Festival had officially ended on August 19, with a peace parade, street dancing, and a huge fireworks demonstration, but thousands of young people were still roaming around West Berlin. Local radio stations and newspapers had run McCloy's announcement, but with only thirty-six hours to publicize the game, no one expected a big crowd. Basketball was not a popular game in Germany to begin with, and German teams were the worst in Europe. McCloy told Abe he'd be happy if 10,000 people showed up.

The Globetrotters flew into Berlin on the morning of the game and were bused to the stadium with a U.S. Army escort. About a mile away, a crowd of young Germans surrounded the bus, blocking the road. Some tried to climb through the windows to get at the players. Abe was convinced that a riot was about to erupt, and was wondering when "the G.I.s would get us the hell out of there before we were lynched." He was also kicking himself for being so stupid, to have brought Jesse Owens back to Berlin. Before long, however, it became clear that what the young Germans were trying to do was *touch* the players, not hurt them. It was the first clue that the day might hold something special.

The bus could hardly move the rest of the way to Olympic Stadium, but when the Trotters finally arrived, a shocking sight awaited them. The crowd had begun filing into the stadium before noon, and by game time, at two-fifteen, instead of the 10,000 people McCloy had been hoping for, the stands were nearly filled. An estimated 75,000 Germans were sitting in the great Olympic Stadium that Adolf Hitler had built as a monument to Aryan superiority; it was the largest crowd ever to watch a basketball game. As one commentator noted: "The largest crowd ever to see a basketball game in the world was drawn in the former Nazi capital by a group of Negroes coached by a Jew."

When the Trotters and Boston Whirlwinds began the game, the crowd cheered every shot, every pass, every basket. Some fans even tried to break through the police barricades to shake hands with the players. But the moment everyone was waiting for was yet to come.

At halftime, a U.S. Army helicopter appeared over the stadium, circled it three times, then slowly descended into the middle of the field. The cockpit door opened and Jesse Owens climbed out, wearing a stylish cream-colored suit. The crowd rose and gave him a standing ovation. Owens bowed and waved, and the cheers grew even louder. Then, with the Globetrotters shielding him from view, Owens did a quick change, slipping out of the business suit, and emerged onto the track wearing his original Olympic track uniform. The crowd went wild.

Owens began jogging around the track, taking a final victory lap at the scene of his greatest triumph, and as he approached each section of the stands, the people gave him a thunderous ovation, each section louder than the one before, until the cheers all merged together into a mighty wave of sound that rolled across the great bowl of the stadium and echoed back again, a primal roar of redemption from the ghosts of Germany's past. Jesse Owens ended his victory lap with a symbolic broad jump and then was escorted off the field by the Globetrotter players.*

A microphone had been set up on the track, directly below *Der Führer*'s box, where Hitler had made the opening speech of the 1936 Olympics. Owens approached the mike and began speaking in meas-

---

* *Owens landed awkwardly in the broad jump pit and hurt his ankle and had to hobble off the field, assisted by Marques Haynes and Sam Wheeler. He was later treated by a doctor.*

ured tones, obviously moved by the crowd's reception. "Words often fail on occasions like this," he began. "But I remember the good that happened here. I remember the fighting spirit and sportsmanship shown by German athletes on this field, especially by Lutz Long of Germany, the man I managed to beat in the broad jump on my last jump."

Lutz Long had been Owens's main competition in the broad jump. When Owens beat him, with a record jump of 26 feet 5 5/16 inches, Long had come over and shaken his hand, then he draped his arm around Owens and hugged him, and the two men had walked off together, laughing and joking—the blond, blue-eyed Aryan and the American Negro. All of this happened under Hitler's baleful stare, as he paced impatiently in his box, waiting to shake Long's hand— but not Owens's. Lutz Long, a national hero, had been killed in World War II, and when the Globetrotters played in Munich earlier in August, Jesse Owens had met Long's widow and visited with her.

Continuing, Owens pointed above him to *Der Führer's* old box. "Hitler stood right up there in the box," he said. "But I believe the real spirit of Germany, a great nation, was exemplified down here on the field by athletes like Long. I want to say to the young people here to be like those athletes. I want to say to all of you to stand fast with us and let us all work together to stay free and God Almighty will help us in our struggle. That is what the United States stands for and I know you are with us. God bless you all." By the time he finished, Owens was overcome with emotion. At that point, the acting mayor of West Berlin, Walter Schreiber, spontaneously came out of the stands and walked over to Owens. Leaning into the microphone, he said, in German, "Fifteen years ago on this field, Hitler refused to offer you his hand. Now I give you both of mine." He turned to Owens with outstretched hands, and they embraced. The crowd roared again, even louder than before. Some fans jumped out of the stands and rushed up to Owens, wanting to shake his hand, too. More people came, completely surrounding him, to the point that the police had to rescue him from the crowd.

By the time it was over, there were few dry eyes in Olympic Stadium. The Globetrotter players didn't understand German, so they didn't know until later what Schreiber had said, but the message came through clearly. "I think everybody was teary-eyed," Marques Haynes would say years later, in a *Sports Illustrated* interview. "And the longer you live, the more you know that you will never see anything like that again. . . . If they had had cameras like we have now, they would have had something that people could cherish till the end of time."

The second half of the game was completed with the Trotters winning, as expected, but everyone knew that the real winner that day had been Jesse Owens. After the game, the crowd poured onto the field, wanting just to touch the players, to shake their hands. The Trotters had to hole up under the stands for an hour, waiting for the crowd to disperse, and then slipped out through a side exit, trying to reach their bus. But the crowd was waiting for them, and it took another hour to make their way through the masses of people to the bus, even with U.S. Army MPs leading the way. When the team was finally able to board the bus, Jesse Owens was the only person missing. They looked out and saw him, still standing in the sea of German people, signing autographs until the end.

The U.S. State Department could not have been more pleased with what had occurred in Berlin. The Berlin office wired Dean Acheson, reporting: "Appearance Harlem Globetrotters with Jesse Owens in Olympic Stadium August 22 even more successful than anticipated." In appreciation, the State Department sent a letter to Abe, declaring: "The Globetrotters have proven themselves ambassadors of extraordinary good will wherever they have gone. On any future tours please call on the State Department of the United States for any help we can give."

When the Globetrotters returned to New York, they were given a rousing welcome at Idlewild Airport and presented with the keys to the city. Jesse Owens told the assembled press, "We did a great job in selling America."

Indeed, they had. The Globetrotters, and Owens, had done a great job of selling America as a land of freedom, equality, and opportunity for all. Unfortunately, some Americans were still not buying. At the very moment that Owens was being lauded in Berlin and the Globetrotters were being promoted as examples of America's treatment of its Negro citizens, their hometown was engulfed in a horrifying episode that painted a very different picture of America and of the festering race hatred that would explode in another few years.

In the Chicago suburb of Cicero, an African American bus driver attempted to move his family into an apartment he had legally rented, but a mob of 4,000 angry whites began rioting in protest. During three nights of violence, the mob destroyed the family's furniture, smashed windows, set the apartment complex on fire, attacked policemen and firefighters called to the scene, and eventually forced Illinois' governor Adlai Stevenson to call out the National Guard to restore order.

The Cicero riot was front-page news around the world, even though New York's governor Thomas E. Dewey insisted that it was a Communist "distortion of life in America" to claim that such a "rare incident of ruffianism represents anything basic in our country."

The *New York Times* was not so sure. While rejoicing over Jesse Owens's glorious return to Berlin, the *Times* cautioned that "we cannot forget that here at home the Hitlerite attitude toward Negroes as 'inferior beings' is still not entirely eradicated," and pointed to the Cicero riots as an example. "It is good that Jesse Owens has received his due as an individual; it will be infinitely better when his people, our Negro fellow citizens, receive everywhere and at all times their due as equal citizens of our Republic."

The Globetrotters and Jesse Owens might have been treated like royalty in Berlin and in the rest of Europe and South America, but they still could not live where they wanted in their own hometown.

★

Into the middle years of the "quiet fifties," the achievements and successes of the Harlem Globetrotters kept piling up, almost too numerous to record.

By 1951, basketball had become a year-round operation for the Trotters, and so had their marketing and merchandising. Fans could now purchase Globetrotter neckties, T-shirts, pennants, autographed photos, 45 rpm records of "Sweet Georgia Brown," and even a Globetrotter Lucky Rabbit's Foot.

That year, after returning from Berlin, Abe came up with another marketing innovation to make money during the slow period in late summer: the baseball park tours. In late August, the Trotters played a series of night games in baseball parks around the country, including Griffith Stadium in Washington, D.C., and Forbes Field in Pittsburgh. Their opposition was the United States Stars, a pickup team headlined by George Mikan, who served as player-coach, and a short, dead-eye shooter named Red Klotz.

The outdoor tour was so successful that Abe expanded it over the next few summers, eventually sending out two different teams—one playing in the South and the other in the North and Midwest (and as far north as Montreal). They played in every size ballpark, from minor league parks in Tallahassee, Birmingham, and Galveston to the most famous parks in America, including the Polo Grounds, Connie Mack Stadium, Fenway Park, and Wrigley Field. They even played a doubleheader with a major league club, the St. Louis Browns, on the final day of baseball's regular season. Bill Veeck, Abe's longtime friend, had bought the hapless Browns earlier that year, with Abe as a partner. The combination of the two most creative promoters in sports—Abe Saperstein and Bill Veeck—would create a synergy that was good for both organizations. Abe arranged for Veeck to sign Satchel Paige, Luke Easter, and other black ballplayers. And Veeck, who would go to his grave known as the "man who sent a midget to the plate," would help with Globetrotter publicity, particularly during the College All-Star tours.

When the Harlem Globetrotters had first formed in the late 1920s, basketball was a fourth-rate sport that couldn't begin to compete with major league baseball, but now Abe was going right into baseball's most hallowed shrines, in the middle of the baseball season, and drawing the crowds.

On October 24, 1951, Columbia Pictures released *The Harlem Globetrotters* in theaters across the country. Columbia had been so impressed with the final cut that it gave the film a "double A" rating, meaning it would be promoted as if it were a million-dollar film, although it had cost only $250,000.

"Those Champs—Those Scamps—in a Full-Length Fun Hit!"—the movie posters read. "The Miracle Men of Sports . . . All Their Arena Razzle Dazzle in a Rousing Big Drama!"

The movie opened to favorable reviews and even better crowds, playing opposite such films as *Death of a Salesman* and *High Noon*. It would enjoy a long shelf life, particularly in drive-in theaters, where it would still be showing late in 1952. Since Abe was getting a percentage of the gross, he was delighted with the film's success, but he was proudest of a letter from a G.I. stationed in Japan, who wrote: "I have just seen your movie. I liked it much better than 'Death of a Salesman.' "

The film's producer was Buddy Adler, who had just made *Woman of Distinction* with Rosalind Russell, and would later produce such classics as *From Here to Eternity* and *South Pacific*. It was directed by Phil Brown, a veteran actor but first-time director, who would soon get swept up in the hysteria of the McCarthy hearings and, at the urging of Ronald Reagan, president of the Screen Actors Guild (SAG), be placed on the Hollywood blacklist in 1952. Unable to work in America, Brown moved to London. Years later, he would be known to later generations for playing Uncle Owen Lars in *Star Wars*.

The Globetrotters' film was so successful in the United States that it was distributed overseas, with the encouragement of the United States Information Service (USIS), which saw it as effective propaganda. In October 1953, a USIS public affairs officer in Martinique, where the film was showing, sent a memo to his Washington headquarters entitled "Commercially Distributed Film Advances USIS Objectives," urging that the film be distributed widely around the world to "enlighten members of the local populace who have been led astray by Communist depiction of the U.S. Negro as a downtrodden, persecuted, 'second-class' citizen." In a glowing review, he described particular scenes that showed Billy Townsend being welcomed in an American university, allowed to "frequent acceptable hotels," live in a modern apartment, and be offered over $1,000 per month to play basketball.

In the kind of supreme irony that Hollywood could appreciate, by the time that memo was written, both the producer and director of this effective weapon in the battle of Americanism versus

Communism had been blacklisted, their film careers destroyed, and the African American stars of the movie—the Globetrotter players, including Bill "Rookie" Brown, who played the part of Billy Townsend—had received only two weeks' salary for the ten days of shooting.* In Brown's case, Abe paid him a total of $275 for the two weeks, but while enjoying himself in Hollywood, Brown asked for $330 in advances, which was deducted against his salary. In the final accounting, the star of the film ended up *owing* Abe $55 for making the movie. And despite the favorable depiction of the "U.S. Negro" on the screen, during the shooting of the film Brown and the other Trotters were forced to stay in a "colored" hotel in Los Angeles, and Brown himself would not have been allowed to enroll in many universities, frequent many "acceptable hotels," or live in many "modern apartments" in America (certainly not in Cicero)—and he would never make $1,000 a month playing basketball for the Harlem Globetrotters.

What mattered most, however, was that it all looked good on the silver screen.

The Harlem Globetrotters were now so popular that it was becoming difficult to top their past exploits. In 1952, however, Abe came up with the grandest scheme of all: an around-the-world tour, spanning 50,000 miles, thirty-three countries, and four continents. He had been intrigued by the idea since the Trotters' first visit to Europe, and by the fall of 1951, he was ready to make it happen. And after the success of the Berlin game, he figured the U.S. State Department would eagerly sign on as a cosponsor.

For twenty-five years, Abe had been selling the Trotters to promoters and sportswriters in every hick town in America, and he had no trouble closing the deal with the U.S. State Department. In November, he first broached the idea of a world tour in a letter to Assistant Secretary of State Jack K. McFall. In December, Abe met in Washington with officials from the State Department and the Inter-

---

* *Abe's contract with Columbia Pictures called for him to pay the players, rather than the studio, supposedly at the minimum rates in the Screen Actors Guild contract.*

national Information and Educational Exchange Program. Soon thereafter, Secretary of State Dean Acheson sent a circular airgram to diplomatic and consular officers around the world, saying that the department was backing the Globetrotters' world tour as "ambassadors of good will, particularly in countries that are critical of U.S. treatment of Negroes." Acheson was optimistic that the Trotters would be "an effective answer to Communist charges of racial prejudice in the U.S.A."

By February 4, 1952, the State Department sent out a schedule to sixty-nine foreign service posts, listing every date and city on the tour. American consulates in Belgrade and Bangkok wrote back, begging to have Yugoslavia and Thailand added to the list.

The scale of what Abe was attempting to do was enormous. The Trotters would leave New York on April 19 for the Panama Canal, play their way across South America, Europe, North Africa, the Middle East, Asia, the Philippines, Singapore, Hong Kong, Korea, Japan, Okinawa, Guam, and end up in Hawaii on October 15. Only two years earlier, they had managed the first transcontinental College All-Star tour, with 18 games in 17 cities, but now they were increasing that exponentially to 141 games in 168 days!

Marie Linehan and the front office staff in Chicago had developed a basic template that could be extrapolated to any tour, but this was taxing their capabilities to the limit. Marie started cranking out letters to everybody making the tour, detailing the requirements for passport applications, passport photos, birth certificates, smallpox inoculations, and visa applications for every country. Abe pulled in other people to help with the logistics, including his sister Fay and Walter Kennedy, who ran the New York office; Harry Hannin, who handled much of the advance work before the Trotters would arrive; Eddie Gottlieb, owner of the Philadelphia Warriors; and Bob Karstens, still playing on the opposition team, who also built the portable wooden floors, weighing seven tons apiece, that would be shipped to venues without basketball courts. In the middle of the night, Abe telephoned Dave Zinkoff, a noted Philadelphia sports announcer (who had gone on both European tours), and browbeat him into taking a job as the "general manager–traveling secretary–announcer–transportation manager–room reservation clerk–treasurer." Also, he wanted Zinkoff to keep a running diary, which eventually would be turned into a book, *Around the World with the Harlem Globetrotters*.

"This is going to be the greatest tour in sports history," Abe declared, and who could possibly disagree? On April 19, 1952, one unit of Trotters flew to Panama and played the next five weeks in Latin America. On May 30, the main entourage—twenty-nine people, including eleven Trotters, the New York Celtics (led by Red Klotz and Tony Lavelli, who also played accordion at halftime), two referees, four halftime acts, plus Abe, Gottlieb, Kennedy, and Zinkoff—left New York for the European leg of the tour. Goose Tatum and Sweetwater Clifton would be joining up with them later, due to family illness. Abe had bought two buses and had them shipped over ahead of time, along with his red Cadillac—"To add a touch of class," he would say—which would draw crowds wherever they went.

They landed at Shannon Airport, in Ireland, and the only Irishman on the plane, Walter Kennedy, kneeled down and kissed the Auld Sod. The tour had officially begun. They would be gone for four months, playing nearly every night in another city. Airfare alone would cost nearly $200,000. In each country, they had to deal with monetary exchange rates, not just to live but to figure out how to take their gate receipts out of the country when they left.

They played in a driving rainstorm in Reims, France, with the players wearing vinyl rain hats and jackets and holding umbrellas. They played before fans in Egypt, who, as Zinkoff put it, "didn't know a dribble from a Dodge." They played midnight games in Spain, following the afternoon siesta and dinners that began at 9 P.M. They went for camel rides in Egypt, visited General George Patton's grave in Luxembourg, and had their luggage stolen in Madrid. In addition to their basketball games, Abe and the Trotters held press conferences, did interviews on local radio, appeared at schools and factories, and were hosted at receptions in many countries.

All along the way, U.S. foreign service posts were sending back enthusiastic reports to Foggy Bottom about the fantastic publicity the Trotters were generating, often attaching newspaper clippings to prove it. "The visit of the Globetrotters thus pointed out a brighter picture of the negroes' place in American life," wrote the U.S. consul in Asunción, Paraguay. The Algerian consulate wired for permission to spend $300 on a reception for the Globetrotters, in order to counteract "local Commie output on U.S. race relations."

Local press coverage was equally impressive. In Beirut, for instance, *L'Orient* reported that nearly 8,000 spectators "were unanimous in describing the visitors as artists rather than players"; *Le Soir's* report even bordered on the supernatural:

> Rivaling the form and ability of "black devils" . . . the spectacle of the Harlem Globetrotters is impossible to describe. One must see it. . . . Teamwork between the different elements reached such a degree of perfection that one began to wonder for a while whether they were human beings of flesh and blood, or automatons, or even a faked film. That is to say a strong impression of the unreal and the superhuman mastered the public and made them utter "ohs" of admiration and "Is it possible?"

In Malaysia, even the usually anti-American *Straits Times* admitted: "Whoever thought of sending the Harlem Globetrotters, those very likeable gentlemen, to Asia certainly hit upon a splendid propaganda stunt. Here was living proof that the American Negro was no downtrodden wretch though, apparently, it's a bit harder for a coloured man to buy a cup of coffee in certain U.S. cafes than it is to make good at basketball."

By the time the Globetrotters played their final game in Honolulu, on October 5, and flew back to San Francisco on a Pan Am Stratocruiser, passing the Golden Gate Bridge, they had traveled 51,000 miles and played before an estimated 1.5 million people. "I'll be lucky to break even on the whole thing, but who cares," Abe said, although he predicted that he'd never try it again. "A trip like this is too hard on everyone who makes it. But it has been the supreme thrill of my lifetime." Recalling how people had laughed at him for naming his team the Globetrotters, he added, "Now I've done it."

Two months after returning, the Globetrotters got a shocking reminder that America had not changed in their absence: they were banned from playing at Louisiana State University by Troy H. Middleton, the university president. Middleton, a retired U.S. Army general and the hero of the 1943 Sicily campaign, refused to allow a black team to play in the LSU gymnasium for fear it would destroy "our way of life." The Trotters had been invited to LSU by the Baton Rouge Kids' Baseball Clinic, a nonprofit group, and the LSU letterman's club. Newspapers in France and elsewhere around the world gave big play to LSU's snub of the Globetrotters, but most American papers, including the *New York Times,* ignored it completely.

"Welcome home, Ambassadors of Goodwill."

CHAPTER 13

"Freedom Now!"

In an organization as old and storied as the Harlem Globetrotters, it is difficult to single out one defining moment when everything changed—when the organization changed course and began heading in a different direction. Moments like that are sometimes too subtle to detect, or they are obscured by the passage of time, fading memories, or the deaths of those who were there. But there is one such moment in the history of the Harlem Globetrotters. It is the point, if one were graphing the nine decades of Globetrotters' history, where the line would turn downward. Not permanently, because there would be later points when the line would turn upward again, but nonetheless, a slow, gradual descent would begin at this moment in time.

That point occurred on October 31, 1953, when Marques Haynes quit the team. There would be no official announcement for another ten days, but it was over long before that. On October 8, when fifty-seven Trotter vets and rookies had reported to training camp at St. Anselm's gym on the South Side, most of the buzz was about two rookies: seven-foot-one All-American center Walter Dukes, whom Abe had managed to sign after a bidding war with the NBA, and Junius Kellogg, from Manhattan College, who had blown the whistle on the 1951 point-shaving scandal that had nearly destroyed the college game. Marques Haynes was mentioned, in passing, as being the captain of the team. One would never suspect that there were any problems. In another few days, however, he would be gone.

Abe had every reason to keep quiet about Marques's departure. For one thing, a new Hollywood movie on the Globetrotters was in the works, with most of the footage having already been shot the previous spring, and, like the first film, it was *supposed* to feature Goose and Marques. Telling the studio that Marques was gone might queer the deal, yet a film about the Globetrotters *without* Marques Haynes seemed inconceivable. Second, the preseason publicity packets were already in the mail, and Abe had been advertising Goose and Marques all over the country, and doing it so cleverly that it sometimes appeared as if they would be playing in two or three cities on the same night. If those weren't reasons enough to keep the bad news under his hat, Abe was an eternal optimist, and was still hoping that Marques would change his mind and return.

But in his heart, Abe had to know better. Marques Haynes was a man of conviction, and he had told Abe, flat out, as Abe was walking out of their one and only contract discussion, "You'll never have to worry about me again."

Which led to the most important reason for keeping the news quiet: if Marques had truly quit the team, then Abe was hoping to get something for him. To trade him or sell him to another team, as he had done with Sweetwater Clifton in 1950, when it became clear that Clifton was dissatisfied and was going to leave when his contract expired.

When the word finally did get out, Abe would claim that his problems with Marques had begun last spring, after the College All-Star tour, when Marques refused to go on the European tour.★ But in reality, their problems started long before that. One could go back to the time when Abe told Marques, "A Negro doesn't need as much money as a white man"—a comment that Marques would never forgive or forget. Or to the time Abe sold Clifton to the New York Knicks, and Clifton complained that he didn't think Abe had "the right to deal me off like that" without his sanction. Or the time when Abe *refused* to sell Marques to an NBA team, when he could have been the first black player in the league. Or even to the times when

---

★ *The Globetrotters had been invited to London as part of Queen Elizabeth's coronation.*

Abe had come in the locker room after a big win and, in a generous moment, tried to give Marques a bonus—stuffed a twenty-dollar bill, or maybe even a fifty, in his hand, and said, "Great game, Marques, have yourself some fun tonight"—and Marques, instead of saying, "Thanks, Skip," like the other players, had handed back the cash and said coolly, "No, Abe, just put it on my salary."

Marques Haynes was a different breed of cat. When he signed on in 1946, he was the first college graduate ever to play for Abe, and he had not lost his perspective—or his business sense—in the intervening years. He was a star, he had a singular talent, he could have played for any team in the country, and he knew it.

In the end, Abe waited until the season was nearly three weeks old to announce, in a tiny one-paragraph release, that Marques Haynes was no longer a Harlem Globetrotter and had been sold to the NBA's Philadelphia Warriors. It was no coincidence that the Warriors were owned by Abe's good friend Eddie Gottlieb, and that Abe was a major stockholder in the team. No selling price was announced, although a figure of $30,000 was later reported.

That could have been the end of it. But when a reporter called Marques the next day at his home in Sand Springs, Oklahoma, he declared, unequivocally, that he would not report to the Warriors and, furthermore, might even start his own team.

This was getting messy.

Eager to tell his side of the story, Abe sought out his most loyal black sportswriters, including the *Chicago Defender*'s Fay Young, who was on Abe's payroll as a talent scout, and Wendell Smith and Rollo Wilson of the *Pittsburgh Courier*. Abe's explanation was that a "new form of contract" had been devised that season, and forty out of forty-one players had signed it. Marques was the lone holdout. According to Abe, Marques had one year left on a three-year contract and the new contract would have included a substantial raise for Marques, for the fourth year in a row. Given Marques's refusal to sign, Abe had dealt him to the Warriors, who needed a point guard. "If he refuses to report, I will suspend him," Abe said. "And I hope he will change his mind."

A week went by with no word from Marques, so Abe turned up the heat. Speaking to reporters at a press luncheon in Chicago, he insisted that the "new form of contract" had been necessitated by a recent U.S. Supreme Court ruling, and included a clause whereby Marques could be traded or sold to any other team at Abe's discretion. "He is legally bound to go through with the deal," he said. "If he refuses to play with [the Warriors], he won't play with any team." Afterward, Wendell Smith relayed Abe's threat in a sensational headline: "Report to Philly Warriors or You Won't Play at All!"

The Supreme Court ruling that Abe referred to had upheld major league baseball's standard player contract, including its controversial "reserve clause," which bound a player to his original team owner for life. The court also upheld the legality of the "ineligible list," which blacklisted players who refused to report to clubs to whom they had been sold or traded.

There are inconsistencies in Abe's argument, however, even on its face. First of all, the Supreme Court ruling had been handed down only the day before Marques was traded, on November 9, and he had quit ten days prior to that. So any "new form of contract" must have been designed prior to the ruling. Further, the ruling applied to baseball's major *leagues,* whereas the Globetrotters were an independent organization, further weakening Abe's claim that this had anything to do with the Supreme Court. More likely, Abe wanted to make it explicit in all player contracts that he had the right to trade or sell any player at any time.* Finally, Marques's contract was an *individual* agreement with Abe Saperstein, not with any league. Unlike the NBA and major league baseball, which had standard player contracts, Abe did not have draft rights or territorial rights over his players, or any kind of reserve clause. The idea that he could sell Marques Haynes to another team would be like him "selling" Marie Linehan to Phil Wrigley, the owner of the Cubs, or the owner of a hometown grocery store selling his employees to a tire dealer. Aside from the legal restrictions of his contract, Marques Haynes was a free agent.

The controversy continued to simmer for several weeks, with still no word from Marques, although Wendell Smith did report, quoting "reliable sources," that Marques had "objected to that particular part of the contract" and had "warned Saperstein that he would

---

* At least by 1961, if not before, Globetrotter player contracts did contain such language.

balk if he was sold elsewhere." For his part, Abe kept throwing fuel on the fire, telling the *Defender*:

> "Haynes, personally, is a very nice fellow. I've done more for him than any athlete I've had. He is an intelligent person, but has not had the courtesy to answer my wires and letters. This has rankled me no end. . . . His salary has quadrupled in the past four years, and he owes me money. I'm going to send him another telegram. If he doesn't answer I'm through with it. . . . I'll make a move to protect my contract if he plays with someone else."

In the fifty years that have transpired, Marques Haynes has never told his side of the story—and still refuses to discuss some details—but based on what he will say, his position becomes fairly clear. To begin with, he disputes nearly everything Abe said, and every word Fay Young or Wendell Smith wrote about the situation (neither reporter ever interviewed him about what happened, and Marques didn't trust them anyway, given their relationship with Abe). According to Marques, he did not have another year left on his contract, but had already fulfilled the terms of his previous multiyear deal. His "refusal" to go on the 1953 European tour had nothing to do with his contract negotiations; in fact, he hadn't gone to Europe in 1952, either, during the "around the world" tour, because he wanted a break from the daily grind. He finds the idea that Abe offered him a "substantial raise" laughable. "Abe Saperstein never gave anybody a substantial raise," he says, and denies that his salary quadrupled in four years, although "that wouldn't have been hard to do."

"I started out [in 1946] only making $250 a month, and even in 1950 I was only making $350 or $400 a month," he says. However, his decision to quit had nothing to do with his salary or with any "new" clause giving Abe the right to sell or trade him. He never saw any such clause, although he would have refused to sign any contract that contained it. "It may have been in there, but we never got that far," he says.

What actually happened, according to Marques, was that he came to training camp in October without a contract, as his previous one had expired. He and Abe were supposed to sit down and discuss a new deal, but the meeting didn't happen until after the season began. Finally, after a game in Wilmette, Illinois—just outside Chicago—they sat down in Abe's office to talk. The entire meeting lasted ten minutes. Abe handed Marques a new, multiyear contract to sign, but there were a couple of clauses that Marques wanted to discuss. Abe refused. "He wouldn't even talk about them," Marques says. "It was 'take it or leave it.'" Exactly what those clauses were, Marques has never said, but he did complain later about "fringe issues," such as appearance fees, endorsements, and movie deals. By 1953, Marques's and Goose's photos were being used in newspaper ads and on posters for various products (they appeared together on a Coca-Cola ad, Marques also endorsed a hair-straightening cream, and Goose endorsed Beechnut gum), but Abe was allegedly getting most, if not all, of the income. In addition, some former Trotters believe that Abe had promised to sell Marques and Goose a percentage of the team, but then refused.

Whatever the issues were, Marques refused to sign the contract. Abe got mad, stood up, and started to walk out. As he was leaving, Marques told him, "Once I leave this office and that door closes, you'll never have to worry about me again."

Abe kept right on walking. And so did Marques. He went back to the hotel, packed his stuff, and caught a flight to Tulsa, where his wife picked him up at the airport and drove him home to Sand Springs. "It was time for me to leave," he says today.

Marques spent a few weeks at home, considering his options, and decided to put together his own team. He had only $252 to his name, and bankers in Sand Springs and Tulsa wouldn't loan him any money, but his wife's teaching job was enough for them to live on, so he decided to take the gamble. He pulled together some of his old friends from Oklahoma, guys he had played with in high school and college, and named his team the Marques Haynes All-Stars. Within a month, he was back on the road again, playing ball, as he would be doing for another forty years.

As for Abe, Inman Jackson reportedly tried to convince him that Marques's issues were legitimate and he should negotiate, but Abe wouldn't budge. He had been through this so many times before, with Runt Pullins, Sonny Boswell, and other players who had quit him over the years, that he knew the drill by heart. And he used the same approach this time as in the past: find a replacement, tell the world he was the best ever, and sell the hell out of it! He already had a replacement dribbler in the pipeline named Leon Hillard, who had signed right out of high school, and had been understudying Marques for two years. By early December, Abe's loyalists at the *Defender* and the *Courier* were already trumpeting Hillard as the second coming. "Replacing Haynes for the Trotters was a new Chicago dribbling marvel, Leon Hillard. . . . Although he has not attained the professional finesse of Haynes, Hillard was quite a sensation," the *Defender* wrote.

Hillard was a fine dribbler, but he was no Marques Haynes. In fact, he didn't try to be. From that point on, Globetrotter dribblers relied on a standardized, choreographed seventeen-second routine that borrowed a few of Marques's slides and his one-knee action, but it was the same every night. They would never again attempt the spontaneous, improvisational style that Marques had invented. They didn't have the creativity or the freedom to break out of that formulaic mold. It was entertaining to the fans, but it was no longer true artistry.

In public, Abe acted as if he didn't miss Marques at all, but behind the scenes he spent months trying to convince him to return. "He wasn't man enough to contact me himself," says Marques, "but he did it through other people." Abe dispatched various emissaries, including road secretary Winfield Welch; his lawyer, Allan Bloch; and his brother Morry Saperstein to contact Marques. They sent letters and telegrams and, when the Trotters played Tulsa in early 1954, Morry Saperstein even tried in person. "But the reason I left was because of Abe—not anybody else," Marques says. "Abe's mind was too small to make those attempts himself."

What happened with Marques Haynes was symbolic of a larger metamorphosis that was occurring with Abe. Beginning around this same time, he began to change as a person. The Trotters were on top of the world—they were packing Madison Square Garden, they were in the movies, appearing on Ed Sullivan's *Toast of the Town,* playing command performances before kings and popes—and Abe was making more money than he ever had in his life. After all the years of struggling to survive, that newfound wealth may have gone to his head.

To the outside world, or at least to the white people around him, the change may not have been noticeable. He was still the same jovial, generous, hardworking little guy with the big ideas. Still the same old Abe. But some of his players noticed the difference.

"When I first went out [with the Trotters], Abe was a great person," recalls Frank Washington. "He used to take the guys to dinner, buy us steaks anytime. . . . But he changed after he started making money. He wouldn't do anything for you, and didn't have respect for us."

At the beginning of every season, Abe would still have the players over to his house for dinner, but at other times he seemed colder, more distant, and more concerned with the trappings of money and power. And clearly, the gap between his lifestyle and that of his players was growing wider. In the old days, he had eaten the same lousy food and had even stayed in "colored" hotels with them on a few occasions, but now he was staying at the swankiest hotels in every city. In Los Angeles, he always booked a room at the Hollywood Roosevelt Hotel, the fabulous "Hotel of the Stars," while the players were at the Watkins Hotel in South Central.* He was driving his bright red Cadillac down the Champs-Elysées in Paris, with beautiful singers on his arm, and traffic backed up, gawking at the little man in the fancy car, while the players were still riding in converted school buses with seats too cramped to stretch their legs. He was eating his favorite chopped liver at Isow's in London's Soho district, wild strawberries in the Rotisserie Perigourdine in Paris, or roast beef at Toots Shor's in New York, while they were still picking up greasy burgers from the back door of slophouses in Mobile and Des Moines, and spending their own money to boot (the players got no meal money in the United States, except on the College All-Star tour). He had

---

* *The Watkins was the most celebrated black-owned hotel in L.A.; it was where Duke Ellington and other famous entertainers stayed in the 1940s and '50s.*

traded in his rumpled black suit and high-water pants for sharkskin suits, alligator shoes, and a Globetrotter tie, while they were still forced to wear the same stinking uniforms night after night, which they rinsed in hotel sinks or doused with French colognes when the uniforms became calcified with sweat and funk. He was hanging out with celebrities and movie stars, syndicated columnists and senators, getting his picture snapped with dignitaries from around the world. In fact, *he* was a celebrity himself, or desperately wanted to be, and spent a lot of time and money pursuing it. He cultivated celebrities with the same doggedness that he cultivated sportswriters and promoters. Every time he met a famous person, a photographer was always handy to take the requisite publicity still, which was then autographed and hung on the wall of his office. He wrote repeated letters to the celebrities he met, whether they responded or not; sent Christmas gifts, thank-you notes, and postcards from his travels.

And slowly it all began to go to his head. A cult of personality began to develop in the Globetrotter organization. It even showed up in the Globetrotter yearbooks, the programs that were sold at every game. The players each got a one-paragraph bio in eight-point type and a thumbnail photo in the centerfold, but Abe got a two-page spread with slick Madison Avenue photos, fawning testimonials, biographical profiles, even articles on his favorite foods and restaurants. The yearbooks had started out being about the Globetrotters, but increasingly they were about Abe. His picture was plastered everywhere, usually hanging out with someone famous. There was even a regular feature called "Abe and His Friends," which showcased him with Bob Hope, Joe Louis, Steve Allen, Hank Greenberg, and assorted pretty women. Abe was always beaming, with the same winning smile he'd had since childhood, but sadly, more and more, it looked staged and frozen, almost robotic, as if the smile were held on with Scotch tape. Abe had always had an ego, which was part of his drive and ambition, but in the old days he had promoted himself as a way to promote the team, as a means to an end—but now *he* was the end.

The players noticed it because they were around him in unguarded moments, when the cameras weren't there. Abe liked the players to call him Skip (as in Skipper), but they called him "Little

Caesar" behind his back and joked about his Napoleon complex. He was the boss, however, so they catered to his ego. Players let him win at gin rummy or whist. They laughed too hard at his jokes. When he came to the gym and tried to show off his basketball skills—taunting some six-foot-eight newcomer, "See if you can block my shot"—the old-timers would have already warned the rookies, "Don't you dare, or you'll be going home." The players pretended to pay attention to his coaching instructions, but ignored them when he left.

One problem was that the organization was now so large, and Abe was so busy, that he didn't really get to know the players as he had in the past. They might not see him for weeks, and then he'd show up for one game, in a big city, and be gone again. Also, he was now much older than his players. In the beginning, he and Inman Jackson, Kid Oliver, Toots Wright and the original Trotters had been from the same generation, but, other than Inman, all those guys were long gone. Even most of the veterans from the 1940s were gone. Ted Strong and Bernie Price had retired, and Babe Pressley, Duke Cumberland, Ermer Robinson, and Pop Gates were Trotter coaches.

With as many as four units operating year-round, plus the farm teams, there had been a huge influx of new players in the past few years. And these players were from a different generation. They were young black men who had come of age *after* World War II, with higher expectations about what the world owed them and what life should be like. They were unwilling to put up with restrictions and barriers that their fathers had accepted in the past, whether from American society at large or from their boss. More and more of the players had gone to college, and were more educated and sophisti-cated than the players Abe was used to. After signing with the Trotters, they had traveled to Bangkok and Buenos Aires, had expe-rienced the night life of Amsterdam and Copenhagen, had seen Gay Paree—and were not inclined to be kept down on *anybody's* farm. These ballplayers had other options now: the NBA was out there, just beyond the horizon, and although the league had an unwritten quota system, allowing only one or two black players per team, every ballplayer believed that he was that one.

This new generation of players included: J. C. Gibson, a six-foot-eight baby-faced giant from Los Angeles, who signed with the Trotters out of high school; Bob "Showboat" Hall, another Detroit player, only six-foot-two but built like a Sherman tank, who was the show-man on the western unit and was developing his own legions of fans; "Tex" Harrison, one of the first black players selected for the Col-lege All-Star team, who had averaged 25 points a game in college and had immediately hit it off with Abe; Bobby Milton, from Fort Wayne; Alvin Clinkscales, from the University of Bridgeport; Willie Gardner, one of the most highly regarded players ever to come out of Indi-anapolis; Chuck Holton, a bright college grad who would be made a player-coach after his second year; Harry Sykes, from Kentucky State; Andy Johnson, a six-foot-six bulldozer from the University of Portland (who later played in the NBA); two New Yorkers, Carl Green and Stanley "Chico" Burrell; and "the Big Three," a trio of stars from Wayne State University, including "Jumping Johnny" Kline, an Olympic-class high jumper who could, according to leg-end, pick a quarter off the top of the backboard, and backcourt mates Charlie Primus and Ernest Wagner.

During the war, Abe had been paying his *top* players, including Pressley, Strong, and Bernie Price, less than $200 a month, and by the early 1950s, the average player salary was $400 a month. In 1952, Ducky Moore, starting his eighth season, was still stuck at $400. (Goose Tatum was making five times that, but he was the exception.) But this new generation wanted more. In 1953, when Abe offered Johnny Kline a $400 starting salary, he turned it down. "I was mak-ing more than that working in my family's business in Detroit," Kline recalls. "He raised it to $500, so I decided to try it for a year."

In some ways, Abe was losing touch not only with his ballplay-ers, but with the game of basketball. As late as 1951, he was calling for a return to the center jump after every basket, arguing that the game was being ruined without it. And he still wanted his players shooting the traditional two-hand set shot, instead of the jump shot that was revolutionizing basketball. Even in the 1960s, Trotter players reportedly were still afraid to shoot jumpers if Abe was at the game. "The thing about Abe you gotta remember, basketball had changed," says Kline, now a Ph.D. and the director of the Black Legends of Pro-fessional Basketball foundation in Detroit. "Abe came from an era where two-hand set shots were the main weapon, but now guys were shooting jump shots on the run. Even when we were running the weave, Abe wanted you to come to a full stop and shoot a set shot. But now guys were playing *above* the rim. Black players had a lot of rhythm to their game, they wanted to be moving."

As the players became more demanding and the game more complicated, Abe seemed to wall himself off, to become more hard-shelled, more of a tycoon. He could still reach out, at times, and form close relationships with some of the new players, such as Tex Harrison. And he still had tight bonds with some of the old-timers, particularly Inman Jackson, Ermer Robinson, and Pop Gates, guys who were still on his payroll and beholden to him, yet who shared a loyalty and mutual respect that transcended their paychecks. With the younger guys, however, it was a different story. Abe could still turn on the old charm, but it was increasingly reserved for the spotlights and the stars, while his players retreated ever further into the background, standing in his shadow.

In January 1954, Abe's ego got another huge boost when *Go, Man, Go* opened in 11,000 theaters across the country. It was the second full-length motion picture about the Globetrotters in three years. After the success of *The Harlem Globetrotters,* screenwriter Alfred Palca had written a second script, formed an independent production company, and raised $175,000 to shoot the film. He managed to line up Dane Clark, a well-known Hollywood actor, to play the part of Abe Saperstein, and distinguished cinematographer James Wong Howe to direct his first film. Looking for a black actor to play Inman Jackson, Palca hired a relative unknown, Sidney Poitier, who owned a rib joint in Harlem. Once again, the Harlem Globetrotters played themselves. The film was shot in New York in May 1953, with the game footage taken in New Jersey, Boston, and Madison Square Garden (including footage cobbled together from the College All-Star tour).

One morning, as Palca was leaving for the set, two strangers were waiting for him in the lobby of his Manhattan apartment building. They were FBI agents, who accused him of being a communist. Among their charges was that he had hired a black man, Poitier. In the 1940s, Palca had joined several left-wing groups, signed various petitions, and contributed money to Russian war relief, but he was no communist. It didn't matter. With McCarthyism sweeping the country, several studios refused to distribute the film. Finally, United Artists agreed, provided Palca take his name off the film. He reluctantly agreed. When the film was released, Palca's brother-in-law was credited as the producer, and his cousin, a Connecticut pediatrician, was listed as the screenwriter. Palca's movie career was over, but forty-three years later, in 1997, his screenplay credit would finally be restored. He died a year later.

Go, Man, Go was very different from the first film. *The Harlem Globetrotters* had been about the team and fictional player Billy Townsend, but *Go, Man, Go* was the Abe Saperstein story, or at least a Hollywood version of it. The emphasis was clear from the opening crawl: "This is the story of a sports wonder of our time. More exactly, it's the story of the man who made it so—one of those fellows with a stubborn idea, who never knows when he's licked—a combination hard to stop."

The film was a box office hit and received favorable reviews, including in the *New York Times,* which described it as "the story of the faith and tenacity of one man." In another ironic twist that only Hollywood could imagine, the film ends with Marques Haynes making a game-winning shot; then he and Abe walk slowly off the court together, their arms around each other. Of course, by the time the film was released, Marques was no longer on the team, and he and Abe were engaged in a bitter court battle (the first of many), as Abe had sued him for using the word "Globetrotters" in his advertising and for copying the Trotters' uniforms.* But Hollywood loves a happy ending.

On May 17, 1954, the U.S. Supreme Court handed down the landmark *Brown v. Board of Education* decision that sounded the death knell for segregation in public schools, although it would take

---

* *In February 1954, a federal district court judge ruled in Abe's favor, ordering Marques to discontinue using any variation of "Globetrotters" in his advertising and remove stars from his uniforms, which were similar to the ones on the Trotters' uniforms.*

decades to actually end it. A year later, Rosa Parks refused to move to the back of the bus and the Montgomery bus boycott was launched, bringing a young Baptist minister named Martin Luther King Jr. to national prominence.

The world was changing. There was a sense of anticipation, a quickening of the spirit and the mind, as a *movement* began to take shape. A great seismic shift was under way, still mostly indiscernible, but the underground plates were grinding against each other, the pressure building toward a quake that would shake the foundations of American society.

The Harlem Globetrotters were ballplayers, not activists, but they were *out there* in America every day, crisscrossing the country, traveling on every highway in every state, stopping for food and gas, checking into hotels, and trying to buy a cold beer after a tough game. If any blacks had their fingers on the pulse of America, it was the Globetrotters. They felt it every day. And if a change was coming, they would sense it first.

What they saw, however, was disheartening. They were among the most celebrated black men in America, so one might expect their treatment to be better than the norm. And while the ball games were going on, it was. By the mid-1950s, they were beyond the point where local teams might try to rough them up or local refs try to cheat them out of a win. In fact, by that time they seldom played local teams, as they were usually bringing both their opposition team and the ref with them. The last egregious incident of racial prejudice affecting a game had occurred in 1952, when the president of LSU refused to let the Trotters play on campus, but there had been no other incidents since.

In the South, however, there were still many places that refused to let blacks and whites play each other, so the Trotters would have to play another black team, such as the Kansas City Stars or Chicago Brown Bombers. It was sometimes hard to tell where the demarcation line was on a map, as the rules varied from city to city and state to state. In 1954, for instance, the Trotters were allowed to play white teams in Savannah, Raleigh, and in Spartanburg and Greenville, South Carolina; but had to play black-on-black in Memphis, Atlanta, and Miami.

In Jackson, Mississippi, segregation was carried to such an extreme that when the Trotters played the Brown Bombers, no white people were allowed to be in the building. There was even a black referee and scorer, and the sheriff guarded the door to keep whites at bay. In Birmingham, the Trotters still played a day game for a white audience and a night game for blacks. Atlanta was slightly more progressive, as whites and blacks could watch the same game, but blacks had to enter through a side door and sit in a segregated balcony.

Once the game ended, however, the Trotters' fame provided no buffer against racial discrimination. They may have been the "Fabulous Magicians of Basketball" while the game was going on, but they were just like any other Negroes once it ended. W. E. B. DuBois described the phenomenon of "double-consciousness," in which African Americans are always aware of being American *and* black, no matter what they're doing. For the Globetrotters, it didn't take long after the final gun sounded to be reminded.

In Jacksonville, Florida, they tried to get a room at a nice downtown hotel, but were refused. The next morning, on their way out of town, they saw in the local paper that "Judy, the Bowling Chimpanzee," who once appeared on the television show *I've Got a Secret*, was staying at the hotel that had turned them away. As Tex Harrison recalls, "They gave the Bowling Chimp the biggest suite and all the bananas she could eat, but they wouldn't let us stay."

There were many times when the Trotters were prohibited from eating or sleeping where they wanted, which was demeaning, but not inherently dangerous. But there was one forbidden object that could get you killed if you were even suspected of desiring it: white women. In one southern town, shortly after Johnny Kline joined the team, he and Inman Jackson were selling programs before the game. When an attractive white woman walked by, Kline eyed her as she passed. Inman Jackson started sweating and looking around nervously.

"What's wrong?" Kline asked innocently.

"Listen," Inman said gruffly, "down here, if we see 'em coming, we don't see 'em leaving." Just as he taught every rookie how to do the Globetrotters' ball-handling tricks, Inman was teaching Kline about the social customs of the South.

But racial prejudice was not limited to the Deep South. Chuck Holton, who had lived in the North all his life, was shocked to find that a hotel in Indianapolis wouldn't let the Trotters stay. "I remember that vividly," he says. "Ducky Moore, our business manager, came out and said, 'We can't stay here.' I looked up at the neon lights and it was the Abraham Lincoln Hotel. I thought, 'Abe, where are you now?' "

"You didn't have to go down South to find prejudice," says Charlie Primus, from Detroit, who played five years in the mid-1950s. "There were places right here in Detroit that wouldn't serve blacks." In some ways, the discrimination in the North was more insulting, because it was unexpected. "I found the worst prejudice in upper Michigan," recalls Vertes Zeigler. "Silent prejudice is worse than straight-out prejudice, because down south they'd have a sign [No Colored Allowed]. But if you go in a place and you sit there and sit there, and nobody's looking at you, and finally they come and say, 'I'm sorry, but the management doesn't allow us to serve coloreds,' I'd tell them, 'We didn't come here to eat no coloreds, you got any food?' Now if they'd had a sign—I've got a pocketful of money—I wouldn't have gone in there."

The greatest disparity in how the Globetrotters were treated came in Europe. On the European tours, where the State Department was promoting the Trotters as exemplars of America's treatment of blacks, Abe put the Trotters up in the same four-star hotels where he was staying, such as the Hotel Claridge on the Champs-Elysées in Paris. But it was entirely different when they returned home. In the old days, Abe had allegedly walked out of a few hotels if they wouldn't let his players stay, but in the mid-1950s, when the Trotters began touring heavily in the Deep South, he did not challenge the Jim Crow customs. Abe was powerful enough, and the Trotters were popular enough, that he might have been able to pressure hotels to integrate, but he didn't try.

During the 1954 summer baseball park tour, one Trotter unit played twenty-four straight games in the Deep South, starting in Miami and working its way through nearly every state of the old Confederacy, including Florida, Georgia, Alabama, South Carolina, Louisiana, Texas, Arkansas, Tennessee, and Kentucky. Abe scheduled doubleheaders in every city on the tour, but the Trotters always played a black team (the Chicago Brown Bombers), while two white teams (the Hawaiian Stars and Boston Whirlwinds) played the second game. In most of the towns, even Miami, they played two segregated games—one for white audiences and one for blacks.

After the games were over, the white and black players went to separate hotels. And sometimes the Trotters and Brown Bombers didn't get a hotel at all. In Tallahassee, Florida, for instance, the white teams stayed at the Floridan Hotel, the favorite haunt of state legislators, while the black players slept in a dormitory at Florida A&M University. In other cities, the Trotters had to stay in private homes, sleeping on roll-away beds or couches, or in community centers.

Abe's timidity in challenging segregation cost him with his players, in terms of respect, and it even cost him good players. One of the reasons that Chuck Cooper and Earl Lloyd gave for signing with the NBA, in 1950, instead of with the Trotters, was the disparity between the hotels for the Trotters and their white opponents. "Saperstein had his players staying in dirty, roach-infested holes in the wall," Cooper would later say, recalling the months he spent with the Trotters. "I used to point this out to the Globetrotter players. . . . For doing that I got the reputation as a troublemaker."

Hall of Fame coach Clarence "Big House" Gaines, the second winningest coach in NCAA history, who spent forty-seven years at Winston-Salem State University, had a number of players who signed with the Globetrotters. He would sometimes call Abe to recommend a player, but on a couple of occasions, when Abe sent a contract to sign, Gaines tore it up and never even told the player. "[He] treated them pretty much like animals," Gaines says today. "Didn't pay them much, didn't give them money for meals—it was a hard life."

In Cincinnati, the Globetrotters had to stay in an old, dilapidated hotel that was like something out of a horror flick, with creaking stairs, spiderwebs, broken windows, and bats flying everywhere. The players would enter the rooms armed with insect spray, and douse the mattresses to kill the bedbugs. The Foster Hotel in Indianapolis had half-inch cracks in the windowsills, and mattresses that were only two inches thick, and players would climb in bed with their clothes on, to keep from freezing. Some black hotels had so few rooms that the Trotters had to sleep four players to a room, stretched out sideways across the beds. In other hotels, the beds were so lumpy, or the stench in the rooms so bad, that players would rather sleep in the bus. One night in Kentucky, they actually slept in a slaughterhouse, and woke up to the screams of hogs being butchered.

If the players wanted to go out after a ball game, they found Jim Crow waiting for them around the corner. In Abilene, Texas, Johnny Kline and some other players decided to take in a movie, but were escorted to the "buzzard's roost," high in the balcony. "We sat so far up we could barely see the screen," he wrote in his memoir.*

In the face of these indignities, the Trotters pulled together and made the best of their circumstances. They developed their own secret code to deal with prejudice. They called black people "rocks" and whites were "you-alls." If a restaurant refused to serve them, they'd say, "We're going Dutch tonight," which meant going to a grocery store and buying Vienna sausages and cold cuts. When racist hecklers were giving them a hard time in Birmingham or Montgomery, they'd give each other a special nod as they lined up for the Globetrotter baseball routine, and the pitcher would "accidentally" bean the heckler in the head with the ball.

And it wasn't all bad. To be fair, they resented not having a choice, but sometimes they *preferred* staying in black hotels because it was a much hipper scene. The Watkins Hotel in Los Angeles was the hub of the West Coast jazz scene, and Duke Ellington, Charlie Parker, and Billie Holliday were often staying there. When they got to a new town, they would seek out the black neighborhood, asking a local black resident, "Where's the Zone?" The food in Paris and Rome was enjoyable, but they couldn't wait to get back to Chicago, where the fried catfish at the Pershing Hotel would make a grown man beg for more. And Skippy's restaurant in Cleveland had the best short ribs, ham hocks, greens, and biscuits of any place on earth.

The Globetrotters would not notice a significant improvement in hotel accommodations in the South until the late 1950s, and even then it was sporadic. In some cases, they broke the color line them-

---

* *Kline's autobiography,* Never Lose, *is an inspiring memoir of his years with the Trotters, his battle with drug addiction, and his eventual attainment of a Ph.D.*

selves, becoming the first African Americans to integrate hotels in a number of cities. "We broke lots of racial barriers," says Tex Harrison. In Norfolk, Virginia, for instance, Harrison caught a cab and told the black cabbie to drive him to the local Holiday Inn. "You work out there?" the man asked. When Harrison told him that he was a guest there, the cabbie was incredulous.

In their own way, the Globetrotters helped break down some of the fears and stereotypes that many whites had about blacks. "Just to see black players out there on the court caused people to be less anxious and have less bigotry," says former player Hallie Bryant. "And once they got to meet you, they saw that you were not that different than they were. So laughter helped break down barriers."

Almost imperceptibly, the world *was* changing. The civil rights movement would soon explode across America, challenging all the conventions of the social order. But for the Harlem Globetrotters, the changes were coming painfully slow, even in their own organization. Abe was an innovator in many areas, both in basketball and business, but in the realm that was most demeaning to his players, he would sit on the sidelines, waiting for others to act. The Harlem Globetrotters' bus kept rolling across America, and throughout the Deep South, but the Freedom Riders were not on board.

★

By the midpoint of the decade, the NBA was opening up new opportunities for African American ballplayers, and the best players in the country were being drafted by the league. Abe's monopoly on black talent was gone, but the Trotters were still the most successful basketball team in the country, so Abe had the financial resources to compete for players with any NBA team.

In 1953, the New York Knicks drafted Walter Dukes, a six-foot-eleven consensus All-American from Seton Hall, in the first round. Knicks coach Joe Lapchick and owner Ned Irish were counting on Dukes as the big man they needed to win the NBA crown. What they hadn't counted on, however, was Abe Saperstein. Irish had offered Dukes approximately $12,000 for the five-month NBA season and thought they had a deal. But Abe reportedly offered Dukes $2,000 a month (albeit for a much longer season) and convinced him to sign a one-year contract. At Dukes's signing ceremony in New York, Abe carted in three thousand silver dollars in a wheelbarrow, a clever publicity stunt that the photographers loved. He immediately shipped Dukes overseas, to catch up with the European tour; later that summer, Dukes played on the outdoor baseball park tour as well.

The following year, Abe showed the same flair in signing a famous white player, the legendary Bevo Francis, who still holds the NCAA single game scoring record of 113 points. Francis, who some say was the best pure shooter of all time, had averaged 46.5 points per game in 1953 for tiny Rio Grande College in Ohio, which had only ninety-two students. After the school expelled Francis for missing too many classes, Abe signed him—and his coach, Newt Oliver—to a one-year deal. This time, at the signing ceremony, Abe hauled out a bushel basket filled with four thousand crisp dollar bills. He told the press that the package deal was worth $30,000, but that was an exaggeration, as Francis made only $10,000 and Oliver's annual contract was for $8,000. That summer, Abe showcased Bevo Francis on the baseball park tour, playing for the Boston Whirlwinds.*

After these successes, Abe turned his sights on the most acclaimed college player in the country, Bill Russell of the University of San Francisco. In 1954, when the Trotters played the Cow Palace in San Francisco, he invited Russell to sit on the Trotters' bench as a special guest, and a local paper reported that Russell was "nearly convulsed with laughter on several occasions." Russell had two more years of college eligibility remaining, but Abe was already starting to court him.

Having outbid and upstaged the NBA, Abe now felt that he could get any player in the country he wanted.

Except one.

In April 1955, he lost Goose Tatum. On April 20, Abe announced that he was giving Goose his unconditional release and would not

---

* *Bevo Francis spent two years playing for the Boston Whirlwinds, an opposition team, then was drafted by the Philadelphia Warriors but turned down Eddie Gottlieb's contract offer and went home to Ohio, where he worked in the steel mills.*

renew the option on his annual contract. It might have been the worst day in Harlem Globetrotter history.

"The 'Goose' who lays the golden eggs for the Harlem Globetrotters basketball team has flown away," Wendell Smith lamented in the *Courier*. And that pretty well summed up the feelings of the fans. A month earlier, when Goose was serving a thirty-day suspension, the Trotters had opened the 1954 College All-Star tour with a doubleheader at Madison Square Garden, and the fans had started chanting, "We want Tatum! We want Tatum!" Even Abe, who had never previously acknowledged *any* negative impact from losing *any* player, was forced to admit that his team was "hurting for laughs" without basketball's Clown Prince.

Now, in an eighteen-month period, Abe had lost his two most famous players, Marques and Goose. How it could have come to that is one of the most provocative questions in the Globetrotters' story.

For fourteen glorious years, Abe and Goose had formed a synergistic partnership that created a form of entertainment the world had never seen, and each man made the other greater than he ever could have been alone. Abe's vision merged with Goose's talent to carry them both to worldwide fame and popularity, and, at least in Abe's case, to great wealth. In some respects, it is surprising they stayed together as long as they did. On the other hand, it is almost unfathomable that Abe would let Goose get away.

Goose and Abe's relationship was complicated by their personal histories. Both men had languished in obscurity for decades, only to be catapulted to fame in a few short years, swelling their egos even faster than their pocketbooks. From the beginning, it was a tempestuous marriage, with cycles of betrayal and forgiveness, rage and affection that finally disintegrated in a bitter divorce.

There were symptoms of problems early on. Goose had a wanderlust that could not be assuaged or controlled, especially in the early years. This deeply quiet man, a true loner, who could flip a switch when a ball game began and become the world's greatest showman, had a habit of just disappearing. Perhaps it was a release valve for those conflicting forces in his own personality—the loner and the clown—but whatever was driving him, he would just leave. It happened over and over again.

On March 21, 1948, the Trotters played a game in Chicago Stadium, defeating the New York Celtics, then boarded the Chicago Northwestern train heading for Omaha, Nebraska, where they had a game the next night. About a hundred and fifty miles out of Chicago, the traveling secretary, Winfield Welch, suddenly noticed that Goose was gone. He hadn't told anybody but had apparently gotten off the train at the previous stop, in Clinton, Iowa. Ten days later, he still hadn't been heard from (Welch suspected he was playing baseball). Three thousand "disgruntled fans" showed up to see him in Creighton, Nebraska, where Jesse Owens told the crowd, "The Trotters don't think so much of Goose anymore." Abe fined him $200 and suspended him without pay. Goose didn't play the rest of the season, and he missed the Trotters' Hawaiian tour.

The next season, Abe and Goose's problems got worse, to the point that the relationship nearly ended. On December 7, Goose scored 26 points in a game in Tulsa, then told Abe he needed a "few days off" because his wife, Nona, was about to deliver a baby. Abe gave him a week off, with pay. Two weeks later, he was still gone, and sent Abe a note, claiming he couldn't leave home (Gary, Indiana) because his wife was in the hospital. Abe wrote back, sympathizing with his desire to be home for the "blessed event," but chiding him for missing advertised games and forcing Jesse Owens and Marques Haynes to apologize to the fans. "There is a trouper's axiom 'The show must go on,'" Abe said, and suspended him without pay for the prior week.

Goose was furious. He rejoined the team a week later, then fired off an angry, three-page letter, insisting that his wife had been hospitalized and that he had been forced to work at the local Bendix plant over the Christmas holidays to make enough money to pay her bill. He also contended that he'd been playing for weeks on a "broken ankle" and needed time to recuperate. Finally, he poured out his resentment about the "unfair" suspension:

> If you want to take my money I can't stop you because
> you are the boss. I say my money because I've earned every
> penny that you've ever given to me and more because I

love to see people leave the gyms happy. I am going to play
harder now than ever. But I will never forgive you for
taking my money as long as I live. I think you have done
me a great injustice.

Then, as always, no matter how angry he was, he signed the letter:

Your friend
"Goose"

Abe was equally passionate in his reply:

I have been very, very fair with you whenever you had a
problem or got in a crack and was never found wanting
and if you will be equally fair with me we will get along in
great shape. . . . Just buckle down and do your damnedest
night in and night out and if your ankle bothers you you get
the treatment every day. . . . I only ask a fair break and I
am entitled to same.

Three weeks later, Goose disappeared in Denver. Abe suspended him
for two more weeks and demoted him to a farm team for another
month. That seemed to get the point across, because Goose became
more reliable for the next few years. He still had the wanderlust, but
controlled it enough not to miss so many games.

Still, one could never tell when he might take off. In 1950, on
the Trotters' first overseas tour, Goose disappeared before a game in
Casablanca and nobody could find him. Fearing that he might have
been kidnapped or killed, Abe and the Trotters organized a search
party in the middle of the night. Around 4 A.M., Abe was about to
give up when he heard a yell, "Hey, Boss!" and turned around to find
Goose driving a horse-drawn taxi full of Moroccans. A few nights
later, in Algiers, Goose disappeared into the notorious Casbah and
was gone for a week. Most of the Trotters were terrified to set foot
in the place, with its narrow streets and reputation for banditry, but
Goose found some kind of solace in the mysterious alleyways. "I just

wanted to see what it was like, so I took off," he said later. "I must have roamed around there for a week. It was very dirty and nasty there but I thought the people were nice."

He was as unpredictable off the court as he was on it. Once, the Trotters were driving through Indiana, and Goose told the bus driver to pull over at a drugstore; he wanted to buy something. Twenty minutes later, one of the players went in to check on him and he was gone. They didn't see him again for six nights, until they walked into their locker room in White Plains, New York, and there he was.

Why he disappeared, no one really knew, and even Goose struggled to explain it. "I just used to get a notion I wanted to go some place, so I went," he said. His doctor attributed one such disappearance to "nerves," as Goose reported to Abe: "Doctor said I was working too hard playing both winter and summer and it kept my nerves on edge."

Whatever urges were driving him to leave, there is a clearer picture of why he came back, and why this shy, lonely man became the Clown Prince of Basketball: he loved making people happy. In the angry letter to Abe about his injured ankle, there's a revealing passage where he talks about what it meant to perform for the crowds. "[I] put on a great show," he wrote. "The people thought it was great anyway and they are the ones that count. . . . I hobbled out on a broken ankle and made them love it."

There it is. Goose Tatum may not have shown up for every game, but when he did, he "made them love it." He played with a "broken" ankle, with a broken hand in a cast, in a back brace, and once, in Paris, with a 102-degree fever, against doctor's orders.

By 1950, Abe and Goose had reached a détente of sorts, and Abe rewarded Goose for his new dependability with dramatic salary increases. He went from making $600 a month in 1949, to $1,500 in 1950, $2,000 in 1951, and $2,500 in 1952. His last three years, he was earning $3,500 a month, at a time when the average American worker made approximately $3,000 a year. Abe enjoyed bragging about how much he paid Goose and, at various times, told the papers that Goose was the highest-paid basketball player in the country, made $50,000 a year, and made "twice as much as George Mikan." He was exaggerating again, but not by much. Mikan's top salary, reportedly, was $35,000 a year, but that was for a five-month, sixty-eight-game season, whereas Goose was playing year-round and nearly every night. Still, Goose was one of the highest paid, if not *the* highest paid, players in the game.

The problem was, he didn't know how to handle it. He'd grown up with nothing and didn't understand money. He wasn't a boozer (at least while he was with the Trotters) or a gambler, but he did love to spend money. "He spent it faster than he could make it," Marie Linehan would say years later, and she was the one keeping the tab. He bought a beautiful new home in Gary for Nona and his stepdaughter, Marjorie, and young son, Reece Jr. With his travel schedule, he might only make it home a half dozen times a year, but he sent Nona money regularly, asking Abe to deduct it from his check. He bought new carpets and jewelry on layaway. He bought thirty acres of land in Chihuahua, Mexico, on which he planned to build a vacation home. Sometimes, if he was in a good mood, he'd drop a fifty-dollar tip on a headwaiter, and once bought Easter dresses and bonnets for some little girls who couldn't afford them. When panhandlers hit him up for money on the street, he would refuse to give them cash but would take them into a diner and buy them a meal.

Living up to being the fabulous Goose Tatum, and maintaining the image that went with that, cost a lot of dough. He developed his own style in clothes, wearing black jackets and a black beret, like Art Tatum or other jazzmen he loved. He wasn't a flagrant womanizer, but the women were always available, and he would show up sometimes with beautiful women on his arm.

By 1953, Goose was one of the highest-paid black men in America, not just in sports, yet he never seemed to have enough money. After one of his suspensions, he wrote to Abe, pleading to be reinstated: "Will have to get back with team or starve, heavily in debt." To this day, some former Trotters insist that Goose couldn't have made more than $1,500 a month (although he was actually making twice that by 1953), because he was always living from paycheck to paycheck. And eventually, he started falling behind. He sent a note to Abe, listing the monthly payments he wanted deducted from his check—to a savings and loan, rug company, and car dealership—again signing the note, "Your friend, 'Goose' Tatum." By 1952, the dunning notices from creditors and collection agencies started arriving at the Globetrotters' office: $75.52 to Block Brothers Jewelers, $41.97 to Tobertson Brothers Department Store, $25.21 to Horwich and Haller for a rug. Sometimes Abe turned the bills over to Goose; other times he paid them himself.

Because he was the "Golden Goose," Abe let Goose get away with things that no one else could. Abe had a hang-up about his players driving Cadillacs, and would harangue them about not buying Cadillacs. He didn't even want them to be seen *riding* in one, so the players would park their Caddys blocks away, so he couldn't see them. But Goose flaunted his in Abe's face. He bought himself a new white Cadillac and drove it everywhere he went.

Abe even let Goose take his Cadillac on the road, instead of riding the team bus, with one of the other Trotters as his driver. Goose would often arrive late for games, brushing off the anxious road secretary by saying, "They can't start without me." Once the game began, however, he demanded perfection from the other players. If a player messed up a ream, Goose would holler, "I can't play with this dummy!"—and it didn't matter if 18,000 people in Madison Square Garden heard him.

Off the court, he pulled stunts that would have gotten other players fired. He couldn't stand Abe's brother Rocky, the business manager for one of the Trotter units, and had numerous run-ins with him. Rocky was a retired army sergeant who used to march up and down hotel hallways in the morning, blowing a whistle to wake up the players, then make them line up in formation as he checked their names off on a clipboard. One morning, Goose was late getting to the bus, and Rocky said something about it that Goose didn't like. "Goose slapped him to his knees!" Vertes Zeigler recalls, laughing. "And we were all making bets on who was gonna go home—Goose or Rocky." Winfield Welch, who had worked for Abe a long time, predicted confidently, "Naw, Rocky's going home. If Goose slapped Abe's mama, he ain't gonna fire him." Sure enough, Abe sent Rocky to a different unit.

Another time, Goose told Rocky that he wanted ten tickets for a game. Rocky told him, "I can't give you ten tickets." Goose responded, "You little son of a bitch, now I want a hundred!" Rocky bowed up and still refused, so Goose said, "I ain't stopping till I get to a thousand." Finally, Rocky got on the phone and called Abe in Chicago, and Abe said, "Give him the hundred." Goose took the hundred tickets and tore them up.

In 1951, Goose and Rocky had one final altercation, in Colorado Springs, when Goose asked Rocky for an advance. Rocky said he'd have to check with Abe first, and Goose punched him so hard he broke his hand.*

Goose and Abe's uneasy alliance still seemed to be holding during the 1953–54 season. After the regular season and the College All-Star tour, Goose played in Europe, then spent five weeks on the summer baseball park tour, making $650 a week. On August 21, Abe even honored him with "Goose Tatum Night" at Wrigley Field, in the final game of the ballpark tour, and presented Goose with the keys to a new Cadillac as a "gift from his fans."†

Goose began the 1954–55 season in spectacular form. He was thirty-seven years old (although he claimed to be much younger) and the grind of playing almost every night, all year round, had punished his body beyond its years. Yet he was playing like a twenty-year-old, scoring more points than ever before, having the greatest season of his career. He hit for 28 points in Omaha, 21 in San Francisco, 25 in Sacramento, and an amazing 56 points on a return visit to San Francisco, the most points he'd ever scored. Through the first four months, he was *averaging* 25 points a game.

He was in "the zone," that mystical place that top athletes sometimes reach, where everything comes together in slow-motion perfection. Here, at the pinnacle of his career, Goose was in complete mastery of his game, his gags, and the fans who marveled at the artistry unfolding before them. Sometimes he'd pull off something so amazing that one of his Trotter teammates would be standing there with his mouth open, and Goose would say, "Buy a ticket, dummy, if

---

* *Tragically, Rocky Saperstein died two nights later, in Denver, when he collapsed just before halftime and died of a heart attack in the locker room.*

† *The House of David team, which played on the doubleheader, supplied portable lights for this game, making it the first night game in Wrigley Field history.*

you wanna watch the game." The other players had to stay on their toes because he would snap off passes so fast that they'd hit an unsuspecting player right between the eyes. But like the audiences, the players understood that they were witnessing a genius at work. And like all great masters, in sport or art, he made those around him better. They just had to trust him, go *with* him, and he would take them on a ride they would never forget. "Give me your mind!" Goose would tell them. "Don't think!" As Leon Hillard recalled, years later, "You never had to wonder when to cut because he told you with his eyes. And he was so darn good and he made you play better than you ever thought you could play."

There were no signs, outwardly, of any trouble between Goose and Abe. But in March 1955, after three years of relative calm, and without any warning, their relationship exploded. As with Marques Haynes, the exact details have never been revealed, but money was certainly part of it. Abe hadn't given Goose a raise in three years, although he was making $3,500 a month. According to his son, Reece Tatum III, one point of contention was Goose's share of endorsement money from advertisers. What is certain is that Goose's old wanderlust returned in full force.

The climactic moment occurred on March 12, when the Trotters played a memorable benefit game for the U.S. Olympic Fund at the Great Lakes Naval Training Station, outside Chicago. It was an all-navy crowd, from admirals down to seamen first class, with no civilians allowed. Abe was going to donate $4,000 to the Olympic Fund, but what made the game historic was that CBS-TV was broadcasting it live, on a coast-to-coast hookup reaching eighty-three cities and 26 million homes. It was the first nationwide telecast of a Globetrotter game in the team's history. They had been on Movietone News, on the silver screen, and on *The Ed Sullivan Show*, but now an entire game was being beamed to the nation. It was the dawning of a new era in which the Globetrotters would become *institutionalized* in American popular culture, with "Sweet Georgia Brown" and the Magic Circle as familiar on TV as *The Wizard of Oz* and baseball's *Game of the Week*. And the person who would usher in this new age—the *only* person who could captivate those millions of Americans sitting in their living rooms, as he had captivated kings and queens and beggar children around the globe—was the Clown Prince of Basketball, Goose Tatum. This was the grand stage that Goose had been building toward his entire life, and he was spectacular. He scored 34 points and had the navy brass and sailors completely under his spell. He was shooting his hook from all over the court, mugging for the TV cameras, autographing programs in the middle of the game, stealing a flash camera from a sailor to take his own picture, and pulling out all his favorite reams—the string ball and the wobbly ball and the pantomime baseball game. He put aside whatever grievances he had with Abe, his chronic worries about money, and his own personal demons and strutted out upon that stage and "made them love it." He put on the greatest show of his life, before the greatest audience of his life.

And then he disappeared into the night.

He missed the team plane the next morning, and nobody had any idea where he was. Like so many times before, he was just gone. He didn't show for the next three games, so Abe suspended him for thirty days, the longest punishment he'd ever imposed. Abe had to pull in the showmen from the other units, Sam "Boom Boom" Wheeler and Bob "Showboat" Hall, to substitute for Goose on the big team. A week went by, with still no sign of Goose. Then, out of the blue, he called a friend in Chicago and said he was in Little Rock, at his sister's house, "taking a rest."

On March 27, two weeks after his disappearance, the Trotters were forced to open the College All-Star tour in Madison Square Garden without him, and when fans rocked the Garden with chants of "We want Tatum!" Abe took his case to the press, as he always had. "I would take Goose back if he promises to show some responsibility," he said. "We advertise that he plays for us and the public deserves to be protected. We pay him $53,000 a year and I think only two major league baseball players make more."

Goose remained silent. On April 3, Abe told the papers, "I haven't heard a single word from Goose. His suspension will be over April 12th and, frankly, if I don't hear from him I'll just have to release him."

On April 20, Abe issued a statement giving Goose his unconditional release. By then, Goose was already putting on exhibitions in

Arkansas and Louisiana with a team called the Fabulous Harlem Clowns. A reporter for the *Arkansas Gazette* caught up with him in Little Rock, staying at the Charmaine Hotel, and asked him if there was any chance he'd return to the Trotters. Goose shook his head and said, "After fourteen years, you want a change." That was the only explanation he would ever give. He estimated that he'd played 3,500 games in his career and now planned to "take it easy," perhaps spending some time down in Mexico on the thirty acres he'd bought.

By the next season, he had joined up with Marques Haynes, as a co-owner of the Harlem Magicians, reuniting the two great players on the same team. The nationally televised game at the Great Lakes Naval Training Station would be Goose Tatum's final game as a Harlem Globetrotter. He had led the Trotters to the promised land, but he would not cross over Jordan.

Even Abe had to acknowledge, in a candid moment, that he missed Goose being on the team. "Sure, who wouldn't miss him," he told Wendell Smith. "Would the Boston Red Sox miss Ted Williams? Would the Cardinals miss Stan Musial? Would the Giants miss Willie Mays? Sure I miss him!" But then he caught himself and immediately reverted to his old standby, the familiar incantation that had worked so many times in the past: the Trotters would be fine without Goose, the new showmen would have audiences laughing just as hard, and the Trotters were bigger than any one player. Abe would have never subscribed to the old racist stereotype that "all Negroes look alike," but there were subtle elements of that at work. All he had to do was find some guy who looked like Goose, walked like Goose, could imitate Goose, and the Globetrotters' white audiences would never know the difference.

"I'm not worried in the least," Abe said cheerily. "We've been packing 'em in since the season started." He already had his eye on a young player, only twenty-three years old, who wanted desperately to be a showman. "He's a natural," Abe said. The youngster's name was Meadow Lemon.

CHAPTER 14

Wilt

On a summer afternoon in Moscow in July 1959, a group of American sightseers was touring the Kremlin, the 500-year-old medieval fortress once occupied by the czars, with its multihued palaces and the fantastical swirled turrets of St. Basil's Cathedral, which now served as the seat of power of the Soviet state. The weather was pleasantly mild and the Americans were dressed in summer suits and ties. Their Russian tour guides were showing them an ancient cannon that the czars had used to drive off mobs of hungry peasants gathered in Red Square. A group of Russian passersby followed behind the Americans, drawn out of curiosity.

Suddenly, a gate opened in the Kremlin and a motorcade of drab Soviet-made limousines headed out across the cobbled streets. As the last car passed the group of American tourists, it suddenly stopped in the middle of the road. The rear door was flung open and a squat, bald man in a suit jumped out and walked briskly toward the Americans. The leading cars also had stopped and were disgorging their passengers. Grim-faced men in dark broadcloth suits, some carrying weapons, hurried to catch up with the chubby man in the lead.

The Americans noticed him and moved in his direction. Behind them, the curious Russians who had been following them stopped and, recognizing the man in the suit, pulled back warily to a safe distance.

The little man rushed up to the Americans and raised his hand, smiling broadly. "Harlem Globetrotters?" he called out in halting English.

It was Nikita Khrushchev, premier of the Soviet Union.

"Yes, the *famous* Harlem Globetrotters," replied Parnell Woods, the Trotters' traveling secretary and the nearest man in line.

"Ah, American basketball!" Khrushchev said, beaming.

Eagerly, he shook hands with the Globetrotter players: Tex Harrison, Showboat Hall, Clarence Wilson, Bobby Jo Mason, Joe Buckhalter, Norman Lee, and Meadowlark Lemon. Abe Saperstein was pushed forward and introduced as the team owner, then the rest of the traveling party took turns shaking hands with the premier. Khrushchev seemed particularly fascinated with one of the Globetrotter players, whom he stared up at with a look of amazement. At seven feet, one inch, Wilt Chamberlain was the tallest player in Globetrotter history.

By now, a crowd was gathering and Khrushchev's security guards were trying to keep it at bay. Turning to an aide, Khrushchev said something in Russian, then pantomimed dribbling a basketball. He laughed at his own joke, and the other Russians laughed along.

A photographer appeared out of nowhere. Khrushchev, who had survived a coup attempt the previous year, understood the importance of good PR and was eager to counter his image as an uncouth boor. But he had just met his match when it came to garnering publicity. Abe squeezed in beside him, and Tex Harrison and other players and staff peered over their heads as the flashbulbs began popping. Khrushchev was looking slightly off to one side, with a squinty smile, but Abe always knew where the camera was pointing and was grinning right at it.

Through an interpreter, Khrushchev asked whether the Americans were enjoying their trip, but most of the conversation was lost in the translation. Then his security guards whisked him back to the limousines, and the motorcade drove away. The whole thing was over in five minutes.

But that photo of Abe and the Trotters with the Soviet premier would be sent out by the international wire services and published all over the world. It would become the most famous, and widely distributed, photo in the team's history. And this trip to the Soviet Union would stand as the greatest media bonanza in Abe Saperstein's career.

For eight years, he had been trying to arrange a trip to the Soviet Union, after Bill Veeck first proposed the idea to the Russian embassy in 1952. The idea went nowhere until Abe was contacted in London by an American promoter, Morris Chalfin, who had just succeeded in booking the "Holiday on Ice" show for seventy-four days in the Lenin Sports Palace, where the American skaters drew 900,000 spectators. Chalfin suggested that Abe go straight to the stadium director, Vasily Napastnikov, instead of working through bureaucratic channels. After several three-way phone calls, with a translator in between, Abe and the Russian tentatively agreed on the terms and logistics for a tour. Then Abe waited five days, on pins and needles, to see if Soviet officials would approve.

He was in Paris when the telegram from Napastnikov arrived: "This cable will confirm our consent to Harlem Globetrotters tour Moscow July 6 to 12 inclusive for nine performances on terms agreed in earlier memorandum." Abe was so proud that he had the cable blown up to three feet high and had photos taken of himself, wearing a Russian mink fur cap, pointing proudly to the cable.

Once Abe had the dates locked down, he set out to tell the world. And he succeeded royally. He got wall-to-wall press coverage before the Globetrotters even left for Moscow, with Drew Pearson taking the lead. Pearson called the Trotters "Diplomats in Short Pants" and suggested that the tour might portend a thaw in U.S.-Soviet relations. Abe ensured full coverage of the actual trip by inviting reporters along, including Wendell Smith, who filed daily reports for the *Chicago Herald-American*. And Abe got tremendous coverage when the Soviet tour was over, if for no other reason than he personally sent cables and letters to his network of sportswriters around the country.

Thirty-seven people made the trip, including the San Francisco Chinese, the Trotters' opposition team (the Soviets would not allow any of their teams to play the Trotters), ten halftime entertainers, and Abe's son, Jerry. The Soviets sent a plane to pick up the Trotters in Vienna and fly them to Moscow, where they were met by a welcoming throng of Soviet officials, reporters, and thirty-seven Russian girls with bouquets for each of the guests.

That night, 15,000 people filled the Sports Palace for the first game. Abe would later say that one of the highlights of his life was standing at attention in the arena that night as "The Star-Spangled Banner" was played. When the game began, the Trotters got a curiously stoic reaction from the Russian crowd. No one was laughing. In sixty-eight other countries, they had never experienced dead silence. The Russians took their basketball very seriously, as evidenced by the Soviets' dominance in international play, and the audience was expecting the Trotters to play straight basketball. They didn't understand the show. After that first game, Abe had the announcer read a pregame statement, explaining that the Trotters were ballplayers *and* entertainers, and the crowds finally got it. From then on, the Trotters got the wild reception they had come to expect, with every game sold out and tickets being scalped outside the arenas. The fans mobbed the players for autographs, particularly Wilt Chamberlain, and the Trotters shook so many hands that they had to soak their swollen paws in hot water at night.

As elsewhere, the Trotters did their part to sell America to the world. When Radio Moscow interviewed some of the players for a broadcast to Africa, Trotter captain Clarence Wilson said, "We have nothing particularly in common with Africa, other than color. We're Americans in every sense of the word. We don't like the idea of you people trying to use us as propaganda pawns just because we happen to look like the people you are trying to win from the West." On a tour of Moscow University, the Russian guides pointed out that Soviet universities were free and open to everyone, without discrimination, whereas American Negroes were still enslaved, as evidenced by the protests in Little Rock, Arkansas, over integration of schools. "Did you ever hear of a slave owning thirty suits, twenty pairs of shoes, a Cadillac, and a ranch house?" Wilt Chamberlain responded, with a smile. Most subversive of all, Abe had brought over several rock-and-roll musicians among the halftime entertainers, who held surreptitious nightly jam sessions with Russian musicians who were accompanying the tour. At the final game, the Russians cranked out their own rock version of "Sweet Georgia Brown."

The Soviet tour was an extraordinary success, with an estimated 135,000 people watching the nine games. The last game was broadcast live by the Moscow Television Network, reaching 1.75 million homes. The Soviets hosted a gala farewell banquet, at which Vasily

Napastnikov, the director of the Lenin Sports Palace, predicted brazenly that the Soviets would dominate the world in athletics, surpassing the United States, by the 1960 Olympics in Rome. Wilt Chamberlain did his part to prevent that by besting three Russian diplomats in a vodka-chugging contest. The only diplomatic snafu on the tour was that the Soviets had paid Abe 40,000 rubles (approximately $11,500) and refused to let him exchange them for dollars. He had to either spend the rubles or deposit them in a Soviet bank. Abe spent them: he bought $9,000 worth of sable furs and $2,500 worth of Russian postage stamps, as collectibles. The Globetrotters climbed aboard their return flight from Moscow loaded down with Russian furs.

★

The 1959 Soviet tour and the signing of Wilt Chamberlain were two of the crowning achievements of Abe's life. Wilt was the first true *national* high school phenomenon. When he came out of Overbrook High School in Philadelphia in 1955, he was coveted by every college in the country. He was seven-foot-one, strong, intelligent, and amazingly nimble for a big man. He could run the court, dribble, pass, and control a game to a degree never seen before. He may have been the best all-around athlete of his time, as he was also a high jumper and a decathlete. The "Dipper" was a legend on the playground courts of Philadelphia, and up and down the East Coast, as he had played summer ball in Washington, D.C., and in New York City's Rucker League, a famous proving ground for playground hoopsters, as well as college and professional stars.

After an intense recruiting battle, he signed with the University of Kansas. Freshmen were still ineligible to play varsity ball, but in his sophomore and junior years he was a unanimous first-team All-American, averaging 29.9 points and eighteen rebounds per game, and led the Jayhawks to the 1957 NCAA championship game, where they lost to North Carolina in triple overtime.

But Lawrence, Kansas, was a long way from Philadelphia, culturally and geographically, and Wilt was homesick and bored with the college game. He was ready to move on.

At that time, NBA franchises had territorial rights to the high school and college players in their region of the country. Eddie Gottlieb, owner of the Philadelphia Warriors, had cleverly drafted Wilt when he was still in high school, to establish his territorial claim even after Wilt went to Kansas. But the NBA prohibited college players from signing pro contracts until their college class graduated. In Wilt's case, he couldn't play in the NBA until 1959.

Wilt was looking for a way out. While at Kansas, he had become friends with Goose Tatum, who was then living in Kansas City and touring with his own team, the Harlem Clowns. Goose had tried to convince Wilt to play with him, and had offered a $100,000 salary, but couldn't find backers to put up the money.

Eddie Gottlieb offered Wilt more than $25,000 to join the NBA right then, which would have made him the highest-paid player in the league, but Gottlieb couldn't convince the NBA to grant a waiver to Wilt on its underclassman rule as a hardship case.

So Gottlieb called Abe Saperstein. Abe was a stockholder in the Warriors and had been friends with Gottlieb since the 1930s, when they both started promoting Negro League baseball. Gottlieb also booked Trotters games on the East Coast and often accompanied the Trotters on their European tours. According to Gottlieb, he explained the roadblock with Chamberlain and the NBA, and suggested that Abe try to sign Wilt to play with the Trotters for one year, after which he would come to the Warriors. It would be a beneficial deal for both of them. Abe agreed to try.

Abe had a lot riding on signing Wilt. Two years earlier, he had made an all-out run at signing Bill Russell, who had led the University of San Francisco to two straight national titles. Abe had started courting Russell when he was a sophomore, and by March of his senior year, Abe was telling the San Francisco papers that he would offer Russell $10,000 to sign with the Trotters. Then, as Abe was wont to do, the salary figure kept creeping higher in the press: first $20,000, and eventually $30,000.* When USF came to Chicago to play in a tournament, Abe invited Russell to come to his office for their first face-to-face meeting. According to Russell, Abe made his

---

*Years later, Russell would write in his memoirs that Abe had purportedly mentioned a figure of $50,000 in the press.

sales pitch about joining the Globetrotters, but Russell was noncommittal. So Abe opened his desk drawer and pulled out a packet of pornographic pictures. "If you sign with the Globetrotters," he said, "you can have all this and more."

Russell was repulsed. As he described his reaction in his autobiography: "Is this what he thinks Negroes are?" Unfazed, Abe continued expounding on the "social advantages" of being a Globetrotter, then suggested that they meet later that day at Russell's hotel, with his USF coach in attendance "to keep everything on the up and up." But when Abe arrived (along with Harry Hannin), he talked only to USF coach Phil Woolpert, who was white, and completely ignored Russell, who was sitting on the couch being bombarded by Harry Hannin's jokes. For Russell, a proud, outspoken man, that was the final insult. He decided that if Abe considered him too dumb to talk to, then he was too smart to play for Abe.

Abe's disastrous courting of Russell was a metaphor for the clash between the old and the new—between the old-school sports mogul and the young, strong-willed "New Negro." Abe probably thought he was doing the "boy" a favor, talking money to his coach, who could help Russell make the right decision. But Russell would make his own decisions, then and always. And when Abe offered only $17,000, Russell realized that he would have to play year-round to earn that much, compared with the NBA's five-month schedule. That fall, Russell signed with the Boston Celtics and led them to eleven NBA championships.

Abe had lost the best player in the country in 1956, but now he had a second chance to sign the best player in the country in 1958. And where Russell was known primarily as a defensive specialist, Wilt Chamberlain was an offensive scoring machine and would be much more of a drawing card.

Abe and Wilt needed no introduction. Abe had first tried to sign Wilt right out of high school, reportedly offering him $12,000, and had been keeping tabs on him ever since. In May 1957, at the end of his sophomore year, rumors started flying that Wilt might leave Kansas two years early. Retired Kansas basketball coach Phog Allen told the press that Wilt was definitely leaving to sign with the Trotters. Wilt denied it and said he would be staying at Kansas to "secure a degree," but in truth, Abe was actively pursuing him. In June 1957, they had a meeting in Abe's New York office. Afterward, Abe enlisted the aid of former Trotter Zach Clayton, a lieutenant in the Philadelphia fire department,* to reach out to Wilt. On Abe's behalf, Marie Linehan wrote to Clayton, asking him to approach "this big boy, Chamberlain" about what the Trotters "might mean to him prestige-wise . . . not only in active playing days . . . but in the future."

Now, a year later, with Chamberlain definitely leaving school, Abe was pulling out all the stops. If he could sign Wilt, it would be the biggest coup of his career, and could return the Trotters to the glory days of Goose and Marques. In May 1958, Abe called Wilt and suggested that they meet again in New York.

When classes ended at Kansas, Wilt and Elzie Lewis, a friend from Kansas City, drove cross country to Philadelphia, and then to New York, for the meeting with Abe. Wilt asked Lewis and Vince Miller, an old Philly friend, to accompany him to the Trotters office in the Empire State Building. The two friends waited in the outer office while Wilt went in to see Abe.

In late May, Wilt had announced that he was forming his own barnstorming team made up of former college players; he had already asked Elzie Lewis to join it. Abe's first goal was to dissuade Wilt from that plan. "Why would you want to have to worry about booking dates, paying players, finding guys to play against?" Abe asked. "Just come play with me. I'll pay you a good salary and you won't have to worry about any of that." Wilt was listening. From their initial contacts, Abe knew that Wilt was going to cost him more money than any player he'd ever had, including Goose. But Abe had done his homework. He had prepared a detailed chart listing a range of salaries, from $42,000 to $65,000, and breaking down how much income tax Wilt would have to pay and the net amount he'd receive. It was all rather convoluted, so he added simplistic column headings: "Abe Pays," "Government Gets," "Wilt Gets." Abe argued that the

---

* Clayton was also a boxing referee, and he was the first African American to referee a heavyweight championship fight: the Ezzard Charles–Jersey Joe Walcott bout in June 1952.

more money Wilt made, the higher tax bracket he would be in, so he was better off making less money and paying less tax.*

They ended up splitting the difference. Wilt agreed to a base salary of $46,000, but with side agreements and bonuses he would still end up with $65,000. To seal the deal, Abe handed Wilt a fat roll of bills. It was $10,000 in cash. "I'd never seen ten thousand dollars in my life!" Elzie Lewis recalls. "In 1958, that was a *lot* of money."

Now it got tricky. Wilt had signed a contract, but he had a deal with *Look* magazine for an exclusive story on his decision to leave Kansas. The next issue of *Look* wasn't scheduled to come out until June 10, so Wilt and Abe had to keep the story quiet for almost two weeks. The editors didn't want Wilt to say anything to the newspapers about his plans, and wanted him to hide out until the magazine was published. Hiding Wilt Chamberlain in New York City was easier said than done. *Look* put him up in a hotel and, once again, he invited Elzie Lewis along. They spent their days playing basketball around the city, then returned to the hotel, took a shower, and ordered room service. After about six days of this, the manager of the hotel came to see them. "You know, you guys are allowed to come downstairs and eat in the restaurant," he said.

Wilt and Lewis played ball all day and hung out with Wilt's friends at night. The $10,000 was burning a hole in Wilt's pocket, but he resisted the urge to spend it. "I bet he brought $9,900 of that back to his mother and father," says Lewis, who later married Wilt's sister.

Finally, on June 18, the big announcement was made at a press conference in Toots Shor's. "Gentlemen, I'd like to introduce the newest member of the Harlem Globetrotters," Abe said. Wilt emerged from behind a curtain wearing a Globetrotters warm-up suit. Abe climbed up on a chair, with a tape measure, to show that Wilt was still taller than he was. After Abe's debacle with Bill Russell, some had questioned whether he was still a major player in the basketball world, but he had just proved the skeptics wrong. The Big Dipper was now a Globetrotter.

---

* At that time, a person making $42,000 was in the 69 percent tax bracket, but at $65,000 the rate was 78 percent.

The big question now was where to play him? In July, Wilt flew to Italy and joined up with the Trotters in Milan, where he made a successful debut. It would seem only natural that a seven-foot-one player would play center, which was the only position Wilt had ever played. But there was one problem with putting Wilt in the pivot: Meadowlark Lemon.

Lemon was the new Clown Prince of the Globetrotters, and he didn't want to share the spotlight with Wilt the Stilt or anybody else. So Abe came up with a novel solution: to play Wilt at point guard. He was the first, and only, seven-foot-one point guard in history. It was actually an inspired move because it showcased Wilt's range of talents. Instead of just standing in the lane and making easy dunks, he was bringing the ball up the court, dribbling behind his back, dishing off passes, shooting a soft jumper, and running the weave.

But the problem with Meadowlark was bigger than Wilt.

George Meadow Lemon was born April 25, 1932, and raised in Wilmington, North Carolina, where he played high school basketball and football. When he was eighteen, he watched the Paramount newsreel about the Globetrotters playing in Madison Square Garden and reportedly decided, at that moment, that becoming a Harlem Globetrotter was his life's ambition. He wrote a letter to Abe, begging for a tryout. After high school, he was drafted into the army and stationed in Austria, where he ended up playing a few games with the Trotters on their European tour. He did well enough that Abe offered him a tryout when he got out of the army, and he made the cut. He was assigned to the Kansas City Stars, and then to the Trotters' southern unit, where he began to apprentice as a showman.

When Goose Tatum quit in March 1955, Abe began auditioning players to take his place on the eastern unit. Sam "Boom Boom" Wheeler had the most experience but was past his prime. The heir apparent was Bob "Showboat" Hall, who had joined the Trotters in 1948, coming out of Detroit's famed Brewster Center. Showboat Hall was a better pure basketball player than Goose and perhaps a better ball handler, but he was a crotchety, bad-tempered guy. Nobody could ever get too comfortable around him, even his friends.

"He's mean as a snake," says one former Trotter. "He was the most arrogant son of a bitch alive," says another. Goose was also notoriously moody, but Goose was Goose. Showboat had his own unique style as a showman, and would win thousands of loyal fans on the West Coast and in Canada, but nobody was ever going to mistake him for Goose Tatum. Abe even paid some of Hall's friends to try to keep him in line, but it didn't work. "If Showboat hadn't been such a prick, he could have been the top showman," said one Globetrotter expert.

In 1956, Abe was still casting about for the lead clown. Meadow Lemon, who had been nicknamed Meadowlark by veteran Josh Grider, started getting noticed. He had many admirable qualities to recommend him. He was a hard worker and dedicated to his craft. At night in his hotel room, he would practice ball-handling skills and facial expressions, to the point of exasperating his roommate, Alvin Clinkscales. He was also extremely ambitious, and made no secret of his plans to be a star. "When he was a raw rookie, he had a desire to be exactly what he got to be," Clinkscales recalls. "He wanted to be the man. I used to kid him, 'You ain't gonna get up there with Goose,' and he'd say, 'Yes, I am.'" Also, Lemon was a perfectionist, who would rehearse a ream until it was exactly right, and he was dependable—the antithesis of Goose—and could be counted on every night to show up and perform.

His most important attribute, however, was that he could imitate Goose Tatum. He even looked like Goose. He was dark-skinned, with long arms (not as long as Goose's, but no one's were), a lanky frame, a huge grin, and sad, hooded eyes. To put it bluntly, he fit the image of the stereotypical Negro: black skin, thick lips, wide nose, and a shambling gait. Some Trotters believed that Abe required all his showmen to look that way, because that's what white people wanted to laugh at. "Meadowlark had the appearance of a clown," says Charlie Primus, who played with him. "The public wanted a clown to be real black. Abe knew that. The showmen were all dark-complexioned." Even today, that belief still persists among current Globetrotters. "You look at all the showmen that have ever been," says one current player, "and you don't see any light-skinned, thin-lipped guys."

This belief strikes at the heart of the most complex issue in the Globetrotter saga, which would come to the fore in the heat of the civil rights movement: are the Globetrotters a minstrel show for white people? And is the showman the "interlocutor" of the minstrels, the Stepin Fetchit of the hardwood? Those issues were not yet being raised, however, when Abe promoted Meadowlark Lemon to the top showman job on the eastern unit at the start of the 1956–57 season, introducing him as the new "Rajah of Comedy."

What was certain then was that Meadowlark had an uncanny ability to copy Goose's moves and reams. Lemon worked on them constantly: the strut, the smile, the hook shot over the head. He practiced until he could do them *almost* as well as Goose. As early as December 1955, his first year as a showman on the southern unit, he was being compared favorably with Goose. "[The Globetrotters were] sparked by one Meadow Lemon . . . whose act and actions closely parallel those of ex-Trotter star 'Goose' Tatum," the *Dixon* [Ill.] *Telegraph* wrote. "The 6-2, 180-pound Lemon, only in his second season with the famed clowning troupers, performed all the Tatum tricks from the pivot and was also the pivotal man in the Globetrotter comedy routine."

His copycat act was good enough for Abe. "Meadow Lemon is coming along and is proving sensational," Abe reported in June 1956. It was good enough for Abe and for audiences that didn't know the difference. But that was exactly what the players *did* notice: the *difference* between Goose and Meadowlark. The most glaring one, which mattered most to the players, was that Meadowlark couldn't play ball. "Oh, he couldn't play—not even a little bit!" exclaims one former Trotter, repeating the phrase over and over for emphasis. "Not even a little bit! Oh, he couldn't play! Not even a little bit! Yeah, he was athletic and could run a little, but he could *not* play basketball. He could not have made a good high school team. He could not play at all."

Meadowlark would gradually improve as a player, particularly with his hook shot, but Abe and the coaching staff recognized his shortcomings and covered for him. He might score 15 or 20 points in a regular season game against the Washington Generals, but when the Trotters had to play straight basketball, Meadowlark was on the bench. It was most noticeable on the College All-Star tours, which were straight-up ball against the best college players in the country.

Goose had often been the Trotters' leading scorer against the All-Stars, but Meadowlark was played sparingly, and usually only in the last few minutes if the Trotters were far enough ahead to put on the show. In Seattle, for instance, during the 1957 tour, the Trotters beat the All-Stars 81–68, and the local paper reported: "Meadowlark Lemon was inserted for the final three minutes and ran through a series of comedic hi-jinx." For the entire tour, Meadowlark averaged a paltry 1.8 points per game. Today, there are still debates about just how good a ballplayer Goose Tatum was, but there is no debate about the basic premise: he could play and Meadowlark couldn't.

The other difference, which was even more profound, was in creativity. Goose was a comic genius, an original, while Meadowlark was a clone. Meadowlark was a great technician and a talented imitator, but he had little spontaneity or improvisational feel. It was all purely derivative from Goose's legacy. If Goose was a jazz soloist, like Bird or Coltrane, creating new riffs and progressions every night, Meadowlark was a trombone player in the high school marching band, who had to flip the sheet music over to know what note to play next. He was an actor reading his lines, and doing it very well, but it was the same script, the same dialogue, the same show every night. It was timed and choreographed down to the second. As Frank Deford once described him in *Sports Illustrated,* Meadowlark was a "contrived character."

Goose cracked up his own teammates because they never knew what he was going to do, but Meadowlark's teammates knew *exactly* what he was going to do, at exactly the same point. And as he became more popular, heaven help the player who didn't deliver *his* line or *his* move at just the right moment.

Again, the typical audience could not tell the difference. If they saw the Globetrotters play only every couple of years, how would they know that Lemon's show was an endless repeat, night after night? But the players recognized the difference between an original and an actor, and described it in eloquent, forceful terms. Leon Hillard, who died tragically in 1977,* may have summed it up best: "Meadowlark couldn't carry Goose's jockstrap to the Laundromat."

---

* *Hillard was shot to death by his wife in March 1977, at age forty-five.*

When Abe signed Wilt Chamberlain to a one-year contract in May 1958, there is no indication that he ever talked to Wilt about the "social advantages" of being a Trotter, as he reportedly had to Bill Russell. It was unnecessary. There was nothing Abe, or anyone else, needed to say to encourage Wilt's pursuit of sexual conquests. Long before his death in 1999, Wilt's name would forevermore be linked with two all-time scoring records: the 100 points he scored in an NBA game, and the 20,000 women he claimed to have bedded. When Wilt first made the latter claim, in a controversial memoir, some critics disputed his math or railed against the objectification of women, but no one challenged the fundamental assumption: Wilt Chamberlain slept with an extraordinary number of women.

And without a doubt, the Harlem Globetrotters helped him achieve what may be a world record. In three separate autobiographies, the Dipper described in vivid detail his apprenticeship with the Trotters in learning to pick up women. What emerges from his stories, and those of many former players, is an indisputable truth: playing for the Harlem Globetrotters may be the world's greatest party.

As Wilt described his initiation to the Trotters on his first day in Milan:

> I soon learned that basketball and comedy were only the second and third most important things in their lives. The first, by far, was girls. The Globies, individually and collectively, were the greatest girl hounds I've ever seen. They spent almost every waking moment trying to figure out how to cop good-looking girls they'd meet on tour—and they damn near always succeeded, despite language barriers that would have stymied most men.

Today, no one would be surprised to learn that professional athletes, movie stars, hip-hop artists, rock stars, and even politicians have access to sexual favors beyond the norm for the average Joe. Money, fame, looks, and power are intoxicating stimulants that attract some members of the opposite sex. The Harlem Globetrotters had no monopoly on this phenomenon, but they may have been in a unique position to take advantage of it.

"There's one thing that's undeniable," says Mannie Jackson, the team's current owner, who played with the Trotters in the 1960s, "the access to sexual opportunities in this kind of life is endless. It's only limited by a person's stupidity and their capacity. And as you would probably expect, these guys have great capacity. That's part of what makes them [great ballplayers]—you couldn't do it without this kind of physiology."

According to Wilt, the Globetrotters were looking for postgame action no matter where they were, but it was harder on the U.S. tour, where they were traveling every day and playing games every night. That didn't prevent them from going out clubbing until the wee hours when the games were over, but it was tough. On the overseas tours, however, they often stayed five or six days in one city—in Paris, Rome, Rio de Janeiro, or Manila—which provided more time to party. And overseas, there were fewer strictures on interracial sex.

Just imagine this scene: a dozen young black men in their early twenties arrive in Bogotá, Colombia, in 1954—or 2004, for that matter—all of whom are impressive physical specimens and world-class athletes, and they are paraded through the streets to the fanciest hotel in town, welcomed by the mayor, and then perform every night before thousands of adoring fans, exhibiting remarkable feats of agility and skill, and when the game is over at nine-thirty or ten, go out to the local nightclubs to relax. Is there any doubt what would happen?

"At first, it was a novelty kind of thing," says Jackson. "You just didn't see guys packaged like this and have access to them. And the testosterone level is so high around the guys, it attracted all kinds of people."

The Globetrotters capitalized on what was offered. For some of the players, the sex made up for not being paid well. "My first few years, I had so much fun on the road that I couldn't wait to get back out there," says one former Trotter. "It took me a few years to realize that I wasn't making any money."

Wilt Chamberlain described how the Trotters developed their own secret language around picking up women. Before the games, players would scan the audience, looking for attractive women, and figure out a way to "drop the bomb" during the game—which meant giving the women their phone numbers. "Did you drop the bomb on that girl yet?" they would ask. Sometimes they would incorporate "dropping the bomb" into one of their reams, finding an excuse to go up in the stands and slip their number to a woman. And the one unforgivable sin for any player was to be caught with a "mullion"—Globetrotter code for an ugly woman. Guys would hide or run around the corner to keep from being seen with a mullion. When the Trotters returned from their historic 1958 tour of the Soviet Union, Wilt Chamberlain summed up Russian women as "100 million mullions."

In 1947, when the Trotters made their first trip to Havana, Cuba, in the heyday of the Fulgencio Batista regime, prostitutes lined the streets near El Ciboney Hotel, and the *fanciest* brothels, where each whore dressed like a different movie star, cost only two dollars. For half that, the regular whorehouses provided a shot of habanero rum and a pallet on the floor.

But once the Globetrotters became celebrities, they no longer had to pay for sex. It was free and plentiful. They would scope out pretty women during the games and arrange to meet them later, or pick up women in bars and clubs, or just meet them on the street. The Globetrotters could draw a crowd just walking down a boulevard in Rome or Madrid. Mannie Jackson believes that some of the sexual attraction was a subtle form of misplaced trust. "Over the years, the aura that built up around the Harlem Globetrotter brand meant that you could trust them," he says. "It's not like you're a jazz guy or a hip-hop artist or have a reputation of being that way. The Globetrotters attracted women who wouldn't ordinarily take a chance, because they think, 'He's a Globetrotter.' "

Some Trotters were notorious for concocting all sorts of elaborate seduction schemes. Duke Cumberland, for instance, would buy cheap rings at pawn shops, give one to his date, and beg her to marry him. He was such a good actor that he could cry on command, so he would get down on his knees and blubber, "Oh, baby, I'm tired of the road, I'm gonna settle down and marry you." Other times,

Cumberland and Ducky Moore would entice women to their hotel rooms with a Brownie flash camera to compete for the title of "Globetrotter Queen," which would begin as a cheesecake photo shoot and usually lead to more.

Women were plentiful on the road, and so were drugs. Even in the early 1950s, when the Trotters started playing in Colombia, Panama, and Mexico, marijuana was widely available. Most of the Trotters preferred beer or whiskey, but some tried reefer and even cocaine.

The frenetic pursuit of sex on the road was not limited to the players; it started at the top. "Abe didn't drink or smoke," says Harry Saperstein, his ninety-one-year-old brother. "His only vice was women—lots of them! He had women stashed all over the world." Abe made no effort to hide his womanizing, and bragged about his sexual prowess. "He thought he was the greatest lover in the world," Johnny Kline recalls. Abe had girlfriends in different cities that he would date whenever the Trotters came to town. They were gorgeous women, some of them actresses and singers. And he seemed to have a particular fondness for black women.

It was one of those troubling paradoxes about the Trotters. Abe would insist that his players not date white women, and would constantly warn them, "Stay away from those white girls!" Yet he openly dated black women. One former Globetrotter first encountered that dichotomy in France, when he got up in the middle of the night to find something to eat, and ran into Abe on the elevator. "I see this black woman standing there," the player recalls. "She's beautiful, about five foot ten. And she says something to Abe, and I realize they're together. And I watch them walk out together, and he puts his hand on her, and I thought to myself, What a revelation."

From a business perspective, some of the players could understand, and even accept, the double standard, realizing that black men dating white women would not play in Peoria or Biloxi and could blow up in Abe's face, but they felt disrespected when Abe flaunted his black girlfriends in front of them. Once, while touring in Washington State, Abe put a well-known black piano player, Hadda Brooks, on the Globetrotter bus, and let everyone know that she was "his woman." Brooks traveled on the bus with the players for several days. "He was putting his business on the street," says Frank Washington, "and rubbing our noses in it."

★

During the one full season that Wilt Chamberlain played with the Globetrotters, in 1958–59, attendance soared. Wilt scored points at a phenomenal pace, and the fans were breaking down the turnstiles to see him. In his regular season debut at Chicago Stadium, he scored 25 points, then pumped in 50 at Boston Garden, and it went on like that the rest of the year. Abe knew that was what the fans were paying to see, and kept urging, "You gotta score more, Wilt."

The more Wilt scored, however, the more insecure Meadowlark Lemon became. "If anyone else stole the limelight," Wilt would later write, " 'Lark' sulked and bitched and threatened to clobber the guy." One night, there was a confrontation in the locker room where Lemon jumped Wilt, who simply lifted him up over his head until Lemon calmed down.

Abe and Eddie Gottlieb's original plan was for Wilt to play the 1958–59 season and then come to the Philadelphia Warriors, so in March 1959, Gottlieb selected him in the first round of the NBA draft. But Wilt was having so much fun with the Trotters, and Abe was making so much money, that Abe tried to convince Wilt to stay. He offered more money, but Wilt eventually signed with the Warriors. Abe and Gottlieb's relationship would never be the same.

Even though Wilt had gone to the NBA, he kept returning to the Trotters. After his first NBA season, he was so fed up with the "roughhouse tactics" used against him that he announced his retirement from the league. Abe immediately offered Wilt $125,000 to rejoin the Trotters. Wilt eventually returned to the Warriors, but for the next eleven years, until 1969, he joined up with the Trotters every summer to play on the European tour. They always kept his number thirteen jersey ready, because he might appear at any time.

Even when he wasn't there, just the mention of his name was enough to inspire fear in the minds of the Trotters' opponents. During the College All-Star tours, if the All-Stars won several games in a row, Harry Hannin would start spreading the word, "Wilt's coming!

Wilt's coming!" As Ray Meyer recalls, "If we beat them, then [we'd hear] 'Wilt is coming'—and then school was out! They always used that threat. I don't remember if he ever actually played, but we were scared to death." In fact, the threat was real. On April 3, 1960, Wilt scored 28 points to lead the Trotters to an 88–82 victory over the All-Stars.

In 1974, near the end of his NBA career, Wilt once again announced that he was thinking about retiring from the NBA and joining the Trotters. Until his death in 1999, Wilt would say that playing with the Harlem Globetrotters was the most fun he ever had in sports.

Abe Saperstein's signing of Wilt Chamberlain was one of the great coups of his career. Sadly, it would be his last great hurrah. Abe made a concerted effort to sign Elgin Baylor in 1958, and Oscar Robertson in 1959 and 1960, but Baylor and the "Big O" both chose the NBA. In later years, the Trotters would attempt to sign Cazzie Russell, Elvin Hayes, Lew Alcindor (aka Kareem Abdul-Jabbar), and even Bill Walton and Pete Maravich. They failed. After the splendid year of Wilt the Stilt, the Harlem Globetrotters would never sign another premier player that the NBA coveted. The league that Abe had kept afloat for so many years had passed him by. The Harlem Globetrotters would still have great ballplayers, many of them NBA caliber (and some who actually played in the league), but their talents would henceforth be secondary to the show. If players had a choice, most went to the NBA. The Trotters were strictly for show.

CHAPTER 15

"Show's Over"

On Sunday, January 16, 1966, the Harlem Globetrotters appeared on CBS's *Sports Spectacular,* on a live broadcast from the campus of Michigan State University in East Lansing. The show, which started at two-thirty in the afternoon, was a ninety-minute extravaganza featuring the Trotters against Red Klotz's Washington Generals, with halftime entertainment by the Czechoslovakian Folk Dancers.*

The Globetrotters were led onto the court by Meadowlark Lemon, the reigning Clown Prince of Basketball, who had become a huge international star. Lemon was surrounded by a talented squad of ballplayers: Fred "Curly" Neal, a dribbling specialist whose bald pate and incandescent personality were already making him one of the most popular and recognized sports figures in the world; Hubert "Geese" Ausbie, Lemon's backup and the most spontaneous showman since Goose; Hallie Bryant, a former "Mr. Basketball" from Indiana; Bobby Jo Mason, an All-American guard from Bradley University; the lovable veteran J. C. Gibson; and two of the most legendary school-yard players in New York City history, "Jumping Jackie" Jackson and Connie Hawkins.

This was a spectacular group of players, with as much pure basketball talent as the Trotters had ever had. Curly Neal could shoot

---

* When the Trotters made their first visit to Czechoslovakia, they were not allowed to bring any Czech money out of the country, so Abe bartered to bring Czechoslovakian folk artists on tour with the Trotters.

jumpers from half court with unfailing accuracy. Connie Hawkins, considered by some as the greatest one-on-one ballplayer in history, was playing his third season with the Trotters, after having been banned unfairly by the NBA for alleged involvement in gambling.* Ausbie had averaged 28 points per game in college. And stories about Jumping Jackie Jackson's exploits in the Rucker League would be talked about for years to come.

These were great ballplayers, but they were clearly a supporting cast in what had become, by 1966, "The Meadowlark Lemon Show." Meadowlark was terrific in his starring role: he controlled the flow of the game, working the reams and the ref and the fans with equal aplomb. He also had improved as a ballplayer, and his quirky, over-the-shoulder hook shot, which he could hit from half court more often than not, was being imitated by young boys all over America. Goose Tatum had set the stage for Meadowlark, carrying the Trotters right up to the edge of the Information Age, and Meadowlark had reaped the rewards. He was a made-for-TV showman in the right place at the right time, and his face was now familiar to *millions* of people around the world who had never heard of, or had forgotten, Goose Tatum.

By 1966, the Trotters were a regular staple on American television. They had been on the talk show circuit, appearing once on Jack Paar and three times on the Steve Allen show, where they played basketball against a celebrity team of Allen, Peter Lawford, Julius LaRosa, and Leo Durocher. They had done variety shows, appearing on ABC's *Hollywood Palace* with comedians Mel Brooks and Carl Reiner, and singers Vic Damone and Edie Adams. They had even reached the long-hair music crowd on CBS's *Omnibus,* hosted by Alistair Cooke, splitting time with Leonard Bernstein and a sixty-two-piece orchestra. Even their old movies were on TV; *The Harlem Globetrotters* and *Go, Man, Go* were still showing up at 1 A.M. on *The Late, Late Show.*

And the Trotters had practically taken up permanent residence on *The Ed Sullivan Show,* having made six different appearances, to the point that "Sweet Georgia Brown" was nearly as familiar to Sullivan's audience as Topo Gigio's "Hey, Eddie, you keesa me good

---

* *Hawkins sued the NBA and won reinstatement in 1969.*

night!" Their most recent appearance, on Halloween 1965, was their first color TV broadcast, and the Sullivan show had just installed revolutionary Plumbicon tube cameras that brought "stunning" clarity to color broadcasts. Guest stars Liza Minnelli, Allan Sherman, and the Harlem Globetrotters had never looked so good.

But their appearances on CBS's *Sports Spectacular* are the most important of all. In 1960, CBS contracted to broadcast one Globetrotter game per year across the country. In fact, the Harlem Globetrotters were so popular that CBS put them on the premiere broadcast of *Sports Spectacular*. Over the years, CBS would broadcast Globetrotter games from New York, Rome, Mexico City, Washington, D.C., and, in 1967, from the decks of the U.S.S. *Enterprise,* recently returned from Vietnam.★

So this game in East Lansing, on *Sports Spectacular,* is a homecoming for the Globetrotters. Television has become their best friend. CBS is paying Abe $150,000 a year on this contract, and the network is getting its money's worth. On this Sunday, for instance, the Trotters' game is competing against a movie on NBC and, most intriguing, the *NBA Game of the Week* on ABC, which matches up the league's two best teams, the Boston Celtics and Philadelphia Warriors, and the two biggest rivals, Bill Russell and Wilt Chamberlain. At the end of the day, the Trotters will earn a whopping 16.2 Nielson rating, compared with a pathetic 3.2 rating for the NBA. The Globetrotters can no longer compete with the NBA for the best players, but they still put on a better show.

And Meadowlark Lemon is the perfect showman for TV. His rote, scripted performance is exactly what CBS wants. In fact, *Sports Spectacular* will actually use a written script, with already prepared lines for announcer Pat Summerall and special guest Pat Harrington, the Washington Generals' "coach." Goose Tatum would have been too "hot" for TV; he would have driven the CBS cameramen nuts

---

★ *The most unique* Sports Spectacular *broadcast took place in November 1963, in London, when the Trotters played the "Lord Taveners," a group of "sporting rogues" made up of actors, journalists, and TV personalities, whose "Twelfth Man" was Prince Philip. The game, a complete spoof, was a benefit to raise money for youth sports programs, and ended with Prince Philip serving champagne to the Globetrotters.*

because they would have never known what he was going to do next—the very source of his humor. But they never have to worry about Meadowlark: he always knows his lines, hits his marks, and does it just in time for a commercial break.

★

The one person missing from this game at East Lansing is Abe Saperstein. In the past, it would have been unthinkable for him to have missed a national TV broadcast. He would have been there with bells on, being interviewed before the game, rattling off the litany of Globetrotter successes, flashing that million-dollar smile.

But Abe is dying.

He has been in declining health for the last two years, and is now on a quickening slide from which he will not recover. After forty years of nonstop travel, of working harder than anybody in sports, his body is giving out. He is officially the Most Traveled Person in the world, having been recognized as such by the commercial airlines; he has flown over 5 million miles and visited eighty-nine countries. Recently, he said he has only two remaining goals in life: to make it to 100 countries and be around for the Trotters' fiftieth anniversary.

He has ten years to go. The 1965–66 season was officially declared the fortieth anniversary of the Trotters,* a milestone that was promoted with great fanfare. From the outside, watching them on *Sports Spectacular* or reading the press releases churned out by publicist Bill Margolis, it would appear that the Globetrotters are more successful than ever before. There is no question that more people have seen them play, counting their enormous TV audiences. And there have been many highlights in the past few years.

Just since 1958–59, the Year of the Big Dipper, the Trotters have had audiences with two popes (John XXII and Paul VI); have accompanied Drew Pearson on Christmas tours to U.S. military outposts in Alaska and North Africa; have made their first visits to India, Pakistan, Tasmania, and continental Africa; and have pushed farther behind the Iron Curtain, to Bulgaria, Romania, Hungary, Yugoslavia,

---

* *Based on Abe's oft-repeated claim that the Trotters played their first game on January 7, 1927.*

Czechoslovakia, and Poland. In 1963, the "international unit" of the Trotters made a circumvention of the world, playing the entire season overseas. In 1964, the Globetrotters were the first sports organization invited to play at the New York World's Fair. And playing almost exclusively against stooge teams like the Washington Generals and Hawaiian Surfriders, the Trotters haven't lost a game since 1962.

But even reading the Trotters' own flack, there is a sense that for the last few years they've been repeating themselves. They keep adding new countries and planning new tours, but there's a hint of weariness to it all, as if they realize they can't keep topping themselves. They've done it all so many times, it's a variation on the same familiar theme. How many times can they play Wembley Stadium before they lose their edge? How many times can Aretha Franklin sing "Respect" before it gets a little stale?

So much of the Trotters' expansion has been fueled by Abe himself, by the white-hot fire burning within him, and there has been a noticeable slackening as that light has dimmed.

Abe has always been extremely healthy, the kind of guy who was too busy to get sick. But in 1959, he had his first serious medical problems, when he underwent routine surgery and nearly died from complications. As Marie Linehan described it, "[Abe] was very, very sick. He had a mighty close call—too close for comfort." After seventeen days in Mount Sinai Hospital in Chicago, he hopped back on a plane to London as soon as the doctors released him, but it was enough to scare him. "It was nip and tuck," he admitted to Ermer Robinson.

His doctors told him that he needed to slow down, but he wouldn't, or couldn't. "Everybody was telling him he had to slow down," says his sister Fay, "but that didn't mean anything to him." He kept barreling ahead, working as hard as ever, and developed a serious heart condition. His cardiologist prescribed daily medication, but Abe would forget to take his pills. "I'd go by his office and see the pills on his desk," says Wyonella Smith, one of his secretaries. "I'd say, 'Abe, did you take your medication?' And he'd say, 'I'll take it, I'll take it,' but I'd go back at four-thirty and the pills were still there." If she reminded him again, he'd take all the pills at once. "He'd just throw them down, and say, 'Aw, it doesn't matter.' "

By 1963, he looked like a sick man. In March, the British amateur basketball association honored him by mounting a plaque at his birthplace in London's East End, on Flower and Dean Streets. Abe was ill and unable to attend the unveiling, but when he flew over later, they took a picture of him standing under the plaque. He looked terrible. His face was ashen, his cheeks hollow. And he wasn't even making an effort to smile, which was a dead giveaway.

Even if he had been a dutiful patient and taken his pills, his lifestyle was enough to kill a healthy man. He was traveling constantly, living on gourmet restaurant food and frozen airplane dinners. He kept a detailed Air Travel Log in which he recorded every flight he made, with arrival and departure times, total mileage, and comments on the weather, service, and food. His reviews of airline fare were brutal: "real 'slum' food not even fit for pigs," "usual American Airlines 'dog food' breakfast," "pure hogwash!"

The Travel Log is a diary of the cumulative effects of forty years on the road and how he was finally wearing down. Commenting on a short flight from Berlin to Frankfurt on Pan Am, his growing exasperation showed: "Cheesiest equipment in Europe. Eighty sardine-packed customers (most could use a bit of cologne). . . . [Pan Am] 'junk' equipment. Oiy vay!" And when he left Paris after one of his final visits, he wrote poignantly: "The skies were sad—the winds were sad—and I was sad—leaving Paris!"

Abe had always been a prodigious letter-writer, producing a voluminous amount of correspondence to promoters, business associates, and old friends, but in these last years his letters had become more reflective, as if he were taking stock of his life.* He wrote lyrical descriptions of Paris, Athens, and London—and then, predictably, would send the identical letter to a half dozen people. He wouldn't follow his doctors' orders to slow down—he couldn't seem to

---

* His letters had a characteristic style and structure, with the opening paragraphs taken up with a travelogue description of where he'd been; and he favored Walter Winchell's trademark use of ellipses to set off sentences or clauses—so much that Marie Linehan adopted it, too.

manage that—but he was taking time to reflect. From Budapest, after a visit to Auschwitz, he wrote:

> I thought places like the filthy Casbah in Algiers, the cesspools and slums of the larger cities of India . . . the squalor that is part of Hong Kong, and like nauseating parts of the world bothered me . . . but I came out of the barbed wire enclosure of barracks that make up this cemetery of millions of human beings . . . absolutely sick at heart . . . a monument of infamy to people who (whether they could or not) did nothing at the time for their less fortunate brothers. . . . Four million piles of bones and ashes now residing on the bottom of the very pretty little lakes adjacent to this place of "no return." . . . I must carry a mental picture with me of Auschwitz the remainder of my life. . . . It has been a week since the Auschwitz death scenes were before me . . . food has not tasted the same . . . I want to "fight" my fellow man . . . and generally am all out of sorts. The bouncing basketball keeps dribbling along . . . one day sad . . . the next pleasant . . . but how does one go about erasing from his mind the picture of the systematic liquidation of four million people.

His deteriorating health was compounded by a series of bad business decisions. No promoter is successful with every venture, and over the years Abe had had his share of flops. His attempt to start a Negro Baseball League on the West Coast in the late 1940s never really got off the ground; and in 1955, his love affair with vaudeville prompted him to stage *The Harlem Globetrotters Varieties of 1955*, a ten-act variety show starring Earl "Fatha" Hines and "the luscious Hadda Brooks," which cost him $15,000 a week and folded quickly.

Beginning in the early 1960s, however, Abe seemed to have lost his Midas touch, and made a series of much costlier mistakes. The biggest was the American Basketball League (ABL). Abe had been yearning to own an NBA franchise since 1950, when he had contracted to buy the Chicago Stags (but the deal fell through). Around 1959, the NBA reportedly promised him a franchise in Los Angeles when the league expanded, as repayment for all the years he'd kept the NBA afloat with doubleheaders. Instead, the NBA allowed the Minneapolis Lakers to relocate to Los Angeles. Then Abe was supposedly offered a San Francisco franchise, but the NBA demanded a $250,000 franchise fee. Abe blew up, feeling that the fee was unjust, given his contributions to the league. Compounding this, he and Eddie Gottlieb had fallen out over Wilt Chamberlain, and Abe got so mad that he sold his stock in Gottlieb's Philadelphia Warriors and began testing the waters for a new league. It took him a year, but he pulled it off.* He called the ABL a league for "the little guy," and proposed innovations such as the three-point shot, a redesigned foul lane, a thirty-second shot clock, and a bonus rule after five team fouls. He was the obvious choice for league commissioner and ran the ABL out of the Globetrotters' office, with Marie and her front office staff doubling up on their work.

The ABL started play in 1961, with eight teams, including the Cleveland Pipers, owned by thirty-year-old shipping magnate George Steinbrenner. But the new league was in trouble from the beginning. Abe scheduled the Globetrotters for doubleheaders, to draw crowds, but the ABL lost $1.5 million in its first season. Halfway into its second season, Steinbrenner attempted to bolt to the NBA and in January 1963, the ABL collapsed. Abe lost $300,000 of his own money.† Five years later, the American Basketball Association (ABA) would be formed and would incorporate most of Abe's innovations, including the three-point shot and a red-white-and-blue ball.

In the middle of the ABL fiasco, Abe tried again to single-handedly revive vaudeville. In April 1961, he launched the "World of

---

* The commonly accepted view of the ABL's origin is that Abe got angry after the NBA refused to sell him the Minneapolis Lakers in May 1960, but he was actually sending out query letters to prospective owners a year before that, in April 1959, just one month after Gottlieb convinced Wilt Chamberlain to leave the Trotters for the NBA. Abe held a meeting in Los Angeles with interested arena owners, and undertook negotiations with NBA commissioner Maurice Podoloff. By the time the NBA's Board of Governors approved the Lakers' move to Los Angeles, in May 1960, Abe had already announced his new league.

† Connie Hawkins, who led the ABL in scoring with a 27-point average, signed with the Trotters after the ABL collapsed. Several former Trotters, including Sweetwater Clifton and Govoner Vaughn, played for the Chicago Majors or other ABL teams.

Music," a two-month-long tour headlined by three obscure singers from Europe and Olga James, an African American singer who had starred opposite Harry Belafonte in *Carmen Jones*. The show was a disaster, folded after only a few weeks, and cost Abe another $75,000. He was stuck in the past and still in love with vaudeville, which blinded him to new opportunities. He was reportedly approached about booking a rising young foursome from Liverpool, England, for a tour of the United States, but declined, saying skeptically, "What's a Beatle?"

Instead of focusing on the Globetrotters, he kept expanding into other sports or show business ventures. In 1965, he bankrolled an overseas tour of the Ice Capades, which, in his words, turned into "a Frankenstein." The Ice Capades lost $24,000 in Hawaii, another $30,000 in Europe and Australia. With the losses mounting, Abe sent a telegram to Joe Anzivino, a Globetrotters' advance man who was managing the Ice Capades tour, suggesting desperate measures:

IF COUPLE ICE CUTIES MUST DO LADY GODIVA ACT TO STIM-ULATE LAGGING BOX OFFICE LET'S GET GOING STOP REMEM-BER OUR MOTTO DO IMPOSSIBLE EVERY DAY MIRACLES TAKE LITTLE LONGER.

It was bad enough to lose money on peripheral ventures, but he also was having setbacks with the Globetrotters. The College All-Star tour, which had been one of his most successful promotions since 1950, came to an abrupt end in 1962.* The AAU's gray eminences, who had been haunting Abe for decades, effectively killed it by rul-ing that college seniors who played on the All-Star tour would lose the remainder of their college scholarships. Since the tour was sched-uled during spring break, players would have had to front their tu-ition and room and board for the last few months of college. Even prior to that ruling, attendance for the College All-Star series had been dropping steadily since the mid-1950s, as the NCAA and NIT tournaments grew in popularity, but the AAU ruling was the final

---

* *The All-Star tour had not been held in 1959, because of the Pan Am Games, or in 1960, because of the Olympics.*

blow. Another of Abe's old standbys, the summer baseball park tour, also ended in 1964; once again, lagging attendance was the culprit.

In some ways, the Trotters' increased TV exposure was hurting them at the box office, as fans now had the option of sitting in the comfort of their living rooms, instead of buying a ticket, to watch the show.

In 1964, the Globetrotters had one of the worst seasons in their history. The regular tour did so poorly that Abe was forced to lay off one entire unit and some of his staff. Among the casualties was Ermer Robinson, one of the all-time Trotter greats, who had been coaching for Abe since the mid-1950s.* Over the years, Abe had released hundreds of ballplayers, and had become so inured to it that he often used a form letter to break the news. But Ermer Robinson had been one of Abe's most loyal employees for nearly twenty years. It was Robinson who had made the winning shot in the 1948 triumph over the Lakers, perhaps the greatest single play in Harlem Globetrotter history. Now Abe was cutting him loose. In a wrenching two-page letter, Abe tried to explain his reasons:

> First of all, I don't have to tell you that last season
> [1963–64] was a most disastrous one . . . probably the worst
> in our history . . . creating omens for me which cannot be
> ignored. I have got to do two things this coming year . . .
> one, a complete revision of the show from the top to the
> bottom . . . and two, draw up and adhere to an operational
> budget which is reasonable and logical . . . I am trimming
> [personnel] to a minimum with most everyone doubling
> up on chores. . . . I am under the gun to follow certain
> rules now set down by better business heads than I. I am
> terribly sorry. . . . You will always be one of our
> Globetrotter family, but like so many who have been in the
> family and who have gone their own ways and left the
> "nest" . . . I hope with all my heart that you can go on to
> even bigger and better things. . . . I guess my greatest
> weakness in the past has been the eternal effort to look

---

* Robinson had also coached the Oakland entry in the failed American Basketball League.

after everyone I felt I should, regardless of whether it fit
the picture or not . . . and on the heels of the frightening
problems of last season, my business and financial advisers
have "laid the law down" to me once and for all to start
thinking of budgets and the specific needs of the business
itself . . . or it will ALL end up in a sad state.

For decades, Abe had run the Globetrotters based on his gut instincts
and his relationships with people, but now, as the organization grew
larger and he grew more frail, his attorney, Allan Bloch, and his "business advisers" (including Marie Linehan) were starting to have more
say. "Abe was not good with money," says Red Klotz. "He would give
away thousands and thousands of dollars in gifts. He'd bring editors
to Paris with their wives. He treated everybody wonderful. Made
them feel good. But it cost him a lot money."

There were other pressures closing in, as the world changed
around him. The drug culture was exploding across America, and the
Globetrotters were not immune. When the Globetrotters flew home
from a trip to Mexico, one of Abe's favorite players was busted at the
airport by U.S. Customs officials for possession of marijuana and
hashish. NBA players were hiring agents to negotiate their contracts,
and there were rumblings that some of the Trotters would try to do
the same. "I'll never deal with any agents!" Abe growled. "He was a
man of his time," says Wyonella Smith, "and [agents were] something
new and different."

The strain of the failed business ventures and the "dog food" dinners and grueling travel all combined to hasten his decline. Judging
from his correspondence, he seemed to be growing weary of the in-
cessant problems and logistical complications of running the tour—
the worries about portable floors that had to be shipped halfway
around the world, incomplete visa applications, contract squabbles
with union musicians, and the never-ending stream of personnel
problems.

In 1965, it all came to a head. Instead of slowing down, as his
doctors and family had been urging, he booked himself on a Herculean four-month-long "around the world" tour to meet with promoters in Europe, Turkey, India, Thailand, Hong Kong, Japan, the

Philippines, Singapore, Australia, New Zealand, and Hawaii. It was enough to break a man half his age, but Abe seemed to be testing himself, to see if he could still cut it—or die trying.

On July 20, ninety days into the marathon, he was starting to realize the enormity of what he had brought on himself. In a letter to Red Klotz, from Tokyo, he wrote: "I thought over a period of 20 years of travel to almost a hundred countries around this little old globe of ours . . . and every major city on the face of that globe . . . that I knew what travel was . . . but this past 90 days have beaten anything ever attempted."

He pushed on to Australia, where it all caught up with him. He came down with a severe cold, refused to see a doctor, and nearly died. "We learned later that he had suffered a mild heart attack there," says Fay Saperstein. By the time he made it home to Chicago, he was in terrible shape. "He should have never gone to Australia," says Red Klotz. "He messed himself all up. He knew he was gonna go. I used to bring soup up to him in his hotel room, and he'd sit in a dark room and drink some soup. But he just didn't want to let up."

Explaining Abe's condition to a player, Marie wrote: "He has been quite ill for several weeks and although he is recuperating nicely right now, his daily working hours are very short and isn't getting involved in too much correspondence work." Unable to travel and forced to abide by a restricted work schedule, he had more time to reflect. In January 1966, he wrote to a promoter in Australia:

The first days of a New Year . . . 1966 . . . and an opportunity to reflect on 1965 which proved to be a year of no end of problems of every nature and description. Contained in that particular year the first serious illnesses of my life in which I was incapacitated much of four months.

During his lengthy recuperation, he turned once again to the man who had stood beside him for over thirty years, through Montana blizzards and player revolts, the one person whom he trusted more than anyone else: Inman Jackson. The two men had been through so much together, and although Inman had stepped away from the limelight for the last twenty years, he had remained one of Abe's closest friends. Abe's only form of relaxation was fishing, and for years he and Inman and Red Klotz had gone fishing in the summers in the wilderness of northernmost Canada, 300 miles from the Arctic Circle. They would fly over the tundra in a bush plane to Great Slave Lake, where they'd live in a log cabin with no phone, and fish for grayling and giant Arctic char. Abe footed the bill for the fishing trips, but Inman handled the money and made all of the arrangements.

However paternalistic or condescending Abe might have been with other black players, there is no doubt that his relationship with Inman was one of deep friendship and respect. "He loved Inman Jackson," says Wyonella Smith. "Abe loved Jack as much as he loved his brothers. He was his closest friend. I'm sure there are things he shared with Jack that he didn't share with anyone. And when he got sick, he wanted Jack to be there."

Abe's recuperation took many weeks, but the front office staff knew he was coming around when he sent Inman out to buy a pair of women's legs off a department store mannequin, which he propped behind the drapes in his hospital room, as if a naked woman was hiding there.

He had refused his doctors' advice to slow down, but he did follow another of their suggestions: to spend the winter in California, away from Chicago's brutal weather. He rented an apartment (which belonged to Steve Allen) in Hollywood, and flew out on several occasions for extended stays, sometimes with his wife, Sylvia.

By mid-January 1966, he was feeling strong enough to resume a limited travel schedule, and made brief trips to San Francisco, Seattle, and Vancouver. In February, he flew to Portland and then to Honolulu, returning to Los Angeles each time. But then he had a relapse and ended up back in the hospital in Los Angeles for ten days. Now, in addition to his heart, he was having other problems. The doctors told him he needed a prostate operation, so Abe made plans to return to Chicago for the surgery. His brother Harry, who lived in Los Angeles, tried to talk him out of it. "I told him, 'Abe, we have good doctors out here, there's no reason to go back to Chicago,' " Harry says. But Abe insisted on going home.

On March 2, before leaving, he wired Joe Anzivino, who was in Florida with the Trotters' eastern unit. "Your . . . telegram received and Florida news most welcome. . . . Returned Monday from another ten day stretch hospitalization. Going into Chicago Monday afternoon. Let's stay in touch. Regards to yourself and host mutual acquaintances down the line. Abe Saperstein."

On March 7, he flew to Chicago on United Airlines Flight 102, which, as he duly noted in his Air Travel Log, left nine minutes late, and arrived in his hometown at three-fifteen P.M. He made one final entry in his log: "Clear sunshiny 70 degrees leaving Los Angeles. Nice ride over."

For the most widely traveled man in the world, it was a fitting commentary for his final journey: "Nice ride over."

On Friday, March 11, he was admitted to Chicago's Weiss Memorial Hospital for the prostate surgery. "He was supposed to come home the next day," says his sister Leah. While being prepped for the operation, however, he had a coughing fit that triggered a heart attack, from which he never recovered. He died on March 15, at seven P.M.

Marie Linehan and Wyonella Smith were still working at the office when the phone rang. "We knew he was quite ill, so we weren't that shocked," says Smith. The Trotters' east unit was playing that night in Greensboro, North Carolina, against their usual foils, the Washington Generals. When Red Klotz, the Generals' player-coach and one of Abe's closest friends, heard the news, he just walked off the court. "I couldn't finish the game," he says. "My team did, but I couldn't. I knew he was dying. He knew it too, but he kept fighting to the end." In the Trotters' locker room, a tearful Parnell Woods, the traveling secretary, told the players, "Skip has died. He would want you to finish the game and the tour." The Globetrotters played on.

In its obituary, the *Chicago Tribune* ran a photo of Abe with the caption "Show's over." His funeral took place on St. Patrick's Day, as 70,000 people marched through the Loop in the city's annual parade. "Abe was a showman to the end," wrote one scribe. "He was born on the Fourth of July, and was buried on St. Patrick's Day." Over the next few weeks, innumerable tributes were composed by his friends in the press. Abe was praised for his generosity, honesty, and contributions to both basketball and American goodwill abroad. "Thousands find it difficult to say good-by to Abe," wrote David Condon in the *Tribune*. "Even in recent weeks, when his face was lean and drawn, Abe still wore a captivating smile. He didn't know many languages, but that smile had universal appeal. The Saperstein smile ignited friendships in each nation that Abe visited."

Earlier in the 1965–66 season, Abe had come up with the idea of scheduling a game in Hinckley, Illinois, as a sentimental commemoration of the fortieth anniversary of the Trotters' "first game" in 1927. There wasn't room for a Hinckley game on the regular schedule, so the Trotters' front office tacked it on as the last game of the season. It was a terrific marketing idea and the perfect ending to the year. On April 13, the Harlem Globetrotters played once more in Hinckley, Illinois, but Abe wasn't there.

★

Ten months and three days after Abe Saperstein's passing, Goose Tatum died in El Paso, Texas, and the two men were reunited again in history.

Goose had been on a roller-coaster ride for years. After leaving the Trotters in 1955, he had joined up with Marques Haynes as a co-owner of the Harlem Magicians, and they barnstormed together for the next two seasons, doing very well financially. On the court, Goose was as good as ever. He scored 44 points one night in Philadelphia, and 62 in Washington, D.C. With Goose and Marques working together, other great ballplayers rallied to join them. Chuck Cooper, who had spent seven years in the NBA, signed on, as did Globetrotter veteran Josh Grider, who told reporters that he was "better satisfied, making a better salary, and less weary than I would be if I were playing with the other team."

Alarmed by the Magicians' success, Abe began pressuring local promoters to block the Magicians from playing big arenas, and was able to keep them out of Madison Square Garden, Chicago Stadium, and Detroit's Olympia. But Abe's old nemesis, Boston Celtics owner Walter Brown, let them play in Boston Garden, and in January 1957, the Magicians set a new Garden attendance record with 13,800 people. Marques couldn't resist taking a little shot at Abe, saying, "We honestly believe we have the finest aggregation of professional basketball players since the heyday of the New York Renaissance Club."

The next season, however, Goose decided to strike out on his own, forming the Harlem Stars in October 1957. It was one thing to be the headliner on the court, but it was altogether different to be the team owner and run the tour, and Goose's temperament wasn't really suited to it. After just one month, players were already jumping ship. Jim Tucker, a former All-American from Duquesne, packed his bags and left, as did Ernie Banks, the Chicago Cubs' popular shortstop, who was reportedly earning $100 a night as the team's announcer. In December, Goose had to cut back on expenses by dropping his regular opposition team, Bill Spivey's New York Olympians (Spivey would later sue Goose for back pay). Goose tried to arrange to play local teams in each city, but it didn't always work out. "Sometimes we'd show up for a game and there'd be nobody to play," recalls Elzie Lewis, who spent that season with Goose.

Over the next few years, he formed one new team after another. In July 1958, he organized "Goose Tatum and His Harlem Trotters," after Bunny Leavitt (the former world champion free-throw shooter) and an outfit called Western Productions reportedly offered Goose a $150,000 guaranteed contract, with incentives that could bring his income to $200,000 a year. This was the same year that Abe signed Wilt Chamberlain for $65,000, and Goose openly scoffed at that puny amount.

In September 1958, Leavitt announced a thirty-nation tour, covering Europe, South America, India, Australia, and New Zealand. But Abe immediately filed a lawsuit, claiming that Leavitt and Western Productions were pirating the Globetrotters' trademarked name and slogans. Abe also launched a full-scale publicity campaign in the international press to ensure that fans did not mistake Goose's team for the real Trotters. By the time Goose limped into Australia, he was drawing as few as 300 people for some games.

The next year, he went back to calling his team the Harlem Stars, but a report made the papers that his "off-court tantrums" had cost him a few players. "One day he'd be the best guy in the world, the next day he wouldn't want you to come near him," says Elzie Lewis. "Any little thing would set him off. If he thought a waitress was giving you more attention than him, or if we were in a nightclub and you'd be talking to a young lady, he'd come up and say, 'Rookie, it's your bedtime, go home.' He always wanted the young ladies, but he didn't want you to have them."

Goose's biggest problem was that he had started drinking. He had been a teetotaler during his years with the Trotters and an infrequent club hound, but now he started hanging out regularly in bars. There were rumors that he was even popping pills. He bought a pink Cadillac and grew a goatee, and when he stepped out of that car, dressed in his black beret and black jacket, he was the coolest dude around. But the combination of alcohol with his already fragile metabolism sometimes led to explosive results—particularly with women.

Goose and his wife, Nona, had always had an unusual marriage, in that he was seldom home, but now he started running around openly with other women. That was too much for Nona. Once, in Chicago, they staged a Keystone Kops–like chase scene in which Nona was running after Goose, shooting at him with a pistol, while two Chicago cops were chasing her. One of Nona's shots clipped Goose's right ear, after which, according to Marques Haynes, an eyewitness, "Goose went into second gear."

Nona divorced him shortly after he quit the Globetrotters in 1955. "I think they had a genuine love for each other," says Marjorie Tatum Byrd, his stepdaughter. "But they just couldn't be together, because there were other women involved." Even years later, when Goose had remarried, he and his new wife would come stay at Nona's house. "Other people thought that was strange, but my mother didn't mind," Byrd adds. "I think she was one of the few people who really understood him."

Unhinged from Nona, his only thread of normalcy, Goose began to spiral out of control. There followed more drinking and more women, in rapid succession. He moved to Kansas City and married a woman named Delores, but the marriage lasted less than two years. Around Christmas 1956, he and Marques Haynes and their Harlem Magicians played a game at the University of Detroit, then went back to the Gotham Hotel, a classy black hotel. An attractive white woman, Naomi Hirsh, showed up at the hotel that night. She was from New York, the daughter of Hungarian Jews, and was an art student and a bohemian. From then on, she and Goose started seeing each other.

That was the final straw for Delores, who filed for divorce in January 1957, alleging that Goose was "quarrelsome, drank too much, and associated with other women." A Kansas City judge ordered Goose to pay $2,000 a month temporary alimony until the divorce was final.

By March, Naomi Hirsh was pregnant. She went back east to New Hampshire, where she delivered a baby boy in December 1957; she named him Reece Tatum III.

By then, Goose had started dating Lotti Graves, a stunning exotic dancer from Detroit who was known as "Lotti the Body." Considered to be Detroit's answer to Gypsy Rose Lee, she was also billed as "The Chocolate Bombshell." Goose took her back home with him to El Dorado to meet his family, and took her on overseas jaunts to Cuba, Australia, and Japan. Lotti the Body let everyone know that he was her personal manager—and her man.

Over the next three years, there were two confusing, quasi-legal marriages. Lotti the Body claimed that she and Goose had gotten married in Mexico in 1958, but then, in 1960, he allegedly married Naomi Hirsh, also in Mexico, when his son, Reece III, was two years old.

If women were complicating his life, that was nothing compared with the affair he had with the Internal Revenue Service. In January 1961, just hours before he was to take the court in Dallas, two U.S. marshals served him with indictments on two counts of federal tax evasion. A grand jury had charged him with failing to file income tax returns in 1956 and 1957 on gross income of $58,869 and $40,924, respectively. The IRS said Goose owed $118,000 in back taxes and penalties. He was arrested and taken before a U.S. commissioner in the Dallas federal courthouse. Dressed all in black, Goose wept softly when he was brought before the judge. Required to post a $5,000 bond, Goose opened a black leather satchel stuffed with bills, and deputies counted out $5,000 on the table. "Basketball, I knows, and knows well," Goose told a reporter. "Money, I don't." His eyes were bloodshot and a reporter described him as "mystified" by the proceedings. He claimed that a Kansas City attorney handled all his bookkeeping. "I can't figure it out," he said, brushing away tears. "You know, I don't worry about money. If I did, maybe I wouldn't be here now. All I've ever wanted in the world is to have the best basketball team, better than the Globetrotters. That's what I'm after and I think I've got that team now."

Ironically, the indictment was good for business, as an overflow crowd of 9,500 showed up that night in Dallas and cheered Goose wildly. That was the thing—he could still put on a show. He was forty-three years old, with flecks of gray in his hair and beard, and sportswriters were referring to him as "ageless" and comparing him with Satchel Paige (who was actually touring with him, providing halftime entertainment). Yet he could still bring it on the court. And good players still wanted to play with him. Sweetwater Clifton, for instance, now retired from the NBA, was touring with him.

But there was an element of unreality about the whole thing. In 1961, he started advertising that his twenty-two-year-old son, "Goose Tatum Jr.," was playing with him, and they'd stage "father-son" publicity shots with Papa Goose giving pointers to Junior. But the real Goose Tatum Jr. (called Sonny) was only eleven years old and living with Nona in Indiana, and the guy in the photos was a fake. His real name was "Tiny" Brown, and he was a dribbling specialist from Detroit. Still, they'd play it up big during the games, with Goose Sr. working the pivot and "Goose Jr."—the "gosling," some reporters called him—dribbling the ball.

Other strange things started happening. Two months after his tax indictment, he got arrested in Henderson, Kentucky, for punching a referee. Goose's team was losing to some ex–college boys in the third quarter, and Goose got in an argument with the ref and hit him, knocking him to the floor. He posted a $1,000 bond and apologized, saying, "You get in the heat of things and you lose your head."

A few weeks later, Lotti the Body "put their business on the street." In a lengthy interview with the *Pittsburgh Courier*'s theater critic, of all people, complete with revealing photos of her on the stage, Lotti begged Goose to take her back. "The Goose Still Loves Me" the headline crooned. His love life had become a national soap opera. The article read like a kiss-and-tell armchair psychoanalysis of Goose, but it did disclose some disturbing insights about his state of mind. Mutual friends described him as a "troubled man, filled with suspicion of almost everyone; a tortured athletic genius who, in the twilight of a fabulous career, feels that almost every man's hand is turned against him." Furthermore, his friends said he was "dissipating large sums of money and maybe his health in a calculated drive of self-destruction" and needed Lotti as a "shelter in his own personal storm."

In May, he pleaded nolo contendere to the tax evasion charges, which the judge described as a "gentlemanly way of pleading guilty." Prosecutors revealed that he hadn't filed tax returns at all in 1956 or 1957, and had filed returns but not paid any taxes in 1958 and 1959. "It looks like this man's skill may be primarily confined to his hands and feet," the judge said. "He may need a manager or a guardian or maybe both." A month later, the judge sentenced him to ninety days in jail and three years' probation. "Goose, you're a fine basketball player," the judge remarked, "but I can't say much else for you."

He went to prison, where he tried to stay in shape by practicing his hook shot in his cell, using an old loaf of bread for a ball. After serving fifty days, he was released early when Texas oilman Cal Boykin offered to underwrite a new tour for Goose's team. Eventually, Goose settled with the IRS by agreeing to pay $15,000—which was less than ten cents on the dollar for the $152,611 in back taxes, penalties, and interest that he owed. Plus, the feds would take 30 percent of his earnings for the next ten years, if he made more than $5,000. One reason the IRS agreed to the settlement was that Goose was broke, and they'd rather get something than nothing at all. He had no bank account, only $100 in cash, and was $169,000 in debt. An accountant began traveling with the team, balancing the books after every game and making sure the IRS got its 30 percent of the gate.

In the midst of all this financial misery, with his world crumbling around him, how did Goose deal with it? He celebrated his release from prison by buying himself a new $7,500 Cadillac. The man needed his ride.

But going to prison seemed to have been a wake-up call for him. He now had a young son who was depending on him. Reece III and Naomi were going out on the road with him, traveling in the Caddy while the other players rode in the team bus. "I grew up in the back-seat of my dad's Cadillac," says Reece, who is now forty-seven. "That was my home." The boy followed Goose around so much that Goose nicknamed him Bird-Dog, which was later shortened to Bird.

In April 1962, *Ebony* magazine did a five-page photo spread about Goose, entitled "A Trio of Goose Tatums," which featured pictures of Goose with four-year-old Reece and the fake Goose Jr. (Tiny Brown). "I've settled down now," Goose said. "I have my sons with me now. I've got to set the right example."

And he did, at least for a while. Goose pulled himself together and stopped drinking. He changed the name of his team to the Harlem Roadkings, which symbolized a fresh start. Naomi started functioning as the road manager, so that Goose could concentrate on the team. She counted the house, collected the gate receipts, and carried the money box. "My dad played ball and my mom was in the money room," says Reece. "That's where she lived."

By 1963, Goose's life was turning around. He was drawing big crowds, his team was traveling in a converted Greyhound bus, and they were making enough money that *all* his players were buying Caddys. "We were playing some big houses in Detroit, Milwaukee, and all around California," recalls Bill Powell, Goose's nephew from El Dorado, who spent three years playing with the team.

The money was rolling in again. "When we were traveling, we'd stop at banks a couple of times a week," says Reece. "My dad was always opening up new savings accounts. We'd stop at a bank, Dad would deposit a bunch of cash, and we'd drive on to the next city."

For the first time in his life, Goose was really functioning as a father. In the past, he might have seen his older son, Sonny, only a couple of times a year, but Reece was with him every day. "My dad was really trying—for me," Reece says. "I showed up during the glory years, and it was an awesome life for a young kid." Whenever they stopped at a hotel, Goose and Naomi would rent one room for themselves and give Reece his own room. By the time he was four, he had learned to read two words: "color TV." As soon as they got to the outskirts of their destination city, Reece would start scanning the billboards, searching for a hotel with color TV. When they checked in, he would ask the desk clerk, "Does this hotel have room service?" "I was so spoiled," he says, laughing. "I had my own room, my own color TV, and was ordering pork chops from room service. I thought that was normal—the way every kid lived."

As they traveled around the country, Goose made a point of sharing his favorite things with his son. One of his great joys was soul food, and Goose would take Reece to the best soul food restaurants in every town. He also loved watermelons and would stop if they passed a U-pick melon field. "We'd load up the whole back of the Caddy with melons," Reece says. "And we'd sit in a park and eat melons—he loved that." The boy became an expert at sighting another of Goose's favorites: Stuckey's restaurants. "We'd buy those Stuckey's log rolls and munch on those," says Reece. "I was an expert at spotting the Stuckey's and the color TVs." When they stopped for gas, Goose would buy grape sodas for Reece and himself, and show the boy how to pour a pack of salted peanuts in the soda and chug it down, the way he did when he was a kid. In Florida, Goose took his son to see an alligator farm. And if they passed some little funky museum along the highway, Goose would stop there as well.

In the off-seasons, they sometimes rented an apartment in San Francisco, Los Angeles, or Mexico, and would just hang out for a month or two. In San Francisco, Goose would take Reece on walks to a nearby park, where Goose would play basketball with local guys to keep in shape. Or he'd take the boy out and play baseball, and even bought him a baseball uniform and glove. In Mexico, they went for boat rides on a canal. Mostly, however, they just hung out together, sitting around their apartment, watching TV. Sometimes, Goose would get out the hot plate he always carried and fry some "gourmet" bologna sandwiches on white bread. "Those times had nothing to do with him being *Goose Tatum*," Reece recalls. "He was probably tired of all the traveling, and was thinking, 'Can't we just sit here for a while?' "

But there were times when being Goose Tatum was cool, however, because of the celebrity status it afforded. Once, at a Ray Charles concert, Charles stopped his performance to introduce

Goose, who stood up in the spotlights and took a bow. Another time, Goose took Reece to a Sonny Liston fight, when he was still the heavyweight champ, and took his son to Liston's dressing room to introduce him. Another time, Goose took Reece to an airport and put him on a plane, and his "babysitter" on the flight was singer Della Reese.

The happiness in Goose's personal life affected him on the basketball court. Goose was able to reach back and tap into a reservoir of creativity that had survived the wasted years. He was now pushing forty-five, but the old man seemed to catch a second wind, and he was his old self again on the court. In fact, he may have been better. At that time, there was a glut of black show teams that were spin-offs of the Globetrotters, including Marques Haynes's Harlem Magicians, Goose's Roadkings, the Harlem Satellites, Runt Pullins's Harlem (né Broadway) Clowns, and Boid Buie's Harlem Stars. They were all playing the same circuit, following right on each other's heels, sometimes just a few days apart. Fans were seeing the same basic show over and over, and were getting bored. "Some nights Goose would say, 'This is not working,' " Bill Powell recalls. "He'd make some switches or adjustments—tell you to do something different than the normal routine. Or he'd start working the crowd and getting people involved."

For the first time in years, the master showman was creating new reams. All the other show teams, including the Trotters, were stealing *his* routines—the gags and trick balls and pantomimes that he had invented twenty years earlier—but instead of sulking about it, or suing somebody, Goose went out and invented new stuff. At a point in his career when he should have been sitting back and resting on his laurels, he was developing brand-new material. "Even while we were traveling on the bus, he would think of new routines he wanted to try," says Powell. "He'd work on it for maybe two or three weeks, just practicing with the ball, thinking about it and visualizing it. And when you saw it on the floor, it'd blow you away."

Some of his comedy was on the cutting edge, particularly for the early sixties. In one of his routines, he'd run up into the stands and "accidentally" trip and fall onto the lap of a pretty white woman. When he stood up, he'd be holding a pair of women's panties, which he would lift up triumphantly and yell, "Where'd these come from?"

(The panties had actually been hidden in his shorts.) He'd run back to center court, stretch out the panties for all to see, and run around showing them off. "The crowd went insane," Reece remembers. "As a kid, I just thought it was funny, but later I realized that he was really pushing the envelope."

Goose's straight game was also undergoing an amazing revitalization. The Globetrotters were playing stooge teams every night, but Goose couldn't afford to bring his own opposition team every night, so he was often playing against *real* opponents—guys who wanted nothing more than to defeat the legendary Goose Tatum. After the ABL fell apart in 1962, there was an abundance of quality ballplayers, former pros who were looking for a game. Goose would show up, not knowing what kind of team he would face, but it wasn't the Washington Generals. He had to really *play*.

After twenty years, Goose had come full circle. It was like the days before the stooge teams, when the Trotters were "playing for their beans" every night. He had to work to get a lead, so he could put on the show against teams that weren't cooperating. It was the real thing. "He would be putting on the show and these guys don't know they're supposed to go along with the program," says Powell. "That's when you would really see what he could do—he'd hide the ball, put it behind them—and it was for real."

By 1964, the year the Trotters had their "worst season ever," the Roadkings were doing better than ever. Goose and Naomi were running the tour together—handling the programs, the transportation, the hotels. Goose hadn't been drinking for three years, and had his old demons under control. He and Marques Haynes, who had maintained a solid relationship through the years, would show up at each other's games when they played the bigger cities, and it was like the old days all over again. With his own team, Goose was still pulling off the father-son act with Tiny Brown, the fake Goose Tatum Jr. In fact, there were *two* fake Goose Tatum Jrs. Goose's nephew, Bill Powell, had also played the role and had his picture published in the paper, standing alongside Goose.

That summer, the *real* Goose Tatum Jr came out on the road for a visit. Sonny, as he was called, was fifteen years old and a rising junior in high school. He and Goose barely knew each other, as Goose had seldom been around when he was growing up. "We were not the Beaver Cleaver family," says Marjorie Tatum Byrd. Goose might come to Gary only two or three times a year, yet Sonny worshiped his dad. What he wanted most in life was to play ball with his father—to *be* Goose Tatum Jr. "My brother heard there was a fake Junior and he wanted to be there with his father to earn his place," Byrd adds.

The kid had talent, and Bill Powell, his first cousin, took him under his wing. "He was going to be a good ballplayer," Powell says. But during his visit, Sonny and Goose had a falling-out—Goose snapped at him, most likely—and Sonny came to Powell in tears. "I want to go home," he cried. "My daddy doesn't like me." Powell convinced him to go talk to Goose, to try and work things out. When the boy returned, Powell asked how it went. "We both started crying," Sonny replied. Goose had taken a look at his own behavior and had reached out to his son. "That was the best thing that could have happened between them," says Bill Powell. When Sonny went back home to Gary, Goose promised him that the next summer he could actually play with the team.

Life was good.

And then a fluke accident set the wheels spinning in motion toward catastrophe. In January 1965, playing in Houston before a full house of 8,000 people, Goose landed awkwardly on his right leg and it snapped. He went down on the floor, writhing in pain. The crowd, thinking it was one of Goose's routines, started laughing. His team gathered around him, but the crowd had seen this before, too, and laughed harder. They were waiting to see the old sneaker-under-the-nose trick, and watch Goose leap up in the air. Over the public-address system, the game announcer asked, "Is there a doctor in the house?" As Reece III recalls, "People were in hysterics, thinking it was part of the act." It wasn't until they carted him off on a stretcher, and then to the hospital in an ambulance, that the crowd realized he was hurt. X-rays showed a fracture of the right leg. Goose told the papers he would be out of the hospital in three or four days.

Then came the bad news. Doctors discovered that he was suffering from a chronic bone infection. Worse, he had liver disease—almost certainly the result of his years of hard drinking. The broken leg healed fairly quickly and Goose went back on the road, but the bone infection wouldn't go away. "We went to doctors all over the country," says Reece Tatum. "That leg was a nightmare."

About this time, Goose and Naomi bought a three-bedroom stucco house in El Paso, Texas, and moved there. Goose started seeing a bone specialist in El Paso, a Dr. Garcia, who was treating the infection. The Tatums spent so much time in Garcia's waiting room that young Reece named a little hand puppet Dr. Garcia. When the Roadkings went back on tour, Goose was still laid up with his leg. But it hurt business to not have the headliner perform, so he had to go out periodically and play, particularly in major cities. Eventually, Garcia performed surgery on the leg and was able to clear up the infection, but it was months before Goose was recovered.

In the summer of 1965, Sonny Tatum—the *real* Goose Tatum Jr.—came back to play with his father. With Goose's help, Sonny had convinced Nona to let him skip his senior year of high school to play with the team. "She didn't want to let him go at first, but they promised her that he would finish high school," says Marjorie Tatum Byrd.

All that summer and fall, Goose, Naomi, Sonny, and Reece were living in the stucco house in El Paso, on Puerto Rico Street. They shared a running joke about having three Reeces in the same house, and when Naomi called for Reece, any one of them might answer. But it was a glorious few months. For the first time, they were like a regular family in a regular house. Young Reece, who was eight, suddenly had a brother. Sonny, who was sixteen, found a girlfriend in El Paso, who would come to visit. Goose brought home two dogs, which he named Kenyatta and Castro, and kept them in the backyard. For that brief time, they *were* the Beaver Cleaver family.

But when basketball season began, they went back on the road. Goose started working Sonny into the games, teaching him the routines. Some nights he would play on the Roadkings, and other nights he would play on the opposition team. He wasn't good enough yet to be the dribbler, so Tiny Brown was still playing the part of Goose Tatum Jr. But Sonny had designs on the job, which was his birthright.

Then, on April 2, 1966, two weeks after Abe Saperstein's death, the Harlem Roadkings were scheduled to play a night game in

Mt. Pleasant, Texas. Goose, Naomi, and Reece had gone on ahead in the Cadillac. Sonny was coming later, riding in a car with several players from the opposition team. They drove through Texarkana, Texas, sixty miles from their destination. Two miles west of town, Sonny's car collided head-on with a chicken truck. He was killed, along with two passengers in the other vehicle.

Goose and the Roadkings had already arrived in Mt. Pleasant. There was a full house in the local gym. The Roadkings came out on the court and went through their normal pregame warm-ups, but the opposition team still hadn't arrived. The crowd was getting antsy. Game time came and went, but the other team still hadn't shown. Goose was stalling for time. Naomi had already collected the money and certainly didn't want to have to give it back. Young Reece was sitting at courtside and realized that something was wrong. Where is the other team? he wondered. Finally, an announcement was made that the game was canceled, but nobody ever said why.

Goose and Naomi couldn't bring themselves to tell young Reece. A few days later, they were in the Cadillac, cruising down the highway. From his usual seat in back, Reece called out to his father, "Dad, I wish my brother didn't give me noogies on my head." It was a typical sibling complaint that any young kid might make—why is my brother picking on me? Goose turned around and looked at him and said, "Your brother is dead." Huge teardrops were pouring out of his eyes and rolling down his cheeks. Goose got out of the car and walked away. "That was something that is etched in my soul," Reece says today. "My father's reaction was so overwhelming; he had nothing but red eyes and baseball-sized tears falling out of his eyes."

Goose could not forgive himself. After reconciling with his older son and having the chance to be the father he had never been, he had let the boy come out on the road, against his mother's wishes, and get himself killed. Goose made all the arrangements for the funeral and had Sonny's body shipped back to Gary, with instructions not to have an open casket, as there had been extensive facial damage. But he couldn't bring himself to face Nona, so he didn't return for the funeral. Nona took it hard that Goose didn't come. Over time, however, she would come to terms with her son's death, saying,

"At least Sonny had that time with his father. That's all he ever wanted."

Goose started drinking again. Those suffering from liver disease have a good chance of recovery, even if they'd been heavy drinkers, if the disease is caught early and they never drink again. However, the American Medical Association warns, "Your liver will remain particularly sensitive to alcohol, so any future drinking should be considered virtually suicidal."

Goose didn't seem to care. "I remember watching my father fall apart after my brother died," says Reece. "It destroyed him. That was it!" The word filtered back to his family in El Dorado that Goose was "drinking himself to death." When Nona heard, she told her daughter, "It's more than he can handle."

Two months after Sonny's death, Goose's liver started shutting down. He was admitted to Providence Hospital in El Paso, the first of many stays. Chronic liver disease is a degrading way to die. Fluid retention causes grotesque swelling of the ankles and stomach. There is memory loss, weakness, confusion, nausea, and vomiting. Men lose their sexual urge and their breasts sometimes enlarge. In its final stages, there can be internal bleeding or hemorrhage. Doctors can reduce the swelling with diuretics, but they cannot reverse the course of the disease. At one point, Goose spent four straight months in the hospital, and had to cancel a South American tour. When he was home, the house on Puerto Rico Street looked like a hospital ward. "There was an entire tabletop filled with pills," says Reece. "There were so many pills—an arsenal of drugs. That period in El Paso was the end time."

Goose's hospital bills were draining his cash, and Nona tried to keep the Roadkings going without him. In January 1967, a Dallas promoter decided to help out by holding "Goose Tatum Day" at the Roadkings' regularly scheduled game on January 19. He invited all former Globetrotters and others who had played with Goose to come back and honor him. Marques Haynes said he would leave his own team in California and go to Dallas to play in Goose's place. Goose had been readmitted to Providence Hospital on January 4, and his doctors told him he shouldn't even think about playing basketball again for at least six months. But from his hospital bed, Goose vowed that he would not only come to Dallas, but play. "They are expecting me to be there and I'll be there," he said. "I think I'll even be able to play some. I want to hear them laugh."

Against doctor's orders, he booked a flight from El Paso to Dallas, then left the hospital and went home to get ready for the big show. On Wednesday, January 18, about nine A.M., he was taking a bath, and felt weak as he climbed out of the tub. He called for Naomi, then struggled to the bed and collapsed. Naomi called for help, and the El Paso fire department responded. Firefighters gave him external heart massage on the way to the emergency room, but he died at 10:17 A.M. An autopsy concluded that he had died of natural causes.

Nine-year-old Reece was at school. "I don't remember saying good-bye to my dad that morning before I left," he says, ruefully. "I always wished I had." During the day, one of his classmates told him, "There was an ambulance in front of your house and they took your dad somewhere." Reece was worried, so he went home. When he walked in the door, Naomi was sitting on a chair, with a neighbor beside her. "Reece, I need to talk to you," she said. She took him in a back room and said, "Your father died today."

"I didn't know what to do with that," Reece says. "I didn't know how to even put it in my head." It had just been a few months since his brother died, and now his father had passed, too. "I must have been in shock, because I did the exact same thing I did every day when I got home from school: I walked in and turned on cartoons on TV. I couldn't deal with it. I didn't cry for my father that year, or the next year. I couldn't get it in, I couldn't comprehend. But years later, it came out!"

Goose had always refused to reveal his true age, but the El Paso hospital announced definitively that he was forty-five years old, and recorded his date of birth as May 3, 1921. Sportswriters around the country would note wistfully that at least one mystery had been solved. But Goose was actually forty-eight, and was still fooling them from the grave.

Naomi Tatum announced that Goose's funeral would be private, following his wishes, and that he would be buried at Fort Bliss National Cemetery at ten o'clock on Friday morning, with full military honors. Dallas promoter Lon Varnell said he was going ahead with plans for Goose Tatum Day on Saturday. "We are going to make it as big a tribute to Goose as possible," he said. "We know that's what Goose would want."

In El Dorado, his sister, Thelma, was devastated. She and Goose had remained extremely close over the years. Their mother, Mary, had died a few years earlier, but Goose had always been a dutiful son, checking on her constantly and paying for an addition on Thelma's house so that Mary could live there. Goose had often returned to El Dorado to visit, and sometimes he brought his team and played a game. He was El Dorado's most famous favorite son. Whenever he came to town, he'd bring the whole team over to Thelma's house for one of her fried chicken dinners, with dumplings and greens and apple cobbler for dessert. Neighborhood kids would gather on the front porch, and Goose would come out and show them a few tricks and talk to them about staying in school and obeying their parents.

When Thelma heard that he was gone, she broke the news to her daughter, Shirley, before she went to school that morning. Thelma and Booker Tatum, Goose's older brother, both intended to be at the funeral, but then they looked at a map. It was over 900 miles from El Dorado to El Paso, a two-day drive, and there was no way to make it by Friday morning. Thelma didn't understand why Naomi wanted to bury him so quickly. "My mom was very hurt by that," says her daughter, Shirley McDaniel. "She didn't get a chance to be there."*

Marques Haynes heard the news of Goose's death on his car radio. He was driving with Josh Grider from Las Vegas to Los Angeles for an upcoming game when an announcement came on the radio that two famous sports figures had died: prizefighter Barney Ross and Goose Tatum. The next morning, Marques and Grider flew

---

* In fact, Naomi's behavior after Goose's death seemed so odd that his family began to question whether Goose had died from natural causes. A week after Goose died, Naomi gave away Reece's two dogs, and two months later, she packed them both up and moved to Barbados, where she opened two restaurants. She cut all ties with Goose's family, and threw away all photos and mementos that referred to him. They stayed gone five years, and by the time they returned to the States, young Reece had lost all traces of the black side of the family. He would not reconnect with them for nearly forty years.

from Los Angeles to Oklahoma, picked up Marques's first wife, then caught an afternoon flight to El Paso for the funeral. They arrived Thursday evening, rented a car, and checked into a hotel.

Knowing that the funeral was scheduled for ten A.M. Friday, they arrived at the Fort Bliss Cemetery early, in plenty of time. There were no signs of a funeral. Finally, they found some gravediggers who told them that Goose had been buried an hour earlier, with no ceremony.

"Did they say a prayer or read scripture?" Marques asked.

"They didn't do nothing," one gravedigger replied. He told Marques that they backed the hearse up to the grave, lowered the casket into the ground, and drove away.

Earlier that month, Marques had called Goose in the hospital and they had talked about touring together again when Goose got better. The two men had played ball together all over the world for twenty years, and now Goose was dead and in the ground before Marques had even had a chance to say good-bye.

He and his wife and Josh Grider drove to a drugstore, bought a $2.98 Bible, and returned to Goose's newly filled grave. Out of respect, the gravediggers wandered over and formed a half circle around the grave, while Marques read the Twenty-third Psalm and they all recited the Lord's Prayer. The most celebrated African American basketball player in the world had at least had a proper burial.

Saturday night, a full house turned out for Goose Tatum Day in Dallas, honoring the memory of basketball's greatest showman. Just a week before he died, Goose had done an interview with an El Paso reporter. When asked if he had any plans to retire, Goose had shrugged and said, "I'll keep playing until the people stop laughing. They're still laughing, so I'll keep playing."

The people were still laughing, but the Golden Goose was gone.

CHAPTER 16

Meadowlark

In the 1970s, America was a terribly fractured nation. The volatility and innocence of the 1960s had hardened into cynicism, polarization, and backlash. A decade of assassinations, which had created a pantheon of fallen heroes—JFK, Medgar, Malcolm, Martin, and Bobby—gave way to a decade of self-inflicted martyrdom—Jimi Hendrix, Janis Joplin, and Jim Morrison. The country was now keenly polarized over Vietnam, busing, abortion, and equal rights for women. The initial upsurge of the civil rights movement, with its victories in Selma and Birmingham, had been blunted by the murder of Dr. King, riots in Watts and dozens of other cities, and the slow grinding battles over court-ordered desegregation. Lunch counter sit-ins and nonviolent civil disobedience had been replaced by Black Power salutes and Bobby Seale exhorting black Americans to pick up a gun. "The Summer of Love" and Woodstock had given way to Kent State and Altamont Speedway. The Supremes and the Beatles had broken up, and John Coltrane, Louis Armstrong, and Jackie Robinson were dead.

Today, the sixties are sometimes romanticized in myth and legend, but the sixties didn't arrive in much of America until the seventies. Marijuana, hashish, LSD, quaaludes, speed, and even heroin moved beyond Haight Ashbury and Harlem into suburban schools and middle-class homes. Hippie communes sprouted in East Tennessee. Women's consciousness-raising groups were birthed in Muskogee and Montgomery.

Every day, the news brought shocking blows to American

confidence and supremacy. In just the first six months of 1971, Lt. William Calley was convicted of murder in the My Lai massacre, the Pentagon Papers were published by the *New York Times,* and the Harlem Globetrotters lost a game.

It sounds silly.

In the context of what was happening in America, it was hard to take the Globetrotters seriously. Abe Saperstein had been dead less than five years, but that seemed like another age—like an exhibit from a traveling museum. Nonetheless, the 1970s were also tumultuous for the Trotters, and three events from 1971 capture that best.

On January 5, the Globetrotters did, in fact, lose their first game in nine years, falling 100–99 to Red Klotz's New Jersey Reds. The game, which took place in Martin, Tennessee, ended the Trotters' 2,495-game winning streak, going back to the final College All-Star series in 1962. But rather than emphasizing the Trotters' dominance over that period, the loss symbolized how far they had fallen. It became a joke. "One of the most discouraging aspects of a sportswriter's professional life is to watch a mighty franchise come apart at the seams," Bill Gleason wrote mockingly. "And now it's happening again with the most awesome dynasty of them all, the Harlem Globetrotters. . . . Somewhere Goose Tatum is grinding his teeth."

Every time the Trotters' front office bragged about their win-loss record, people smirked. The nine-year winning streak just meant that it had been nine years since they'd played a legitimate team. Red Klotz had been providing opposition teams for the Trotters since 1950, when Abe had loaned him $1,500 to buy a used DeSoto to haul around his team, which has been known alternately, over the years, as the New York Nationals, Atlantic City Seagulls, Boston Shamrocks, New Jersey Reds, and, most famously, the Washington Generals. Klotz still insists that his team plays to win, but they're not allowed to contest passes to the showman or interrupt the basic reams; with those restrictions, they're bound to give up enough baskets to lose.

The Martin, Tennessee, game wasn't so much a triumph for Klotz's lovable losers as it was a reflection of everything that was wrong with the Globetrotters. Even knowing the script, they managed to lose. "It was a terrific ball game," Klotz recalls. "Generally in the last quarter the Trotters went into their show, but that night Meadowlark decided to really play. He was going to really whip us." Klotz lets out a satisfied chuckle. "But it didn't work out that way."

The Reds built a 12-point lead with two minutes to play. The Trotters made a furious comeback, aided by the timekeeper, who Klotz insists was stalling the clock, and took a 99–98 lead. But Klotz, who was a legitimate ballplayer in his day (he played on the 1948 Basketball Association of America champion Baltimore Bullets) and one of the best long-range shooters in the country, connected on a two-hand set shot from twenty feet to put the Reds up by one. On the Trotters' final possession, Meadowlark's shot rimmed in and out, and the Reds got the rebound. Klotz dribbled out the remaining seconds, as the crowd counted down: "five-four-three-two-one." When the buzzer sounded, the fans sat frozen, unsure of what had just happened. "They were still waiting for the show," Klotz says. "They couldn't believe the game was over." Finally, when it dawned on them that the Globetrotters had lost, people started booing. Klotz rushed his players off the court and into their locker room, where they hoisted Klotz on their shoulders and poured orange soda over him, since they had no champagne. Later, Klotz would say of the win, "It was like killing Santa Claus." The Trotters had become "The Meadowlark Lemon Show" to the point that if they really needed to play ball, it was hard to turn it on.

Four months after their loss, a second emblematic event occurred: the Trotters hosted an NBC show called "An Evening with the Harlem Globetrotters" at Hofstra University, with Joe Garagiola as the announcer. This was their first prime-time broadcast of a game and their first show on NBC. After eleven years of Sunday afternoon games on CBS's *Sports Spectacular*, the Trotters had leveraged a two-year contract with NBC for *prime-time* specials, hoping to reach an even larger audience. If the Martin, Tennessee, loss symbolized the team's decaying basketball skills, the NBC specials were equally indicative of their emerging *show business* talents. They had become a ubiquitous force in the television industry, blanketing all demographic segments.

On their NBC prime-time specials, aimed at adult viewers, they would host celebrity games against the likes of Bill Cosby, Soupy

Sales, Red Buttons, James Caan, Jackie Cooper, Johnny Mathis, Robert Goulet, and Jo Anne Worley. In 1973, they would jump to ABC, signing a multiyear contract to broadcast annual Globetrotter specials on *Wide World of Sports*. In fact, the Globetrotters would be on that season's premiere episode of *Wide World*, with the game announced by ABC's *Monday Night Football* trio of Howard Cosell, Frank Gifford, and Don Meredith. The show would be the second highest rated show in the history of *Wide World of Sports*, topped only by a Muhammad Ali–Joe Frazier fight.

Over the next thirteen years, ABC's Globetrotter specials would be filmed in exotic locations all over the world, including London, Hong Kong, the 1980 Lake Placid Olympics, Disney World, the Grand Ole Opry, and in 1976, most unique of all, on the grounds of Attica State Prison, where Howard Cosell presented a reprise of the 1971 Attica riots. As the Trotters' TV persona expanded, the basketball games themselves became almost secondary. Feature segments were shot of the Trotters roaming the French Quarter, singing with Charley Pride, boogying with Mr. T and Ben Vereen, riding "Thunder Mountain" at Disney World, touring F.A.O. Schwartz, and schmoozing with the Rockettes and the Broadway cast of *Annie*.

In between their yearly specials on *Wide World*, the Trotters would become talk show regulars, appearing on Johnny Carson, Dick Cavett, Joey Bishop, Mike Douglas, and Merv Griffith. They would appear on variety specials with Goldie Hawn, Burt Bacharach, and Donny and Marie Osmond. And they would play themselves in episodes of *The White Shadow, Gilligan's Island,* and *The Love Boat*.

Having saturated the adult viewing audience, market research showed that the Trotters' strongest fan base was with children, so, in September 1970, they invaded the Saturday-morning kids' market. *The Harlem Globetrotters*, a Hanna-Barbera cartoon, debuted on CBS, featuring six of the actual players (or animated versions of them), with their voices dubbed by Scatman Crothers, Stu Gilliam, and other actors. It was an immediate hit. Airing at 10:30 A.M., opposite *The Pink Panther* and *Here Comes Doubledecker*, the show swamped its competition, typically drawing more viewers than ABC and NBC combined. It became the most watched show on Saturday mornings, was extended for two more seasons, then went into international syndication.* The cartoons had a good-versus-evil theme, as the Globetrotters traveled around the world in their red-white-and-blue-striped bus, accompanied by their canine mascot, Gravy, and their bus driver, "Granny," a plucky senior in a cheerleader outfit.

Already a hit in animated form, the Trotters themselves took to the air in December 1972 with their own variety show, *The Harlem Globetrotters' Popcorn Machine,* again on CBS. The pilot was a one-hour prime-time special featuring eighteen Globetrotter players, led by Meadowlark Lemon, Curly Neal, and Geese Ausbie, singing, dancing, and performing comedy sketches with Bill Cosby, Dom DeLuise, Mama Cass Elliot, Ted Knight, and *All in the Family* stars Jean Stapleton and Sally Struthers. Again, the Trotters ruled the airwaves: the *Popcorn Machine* was the top-rated show in its time slot, outperforming *Adam 12* and *The Paul Lynde Show,* and was viewed in 13.4 million homes.

The pilot was spun off into another Saturday-morning children's show, which premiered in September 1974 and ran until 1976. Each show had a different theme (honesty, kindness, safety, brotherhood, teamwork, discipline, etc.), and the Trotters performed comedy sketches, songs, and dances, assisted by child star Rodney Allen Rippy. A special guest star appeared every week, with such well-known performers as Ruth Buzzi, Arte Johnson, Ted Knight, Sally Struthers, Esther Rolle, and Jim Backus. Sixteen episodes were produced, with memorable sketches of "Little Red Riding Hood," "The Three Musketeers," "Goldilocks and the Three Bears," and "Snow White and the Seven (Globetrotter) Dwarfs."

It was clean family entertainment with redeeming social values, and great marketing, but some old-time Globetrotters had to ask: "What the hell does this have to do with basketball?" And for the Globetrotter fans who still remembered the historic wins over the Lakers, it was hard to connect the dots from Inman Jackson, Goose Tatum, and Sweetwater Clifton to Geese Ausbie and Curly Neal in drag, playing Cinderella's evil sisters. For five decades, the Trotters had

---

* The Harlem Globetrotters *and* Sesame Street *were the only two American children's shows bought by the BBC. In 1979, a new cartoon,* The Super Globetrotters, *debuted on NBC, although it lasted only eight episodes.*

built their image as a great barnstorming team, perhaps the best basketball team in the country, which could also entertain. "First we win, then we put on the show," Abe used to say. The show was always the final affirmation of their basketball supremacy—counting coup on their victims—but now the show was all there was. "First we clown and, if there's time, we play a little ball," seemed to be the new motto. In their *Wide World of Sports* specials, the directors would include the Magic Circle and the corniest reams—the confetti in the bucket and the baseball game—but when it came time for straight basketball, they'd show a few dunks and go straight to commercial. The Globetrotters were no longer a great barnstorming team that could clown, they were just clowns. Or something. "At some point the Harlem Globetrotters ceased being anything in particular," Frank Deford wrote in a 1973 *Sports Illustrated* feature.

Which leads to the third, and most revealing, event of 1971: the Harlem Globetrotters went on strike. It didn't compute. "Smiles, Giggles and Ha-Ha's on Strike," read the headline in the *New York Times*. "In all the laughter, it never occurred to anybody that the Globetrotters might be unhappy," wrote Dave Anderson. "But the laughter has stopped. . . . The thought of the Globetrotters on strike is as incongruous as Snoopy stalking out of the 'Peanuts' comic strip shouting for a larger doghouse. But it's happening."

On November 16, 1971, the Globetrotters' east unit (now known as the National Unit) was supposed to play a game at Port Huron, Michigan. When they arrived in town, nine players refused to play. Their attorney, Elliott Goodman, held a press conference in Chicago and said that he had asked for a meeting with management to discuss the players' grievances. He also set a 5 P.M. deadline for management to respond. If they didn't, the players would strike the Port Huron game. When five o'clock came and went, the players threw up a picket line outside McMorran Sports Arena in Port Huron, in front of the ticket booth. They held hand-lettered signs: "Globetrotters Protest Unfair Treatment!" Even then, the whole scene had a surreal quality, as young children milled around the players, asking for autographs.

Significantly, the star of the team, Meadowlark Lemon, refused to join the strike. Instead, he flew back to Chicago and announced that he was eager to resume "making people laugh."

The sixties had finally caught up with the Globetrotters. Abe Saperstein was turning over in his grave.

⭐

In the first forty years of the Harlem Globetrotters' existence, they had one owner and one boss. In the next twenty-five years, they had five owners and eight different bosses. The one constant through all of the changes was Marie Linehan, who had been there since 1948 and would not retire until 1987.

When Abe died in March 1966, he did not leave the Harlem Globetrotters to his family. Instead, his will (which he wrote in 1951) stipulated that the executors of his estate—Allan Bloch, his longtime attorney, and Continental Illinois National Bank and Trust Company—were authorized to carry on the business for as long as they "deem it to be in the best interests of the trust estate." In other words, his executors had total discretion to keep or sell the Globetrotters, whichever they felt was best for the estate.

Abe died a wealthy man, with the total value of the estate, after taxes and estate fees, assessed at $2.5 million.* But the vast majority of that was the value of the team, and the Globetrotters would generate more value for the estate on the open market, rather than just continuing to operate the business.

The most interesting bequest in Abe's will was that Inman Jackson, Marie Linehan, and his sister Fay Saperstein were each left 4 percent of his estate, or $97,964.50 apiece. He had rewarded Inman and Marie for their decades of service with a financial windfall. His wife, Sylvia, received one-half of the estate, and his two children, Eloise and Jerry, split the rest.

For the first year after Abe's death, Morry Saperstein and Marie ran the business, under the oversight of Allan Bloch. The rest of the

---

* Abe went to his grave still owed money from Czechoslovakia, which had refused to let him take koruny out of the country, and from India. He was also still earning small royalties from The Harlem Globetrotters film.

old front office crew were still there: secretary Wyonella Smith, advance man Joe Anzivino, accountant Marian Polito, and publicist Bill Margolis. Inman Jackson was given the title of consulting coach. But the day-to-day decisions fell to Morry, who handled the scheduling, and to Marie, who had her hands on everything else. The executors had incorporated the Globetrotters as Abe Saperstein Enterprises, Inc., and Marie was put on the board of directors and given the title of vice president of administration. Years later, Anzivino would recall that first year: "We would all sit around and someone would say, 'I wonder what Abe would've done?' Marie would tell us what Abe would have done. She was one of those powerful forces." The extra responsibility took its toll, however, and she would describe those months as "killing ones for me" with "virtually no time off."

In a twist that Abe would have appreciated, they borrowed his old mantra for dealing with the loss of a star player: "We miss Abe, but the Globetrotters are better than ever!" And the results backed that up, as the Trotters broke the three million mark in attendance for the first time since the Year of the Big Dipper in 1958–59.

In the long run, however, Allan Bloch and Continental Bank were not interested in becoming basketball tycoons. Jerry Saperstein, Abe's twenty-seven-year-old son, was working in the front office and hoping to "some day fill the shoes of his showman father," but with a big inheritance tax looming, Abe's executors put the team up for sale. In January 1967, they started receiving bids from prospective buyers. There were three serious bidders, and in May, the executors signed a contract with Metromedia, which owned the Ice Capades and several TV and radio stations, to purchase the Trotters for $3.5 million. But the deal had to be approved by Judge Robert Dunne and, at the last minute, one of the other bidders raised its offer, and the judge accepted it.

On June 8, 1967, the Harlem Globetrotters were sold for $3.71 million to a trio of young businessmen: Potter Palmer IV, thirty-two, part-owner of the Atlanta Braves and a scion of Chicago's most famous family; his brother-in-law John O'Neil, from Miami, who would be a silent partner; and George Gillette Jr., a twenty-eight-year-old Wisconsin entrepreneur and management consultant, who was also the business manager and part-owner of the Miami

Dolphins. In approving the deal, Judge Dunne said, "Abe Saperstein was a shrewd businessman. He saw fit to give the coexecutors of his estate discretion to sell his lifetime enterprise. I will not interfere with the exercise of that discretion."

Gillette, Palmer, and O'Neil had bought *everything* that belonged to the Harlem Globetrotters, from the player contracts and trademarks to Abe's Eiffel Tower lamp and a Naugahyde recliner he'd used just before he died.

Gillette was named president and general manager, and gave up his position with the Dolphins to manage the Trotters on a daily basis. He shared two characteristics with Abe Saperstein: he was very short and he was a workaholic. Otherwise, they were from different worlds. He was the son of a prominent surgeon in Racine, Wisconsin, had gone to college at Amherst, and had worked for McKinsey and Company, a leading management consulting firm. Abe was an old-world immigrant and an old-school boss, who wouldn't have known what to do with a management consultant if one fell in his lap.

One of Gillette's first priorities had to be signing the players to new contracts, as all but Meadowlark had one-year deals that had already expired. When the sale of the team was first announced, the Trotters were on their European tour, and the players decided to ask for a meeting with the new owners to talk about salaries. With fresh young leadership, they were hoping to upgrade their salaries and working conditions. They still got no meal money, had no pension, and had to wash their own uniforms in their hotel sinks. Meadowlark was making $3,333.33 a month (still less than Goose Tatum in 1953), but the other nineteen players averaged barely more than $1,000 a month. Gillette and Palmer agreed to meet with them, which was, in itself, a good sign, as Abe would have had a fit at the suggestion of a team meeting about salaries.

The players knew that having Meadowlark on their side would be critical to their success, so they talked to him about their plans. He said he'd go with them to the meeting. When the meeting time rolled around, however, the players had all assembled in the hotel lobby, but Meadowlark hadn't shown.

"We decided we'd better go on up and Meadowlark could catch up with us," says Frank Stephens, who was in his second year with the Trotters. "Just as we got to the room, the door opened and Meadowlark walked out, with a big grin on his face. He said, 'I got mine, you get yours.' We all looked at each other and knew we were in trouble, because whatever his deal was, we were excluded."

It was a bad omen of things to come. Gillette had used his modern management techniques to play Meadowlark and the other players against each other. Over the next few years, the gap between the public's perception of the Globetrotters and the private reality of the players' lives would become a deepening chasm.

Gillette began modernizing the operation. He moved the front office out of the old Dearborn Street offices into a modern suite in the IBM building, with wood paneling and deep-pile carpets. He upgraded the game programs, replacing the bland testimonials from Abe's gray-haired sportswriters with four-color graphics and snappy layouts. Gillette was fascinated by television and its potential to increase Trotter revenue and attendance.* He met Fred Silverman, at that time a thirty-year-old CBS programming executive,† who was interested in doing a show about the Globetrotters, which became the *The Harlem Globetrotters* cartoon. Gillette also arranged an appearance on the Johnny Carson show and a celebrity game in Los Angeles, which was broadcast on ABC. When attendance improved, it appeared that his strategy was working.

The more popular the Trotters became on TV, however, the more disenchanted the players became. The flash and glitter was seductive, and they enjoyed their new celebrity status, but it was ephemeral, like a façade on a Hollywood set. Behind the false front, the team was boiling with resentment. As early as 1969, they were planning to strike in Portland, Oregon, but Gillette got wind of it and fired Willie Campbell, who was one of the ringleaders. "Persons of your caliber we do not need in the organization," Gillette wrote in his dismissal letter, chiding Campbell for his "organizing activities" and the "un-

---

* In the late 1980s, Gillette would buy up a string of television stations, building one of the largest media companies in the country.

† Silverman would go on to be head of programming at CBS, where he pioneered All in the Family and Maude, and later served as network president of both ABC and NBC.

forgivable incident in Portland." Marie Linehan agreed with Gillette that "making an example . . . of a troublemaker will prove something to all the others," but she warned Gillette that "the problem is severe and deep and involves more than just Willie [Campbell]."

Some of the players' resentment focused on Meadowlark Lemon, who had become even more self-absorbed as his celebrity status increased. He started his own line of clothing, was pursuing a singing career, and resented anyone who took away from his limelight. Curly Neal was especially troubling. Meadowlark and Curly were portrayed as a tag-team act, the two most famous Trotters, but Meadowlark resented Curly's popularity with the fans. Curly had a radiant innocence about him, and fans adored him. His bald head and beaming smile were catapulting him to superstar status. Other than Muhammad Ali, he may have been the most recognizable sports figure in the world. But this was supposed to be "The Meadowlark Lemon Show." One night in Madison Square Garden, the fans gave Curly a standing ovation when he was introduced. "Curly was grinning from ear to ear," recalls Frank Stephens. "Meadowlark started motioning to the announcer, 'Cut it, cut it.' " Curly was stealing his show.

Meadowlark's insecurity led to altercations with Wilt Chamberlain, Connie Hawkins, and some Washington Generals' players. At least one turned deadly. A Trotter player, Murphy Summons, was fired for allegedly pulling a gun on Lemon, and possibly firing it.

The players also resented that Meadowlark was in a special category with management. He was the only player allowed to have an agent (Stan Greeson, who represented Soupy Sales and other celebrities). The other players were still negotiating directly with Gillette, who would call them into his office one at a time, pull out a bottle of Old Grandad, and pour them a drink. After a few minutes of chitchat, and perhaps a few more drinks, he'd slide a blank contract across the table and tell them to sign. "I'll fill in the amount later," he'd say. Some players were so eager to play with the Trotters, they did.

★

It all came to a head at Port Huron in November 1971. The game that night at McMorran Arena had to be canceled, and the striking players said they wouldn't play the next night either in London,

Ontario. George Gillette told the press it was a "classic power play" by the players' attorney, Elliott Goodman (who also represented the Saperstein family), which was designed to sabotage the new owners. Madison Square Garden was still running newspaper ads for two upcoming Trotters' games in early December, but no one knew if they would even be played.

There had been other player uprisings in the Globetrotters' history, going back to Runt Pullins and Sonny Boswell, but this was the first full-blown strike. The leaders, Bobby Hunter and Frank Stephens, were representative of the new breed of Globetrotters. They were college educated, articulate, and attuned to the rising consciousness of "Say it loud, I'm black and I'm proud." Hunter, who was a backup showman to Meadowlark and was being groomed as his eventual replacement, was a sophisticated, street-smart guy from Harlem. After graduating from Tennessee A&I and being cut by the New York Knicks, he joined the Trotters in 1966, the last player Abe recruited before he died. Stephens was the tallest player on the team, at six-foot-ten, and also had joined the Trotters in 1966, after graduating from Virginia State College and playing one year with the NBA's St. Louis Hawks.

The biggest issue in the strike was salaries, but the players had a laundry list of other demands. They wanted meal money, a pension plan, better insurance benefits, limits on travel between games, extra pay for doubleheaders, more amenities on their bus, and their uniforms cleaned between games. Finally, they wanted Gillette to recognize their union and negotiate with it from that point on. To outsiders, the issue of clean uniforms might have seemed insignificant, compared with salaries and a pension, but it was particularly galling to the players. Each Globetrotter had two uniforms, which they were responsible for cleaning. Traveling every day and playing every night, it was difficult to find time, or the means, to clean them. "A lot of our show was interacting with the crowd," says Stephens. "The last thing you want to do is go up there and squeeze a person and you smell like a week of funk and sweat."

The players had timed the strike to do the most damage. Gillette and Palmer had formed Globetrotter Communications, Inc., a publicly held corporation, and were buying up radio and TV stations, hoping to build a diversified communications company. They had scheduled a public stock offering for November 17, the day after the strike.

Clearly, it was going to be a bloody battle.

Gillette told the press that the strike was illegal because "each player had a good and valid contract." When rumors circulated that he was going to field a replacement team to play Madison Square Garden, Bobby Hunter went to the Teamsters Union, which threatened to shut down the arenas it controlled. "All the tactics that they had applied to former players didn't work with us," says Hunter. "We were college graduates, more intellectual, more East Coast."

The players held a press conference in New York. They did interviews for newspapers and television. "We just want to be treated as men and given our human dignity," Frank Stephens told Dave Anderson of the *New York Times*. Internally, however, they were struggling to hold their own ranks together. Meadowlark had already gone over to management,* and as the strike dragged on for weeks, other players began to waiver. "A lot of brothers started telling on each other," says Mel Davis, a longtime Trotter veteran and one of the strikers. "Guys thought they would get ahead by stabbing each other in the back." Indeed, several Trotter veterans cut their own private deals with management. At the time the strike began, the Trotters' International Unit was playing overseas, which made it difficult for those players to stay in touch. The union even tried to get Jesse Jackson and Bill Russell involved, but the players themselves were not united.

Finally, after twenty-seven days, the strike ended. Fourteen games had been canceled, including both shows in Madison Square Garden. The players had won a partial victory, as the minimum salary was increased from $7,800 to $13,200, and they got $12.50 for meal money, soft drinks on the bus, extra sets of uniforms (washed by the team equipment manager), and a stock option plan for all employees.

---

* *Lemon later wrote in his autobiography that he would have joined the strike if the players had invited him, but Hunter disputes that: "He was asked to join, and he said he would go to management and come back and tell us what was happening. And the next time we saw him was when the strike was over."*

The Globetrotters returned to the court on December 13, in Springfield, Massachusetts, but it was not business as usual. Gillette was becoming more interested in his new television and radio acquisitions, and decided to find someone else to manage the Globetrotters. Meadowlark's agent, Stan Greeson, had just negotiated a new lucrative contract for him and had also been involved in the negotiations for *The Harlem Globetrotters* cartoon. In a bizarre move, Gillette and Palmer hired Greeson, who had been an agent for over twenty years, as the new president.

The players saw the handwriting on the wall. Meadowlark was already aligned with management, and now his agent was the new company president. More repercussions from the strike quickly followed. Five of the striking players were terminated in April 1972, including Leon Hillard, a fourteen-year veteran, and four rookies. Then Gillette did something very shrewd: he brought back Marques Haynes. Marques agreed to fold his own team, the Fabulous Harlem Magicians, and rejoin the Trotters. With one stroke, Gillette had brought back into the fold the most respected player in Globetrotter history—on the side of management.

Why would he agree to come back after twenty years? "Well, for one thing, Abe wasn't there," Marques says today. "I dealt directly with Gillette." He was nearly fifty, but he could still play. And nobody, including Curly Neal, could dribble like Marques. He would spend the next seven years with the team, inspiring new generations of young ballplayers, including Isiah Thomas and Magic Johnson, with his dribbling wizardry.

Stan Greeson came on board as president in May 1972, and named Marques the player-coach of the International Unit and Meadowlark the player-coach of the National Unit. That summer, a handpicked group of players ("the [ones] we wanted to build around," Meadowlark would later write) was selected to go on the European tour. While overseas, they formed a new "company union," with Marques elected as president and Meadowlark as vice president. The remaining strikers, including Hunter and Stephens, were left out in the cold, and players now had to make a choice: do we go with Marques or against him?

To this day, there are hard feelings toward Marques from some of the players. "We did exactly what Marques did [with Abe]," says Stephens, "and instead of supporting us, he stabbed us *not* in the back, but in the chest—looking us in the face." Bobby Hunter also felt betrayed, but has reconciled with Marques. "It took us a couple of years to come to grips with each other," he says, "but I can understand why Marques came back, because it was owed to him—as one of the greatest Globetrotters of all time. And you have to move on. It wasn't worth killing anybody over, although at the time it seemed like one of the options."

As for Marques himself, he denies that he came back to break the union, and says he got involved with the union only to try to make things better. "As far as a good strong union contract, what they had was about as weak as water," he says. "They *elected* me president of the union. I really didn't want it."

Marques Haynes was not the only former Trotter to return. In the fall of 1972, Greeson and Meadowlark brought back a whole squad of old-timers, including Tex Harrison and Andy Johnson, who were both forty, and Joe Cunningham, who hadn't played in twelve years. "They brought back all these old fat broken-down men who couldn't play dead," says Stephens. "We needed two benches just to sit everybody." To the strikers, it was clear that Greeson wanted a backup team—"scabs," they called them—if another strike occurred.

With its new company union and cast of players, the Harlem Globetrotters unveiled their new season—and it was a huge success. *The Harlem Globetrotters Popcorn Machine* debuted in December, *ABC's Wide World of Sports* debuted in January 1973, and dozens of new attendance records were established. To the world, at least, the laughter had returned to the Globetrotters.

The labor struggles did not go away, however. Over the next few years, the players' union continued to win concessions on salaries, per diem, life insurance, and better travel conditions. By 1974, the average player salary was up to $30,000 (although Meadowlark's $85,000 salary skewed that number). Stan Greeson and George Gillette made it clear, however, that they would not tolerate a *real* union. In 1974, Bobby Hunter had been elected union president and started bringing more militant proposals to the bargaining table, including full pension benefits at age forty-five, $30 per diem for meals, residual payments from *The Harlem Globetrotters* cartoon and the *Popcorn Machine,* a percentage of endorsement revenue, and pay for TV appearances. Finally, the union's most radical proposal was to set aside one game a year that belonged to the players (they would get the entire gate, to split among themselves). On May 31, 1974, Hunter held a press conference in New York to announce that the players' union was affiliating with Local 189 of the Service Employees International Union (AFL-CIO), which would be negotiating their new contract.

That fall, at training camp, Hunter, Stephens, and Pablo Robertson, another union activist, were all released. "Stan Greeson called me in and said I did not make the team," says Stephens. "I laughed. I knew what the ploy was. He told me one time, 'We could go find a black face in any ghetto in the country and put that uniform on, and nobody would know the difference.' But I was ready to go, I'd had enough. I told him, 'Just give me my ticket.' "

In addition to the three union leaders, Bob "Showboat" Hall was not invited back to camp, after twenty-six years as an active player, the most in Globetrotter history. Hall reportedly wasn't even told directly, but found out when he called to ask about his airline ticket to training camp. Today, he remains so embittered that he would not even attend his induction ceremony into the Harlem Globetrotters' Legends Ring.

HERE INTERRED
LIE THE REMAINS
OF THE MAN
SAMBO

Born three hundred–odd years ago,
the exact date obscured by distorted memories:
danced and pranced and laughed
across the stages of American life
in blackface and bravado;
An image born in the inner reaches of white minds,
extending in childlike grin and gait,
entertaining and regaling
all who came into contact:

that pearly smile, those rounded eyes, rhythmical steps,
that rollicking laughter. . . .
May he rest in Peace,
Never to be resurrected.
Amen

JOSEPH BOSKIN,
FROM *SAMBO: THE RISE AND DEMISE
OF AN AMERICAN JESTER,* 1986

The labor wars raging within the Globetrotter organization remained largely invisible to the public, other than the 1971 strike, but the Harlem Globetrotters were coming under increasing public scrutiny during the 1970s for a very different reason: the Uncle Tom question. As far back as the mid-1930s, Abe had been criticized for putting on a minstrel show that demeaned black players, who lolled on the floor, shooting craps and gambling for their shin guards. But now a fierce debate over racial identity was roiling the black community, which was exploding with "Black is beautiful" slogans, foot-high Afros, and dashikis. Against that backdrop, *everything* about what it meant to be black, from hairstyles to the proper name for the race, was under intense scrutiny, and the Globetrotters became an easy target.

Black critics were particularly excoriating. "White American spectators are perhaps most at ease when they are treated to the rhythmic jabbering of the Harlem Globetrotters, who project a slave mentality for Mr. Charlie's entertainment," Dr. Ross Thomas Runfola, a social science professor, wrote in the *New York Times*. Columnist Lacy J. Banks, of the *Chicago Sun-Times*, was even more critical:

> The slapstick antics, falsetto voices, rubbery-limb motions, toothy grins and yelping dialogue are as modern American as Aunt Jemima and Little Black Sambo, and equally defaming to many blacks. . . . the Trotter drama is a combined sedative-stimulant for black fans taking a beating in housing, employment, health and education benefits each day.

Young blacks were the most dismissive of all. Willie Worsley, who played on the 1966 national championship team at University of

Texas at El Paso (UTEP), was quoted as saying, "The Trotters are clowns, and some of the young Negroes don't like it. . . . Clowning like animals. Acting the fool. Cheating and screaming. They're out there telling the whites exactly what the whites want to hear."

Criticism of the Trotters was coming from outside, and from within their own ranks. In 1972, a biography of Connie Hawkins included a damning chapter on his three years with the Trotters, entitled "Tomming for Abe." "What we were doing out there was actin [*sic*] like Uncle Toms," he said. "Grinnin [*sic*] and smiling and dancing around—that's the way they told us to act, and that's the way a lot of white people like to think we really are." Today, Hawkins has a more positive view of his Trotter years, but his earlier statements are still being widely circulated in articles, dissertations, and books.

It wasn't just the black community criticizing the Trotters, as whites lined up to take their turn. Author Jack Olsen described them as "the white man's favorite black road show. . . . Running about the court emitting savage jungle yells, shouting in thick Southern accents ('Yassuh, yassuh!') . . . they come across as frivolous, mildly dishonest children." Even grandfatherly James Michener offered this disparaging critique:

> What these blacks were doing for money was exhibiting proof of all the prejudices which white men had built up about them. They were lazy, and gangling, and sly, and given to wild bursts of laughter, and their success in life depended upon their outwitting the white man. Every witty act they performed . . . was a denigration of the black experience and dignity. . . . In fact, I strongly suspect that the Harlem Globetrotters did more damage racially than they did good, because they deepened the stereotype of the lovable, irresponsible Negro.

To be fair, it wasn't completely one-sided. There were Globetrotter defenders in the African American community, including Bill Cosby (who played in a 1972 celebrity game against them and was given a lifetime dollar-a-year contract) and Jesse Jackson, who came to their defense in 1978, saying, "I think they've been a positive influence. . . . They did not show blacks as stupid. On the contrary, they were shown as superior . . . they were able to turn science into an art form. I know professionals today who are still in awe of Marques Haynes and Goose Tatum."

Once again, Meadowlark Lemon became a lightning rod for the controversy. His defense was that if he was a Tom, so were all comedians, white or black, but there were elements of his act that offended even some teammates. "He was always screaming—'yeh-yeh-yeh-yeh-yeh-yeh'—and that would permeate the entire show," Frank Stephens recalls. "And he'd give you that Stepin Fetchit walk and that big smile, and we really didn't appreciate it. But who's gonna tell Meadowlark? That's what The Man wanted him to do, and if we question anything, first thing Meadowlark's gonna do is get us fired. So what we used to do was carry ourselves as dignified human beings. He was doing his Amos 'n' Andy shit, but we carried ourselves with dignity."

Even former Trotters who hadn't played in decades were pulled into the debate. "If you look at the showman, the guy looked like a minstrel person," says Dr. Johnny Kline, who played from 1953 to 1959. "It was a stereotypical kind of thing—Meadowlark doing all the clowning, stupid stuff, giving himself up, becoming something demeaning. I heard that many times." And for some former players, the issue once again brought up unfavorable comparisons between Meadowlark and Goose Tatum. "Goose didn't run around screaming like Meadowlark did," says Frank Washington, who played from 1946 to 1955. "Just running up and down the court hollering—I don't think the people like it."

The Globetrotters had always had more whites in their audiences than blacks, partly because of ticket prices, but in the crucible of the 1960s and '70s, as Black Pride became the defining ethos of the age, the Trotters were losing much of the black support they once had. The more popular they became among whites, and the more they were portrayed as buffoons on TV, the less credibility they had in the African American community. A divide formed between the black community and the Globetrotters that would take many years to close. Some black families, who had once considered the Trotters a high calling, now discouraged their sons from trying out. "When I told my father I was going to try out for the Globetrotters," recalls Mannie Jackson, "his words to me were, 'Why would you want to play with that bunch of clowns?' "

By 1974, Wells Twombly of the *San Francisco Examiner* was already composing the Trotters' epitaph:

> They come prancing out on to the floor to the tune of an extraordinary piece of music, their eyeballs rolling, their legs strutting, their bodies moving to the rhythm. They jabber like plantation slaves. They act stupid for the palefaces. They're supposed to be comic, but they end up looking grotesque. They belong to a time when black people had no dignity, no sense of purpose. Their time is long past. . . . In what is, hopefully, an enlightened era, the Harlem Globetrotters are strictly for Archie Bunker and nobody else. They aren't funny anymore.

★

In 1976, the Harlem Globetrotters were sold to Metromedia, an entertainment and communications company that owned the Ice Capades and a chain of radio and television stations. Metromedia had bid on the Trotters in 1967, and finally had them ten years later. CEO John Kluge decided to relocate the Globetrotters to Los Angeles, where the company was based. Most of the old-timers in the Chicago office chose not to go (Wyonella Smith, Bill Margolis, Marian Polito, and Morry Saperstein, among them), but Marie Linehan packed up her file cabinets and her memories and moved to sunny California.

She and Joe Anzivino, who had come to work as an advance man in 1961, were the last of the old guard. Inman Jackson, the only remaining survivor from the Globetrotters' early years, had died in April 1973, at the age of sixty-five. Big Jack had been in failing health for several years, and his friends were thankful that his suffering had ended. "We all miss Jack, of course," Marie wrote to Bob Karstens, "but he was so sick at the end."

With Inman gone, Marie became the institutional memory of the organization. Her surviving correspondence serves as a poignant journal of the gradual deterioration that would bring the organization to the edge of ruin. The Harlem Globetrotters were not the same as they had once been, and Marie Linehan, in the same meticulous fashion with which she had detailed their greatest triumphs, was now recording their demise.

Marie took her role as in-house historian seriously. In 1978, she commissioned a freelance writer, Chuck Menville, to write a "picture book" on the history of the team. George Vecsey of the *New York Times* had written a juvenile book for Scholastic Press in 1970, but the Menville book was intended for the commercial adult market, and was filled with photographs. Even as the book was coming off the presses, however, Marie was saddened that so much of the Globetrotters' history had already been lost. "It is as accurate as we could make it," she wrote to a former player. "Most of the people of the late '20's and '30's are not available and official records really did not undergo any formal compilation until the mid '40's." In a letter to Karstens, she bemoaned the gaps in the story. "So much of the early days were never recorded as there was no real sense of history, so some of it is just [lore]," she wrote. "All of the people who knew all of the stories (Abe, Inman especially) are gone. The real inside stories will never be told."

Marie and Joe Anzivino were the only conduits for old players who still wanted to feel connected to the organization, and she corresponded with many of them. Several times, she included a "Stars of Yesteryear" page in the annual yearbooks, featuring Globetrotters who had made good. There were many success stories—players who had built on their Globetrotter careers to become successful in business, government, or education. Among them were Harry Sykes, an educator and city commissioner in Lexington, Kentucky; Charlie Primus, a director of juvenile detention programs in Detroit; Bob Williams, a supervisor with Pillsbury Flour; Don Barnette, an administrator for the U.S. Office of Civil Rights; and Chuck Holton, a bureau chief for the Wisconsin Department of Family Services. One of the regulars in the "Stars of Yesteryear" was Mannie Jackson, who had risen quickly up the ladder at Honeywell to become its Labor Relations director.

Stan Greeson had continued as president after the Metromedia purchase, but he resigned in January 1980. One of the last major actions he took was to fire his old client Meadowlark Lemon. The official announcement, on October 6, 1978, claimed that Meadowlark had "retired after requesting his release," but he was actually fired. At forty-six years old, he had been showing his age but was still the Trotters' biggest attraction. He was making $225,000 a year, but when he demanded a raise to $800,000, Greeson had had enough. The Trotters were playing in Europe when Greeson sent Meadowlark a telegram relieving him of his duties as the player-coach. Meadowlark was furious and called a meeting of the players. He told them about Greeson's telegram and announced righteously, "We're just not gonna play!"

"Uh, wait a minute, Lem," said Dallas Thornton, a veteran known for his blunt style. "Shit, *we* didn't get no telegram. He sent *you* a telegram; he didn't send *us* no telegram."

After years of being upstaged by "The Meadowlark Lemon Show," the players were not going to stand up for Lemon now. He had cut too many private deals with management, had left the players hanging too many times, had pitched too many tantrums about other players stealing the spotlight he felt belonged solely to him. The players walked out of the room, and played the game.

"Meadowlark was truly upset behind that," says "Sweet Lou" Dunbar, who was in his rookie year. The next morning, as the players were boarding the bus, Lemon was pacing around the parking lot, all alone. Dunbar had never seen Lemon wear sunglasses in a year of playing with him, but on this morning his eyes were hidden behind dark shades. Greeson installed Nate Branch as the player-coach, but Meadowlark continued playing until they finished the European tour. When the European tour ended, Greeson bought out Lemon's contract and cut him loose. "Meadowlark [had] just got out of control," says Red Klotz.

Geese Ausbie was promoted to top showman on the National Unit, with "Twiggy" Sanders and "Sweet Lou" Dunbar sharing the duties on the International Unit. Once Meadowlark was gone, there was an outpouring of criticism by other players, who suddenly felt free to speak their minds. "[Lemon] had become 95 percent of the show . . . and would not allow anyone to do anything to rival him," Curly Neal told Thomas Boswell of the *Washington Post*.

The players made equally candid observations to Boswell about the state of the Globetrotters organization. "For the last couple of years the Trotters were in big trouble," said Nate Branch, the new player-coach. "Most of the guys, myself included, hated being Globetrotters. Promoters were running away from us. The word was out: We were turning into box-office poison." The players claimed that average salaries were still only $35,000 to $40,000 a year, and Branch warned, "We want a different future from the Trotters of the past. . . . In the near future, everybody on this team is going to be satisfied, or we'll see the end of the Trotters."

For the next few years, the Harlem Globetrotters continued doing well at the box office, but on the inside the organization was dying. "Everything seems to be so heavy, almost like a blanket of gloom covering the atmosphere," Joe Anzivino wrote in 1980. Marie Linehan's closest confidant was David Land, a London theater producer who had booked the Trotters for years.* "I cannot wait (but will have to) for August—to get away from this 'un-fun' place," she wrote Lamb. "It hasn't been fun for a long, long time . . . actually I do not fit into the corporate structure of rules and regimentation. And it gets worse . . . No sentiment about it. The organization as I knew it and loved it really doesn't exist anymore. So any separation would be painless at this stage. Our tears were shed a long time ago."

Abe Saperstein had built the organization on the strength of his personality and the relationships he'd built around the world, but such personal connections were now subsumed by corporate policies and procedure manuals. The Globetrotters were part of the Arena Entertainment Division of Metromedia, which included the Ice Capades, and were just another line item in the corporate budget. "The evolution to the impersonal corporate structure is complete," Marie wrote in 1984. "We still sell a product which is recognizable and in demand but the operation mirrors any structured corporate

---

* *Land is best known as the producer of* Jesus Christ Superstar, Joseph and the Amazing Technicolor Dreamcoat, *and* Evita.

operation—for that matter we could be selling shoes or shovels or have a Roto-Rooter service. We are owned by the 'mother' company [Metromedia] and there is a rule for everything we do."

By 1984, the ennui and listlessness within the organization began to show up at the box office. Week after week, gate receipts were falling short of projected revenue. In December, for instance, receipts during the first week were $43,000 short of budget projections, they were $68,000 below budget in the second week, and $21,000 below in the third. For a company that generated approximately $10 million a year, these were negligible amounts, but they indicated a disturbing trend. In March 1984, in a cost-cutting move, Metromedia eliminated the halftime entertainment, a staple of Globetrotter games for forty years; canceled the European tour, which was the first time in twenty-four years the Trotters hadn't played overseas; and cut back to only one unit, which meant that half the players lost their jobs. "It's been rough, real rough," Geese Ausbie told the press. "I hope I'll be back next year. I hope all of us will. But it hurts to see your brothers lose their jobs."

Even for those who survived, the negative vibes were affecting their play on the court. In January 1985, the team's road manager filed a report on two games in Kansas City. "The first show was a bad show, equally as bad as the Friday night show," he wrote. "We had been showing no quality and an obvious lack of enthusiasm. . . . For all intents and purposes, without the help of some reams the Generals could easily have won the game. . . . Not entertaining—not good basketball."

After the Globetrotters lost $500,000 in 1984, Metromedia decided to bring in new leadership. In February 1985, Earl W. Duryea was appointed president and chief operating officer. Duryea, forty-seven, was a former vice president of Ringling Brothers/Barnum and Bailey Circus. He had also been the arena manager for the Nassau Coliseum and the Salt Palace in Salt Lake City. Duryea's résumé had one glaring omission: he had no experience in sports. Marie would sadly note the ascension of "Earl Duryea and his circus cronies."

Duryea announced his intention to "hire better players," and promptly instituted a general housecleaning, releasing the Trotters' popular but aging stars Geese Ausbie and Curly Neal. In June,

Ausbie announced that he was retiring after twenty-four years, but three months later, at a tearful press conferénce, he said that he had actually been fired and was filing a federal lawsuit alleging age discrimination. Curly Neal joined the suit, claiming the company had refused to negotiate his contract in good faith.

The oldest employee in the organization, by far, was Marie Linehan, who at seventy-five was ready to get out herself. She had negotiated an agreement where she would work three days a week until 1987, then serve as a consultant. "Inasmuch as we are on the fourth president and the fourth change of administration in nine years, I have had all the transition periods I want," she reported to David Land.

Duryea's biggest innovation was to hire the Globetrotters' first female player, Lynette Woodard, former Kansas University and Olympic star. Woodard's signing, in October 1985, generated a huge wave of publicity (including an appearance on the *Tonight Show* and articles in *Sports Illustrated, People, Ebony,* and *Ms.*) and a significant bounce at the box office. Duryea added a second woman, Jackie White, the following year, and a total of eight women would play with the Trotters over the next few years. "Sweet Lou" Dunbar, who was now the top showman, had been skeptical about Woodard's hiring, but reported, "This is a grueling schedule for men, and I just felt she wouldn't be able to handle it. But she's the best sleeper on the bus. She's hangin' in there, and we're very proud of her. We consider her our baby sister."

Duryea's "circus cronies" were suggesting other ways to revitalize the Globetrotters, including a remote-controlled trick ball, a helium-filled ball, and a ball that disintegrated on the way to the basket. As one of his marketing people proposed, "The quality of play can't be scripted, but we can 'artificially' produce spectacular plays. Why can't we inject spectacular plays just like we do comedy reams. Every fast break should include a no-look pass. Instead of a layup, throw it off the glass and let a following player slam it home. We control the defense anyway, why can't we MANDATE an exciting style of play."

Despite the upturn in attendance after Woodard's signing, Duryea's relationship with the players and their independent union, the United Basketball Players Association, was rapidly disintegrating. In November 1985, a game in Edmonton, Ontario, had to be canceled when the players refused to travel 500 miles by bus, after their flight from Helena, Montana, to Edmonton had been canceled because of bad weather. Duryea accused the union of violating a no-strike clause in their contract and tried to fire the entire team, but Metromedia refused to back him. The Edmonton cancellation cost thousands of dollars and generated terrible publicity. "The Harlem Globetrotters, it says here, are dying," one Edmonton sportswriter opined. "The Globetrotters used to have a purpose. . . . [but now] they're just a bunch of black guys (and a gal) trying to perpetuate a tired, old—and now—bad act. In this day and age they're preposterously out of place."

In July 1986, Duryea and the union began negotiating a new contract, but over the summer their relationship deteriorated to the point that the entire team, other than Woodard, refused to report to training camp. But within a week, four players went back, including showman Twiggy Sanders, and Duryea had enough to field a team. The remaining five players—Dunbar, Billy Ray Hobley, Ovie Dotson, Jimmy Blacklock, and Osborne Lockhart—stayed out on strike the entire 1986–87 season. They filed an unfair labor practice against the company and even formed their own team, "Basketball Magic," which toured in the Caribbean.

In December 1986, Metromedia sold the Globetrotters and the Ice Capades to International Broadcasting Company (IBC), a Minneapolis company that owned three amusement parks, a Minnesota dinner theater, and the Ice Chalets. The sale price was $30 million. Over the next six years, the seemingly irreversible decline of this once-proud franchise would continue unabated. Marie Linehan, in one of her last letters to her friend David Land, wrote:

I have one more season to spend here (if the Almighty agrees) and then I am off and I must tell you, I just cannot wait. It is over, it is alien, it is discouraging and weakened, it is languishing and withering. There is no rejuvenation each year, no springtime, and there is no jollity, no sharing of accomplishment, no excitement. I stay on only for the most basic reasons which are tied into economic protection. One more year and then a few of a consultancy, and it's over.

On March 23, 1990, Marie Linehan died at age eighty. She had worked for the Harlem Globetrotters for forty-four years, the longest continuous service of anyone in their history. Although she had lived in California for nearly fifteen years, it had never felt like home, and so, at her request, her body was carried back to Chicago to be buried among her Irish kith and kin.

★

In August 1991, IBC filed for bankruptcy protection under Chapter 11, after it was unable to restructure a $66 million debt with its major lender, National Westminster Bank USA (NatWest). In an attempt to recoup its losses, the bank assumed control of IBC, imposed severe cost-cutting measures, and considered selling off some of IBC's holdings, including the Globetrotters, if the price was right. In 1991, the Globetrotters were still making a profit, but NatWest's draconian cost-cutting only accelerated the downward spiral. The Globetrotters were cut back to one unit, laying off ten players, and the schedule was reduced by half. The 1992 South American tour was canceled. The scouting budget was eliminated, training camp expenses were slashed by $30,000, Red Klotz's fee for games was cut 10 percent, contributions to the players' pension funds were suspended for three years, and on it went.

From 1987–88 to 1991–92, attendance had been dropping precipitously in many of the Trotters' major venues: from 25,932 to 12,573 in Philadelphia; from 26,271 to 10,935 in Houston; from 22,667 to 8,247 in Minneapolis; and from 11,275 to 4,279 in Cleveland.

The last of the old-timers, Joe Anzivino, who had been with the Trotters since 1961, was installed as president in March 1992, but he had little authority and was answering directly to the bank's crisis manager, Burton Merical, and to Ice Capades' president, Michael

Booker. "In my 30 years I have never experienced the bizarre leadership we've had in the past four years," Anzivino complained to Merical.

By 1992, the Globetrotters had degenerated into more of a farce than a comedy show, and basketball had been forgotten long ago. They were getting almost as much publicity in police reports as in the sports pages. There were drug busts, assault charges, a fistfight between two players in a bowling alley that had to be broken up by police, a hotel scuffle between a player and his wife that made the papers, even a rape charge against a former Trotter. On the court, it was almost as bad. One player was photographed giving the finger to the crowd, another was drinking so heavily that he was "noticeably tipsy" on the bench, a Washington Generals' player told the referee to "Shut the fuck up!" and a Globetrotter star told a promoter to "go fuck himself." One mother wrote a complaint letter, outraged over her children watching the showman "pretend to have sex" with the referee. Other fans complained about players caressing each other's buttocks and performing a "pantomime of sodomy."

It all spiraled down to the season opener in October 1992, when the players took to the court not in their traditional red-white-and-blue uniforms, but in a new one-piece spandex pull-on suit designed by a costumer for the Ice Capades. The sleek uni-suits were the inspiration of Michael Booker, former British national figure-skating champ and president of the Ice Capades, who had suggested that the Trotters needed to update their look. In the locker room, players would step into their "unis" and ask a teammate, "Would you zip me up?"

It was as bad as it could get.

CHAPTER 17

Mannie

On March 28, 1993, Mannie Jackson took his teenage daughters to see the Harlem Globetrotters play in Boston Garden. He wanted to see the team play one last time before making his final decision. You see, Mannie Jackson was the man who was going to shut down the Globetrotters. Close down the tour and put the Trotters in the museum alongside the Negro Leagues and colored water fountains and other relics of America's Jim Crow past. He had a handshake deal with NatWest, the bank that controlled the Trotters, to buy the team; and he hoped to convince Hollywood to make a movie, he planned to write a book on the Trotters' history, and he figured he could sell Globetrotter merchandise in retail outlets. But the team itself was finished. "It had made a great contribution to the world, but it was over," he would later write.

If anyone was going to shut down the Trotters, Mannie Jackson was the perfect man for the job. He was a former Globetrotter himself, having played in the early 1960s, before going on to a star-studded career in corporate America, first at General Motors and then for twenty-five years at Honeywell, where he had risen to become a corporate officer and senior vice president for marketing and administration, overseeing a $2.3 billion global business unit. He knew business and he knew basketball, and he knew that the Harlem Globetrotters could no longer survive in either realm.

And so he had brought his daughters with him to Boston to watch this game. Mannie's daughters, Candace and Cassandra, who were thirteen and fourteen, respectively, did not think of their father as a basketball player. Their image of him was as a fabulously success-ful Honeywell executive who bought and sold companies over the phone, making $20 million acquisitions before breakfast. They pictured him in his luxurious office at corporate headquarters, or jetting halfway around the world for an afternoon meeting, then returning home at night to their Minneapolis mansion on the lake. To them, his one athletic passion was golf, which he pursued to an eight handicap at exclusive country clubs. Mannie Jackson had a beautiful family, a stellar business career, and all the money he would ever need. He had it all—and basketball was not part of it.

So his daughters held no romanticized image of their father as a Harlem Globetrotter. That part of his life had ended twenty-five years ago, long before they were born. They weren't that thrilled by a trip to Boston in the first place, so Mannie had enticed them by saying, "Listen, we'll check out Harvard while we're there." Fine, the girls said, *that* was worth a trip.

But that night, as they sat courtside in Boston Garden, what they saw unfold before them was so shabby, so bumbling and amateurish, that they could not imagine their father had ever been part of it. It did not jibe with their image of him at all. "Daddy, you used to do *this*?" they asked, in that incredulous tone that only teenagers can summon. "You used to play with *these guys*?"

"Yeah," Mannie admitted, with embarrassment. "I did."

Candace and Cassandra couldn't believe they had come all the way to Boston for *this*—Harvard or no Harvard.

For Mannie, the game confirmed all of his misgivings about the team's future. The attendance was dismal, the players looked lost, and the Globetrotters' front office was so desperate that they had brought Meadowlark Lemon out of retirement for a forty-eight-game "Reunion Tour," even though he was sixty-two years old. A forty-year-old basketball player is considered an old man, but Lemon was old enough to draw Social Security! He was so sensitive about his age that the front office had issued a company-wide memo to deflect any inquiries with the standard response: "Meadowlark is between 18 and 100." Lemon was playing only one quarter in each game, and some nights he was able to recapture flashes of his old magic, but most nights, like this one in Boston, he looked like an old geezer hobbling around the court.

It wasn't just the team that was embarrassing, it was the entire operation. "I realized that every little detail was being mismanaged," Mannie says today. "Every single detail—from the concessions, the box office, transportation, to the attitude of the players and the road staff—was being terribly managed."

Mannie took notes on all the problems he saw and decided to call a meeting of the players in their hotel after the game. The players had heard the rumors that he was going to buy the team, and they knew he was at the game, so he figured it was time to talk to them face-to-face. Few of them actually knew him, but they had heard stories about him and knew his reputation. He was the guy who'd made it big—the former Trotter who'd hit the number and cashed in all his chips. When they assembled, Meadowlark included, Mannie fully intended to give the speech he had been preparing, about closing down the tour, selling licensed products, putting out a movie. "You guys, through no fault of your own, are in a terrible situation," he began. "This is on its deathbed."

But as he continued talking, something unexpected happened. "I saw something in their eyes," he recalls. There was a spark, a yearning, a kind of hunger that he had not anticipated. Mannie found himself thinking back over sixty-five years of Globetrotter history to all the great players who had gone before—Inman Jackson and Goose Tatum and Marques Haynes—and, very subtly, the verb tense of his speech began to change from past to present, from the pluperfect to the conditional. He began talking not about shutting down the team, but about what it would take to resurrect it. He started laying out a business plan of what he would do if he bought the team—and by the end it was not "if" but "when." Instead of convincing the team that the end had come, he had convinced himself to try to bring the Globetrotters back from the dead.

"Mannie came *strong*," recalls Curley "Boo" Johnson, a Trotter veteran who was at the meeting.

"Saving the Globetrotters has got to be a religion for us," Mannie told them. "You guys are my disciples; I'm going to be your leader. If you don't want to join me, get out of here now." No one left the room. "If you guys are with me, I'll make you wealthy, I'll make it popular, I'll make it big, but it's going to be a rough ride before it's over," he added.

Mannie went back to Minneapolis, determined to convince NatWest to sell him the team. He had a handshake agreement, but there were other prospective buyers for the Globetrotters, including Jerry Saperstein, MOMA Concerts USA, and Century Park Pictures Corporation. In November 1992, Mannie Jackson had offered to buy the team by himself, but NatWest refused. "Who have you got with you?" the bankers kept asking.

Mannie read a subtle message between the lines: NatWest was not going to sell to a lone black man, no matter how much credibility he had, without other investors to bail him out if he fell on his face. "I really hate to say that, because you'd think in the nineties you could buy a company by yourself," he says, "but it was really necessary that I had a support group with me." Mannie wanted to put together a black ownership group, so he approached other well-known African Americans, including Isiah Thomas, rap artist M.C. Hammer, and several black CEOs he knew, but none would put up any money. "That was the saddest thing I experienced in the whole process," he recalls. He did get one taker, John L. Jones, a Xerox and Jostens executive, but that was not enough.

So Mannie turned to Dennis Mathisen, a Minneapolis investment banker, and asked him to assist in putting together a local investment group. Eventually, they pulled together twelve investors, mostly friends and business partners from Minneapolis, who had the financial credibility that the bank desired. In addition to Mathisen, these included retired Honeywell chairman Ed Spencer, who had been Mannie's mentor in his early years with the company; H. William Lurton, chairman and CEO of Jostens Incorporated; A. Skidmore Thorpe; Barbara L. Forster; Miller and Schroder Capital Corporation, Dennis Lind; Ruth Busta; Draft Company/Nicholson Boys L.P.; the Sienna Corporation Employees Profit Sharing Plan; and the only African American investor, John L. Jones. These investors contributed a total of approximately $500,000.

The newly formed Mannie Jackson Associates (MJA) then made its pitch to NatWest, offering $5.5 million for the Globetrotters. NatWest accepted, on the condition that the bank would retain a 20 percent ownership of the team, which Mannie could buy out over the next five years. Mannie would hold 35.5 percent of the company and have full control of its operations, Dennis Mathisen would control 34.5 percent, and the remaining investors would split the final 10 percent.

Before the sale was publicly announced, Mannie organized a three-day strategic planning retreat on a farm in southern Minnesota. The participants included Red Klotz and former Globetrotters Hallie Bryant, Curly Neal, Geese Ausbie, Osborn Lockhart, and Tex Harrison. They asked themselves, "What could the Globetrotters be? What *should* they be?" And the answer, they concluded, was that the Globetrotters could be anything they wanted to be. "But we had to believe that internally first," Mannie says today. "The people had lost confidence in themselves, and the company was rudderless."

In June 1993, the sale was announced with great fanfare in the national media. Mannie Jackson became the first former Globetrotter to own the team and the first African American to own a major sports franchise in American history. Those two historical firsts were symbolic of just how far he had come.

There is an old adage that a journey of a thousand miles begins with a first step, but the first steps in Mannie Jackson's journey were taken in more humble surroundings than one might imagine: he was born in a railroad boxcar in Illmo, Missouri, in 1939. A combination of the abbreviations for Illinois and Missouri, Illmo was a railroad hub on the banks of the Mississippi River, in southeastern Missouri, with 1,100 residents. During the bleakest days of the Great Depression, the St. Louis Southwest Railway (later the Cotton Belt Railway) started providing converted boxcars as free housing for its section hands. Eventually, there were as many as twenty boxcar houses near the train station, with both black and white families living there. The boxcars had electricity but no running water, and several families shared an outdoor bathroom. Mannie Jackson's maternal grandfather was a straw boss for the railroad, which is why the family was living there when Mannie was born. His grandmother used plywood and bedsheets to make separate rooms for the eleven members of the family. "My grandmother made it a castle," he later recalled.

He spent his first four years in the boxcar house, then moved to

Edwardsville, Illinois, a suburb of St. Louis, twenty miles across the Illinois state line. Edwardsville had a population of 8,000 people, and everybody knew everybody else. The school system was still segregated, so Mannie enrolled at the Lincoln School, which included kindergarten through twelfth grades. His father got a job at the local Chrysler dealership, and his mother and paternal grandmother worked as domestics, cleaning white people's houses. Mannie would sometimes accompany his mother to her jobs. "My mother was a domestic, and for some African Americans that sounds demeaning," he says, "but the experience I had of going with her and my grandmother was positive for me. Going in those homes, I got to see my mother's work ethic and the relationship she had with the people she worked for, and how much they loved her and respected her. And I was able to see the inside of their homes and walk through their libraries and see how they expressed themselves and how they conducted their lives. It was a source of inspiration and goal setting and envisioning what life could be."

In the first grade, he met the new kid in town, Govoner Vaughn, whose family had just moved north from Mississippi, and the two young boys would forge a friendship that would last for sixty years. On the sandlot basketball courts in front of the Lincoln School, Mannie and Gov played thousands of games together, and by the time Edwardsville integrated its schools, in 1950, Mannie and Gov entered the eighth grade as a dynamic duo. They swept through junior high and onto the Edwardsville High freshman team, where they continued their outstanding play. On January 29, 1953, for instance, Mannie scored 28 points and Gov added 12 to lead the Edwardsville freshmen to a 61–45 win over Belleville.

In their sophomore year, Mannie and Gov made the varsity and had high expectations about starting, but they ran headlong into the diminutive Coach Joe Lucco, who promptly sat them on the bench. The Edwardsville Tigers had finished fourth in the state in 1952–53 and were loaded with talented upperclassmen, including Don Ohl, who would play for the NBA's Baltimore Bullets. Lucco was an extreme disciplinarian who ran the program like a Marine Corps boot camp. He made his players cut their hair the same way, refused to let them play football, forced them to run cross-country to build their endurance, and wouldn't let them date during the season. Players who questioned him or talked back or sulked would provoke a tirade that left more than one of them in tears.

Mannie Jackson was like the *anti*-Lucco. He was a free spirit who dressed in flashy clothes and a big fedora. He had a smart mouth and a quick mind and sometimes engaged the former before the latter. His father was an outspoken civil rights leader and active in the fight to integrate the local schools, and Mannie was primed to challenge any perceived racial slight or slur. "I was outspoken, particularly about racial stuff, and I would challenge anyone," Mannie recalls. "I had a way of looking a certain way or doing a certain thing that would set Lucco off."

Mannie was six feet tall, but a scrawny 150 pounds, and had an unorthodox jump shot that he launched from way behind his head. But he could hit his quirky shot consistently from twenty feet, was blindingly fast off the dribble, and had been dunking since he was twelve. Gov was taller, at six-four, and had an even sweeter outside shot.

Lucco realized what kind of exceptional talents he had in Mannie and Gov, but still made them conform to his system. "Now I appreciate him being tough on me," Mannie says. "The reward was that we won and we were all better for it." By their senior year, Mannie and Gov were the talk of southern Illinois. Mannie had grown to six two and a half and filled out to 170 pounds, and with him on the left wing and Gov in the pivot, they were unstoppable. They had such quick first steps to the basket that opposing coaches were constantly complaining to the referees that they were traveling. When one official kept calling traveling on Mannie, Lucco told the ref, "He may have traveled, but it happened too fast for *you* to see it."

Together, Mannie and Gov led Edwardsville to a 28–6 record, and they lost in the finals of the state championship by 2 points. Mannie averaged 24.4 points per game and finished his career as the greatest scorer in Edwardsville history; he made the all-state team and was voted "Prep Player of the Year" in the greater St. Louis area. He had scholarship offers from sixty colleges, including UCLA, Seton Hall, and St. John's, but he and Gov decided to stick together and signed with the University of Illinois.

Mannie and Gov hoped to carry the Fighting Illini to a national title, but they picked the wrong years to be playing in the Big Ten. Ohio State won the national championship in 1960, with Jerry Lucas, John Havlicek, and Larry Siegfried; and Walt Bellamy was a two-time All-American at Indiana. "We never had a big guy," Gov laments. "If we'd had a good big man we could have gone all the way." Mannie and Gov started for three years, and Mannie was elected the first black captain of the Illinois team and made second team All Big Ten. Gov scored 1,001 career points, making him the third-highest scorer in school history.

After they graduated in 1960, Abe Saperstein tried to sign both of them to the Globetrotters. But Mannie and Gov had dreams of playing in the NBA, and they had an offer from the New York Tuck Tapers, in the National Industrial Basketball League, whose players worked out regularly with the New York Knicks. Tuck Tape would give the players corporate jobs, and they'd play ball on the weekends. Once again, Mannie and Gov decided to stick together.

They played that summer with the Tuck Tapers and worked out with the Knicks. Mannie had a management job in customer service, and liked the exposure to the world of business. "The thing that occurred to me then was that the smart guys were going to the Industrial League," Mannie says. "The smart white guys, the guys that got the As and Bs and were business students and more serious students, they were either going to graduate school or to the Industrial League, where they could get executive positions. The guys that were jocks, they were going to the NBA. . . . I always thought the business guys were cooler."

But Abe kept after them. He sent them airline tickets to the Globetrotters' training camp, and they decided to go. They had a terrific camp, and Abe told them, "I want you both here right now!" He offered them $700 a month, they bargained him up to $1,000, and Gov decided to take it. But Mannie felt he was so close to making the Knicks, and was so enthusiastic about his job at Tuck Tape, that he couldn't go. For the first time, they split up the dynamic duo. A few weeks later, Gov was playing with the Globetrotters at Madison Square Garden, and Mannie went to see him play.

Abe kept hammering at him. "You can always go to work, son," he said, "but you can't always have the thrill of traveling around the world and playing with the Globetrotters."

"You know what, Abe?" Mannie said. "You're right."

He was becoming discouraged about his chances of making the NBA, although he had no doubts that he was good enough. "At the time I came out of school," he says, "prejudice was just accepted—the racism and the quotas on the teams. When I tried out for the Knicks, there were like twenty-five guys trying out, and eighteen or nineteen were black, but we knew that only two or three of them were going to make the team."

On May 1, 1961, he flew to Chicago, and four days later was on a plane to Europe for the Globetrotters' summer tour. He played one full season and portions of the next five, joining the team in the summers or for a week here or there.

Abe took a liking to him, and used to tell the other players, "Keep an eye on this guy, he's going places." Years later, Mannie would say that Abe Saperstein was "one of a handful of white adults at that time who I thought cared about me personally."

For many of the Trotter players, basketball was their life, but for Mannie Jackson it was a means to an end. "It was really fun to play with the Globetrotters," he says, "but it was grueling. And it was really hard on my knees." In 1963, disenchanted with the racism in pro basketball, and worn down from the Trotters, he went back home to Edwardsville to find his bearings. He took a teaching job in St. Louis, teaching junior high biology. He was commuting to St. Louis and playing ball with the Schumacher Saints in the Edwardsville city league but still had a hankering to prove that he could play in the NBA. He moved to Detroit and lived with Earl Lloyd, the former NBA player, who was scouting for the Detroit Pistons. If he couldn't hook on with the Pistons, Mannie hoped to find a job in the auto industry. During a workout with some of the top players in the city, he met John Watson, a white guy who worked for General Motors.

"You seem like a bright guy," Watson said. "I've got a good situation at GM, why don't you apply?"

"They won't hire me because I'm black," Mannie replied.

"No, they test you—if you pass the test, you're hired."

He passed the test. "All of a sudden the world opened up for me, and I never played basketball again," Mannie says. He was hired in GM's Cadillac division, and quickly advanced up the corporate ladder. By 1966, he was director of training and development for Cadillac, in charge of the apprenticeship program for eleven skilled trades. It was a turbulent time at GM, with increasing racial tension in the plants and bad blood between management and the United Auto Workers, in the wake of a five-week-long strike in 1964. But Mannie had great rapport with black workers and built a solid relationship with the white business managers of the UAW local. "Those guys adopted me," he says, "and I could walk into some of the toughest plants and people knew me." He was eventually promoted to Cadillac's director of labor relations, and also took graduate classes in business administration at the University of Detroit.

In 1968, his rising star at GM attracted the attention of Honeywell, the Minneapolis-based manufacturer of building control systems (such as thermostats). He was offered a job as an equal employment officer and moved quickly through the managerial ranks. In the early seventies, he moved to Boston and became director of human resources for Honeywell's computer business. By 1979, he was invited to Minneapolis to run Honeywell's Venture Center, overseeing mergers and acquisitions of new businesses all over the world. It was exhilarating. He was working seventeen- and eighteen-hour days, living off the adrenaline rush from making deals. But in 1991, Honeywell decided to sell off all of its allied businesses, including the Venture Center, to concentrate on its core. Mannie was rewarded with a promotion to corporate headquarters, as senior vice president in charge of marketing and administration. It was the dream of all senior managers: a corporate vice presidency, a plush office at headquarters, and a fantastic salary. "I disliked every minute of it," Mannie says. "I had been running one hundred miles an hour, making deals all over the world, and now I was parked in corporate, looking out the window, being an administrator. I had a burning desire to do the deal, and it killed me to sit."

By then, he was one of the most prominent African American business executives in the country and had taken a leadership role on many initiatives in the black community. In 1986, with twenty-three other black executives, he cofounded the Executive Leadership Council (ELC), which served as a national support network and also developed guidelines for U.S. companies doing business with South Africa. He was an investor and founding member of Stairstep, Inc., a Minnesota corporation that developed and financed black-owned small business initiatives. He served on the board of directors of the Entrepreneurial Development Center at Florida A&M University and on the Dean's Advisory Council at the Howard University Business School.

But he was still craving the thrill of the deal. He bought a failing health club in Minneapolis and turned it around and, in 1989, spearheaded an effort to secure an NBA franchise for San Diego (the league ultimately turned him down).

So when he got a tip that NatWest had put the Globetrotters on the market, he was already trawling for failing companies that he could buy on the cheap, get back on their feet, then flip his investment two or three times over. "There was nothing passionate about buying the Globetrotters," he says. "It was just another business opportunity. I figured for a million bucks, maybe two million bucks, I could leverage a down payment and a loan, and get a good return on it. Plus, I could preserve the legacy of the organization, which was number two on my list."

Some experts questioned his judgment on both counts. The Globetrotters had fallen so low that some people—ones who should have known better—already thought they were dead. A few months after Mannie's acquisition of the team, NBC was broadcasting an NBA playoff game, during which the cameras panned the crowd and zoomed in on Meadowlark Lemon, who was sitting in the stands. The sight of Lemon inspired announcers Dick Enberg and Magic Johnson to reflect on the Globetrotters' legacy. "How many years they've delighted fans," Enberg observed. "And now the NBA has become so good that, in a legitimate game, they've put the Globetrotters out of business."

"It's tough to compete with the NBA," Johnson agreed sadly.

Mannie Jackson called NBC and got the network to issue an on-air apology, with Enberg backtracking and noting the Trotters' "strong pulse," but the damage had been done. If NBC's game announcers thought the Trotters were already dead, how many fans thought the same?

Mannie Jackson's mother once told an Edwardsville sportswriter that she never expected her son to become that good an athlete because "he just didn't seem to have the necessary energy." Somehow in the intervening years he had found it, because when he took over the Globetrotters in the spring of 1993, it was like a tidal wave had slammed into the front office. Everything the Globetrotters had been doing for years—every process, every practice, every assumption—was examined, analyzed, critiqued, and often thrown out with the trash. The evaluation process was so intense that some of the old-time staffers, including Joe Anzivino, would end up leaving, and not always by choice.

Even before the sale closed, Mannie was requesting copies of all contracts with merchandisers, arena owners, foreign promoters, players, and front office personnel. He wanted reports on how players were recruited and how training camp was run. All front office employees were required to write one-page summaries of their jobs and their perceived future with the company. Top executives completed a sixteen-page questionnaire evaluating the organization's culture and leadership. Mannie held an employee retreat to develop a new mission statement and company objectives. Over the summer, reams of data were collected into a "Production Bible" that broke down every item in the Trotters' budget, including the costs for materials, the relationship between fixed and variable costs, overhead, and the break-even point for every venue.

A series of focus groups were convened around the country to assess how damaged the Globetrotters' credibility was with the public, and the results showed that young people didn't know anything about them, and many older people hadn't heard about them in years. Mannie hired musicians to write original music for the Trotters' games, and got rid of the players' hated zip-up uniforms, replacing them with the Trotters' traditional red, white, and blue stripes.

Mannie was convinced that the Trotters had to first reestablish their credibility as a business before they could hope to reestablish any credibility in sports. So he leveraged his contacts in the business press to get articles in the *Wall Street Journal, Forbes,* and *USA Today.* The

Globetrotters had also lost credibility with arena managers, the people who controlled the buildings in which they played. Fortunately, Mannie knew a fair number of them through Honeywell, which supplied their control systems or security systems. "I'm in a new world now, can you help me out?" he asked, and many of them offered the Trotters a cut rate that first year. "Giving us a deal, period, was helpful," Mannie says, "because several had given up on the product."

All summer, the Globetrotter players had been hearing rumblings about the drastic changes Mannie was instituting, but they experienced them firsthand when they reported to training camp. In past years, the players had practiced two hours in the morning, two hours in the afternoon, and had the rest of the day off. But under Mannie's new regimen, they were roused out of bed at six A.M. to run four miles before breakfast. Then, they practiced two hours before lunch, spent the entire afternoon in the classroom, being schooled on African American and Globetrotter history, media relations, and public speaking, and returned after supper for another two-hour practice. Mannie also imposed a zero-tolerance policy on drugs or alcohol abuse, and warned the players that flagrant womanizing or rudeness to fans were grounds for immediate dismissal.

One of Mannie's first personnel decisions was to give Tex Harrison a lifetime coaching contract, and Harrison wrote a detailed assessment of the players and the show. His first recommendation was to drastically improve the quality of players on both the Trotters and the Washington Generals, and Red Klotz responded by firing his entire team. Harrison urged that "slapstick type comedy" be eliminated and insisted that the showmen "must be skilled as basketball players first and comedians second." Indeed, one of the first changes Mannie made to the show was to remove some of the racially stereotyped gags from the Meadowlark Lemon era. Former Globetrotters noticed the changes right away. "One of the things I was thrilled about when Mannie took over was they no longer did that Amos 'n' Andy stuff," says former Trotter Frank Stephens. "That was the first thing I noticed—they had taken out the Stepin Fetchit stuff, that minstrel shit."

To save money, IBC and NatWest had cut back to one Trotter unit, but Mannie reinstated the second squad, thereby doubling the total number of games. When the season began, he instituted a fifteen-minute autograph session after every game, which became so popular with the fans that it was lengthened to thirty minutes. By early 1994, the changes were already starting to pay off. Attendance and gate receipts were up, and instead of mothers writing to complain about players "pantomiming sodomy," Mannie passed a letter around the office from a mother in Indiana who raved about the Globetrotters' postgame autograph session, and said her teenage daughter and her friends had left "with new heroes that evening."

During Mannie's second season, the momentum kept building. The Globetrotters appeared on *Good Morning America* and on Oprah's tenth anniversary show, where they shot baskets with her on an outdoor court; Columbia Pictures optioned a movie deal on the Globetrotters' early history; and Mannie unveiled a new mascot, "Globie," who entertained the kids before the games.

Mannie was still working full-time for Honeywell and running the Globetrotters by fax, phone, and on the weekends. Back home in Minneapolis, his fax machine was burning up, as he required the Globetrotters' road managers to fax him nightly reports, showing the cost, revenue, and operating profit for every game. Honeywell had been his life for twenty-five years, and CEO Michael Bonsignore had been extremely supportive of Mannie's private venture with the Trotters, insisting that there was no conflict of interest between the two jobs. But Mannie came home one night and told his wife, Cathy, "I don't have a conflict of interest, I have a conflict of passion."

He had fallen in love with the Globetrotters. What was supposed to have been a calculated investment had become an all-consuming passion. He had gotten hooked on the challenge of turning around the business, and on the people. In December 1994, he resigned from Honeywell and threw himself into managing the Trotters full-time. Making the move was not without risk, both personally and professionally. Being the owner of the Harlem Globetrotters might bring him additional fame and wealth, but he knew that the corporate world did not consider entertainment to be serious business, and he could lose some standing as a major player in that world. To compensate, he served on the boards of directors of five Fortune 500 companies, including Ashland Oil, Jostens Inc., Reebok, Stanley Tools, and Martech Controls (Honeywell's South African subsidiary).

He soon relocated his family and the Globetrotters' headquarters to Phoenix, Arizona. Now, with Mannie engaged full-time, the intensity level in the front office increased exponentially. For the first time since Abe Saperstein died, there was an owner who was totally and exclusively committed to the Harlem Globetrotters. Indeed, although Mannie Jackson and Abe Saperstein have very different personalities, there are striking similarities in a few key areas. They were both terrific salesmen and marketing wizards, had unusual communication and relationship skills, communicated a vision of where they wanted the Globetrotters to go, infused the organization with their own energy and sense of purpose, and worked harder than anybody else.

Over the next few seasons, Mannie focused on three major priorities: increasing the team's competitiveness and the quality of the show, developing corporate sponsorships, and broadening the Trotters' community involvement.

Improving the team may have been the easiest of the three goals. He cut 30 percent of the veterans in 1994, replacing them with younger, more talented players, and instigated a relentless search for better players. Even with the growth of the NBA, the Continental Basketball Association (CBA), and the European leagues, there was no shortage of talented basketball players coming out of American colleges. "There are so many good basketball players today," says coach Tex Harrison, "but we're looking for great players who also have the right personality to be Globetrotters."

Wun Versher, a current player, believes that it takes a certain kind of personality to handle the constant demands on the Globetrotter players. "You can't turn it on and turn it off," he says. "If you don't really love being around people, you will lose your mind out here."

What Mannie Jackson was trying to do was take the Globetrotters back to their roots, to the days when they had great players who could also clown—not just clowns. "We didn't want to connect back to the cartoon period of the 1970s," he would later say, "but to the period when it was a great barnstorming team that could compete and play against anyone." But convincing the press and the public that the Trotters could play serious ball—and understanding why they would even want to—was a challenge. It had been over thirty years since the

Globetrotters had last played a legitimate game (when the College All-Star series ended in 1962), and to an entire generation of Americans they were strictly a show team—or, worse, cartoon characters on *Scooby Doo.*

In those thirty years, the NBA had *become* the Globetrotters, adopting the flashy style that had once distinguished the Trotters from the "serious" pro leagues. The thrilling dunks and behind-the-back passes that had once been the Globetrotters' exclusive trademarks had now become standard fare at NBA games. Superstars like Julius Erving, Magic Johnson, and Michael Jordan had redefined modern basketball in Harlem Globetrotter colors. Magic Johnson and the Los Angeles Lakers had institutionalized the Globetrotters' style and given it a Hollywood name: "Showtime."

But Mannie was determined to prove that the Trotters could become one of the best teams in the world again. First, he had to find somebody, besides the Washington Generals, who would even play them. And he needed someone with legitimate basketball credentials.

In September 1995, the Trotters opened an eleven-game "Ultimate Challenge" series in Europe against the Kareem Abdul-Jabbar All-Stars, who included the forty-eight-year-old Abdul-Jabbar and former NBA stars Nate Archibald, Artis Gilmore, and Jo Jo White. They were all in their forties, but Abdul-Jabbar still had his pride and some of his game. When Mannie went to his house to talk about the series, Abdul-Jabbar warned him, in his characteristically sober manner, "Now this ain't going to be no show. Nobody's gonna throw a bucket of confetti on *me!*"

Mannie had intentionally scheduled the games in Europe, knowing that American sportswriters would never take the games seriously. "We couldn't do it in the U.S.," he says, "but in Europe they're a little more naive, a bit more open to a fresh idea."

After the Trotters won the first two games against Abdul-Jabbar's forty-somethings, Kareem went out and recruited some younger players, including Bo Kimble, a three-point specialist who had played in the NBA, and a six-foot-nine enforcer from the European leagues. In the third game, in Vienna, Abdul-Jabbar hit fifteen of sixteen shots, scored 34 points, and led his team to a 91–85 victory over the Trotters, ending their 8,829-game winning streak that dated back to Red

Klotz's fabled 1971 victory in Martin, Tennessee. The Trotters rebounded to win the remaining games, but the cynicism of U.S. sportswriters still followed them across the ocean. "What in the name of the Washington Generals is Abdul-Jabbar doing?" *Sports Illustrated* asked skeptically. "And what in the name of Meadowlark Lemon are the Globies doing? Both the sky-hooking legend and the merry-making legends seem out of their element."

Unfazed by the sarcasm, Mannie kept looking for legitimate games. In April 1997, he revived one of the Globetrotters' greatest traditions, the College All-Stars series, and the Globetrotters defeated a team of college stars 126–114 in Phoenix. As an extra drawing card, Magic Johnson played for the Trotters, scoring 29 points and adding eleven rebounds and fifteen assists. Between 1997 and 1999, the Trotters would play, and win, five more games against college all-star squads that included ten future NBA first-round draft picks. In 1998, the Globetrotters also won the championship of the prestigious Los Angeles Summer Pro League, which included international teams from Germany, Mexico, and China.

In January 2000, Mannie scored a major coup by signing an agreement with the National Association of Basketball Coaches to play a series of preseason games against NCAA teams, as well as an All-Star game during NCAA Final Four weekend. Since then, the Trotters' "Fall College Tour" has matched them up against some of the best college teams in the country, including defending champions in every NCAA division. They have played Division I champs Michigan State (2000), Maryland (2002), and Syracuse (2003), and have defeated such Division I powerhouses as Purdue, Iowa, Minnesota, and St. John's. The Fall College Tours have also provided national TV exposure, as ESPN and ESPN2 have broadcast several games. At the end of the 2003 tour, the Trotters had a 20–9 cumulative record,* and had reestablished their credibility on the court.

In November 2003, Kenny Smith, the NBA analyst for TNT television, was sitting courtside with Mannie, watching as the Trot-

---

* *Six of the nine losses came during one disastrous stretch in 2002, when the Trotters lost six games in a row, to Vanderbilt, defending champ Maryland, Mississippi State, UConn, Central Connecticut, and Ohio State.*

ters completely manhandled the Syracuse Orangemen, the reigning NCAA champs. "Mannie, right now you'd be the sixth or seventh seed in the [NBA's] Eastern Division," Smith said.

Off the court, Mannie was equally aggressive in pursuing corporate sponsorships, both to relieve the pressure on ticket sales as the Trotters' primary revenue stream and to give added cachet to the Globetrotters' name, by associating with well-known companies. Northwest Airlines was the first corporation to come aboard as a major sponsor, but Disney, Denny's, Reebok, Monsanto, Dixie Crystals, Valvoline, and Jostens soon followed. In 2001, Mannie signed a five-year-deal with Burger King—the largest sponsorship deal in Globetrotter history—to become the "title sponsor" for the Trotters' world tour. Then, in July 2002, Mannie signed an agreement with FUBU to become the Trotters' exclusive outfitter and to produce a new Globetrotter clothing line. Coming at the height of the "retro" craze, FUBU's Globetrotter jerseys and warm-up suits became an immediate hit and sold over $60 million the first two years.*

The FUBU success proved that the Globetrotters were cool again—and, most significant, they were cool in the African American community. Mannie Jackson had played with the Trotters in the early 1960s, when the black community rejected the team as Uncle Toms, and he was determined to bridge that forty-year-old divide. He had consciously reached out to black organizations, had donated money to the United Negro College Fund and the NAACP, had done all the right things—but the FUBU clothing line did more than any of those to seal that gap. Eighteen-year-old kids, who weren't old enough to remember when the Trotters were considered Toms, were snapping up sixty-dollar Globetrotter retro jerseys so fast the stores couldn't keep them in stock. And older African Americans, who *did* remember when the Trotters were seen as Toms, were still buying $100 fleece warm-up suits with Goose Tatum's name on the back. "[FUBU] sealed the gap," Mannie says proudly. "It's gone."

---

* *The FUBU contract expired in 2004, and the Globetrotters are currently negotiating with other clothing distributors, hoping to expand the Globetrotters' sales in the international market.*

Having rebuilt the Trotters' credibility on the court and in corporate boardrooms, Mannie also set out to reclaim their image as "ambassadors of goodwill," particularly in the black community. In April 1994, he donated $250,000 to the United Negro College Fund, the first of $10 million in charitable contributions he would make over the next decade.★

Since 1998, the Globetrotters have been holding Summer Youth Basketball Camps in major cities across the country, with scholarships provided to inner-city kids. In June 1996, the Trotters were the first professional basketball team to tour the newly democratic South Africa, where they were welcomed by President Nelson Mandela. During their tour, they put on clinics for 300,000 kids, donated 50,000 basketballs and 5,000 hoops, and raised $1.5 million for the Nelson Mandela Children's Fund. The Trotters made a return visit to South Africa in 1997, where they performed for Mandela's seventy-ninth birthday. In 2000, the Trotters had an audience with Pope John Paul II and made him an Honorary Globetrotter.

Further, Mannie hasn't shied away from politically explosive issues. When the South Carolina NAACP called for an economic boycott of the state because of a controversy over the Confederate flag, Mannie donated $50,000 to the state NAACP and has refused to play in South Carolina ever since.

Today, the Globetrotters schedule community service events in every city on their tour. They have performed special Magic Circles with kids from the Foundation for Blind Children, have had cancer victims from the Make-A-Wish Foundation serve as honorary coaches, have given Black History presentations in public schools, and have donated hundreds of thousands of dollars to the Red Cross national disaster relief fund (the Globetrotters donate one dollar for every mile their buses travel, which totaled $92,485 in 2003). In partnership with the U.S. Department of Education, the Globetrotters

---

★ *In 1998, Mannie Jackson established a $100,000 Jackson Family Endowment for the Lincoln School Alumni Foundation, to provide scholarships to local students. He insisted that the program be co-named for Joe Lucco, his old high school basketball coach. In 2003, he donated $250,000 to build a new YMCA in Edwardsville.*

now visit hundreds of elementary schools as spokespersons for the CHEER for Character program.*

In the past ten years, the Harlem Globetrotters have reestablished their credibility on the court and with their fans and with corporate America. They have rebuilt their image in the African American community and reaffirmed their reputation as ambassadors of good-will in the community at large. But the most difficult rebuilding job Mannie Jackson faced was with a much smaller community that held much greater animosity toward the Globetrotters: former players. For an organization whose entire history has been built around making people happy, it is astounding how many former players hold deep, personal grudges toward the Globetrotters, going all the way back to the era of Abe Saperstein. To them, the Globetrotters' demise was not about falling gate receipts or losing credibility with corporate sponsors—it was personal.

Some former Trotters were still mad at Abe for cutting them, or for not paying them what they were worth. Some of them were mad because they felt exploited—because Abe got rich and they just got old. Some of them were angry because they had no pension and no health insurance for their ruptured disks and worn-out cartilage from too many games and too many miles on the bus. But most of all, they were angry for being ignored.

However they felt about Abe Saperstein, at least when he was alive the Globetrotters were a kind of family. Like many families, it was somewhat dysfunctional, with some members not speaking to each other, but a family nonetheless. Even after Abe died, at least Inman Jackson, Marie Linehan, and Joe Anzivino were still there and still remembered them. There was someone who would still laugh at their stories and make sure they had complimentary tickets when the Trotters came to town. Someone who would let them know when one of their old teammates passed on. But in the twenty-five years between Abe's death and Mannie's ascension, the Globetrotter players were ignored. Nobody in the corporate office even knew who they were. And they were pissed.

---

* A character-based education program, CHEER stands for the traits of cooperation, honesty, effort, enthusiasm, respect, and responsibility.

Mannie Jackson inherited that bitterness when he bought the team, along with the company trademarks and the rights to "Sweet Georgia Brown." "A lot of the old players wouldn't even return a phone call," he says. As a former Trotter, he understood their hostility, and attempted to reach out to the Globetrotter audience that mattered most. In 1993, the first year he bought the team, he created a Legends Ring, the equivalent of a Globetrotter hall of fame, to honor former players who had made a lasting contribution to the team. Chosen by an advisory board, the Legends Ring now includes nearly twenty former Globetrotters, including Goose Tatum, Marques Haynes, Meadowlark Lemon, Curly Neal, Geese Ausbie, Bob "Showboat" Hall, Wilt Chamberlain, Connie Hawkins, Bob Karstens, J. C. Gibson, Frank Washington, Dr. Johnny Kline, Tex Harrison, and Lynette Woodard, among others.

That was a nice beginning, but nearly 200 former Globetrotters are still alive, out of an estimated 500 who have played for the team, and Mannie can't put all of their pictures on the wall. Most of them will never be inducted into the Legends Ring.

He had to do more. In 2000, he decided to form an alumni association to try to reconnect with the surviving players and heal the family feud. He knew that only a former Trotter would have the credibility to make the alumni association work, so he turned to the friend he had known longer than anyone else: Govoner Vaughn, who had had a distinguished career as an executive for Detroit Edison. Mannie convinced Gov to move to Phoenix and become the director of alumni relations. Slowly, one by one, Gov started tracking down the old-timers. He compiled an alumni roster, published a newsletter, and became the liaison between the past and the present. "A lot of the guys just want somebody to talk to," he says today, between constant phone calls.

Gov also became the de facto Globetrotter historian, unpacking all the boxes of old files and photographs that Mannie had salvaged from a storage warehouse in L.A., where they were rotting away. He built a Harlem Globetrotters archive in his office, with manila folders for every player and three-ring binders full of old photos and newsclips. With their history and their contributions finally being appreciated, the former players have come around. There are still a few who won't return Gov's calls, but he's slowly bringing them back into the fold.

Many former Trotters have done well in their lives, but many others have fallen on hard times. There are guys who played before there were pension plans and 401(K)s, and guys who had nothing to fall back on—no skills or college degree—when their playing days were done. Mannie Jackson has begun to reach out to them, too. In 2004, he donated $250,000 in seed money to the alumni association to help former players in need.

Today, it has all come together in an astounding resurgence for this nearly eighty-year-old institution. The Globetrotters are playing before two million people a year in twenty-five countries. Attendance was up 15 percent in 2004, the tenth consecutive year of double-digit increases. Total revenues have grown an average of 16 percent a year for the past ten years, and gross revenues have increased fivefold, from $9 million to over $40 million per year.★ In 2000 and 2002, the Globetrotters were recognized as the "most liked and most recognized" sports team in the United States by the "Q Ratings," an entertainment industry survey.

From the brink of collapse ten years ago, the Harlem Globetrotters have firmly reestablished themselves as an American sports icon and an international phenomenon. It would be tempting to say that the story has come full circle, and that the Trotters have recaptured the luster of their glory days in the 1950s and '60s. But that would be too simplistic, and too cute. The world has changed, basketball has changed, and the Globetrotters are not looking to recapture their past.

In the 1950s, the Globetrotters were emissaries who carried basketball around the world, introducing it in countries where the game was as yet unknown. But now basketball has become a global sport. What began with Dr. Naismith and a peach basket in Springfield,

---

★ *Mannie Jackson bought out NatWest's 20 percent share of the team within three years, and has since bought out all of his original investors, at extremely healthy returns. He now owns 100 percent of the company stock.*

Massachusetts, has spread around the world, and the game that America dominated just fifteen years ago—when the 1992 Dream Team swept to Olympic gold in Barcelona—has in many ways passed it by. One need only look at the humiliating defeat of the American men in the 2004 Athens Olympics to know that the world is no longer in awe of American basketball or its self-absorbed NBA millionaires.

And as basketball's popularity creates a new global market, who better than the Harlem Globetrotters to capitalize on it? Fifty years ago, Abe Saperstein had the foresight to take his team around the world, when no one else could envision it, and build the Globetrotters into the most popular sports franchise on earth. Today, Mannie Jackson sees the potential for the Globetrotters to become more popular internationally than even Abe could have dreamed. In August 2004, the Globetrotters signed a five-year contract with the Chinese government to play sixty games a year there, with the possibility of that number doubling. Similar opportunities exist in Japan and across the Asian Rim. The Chinese don't just want the Trotters to perform; they want them to teach values and character development in Chinese schools. The Trotters' unique combination of sport, entertainment, humanitarian work, and family values may catapult them to a level of international popularity that no sports franchise has ever achieved.

At sixty-five, Mannie Jackson is beginning to reflect on the legacy that he will leave behind for the Globetrotter organization. "If I've accomplished anything, it is [to create] the possibility of this American icon exploding worldwide in ways we've never imagined," he says. "No one knows yet what the global market will evolve to be, but the rules will not be defined by the NBA or the American media, but by someone sitting in Beijing or Brisbane or Istanbul. And the Harlem Globetrotters will be a major player. We'll be at least number two in the world, and with the right influences, we'll be number one."

EPILOGUE

Final Circle

It's an hour before game time in Tampa, Florida, and the Harlem Globetrotters are in their dressing room at the Ice Palace, eating a pregame meal of fried chicken and french fries out of Styrofoam take-out containers. The meal would not win any "Healthy Heart" certificates, but there is no time for a sit-down meal this afternoon. The Trotters arrived two hours earlier from Bradenton, fifty miles south, where they played the previous night, then immediately hit the floor for their daily practice and scrimmage against the New York Nationals, their regular opposition team.

The Trotters practice every day, even after long hauls between towns, and those practice sessions are surprisingly intense. Coach Clyde Sinclair, a recently retired player himself, screams at the Trotter guards from the sidelines, "Push it! Push the ball!" The Trotters and the Nationals, who are owned by Red Klotz, have played hundreds of games against each other and the Nationals have never won, yet the players still go at each other hard on the floor.

By the time practice ended, there was only an hour before this Saturday matinee was to begin, so the players make do with the take-out chicken. Curley "Boo" Johnson (Curley is his real name), the veteran dribbling specialist now in his sixteenth year, picks half-heartedly at his food and then starts laying out the oversized knee pads that protect him when he goes into his slides. A reflective, studious man, Johnson has been keeping a daily journal every year since he joined the team, and functions as the Trotters' resident historian. Other players joke around as they eat, showing the easy familiarity of men who spend four straight months traveling together.

Two of the Trotters' stars, Paul "Showtime" Gaffney and Michael "Wild Thing" Wilson, are already out in the arena, talking to about thirty-five adolescents from the Florida Sheriff's Boys Ranch. This is a daily pregame ritual called "Globetrotter University," at which Trotter players talk to youngsters from local boys or girls clubs, scout troops, or AAU basketball teams. Gaffney emphasizes the importance of staying in school and getting a college degree. "The Globetrotters are not just the most entertaining team in the world, we're the most educated," he says, citing the fact that over 80 percent of the Trotters have college degrees.

After their initial presentation, the players field questions from the kids.

"Do Globetrotter players go to the NBA?" one boy asks.

"Yeah, a lot of Globetrotters play in the NBA," says Wilson. "There's not a *talent* difference; it's a *choice* difference. I see more of the world in a month than most people see in a lifetime." Wilson knows something about talent. The six-foot-five beanpole, who starred at Memphis University, is listed in the *Guinness Book of World Records* for an incredible twelve-foot dunk.

"Are you guys sort of like 'And 1'?" another kid asks, referring to the popular street-ball hoopsters who have been featured on ESPN.

"No, 'And 1' is like us, only we're better," Gaffney replies.

Globetrotter University wraps up forty-five minutes before game time and Gaffney and Wilson hurry back to the locker room to gulp down their now-cold chicken dinners and get into their game uniforms. This pregame meeting with kids is indicative of the difference between the Globetrotters and the NBA. There may be more of a talent difference than Gaffney and Wilson would admit, but the *image* difference is truly striking.* Nearly every week, it seems, the press is

---

* *The Globetrotter players certainly can't compete with the salaries of NBA players, but they make a good living. Mannie Jackson has increased player salaries to an average of $120,000 for a twenty-week season, with the highest-paid players making $500,000. The Trotters also receive full medical benefits, a 401(k) plan, and "impact bonuses" that have gone as high as $100,000 per player. They typically stay in four-star hotels, and receive free pregame and postgame meals, as well as free Globetrotter clothing and apparel.*

reporting another scandal involving professional athletes: failed drug tests, wife beatings, murder raps, drunk-driving charges, steroid abuse, and on and on. While the NBA's multimillionaires are notorious for blowing off fans, refusing to sign autographs, and cultivating a gangsta image (which now includes the horrifying spectacle of Ron Artest and other Indiana Pacers brawling with Detroit Pistons' fans in November 2004), Globetrotter players visit schools and hospitals in every town, hold free clinics for underprivileged kids, and sign autographs for at least thirty minutes after every game.

The crowd is starting to fill up the Ice Palace, the 20,000-seat home of the Stanley Cup–champion Tampa Bay Lightning. The Globetrotters' announcer is already hard at work, interspersing music with announcements about the Trotters' Web site and pitches for Burger King, the tour sponsor. The crowd is made up almost entirely of families with children, and with a half hour still to go before game time, the younger ones are getting antsy.

An eight-year-old girl attending her first basketball game asks her father, "Daddy, how does basketball work?"

The father starts to explain, then hesitates, wondering how to translate a Globetrotters' game into regular basketball terminology. He is saved by the announcer, however, who booms out, "And now it's time to meet the world's most popular mascot—heeeerrreee's Globie!!!"

From the north end zone, the Globetrotters' mascot emerges—a young man wearing a gigantic globe-shaped head, a red-white-and-blue uniform, and clown-sized sneakers. Globie is one of Mannie Jackson's creations, a perfect combination of marketing savvy and customer satisfaction. Globie fills the thirty minutes before the game by entertaining the younger kids. It's like having Big Bird in sneakers. After high-fiving his way around the arena, Globie invites a young boy out of the stands and, with "Come On Everybody, Let's Do the Twist" blaring on the PA, coaxes the boy to dance. Then Globie teaches the boy to shoot an over-the-head shot with his back to the basket; every time he misses, hundreds of children in the stands groan in sympathy.

Just before game time, the announcer says, "Globie will be signing autographs in the north end zone," and there's a stampede of youngsters to that corner. The eight-year-old who doesn't know how basketball works turns to her dad. "I want to meet Globie!" she cries, and they're rushing off to join the throng. Of course, the kids need something for Globie to autograph, and there are Globie T-shirts and Globie basketballs and Globie beanie babies for sale—and every kid has to have one.

The Globetrotters and the Nationals come out on the court and, after introductions, the Trotters perform the Magic Circle. For fifty years, the Trotters have been entertaining fans with this same ball-handling routine, but it never grows old. People are tapping their feet and clapping their hands to "Sweet Georgia Brown," and it's the same all over the world. The song and the show are magic.

The game begins, and Showtime Gaffney takes over. Globetrotter showmen are now miked, so they can be heard in the upper reaches of big halls, and Showtime directs the Trotters' weave, feeds Michael Wilson for a rim-rattling dunk, harasses the ref, steals a woman's purse, and hits a hook from half court on his third try. Before halftime, Curley Boo goes into his dribbling routine, sliding across the floor with a Nationals player in pursuit. Later, Curley pushes a young girl in a wheelchair to center court and, with a little assistance, has her spinning the ball on her finger. By the time the game is over, the Trotters will have pulled out most of the old standards—the confetti-in-the-bucket and the slow-motion-football pantomime—and the parents in the crowd will be laughing as hard as they did when they were kids. The father of the eight-year-old wonders if his daughter will ever want to see a regular ball game after this. But then, as he sees the joy on her face, he knows that for her, as for so many millions of fans around the world, this will be a memory that will last forever.

It's the final night of the Harlem Globetrotters' greatest triumph. After seventy-five years, the Trotters have been inducted, as a team, into the Naismith Memorial Basketball Hall of Fame in Springfield, Massachusetts. They're only the fifth team to be inducted, and now join their old rivals the New York Rens. The induction ceremony, on Saturday night, was hosted by Ahmad Rashad and broadcast live on

ESPN2. Besides the Globetrotters, other inductees included coaches Larry Brown and Lute Olson and, most notably, Magic Johnson, who sat in the front row of the Springfield Civic Center, in a place of honor.

When the Trotters' turn came, Rashad introduced a short video about their history, which included highlights of their two victories over the Minneapolis Lakers and interviews with Trotter greats Marques Haynes, Meadowlark Lemon, and Curly Neal. As the video ended and the lights were coming back up in the auditorium, Rashad leaned down toward Magic Johnson and said softly, off-mike, "You know you stole some of that stuff." And Magic nodded and pointed at Rashad, and threw back his head and laughed.

Indeed.

Later, after a jam-packed reception at the Hall of Fame, the Globetrotters' entourage gathered in the lobby bar of the Sheraton Hotel, where they were staying. Mannie Jackson had flown in a group of former players for the big event, including Marques Haynes, Curly Neal, Geese Ausbie, Tex Harrison, Dr. Johnny Kline, Lynette Woodard, and Govoner Vaughn. He had also brought in a squad of current players, who had performed the Magic Circle at the induction ceremony.

Now, around midnight, they were all gathered in the lobby bar. The old guys were clustered together around several small tables, nursing beers, while the young players, still wearing their Trotter warm-up suits, sat nearby at the bar. As happens whenever former Trotters get together, they started telling stories and swapping lies. "He never tells the same lie twice," one old veteran exclaims, disputing a former teammate's recollection of an ancient event. This same scenario is reenacted all over the country wherever former Trotters gather—in Detroit, New York, or Phoenix.

The memories flow, good and bad alike. They tell stories about the Big Dipper, remembering the time Wilt slammed a ball so hard that it hit the ground and bounced all the way back up through the basket. They remember Connie Hawkins taking off from the foul line and swooping down out of the sky so powerfully that the defenders turned and ran.

They make fun of the wanna-be Globetrotters who periodically crop up at big events (one is even here in Springfield), claiming to have played with the Trotters, when all they ever did was try out and get cut, or play one game *against* the Globetrotters.

They laugh now about racial incidents that weren't funny at the time, like the time rednecks in Evansville, Indiana, set the team bus on fire; or the time, in 1983, when Sweet Lou Dunbar, Ovie Dotson, and Jimmy Blacklock were thrown to the ground and arrested by Santa Barbara police, at gunpoint, after a jewelry store was robbed, even though they didn't match descriptions of the suspects in the least.

The racial complexities of being a Harlem Globetrotter are ever-present, even tonight. Two of the current players, Wun Versher and Curley Boo Johnson, are approached at the bar by a white mother with two young boys. She sends the boys up to ask for autographs, which the players give obligingly. But after she leaves, Curley Boo asks reflectively, "Now, do you think she would come anywhere near us, with those kids, if we weren't wearing Globetrotter warm-ups?" At any other time, seeing two young black men sitting at a bar at midnight on a Saturday night, the woman may have run the other way. "I know I get treated different when people know I'm a Globetrotter," he continues, "but I wouldn't say anything to her about it. Because I'm a Globetrotter, maybe people can see me as person."

With the arrival of a second round of beers, the old-timers start loosening up, and the stories about Abe Saperstein come spilling out, even thirty-five years after his death. They are still debating, passionately, how much he actually knew about basketball, and whether he was prejudiced or whether it was all "just business." "Abe was about six different kinds of asshole, but racist wasn't one of them," says Bobby Hunter, who paid his own way to Springfield to be there for the Hall of Fame induction.

More solemnly, they talk about their former teammates—some who are doing well, and others who aren't. If a generalization can be made, the former Trotters who seem to be doing better are those who played only a few years, five or six, perhaps, and then moved on with their lives. These guys built on their Globetrotter experiences, used the connections they made, and the celebrity status it brought them, to forge a new career. "The Harlem Globetrotters were something I *did*," says Frank Stephens. "It's not who I am."

The guys having the hardest time, however, are the ones who couldn't let it go. The longer they played, the harder it became to be something *other* than a Globetrotter. Two of the saddest cases are the two most famous Globetrotters, Curly Neal and Meadowlark Lemon.

Curly Neal is still one of the most recognized sports figures in the world, twenty years after he retired. Everywhere he went in Springfield, peopled recognized his bald head and dazzling smile. "Curly! Curly!" screamed a middle-aged woman working at a local Burger King, rushing out to give him a hug. When the Trotters visited the cancer ward of the Baystate Children's Hospital, he was inundated with requests for autographs by nurses and doctors. Saturday night, at the induction ceremony, a crowd of people stood in line behind a rope to get his autograph; and some of the other former Trotters stood to one side, shaking their heads and marveling at the scene. "Curly could have been a multi-multimillionaire," said Govoner Vaughn, "but he was his own worst enemy." Neal has had financial problems and has been reduced to making appearances for Lowe's; he carries around a little ditty bag of publicity photos, and sometimes seems to be searching for someone to give them to.

Perhaps the saddest case of all is Meadowlark Lemon, who was noticeable by his absence in Springfield. It is hard to find many former Trotters who will say nice things about him, other than that he was "a professional." But Lemon, more than any other Globetrotter, cannot let it go. At seventy-two, he is still trying to play basketball, still going out on tour and doing his old reams. Now a born-again Christian minister, Lemon has his own Web site, on which he sells Meadowlark Lemon nutritional drinks and, improbably, the Meadowlark Lemon home-schooling curriculum. He has recently published a new autobiography, available only through the Web site, for the remarkable price of $350—complete with an authenticated thumbprint.

Inevitably, the old guys start telling stories about Goose Tatum.

They talk about Goose "going fishing" in his make-believe boat and throwing that damn hook shot from the top of the key. They talk about the nights he came up with gags that nobody had ever seen before, and fifty years later he's still making his teammates laugh. They draw comparisons between Goose and other showmen, but even the other showmen realize that there is no comparison. "Goose was the greatest of all time," says Geese Ausbie, who would get some votes himself for that title. But as Marques Haynes says, "Geese Ausbie was a great showman, but Geese is no Goose."

There's something incongruous about telling Goose Tatum stories in Springfield, however, because he is not a member of the Hall of Fame. Abe Saperstein was inducted in 1970, and now, with Mannie Jackson sitting on the Hall's advisory board, more of the old Globetrotters are getting their due. Marques Haynes, Meadowlark Lemon, and Lynette Woodard have all been inducted. Even Bill Cosby, who has a "lifetime" dollar-a-year contract with the Trotters, was inducted in 2004 as an honorary member. But Goose has never made it.

"Goose should have been in the Hall of Fame years ago," says Marques Haynes. "If he doesn't get in, I'll always have the feeling that the Hall of Fame is incomplete."

By now, it's almost one in the morning, and some of the older guys start making noises about turning in. As the evening winds down, however, the talk turns, as it always does, to the Globetrotters who are gone. The ones who have passed on. There are so many of them. Ermer Robinson, who hit the winning shot against the Lakers, and died of throat cancer. Rookie Brown, who starred in *The Harlem Globetrotters* opposite Dorothy Dandridge, who died penniless after too much alcohol. Sweetwater Clifton, the gentle giant, who died driving a hack in Chicago. Bernie Price, who used to bring his grandchildren up to the office on Dearborn Street and show them off. Pop Gates, who is in the Hall of Fame, passed away in 1997. Billy Ray Hobley, "Super Trotter," who dropped dead of an aneurism on the tennis court at age forty-six. All gone now.

The night is ending. One by one, the old Trotters stand up and stretch their legs and say their farewells. Some have early-morning flights to catch back home to Little Rock, Dallas, or Detroit. They shake hands across the table with their old teammates and tell them, "Take it easy, man, I'll see you next time," even though they know there may not be a next time for all of them. But as they turn and slowly make their way across the lobby, some are still here, some have passed on, but the Circle remains.

The All-Time Roster
for the
Harlem Globetrotters

What follows is an alphabetical listing of every player who ever wore a Globetrotters' uniform since their inception. I appreciate the work of J. Michael Kenyon in collaborating with me to compile this list.

Angel Acuna
Gerrod Abram
Melvin "MC" Adams
Joe Adkins
Eli "The Fly" Akin
Tony Akins
Bacari Alexander
Chad Allen
Peter Aluma
Cliff Anderson
Greg "Cadillac" Anderson
Lawrence "Rock" Anderson
Willie "Train" Anderson
Orlando "Hurricane" Antigua
Darnell Archey
Jesse Arnelle
Morris L. Arthur
Robert Aston
George Atkins
Ernest Aughburns
Hubert "Geese" Ausbie
Clyde "The Glide" Austin

Reginald "Rickey" Ayala
James "Jumbo" Bacon
Galen Baker
Milton Banks
Robert Banks
Bill Barnes
Maurice "Stretch" Barnett
Donald Barnette
Shanty Barnette
Floyd Bates
Kenny Battle
Albert Beard
Curtis Bell
Greg Bell
Tavorris Bell
Willie Bell
Arnold "A-Train" Bernard
Jackie Bernard
Jimmy Blacklock
Joe Blair
Anthony Blakes
Larry Bleach
Ben Bluitt
Ruben Bolen

"Jazzy J" Jamie Booker
Tyrus Boswell
Wyatt "Sonny" Boswell
Joseph Bourne
Myree Bowden
Donnie Boyce
Aundre Branch
Nate Branch
Agis Bray
Cleveland Bray
Brad Bridgewater
John Britto
Ernest Brock
Tommy Brookins
Bill "200" Brown
Courtney "The Iceman" Brown
Ernest Brown
George Brown
Gerald Brown
Hillary Brown
J.B. Brown
John (Jack) Brown
Mike Brown
Rickey Brown
Sir Valiant Brown

Thomas "Cochise" Brown
Tyrone "Hollywood" Brown
William "Rookie" Brown
Willie Brown
Kris "Hi-Lite" Bruton
Andre Bryant
Hallie Bryant
Tarise Bryson
Joe Buckhalter
Monty Buckley
Pete "Shorty" Bueford
Boid Buie
Marcus Bullard
Walter Burch Jr.
Frank Burks
Stanley "Chico" Burrell
Ed Burton
Donald Byrd
Roy "ZaZu" Byrd
Cedric Caballos
Harry Caldwell
Don Calhoun
John "Moose" Campbell
Willie Campbell
Derrick Canada
Bruce Capers
Ted "Fist" Carey
Marc Carter
Willie Cerf
Wilt "The Stilt" Chamberlain
John Chaney
John "Bill" Chavers
Nathaniel Chisholm
Wally Choice
Ousmane Cisse
George Clark
Zachary "Zach" Clayton
Nat "Sweetwater" Clifton
Alvin Clinkscales
Keith Closs
Kara Coates
Jesse Coffey
Elvin Coker

Ron "Sugah" Cole
Larry "Shorty" Coleman
Lorenzo Coleman
Troy Collier
Lee Collins
Chuck Cooper
Duane Cooper
Robert Cooper
Bill Cosby
Opal Courtney
Shon Crosby
George Crowe
Jason Crowe
Robert Crowe
Lance Cudjoe
Lawrence Cudjoe
Albert Culton
Roscoe "Duke" Cumberland
Roscoe "Duke" Cumberland Jr.
Alan "Vitamin C" Cunningham
Thomas "Joe" Cunningham
William Cunningham
Jamar Curry
Kevin Daley
Wendyl "Brutus" Daniel
Warren Daniels
Ben Davis
James "Country" Davis
Lorenzo "Piper" Davis
McKinley "Deacon" Davis
Mel "Trick" Davis
Darryl "Chocolate Thunder" Dawkins
Todd Day
Brandon Dean
Dick Dempsey
Blaine Denning
Dan Dennis
Hank DeZonie
Kaniel Dickens
Dwaine Dillard
Al Dixon

Reggie "Air Man" Dixon
Tyrone "Dynamite" Doleman
Cameron Dollar
Jeffery Dollison
Ovie Dotson
James Doughty
Michael "Memphis" Douglas
Robert Dowery
Jessie "Super-J" Drain
Sam Lee Drummer
Walter Dukes
Walter Dumpson
"Sweet" Lou Dunbar
Dwight Durante
Sherwin Durham
George "Easy" Easter
Eugene Edgerson
Damond Edwards
Sidney Edwards
Rodney "Hot Rod" English
Dajuan "Piece" Eubanks
Lamont Evans
Robert "So Smooth" Fairley
Greene Farmer Jr.
Al Fawks
James Felton
"Fast" Eddie Fields
Ronnie Fields
Agusta "Gus" Finney
Jackie Fitzpatrick
Pascal "Frenchy" Fleury
Sterling Forbes Sr.
Sterling "Smooth" Forbes Jr.
Sherell Ford
William "Plunk" Ford
Willie Foreman
Tremaine Fowlkes
Glen Francis
Seth "Hot 'N Fresh" Franco
Reggie Franklin

Robert Frazier
William "Razor" Frazier
Lloyd Gabourel
Paul "Showtime" Gaffney
David "Smokey" Gaines
Erin "Helicopter" Galloway
"Wee" Willie Gardner
Lee Garner
William "The Orbit" Garner
Bill Garrett
Lionel Garrett Jr.
William "Pop" Gates
Reggie Geary
Sammy Gee
Devean George
Gee Gervin
Bob Gibson
Leroy Gibson
Thomas Gibson
Henry Gill
J.C. Gipson
Kenny Glenn
LaMarcus Golden
Elbert "Tree" Gordon
Art Grant
Chudney Gray
Ed Gray
George Gray
Gerald Gray
Carl Green
"Super" Mario Green
Nate Green
Anthony Greenup
Lynn Greer
Josh Grider
Rob Griffin
William Sylvester Griffin
Willie Griffin
Eugene Gutter
Sammie Haley
Simeon Haley
Lorenzo Hall
Robert "Showboat" Hall
Roy Hammonds
Mark Hannabal

Vic Hanson
Barry "High Rise" Hardy
Mike Harmon
Cleveland Harp
Charley Harris
Millard Harris
Rico Harris
C.C. Harrison
Charles "Tex" Harrison
Connie "Hawk" Hawkins
Fess Hawkins
Juaquin "Hawk" Hawkins
Leroy Hawkins
Sherman Hawkins
Jimmy Haynes
Marques Haynes
Curtis Haywood
Carl Helem
Michael Henderson
Jimmy "Pee Wee" Henry
David Hicks
Sean Higgins
Cory Hightower
Kelvin "Special K" Hildreth
Oris Hill
Leon Hillard
Doug Himes
"Mr. Exciting" Exree Hipp
"Supertrotter" Billy Ray Hobley
Sandra "Sweetness" Hodge
James Hodges
Robert Hokett
James Holland
Kevin Holland
General Lee Holman
Charles Holton
Pete Hood
Gary Hooker
James Horne
Willie Horton

Stuart House
John Howard
Tyrone "Mooney" Howard
Charles Hoxie
Harold "Bobo" Hubbard
Eugene Hudgins
Roosevelt "Roosie" Hudson
Solomon Hughes
Vincent Humphrey
Eddie Hunt
Bobby "Zorro" Hunter
Jimmie "Snap" Hunter
McCoy Ingram
John Isaacs
Alvin Jackson
Anthony "Tony" Jackson
Benjamin Jackson
Glover "Action" Jackson
Inman "Big Jack" Jackson
"Jumping" Jackie Jackson
Mannie Jackson
Matt "Showbiz" Jackson
Mike Jackson
Quentin Jackson
Ronnie Jackson
Jerome James
Max Jameson
Shawn "Thunderbird" Jameson
Alvin Jefferson
Seldon Jefferson
Jesse Jemison
Daron Jenkins
Ferguson Jenkins
Al "Big Train" Johnson
Albert Johnson
"Handy" Andy Johnson
Cleo Johnson
Curley "Boo" Johnson
Curley Johnson
Dalron Johnson
Earvin "Magic" Johnson
Harold "Killer" Johnson
Lester Johnson
Lorenzo Johnson

Luther Johnson
Allen "AJ" Jones
Chuck Jones
Chuck "Mighty Man"
 Jones
Collins Jones
Damon Jones
Eric Jones
Ernest Jones
Steve Jones
William "Bill" Jones
Clyde Jordan
Gerald Jordan
Mike Jordan
Reggie Jordan
James "Jamming J"
 Joseph
Roscoe Julien
Charlie Justice
Bob Karstens
Henry Kean Jr.
Junius Kellogg
Walter Kennedy
Otis "OK" Key
Boudreau King
Ezell King
Jeff King
Mike King
Wilbert King
William "Dolly" King
Woudruff "Boudreau"
 King
Robin "Captain Kirk"
 Kirksey
Webster Kirksey
"Jumping" Johnny Kline
Bobby Knight
Ronald Knight
Herman "Helicopter"
 Knowings
Vic Kraft
Darius Lane
John Lane
Herbert "Flight Time"
 Lang
Alto Lark
Granville "Granny" Lash

David "Big Daddy"
 Lattin
Jolette "Jazzy" Law
Edmond Lawrence
Jason Lawson
Floyd Layne
Harry "Bunny" Leavitt
Eric "Big E" Lee
Norman "Junior" Lee Jr.
Theodis "Wolfman" Lee
George "Meadowlark"
 Lemon
Melvin Levett
Brian Lewin
Elzie Lewis
Joe Lillard
John Linehan
Robert Lee Little
Jamal Livingston
Earl Lloyd
John "Licky" Lloyd
Ramel Lloyd
Osborne "The Wizard"
 Lockhart
Rahim Lockhart
Byron "Fat" Long
Thomas Long
Ray Lothery
Corey Louis
LaQuency "Candy"
 Lucas
Emory Luck
Paxton "Sugar" Lumpkin
Bob Lun
Kevin Lyde
Kei Madison
Coata "Big Cat" Malone
Willie Malone
Jack Mann
Chris "Plastique" Manuel
Fred Marberry
Everett "Ziggy" Marcell
Mike Marshall
Darrick Martin
Elmer "String Bean"
 Martin
Bobby Joe Mason

William "Buzz"
 Matthews
Dut Mayar
Ken McBride
Mark McCall
Grady McCollum
Joel McCrea
Darnell McCulloch
Jeremee McGuire
Lowell McHenry
Eural McKelvy
Vernon McNeal
Pat McPherson
Paul McPherson
Bill Meggett
Matthew Merritt
Anthony "Pig" Miller
Oliver "Big O" Miller
Bobby Milton
Davage "Dave" Minor
Howard Mitchell
Thomas Mitchell
Bill Mobley
Max Molock
Michael Moncrief
Howard Lee
 Montgomery
Jamario Moon
Donald "Ducky" Moore
Legolian "Boots" Moore
Sammy Moore
Trey Moore
William Morgan Jr.
Chris Morris
Earl "Sugar" Morrison
Cameron Murray
David Nash
Dave Naves
Fred "Curly" Neal
John Netherly
Ritchie Nicol
Chuck Norris
Ronald Nunnery
Eathan O'Bryant
Kingsley Ogwudire
Terrance O'Kelley
Manny Oliver

William "Kid" Oliver
Townsend Orr
Okeme Oziwo
Robert "Babyface" Paige
  Jr.
Clifton Payton
George Peaks
Fred Pearson
C.J. Pepper
Reggie "Silky" Perkins
Ervell Perry
William "Dink" Peters
Tony Peyton
Silas Phelps
Reggie "Regulator"
  Phillips
Kendal "Tiny" Pinder
William Pippen
Derick Polk
Olden Polynice
Robert "Longie" Powell
Louis "Babe" Pressley
Al Price
Bernie Price
Timothy Price
Charles Primas
Trent Pulliam
Al "Runt" Pullins
Randolph Ramsey
Ty "Mr. T" Randolph
Dedrick Reffigee
Kareem "Best Kept
  Secret" Reid
Johnny "Ace" Rhodes
Kitwana Rhymer
Spencer "Doctor"
  Rhynes
Chris Richardson
Pooh Richardson
Antonio Rivers
Larry "Gator" Rivers
Stanley Roberts
Terrance Roberson
Bailey Robertson
Paul "Pablo" Robertson
Walter Robertson
Doug Robinson

Ermer Robinson
Galen Robinson
James "Tim the Rim"
  Robinson
Dwayne "Legend"
  Rogers
Ron Rollerson
Oliver "Catfish" Rollins
William John
  Roseborough
Warren Rosegreen
Cliff Rozier
Harry Rusan
Mike "The Saint"
  St. Julien
Soumaila Samake
Alex "Big Ticket"
  Sanders
James "Twiggy" Sanders
Keaton Sanders
Mark Sanford
Abe Saperstein
Woody Sauldsberry
Sam Sawyer
Willie Scarborough
Antoine Scott
Antwan Scott
Christopher Scott
Henry Scott
Jack Scott
John Scott
Lee Scruggs
Tom Sealy
Ron Selleaze
Karim Shabazz
Sam Sharpe
Frank Shaw
Clifford Shegogg
Andrew Shepard
Nick Sheppard
Keiron "Sweet Pea"
  Shine
Trazel "Quick" Silvers
Lazarus Sims
Cyde "The Glide"
  Sinclair
Henry "Al" Singleton

Charles Smith
Clarence Smith
Doug Smith
Fred "Preacher" Smith
George "Sonny" Smith
Gerald "Deep" Smith
Herbert Smith
Howard Smith
John Ford Smith
"Little" John Smith
"Fabulous" Leon Smith
Orick Smith
Thomas "Tarzan"
  Spencer
Larry Spicer
Larry Spriggs
Khary Stanley
Frank Stephens
Harrison Stepter
George Stevenson
Jackie Stevenson
Albert Stirrup
Lee Andrew Stoglin
Maurice Stokes
Frank Streety
William "The Prince"
  Stringfellow
Othello Strong
Ted Strong
Murphy Summons
Kevin Sutlon
Shannon Swillis
Harry Sykes
Shon Tarver
Jermaine Tate
Reece "Goose" Tatum
Harry "Trees" Taylor
Herb Taylor
Herman "Honey" Taylor
Fred Thomas
Willie Thomas
Garnett Thompson
Dallas "Big D" Thornton
Murdock Thornton
Homer Thurman
Tony Tolbert
"Shark" Tserenjanhor

"Slick" Al Tucker
Ed Tucker
James Tucker
William Tupelo
Roman "Doc" Turmon
Bridget Turner
Herschell Turner
John Turner
Wayne Turner
Johnny Tyson
Jim Usery
David Vaughn
Govoner Vaughn
Jeremy Veal
Jerry Venable
Conley Verdun
Wun "The Shot" Versher
Quincy Wadley
Ernie Wagner
Joyce "The Juice" Walker
Leroy Walker
Robert "Skywalker"
  Wallace
Charles "Tiny" Ward

Hammie Ward
Andy Washington
Frank Washington
James "Nuggie" Watkins
Johnny Watts
Kenyan Weaks
Winfield Welch
Charles "Bubba" Wells
DuJuan Wheat
Sam "Boom Boom"
  Wheeler
Tyson Wheeler
Jackie White
Vincent White
Charles Whiteman Jr.
Tony Wilcox
Al Williams
Brandon Williams
Donald Williams
Ella Williams
Jermaine Williams
John "Hot Plate"
  Williams
Koney Williams

Orlando Williams
Robert Williams
Sean "Elevator" Williams
Tracy Williams
Clarence "Cave" Wilson
"Jumping" Johnny
  Wilson
Michael "Wild Thing"
  Wilson
Ron Wilson
Willie Wilson
Jackson Winters
Robert "Sonny" Woods
Lynette Woodard
Bruce Wright
David Wright
Kareem Wright
Walter "Toots" Wright
John "Yank" Yancey
Charles Young
George "Jake" Young
Vertes Zeigler

Notes on Sources

★

Ben Hogan once said, famously, that he found his near-perfect golf swing "in the dirt." I thought of that comment many times in the past three years, because I felt as if I was digging this story out of the dirt. The Globetrotters have existed since the late 1920s, but there are *no* records prior to the late 1940s—no schedules, rosters, or correspondence. When I started my research, there was no way to know where the Globetrotters had played in the 1920s, '30s, '40s, '50s, '60s, '70s, or '80s. In the early years, Abe Saperstein ran the tour out of his hat and coat, and until Marie Linehan arrived in 1945, apparently little, if anything, was preserved. And after the team was sold four times between 1967 and 1993, much of what had been preserved was lost.

So I had to find it "in the dirt"—primarily, in old newspapers. The most reliable source, for obvious reasons, was the black press, so I read every issue of the *Chicago Defender* and *Pittsburgh Courier* from 1922 to the late 1960s. The *Defender,* in particular, was the "newspaper of record" for every significant event in early Globetrotter history. I also scoured the *Baltimore Afro-American* and the *Amsterdam News,* although they proved less helpful. Many old newspapers are now available on the Internet, but the grunt work still had to be done with microfilm in the basement of university libraries. My eyesight may never be the same. Fortuitously, J Michael Kenyon found me six months into my research, and he had a thirty-year head start cataloging old newspapers; his archive filled in *decades* of missing Trotter games.

The other great newspaper resource was in the Globetrotters' headquarters in Phoenix, where Govoner Vaughn has filled three large binders with original news clippings, covering games from 1930 to 1945. Unfortunately, the clippings from the 1930s were never dated or identified, but J Michael was able to cross-reference and identify many of them.

The most exciting research discovery was finding the "missing" Globetrotter records—seventeen banker's boxes of material—in the Center for American History at the University of Texas. In the late 1980s, Marie Linehan and Joe Anzivino, the last of the old-time front office staff, decided to preserve the most significant team records before they were tossed in the dumpster by the new corporate owners. Marie filled two boxes, which comprise the Abe Saperstein Collection, and there are fifteen additional boxes in the Joseph Anzivino Collection. These boxes include dozens of press clippings, team yearbooks and College All-Star programs, massive amounts of correspondence and marketing letters, Abe's travel logs and estate records, chronologies of all Globetrotter television appearances, Abe's complete files on the American Basketball League, financial and attendance records, team rosters and schedules (from 1961 on), records of lawsuits and labor-management conflicts, and an entire box of photographs.

A summary of the major sources for each chapter follows:

In chapter 1, details about New Year's Day 1950 and the Globetrotters' first game in Madison Square Garden were extracted from New York newspapers, including the *Times, Daily News, Herald Tribune, Daily Mirror,* and *New York Age;* from Paramount News's "Eyes and Ears of the World," dated January 28, 1950, which is available at the Special Media Archives Services Division of the National Archives in College Park, Maryland; and from interviews with Marques Haynes and Frank Washington.

In chapter 2, historical information on Chicago, Jewish immigration, the Great Migration, and the 1919 race riot was drawn from numerous reference books, including *City of the Century, Land of Hope, Black Chicago, The Negro in Chicago, Jews in Chicago, Maxwell*

Street: Survival in a Bazaar, The Gold Coast and the Slum, Bronzeville, An Autobiography of Black Politics, The Slum and the Ghetto, Race Riot, Kup's Chicago, and *The South Side.* Details about Abe Saperstein's family and upbringing were based on interviews with his three surviving siblings, on U.S. Census records, and on Lake View High School yearbooks. His basketball career was documented in the *Chicago Tribune* and *Chicago Evening Post.* The involvement of Jews in basketball was drawn from *Ellis Island to Ebbets Field* and *City Games.* The history of basketball on the South Side was influenced by Gerald Gems's "Blocked Shot" and *Windy City Wars,* as well as Robert Pruter's *Early Phillips High School Teams.* Biographical information about the first Globetrotter players was drawn from U.S. Census records and interviews with Napoleon Oliver, Timuel Black, and Larry Hawkins.

In chapter 3, the history of the Giles Post American Legion, the Savoy Big Five, and Tommy Brookins's Globetrotters was drawn from the *Defender,* Michael Strauss's interview with Tommy Brookins, Kenyon's archive, and my interviews with Kenyon and Strauss.

Primary sources for chapters 4 through 7 included Govoner Vaughn's clipping files, Kenyon's archive, Globetrotter press releases, numerous interviews Abe gave to sportswriters, and my own interviews with Napoleon Oliver, John Isaacs, Nugie Watkins, and Timuel Black. Descriptions of basketball in the 1930s came from Frank Basloe's *I Grew Up With Basketball, Cages to Jump Shots* by Robert W. Peterson, *24 Seconds to Shoot* by Leonard Koppett, *A Hard Road to Glory* by Arthur R. Ashe Jr., *Elevating the Game* by Nelson George, *Fifty Years of Basketball* by Joe Lapchick, *Smashing Barriers* by Richard Lapchick, and *The Ronald Encyclopedia of Basketball.* Information about the Trotters' rivalry with the New York Rens came from Susan Rayl's dissertation "The New York Renaissance Professional Black Basketball Team, 1923–1950" and from articles in the *Defender, Courier, Afro-American, Amsterdam News,* and the *People's Voice.* The history of minstrelsy and black humor in America was drawn from *Sambo* by Joseph Boskin and *On the Real Side* by Mel Watkins. Information on the World Pro Tournament came from Chicago papers, including the *Defender, American, Herald-Examiner, Tribune,* and *Daily News,* as well as the *Pittsburgh Courier* and the *Sheboygan Press.*

Background on Goose Tatum, in chapter 8, came from inter-views with former teammates, Arkansas friends, and surviving rela-tives, along with U.S. Census records and various newspaper articles. Similarly, information about Marques Haynes, in chapter 9, came from newspaper articles, interviews with former teammates, and with Haynes himself. Langston University's 1946 victory over the Globe-trotters was documented in the *Daily Oklahoman*. Information about the Globetrotters' front office staff came from interviews with Wyonella Smith and Katherine Linehan, and from the Saperstein and Anzivino collections at the University of Texas. Details on the Trotters-Lakers games, in chapter 10, came from newspapers in Chicago and Minneapolis, previously published interviews with key participants, George Mikan's two autobiographies, a sixteen-minute outtake of a 1949 Movietone newsreel, and my interviews with Mar-ques Haynes, Vertes Zeigler, Ray Meyer, and Timuel Black. Informa-tion in chapters 11 and 12, about the College All-Stars and the Globetrotters' overseas tours, was drawn from magazine articles (in-cluding *Reader's Digest*, January 1952; *Negro Digest*, May 1950; *True Magazine*, April 1952; *Collier's*, November 13, 1948, and January 31, 1953; *The American Mercury*, December 1955), Globetrotter year-books, the Saperstein and Anzivino collections at UT, *Around the World with the Harlem Globetrotters* by Dave Zinkoff and Edgar Williams, *Never Lose* by Dr. John Kline, and interviews with former Globetrotters and Ray Meyer. Details about Abe Saperstein and the integration of the NBA came from the Saperstein and Anzivino col-lections and Ron Thomas's *They Cleared the Lane*. The role of the U.S. State Department in booking the Trotters overseas was docu-mented in the National Archives in College Park, Maryland (Records Group 59, Central Decimal File 1950–54); and in "Saperstein's Sambos," by Josh Wetterhahn (a senior thesis at North-western University), "Spreading the Gospel of Basketball: The State Department and the Harlem Globetrotters, 1945–1954" by Damion Thomas, and the books *Race Against Empire* and *Parting the Curtain*.

Background information for chapters 13 through 17 and the epilogue came from interviews with numerous former Trotters, team records in Phoenix, and the Saperstein and Anzivino collections at UT. Wilt Chamberlain's recollections about the Trotters were printed in his memoirs (*Goliath: A View from Above* and *Wilt*) and in *Look* magazine ("Why I Am Quitting College," June 10, 1958). Bill Russell's interactions with Abe Saperstein were documented in his autobiography, *Go Up for Glory;* his claim that Abe showed him pornographic pictures was made in a televised interview in Seattle in 1975, which was later printed in the *Everett* [Wash.] *Herald* (January 9, 1976). Criticisms of the Globetrotters as Uncle Toms were drawn from *Foul: The Connie Hawkins Story, Elevating the Game, Basketball Jones, The Black Athlete: A Shameful Story, Winning Is the Only Thing, Darwin's Athletes, Sports in America* by James Michener, and "The Harlem Globetrotters and the Perpetuation of the Black Stereotype" by Ben Lombardo.

Acknowledgments

★

I am always afraid, in writing the acknowledgments for a book, that I will leave out someone who helped me along the way; and I'm even more afraid than usual with this book because there are so many people in that category.

I want to start by thanking the person who originally suggested the book, my literary agent, Jim Rutman. My first reaction when he called was to ask, incredulously, "There's never been a book on the Globetrotters?" Today, I'm still incredulous that an organization that has been around for nearly eighty years has never engendered a comprehensive history. I have felt thankful, on many occasions, for being the writer who got to do that book, and for Jim's thoughtful guidance from beginning to end.

I felt a sense of responsibility to get the story right, and also a sense of urgency. Many of the principal characters in the story are already dead, and many of the surviving Globetrotters are in their seventies or eighties. If the book didn't happen soon, I was afraid that it might not happen at all.

In that respect, I want to thank HarperCollins, and Dawn Davis, the executive editor of Amistad Press, in particular, for appreciating the importance of the story and for being committed to seeing it into print. I've felt lucky to be the one writing this book, and lucky as well to have Herb Schaffner as my editor. I have never had an editor who was so engaged, enthusiastic, and dedicated to making this book the best it could be. I've felt as if I had a partner, a colleague, and a friend at every step along the way.

Next, I want to acknowledge the contributions of the Harlem Globetrotters' staff, including Colleen Lenihan, Eve Miner, Brian Killgore, Cassandra Jackson, and Jeff Munn. Most important, I want to appreciate Govoner Vaughn, the Globetrotter's director of alumni relations, who put up with me camping out in his office and rummaging through his file cabinets, and Brett Meister, the vice president of communications, who has been my number-one point of contact for the entire project. We have shared long drives, cold pizza, baseball sagas, faulty cell phone connections, stories about our daughters, and two years of hard work to make this book happen.

One of my most pleasant surprises was discovering a network of researchers, journalists, and Globetrotter fans across the country who have been collecting information about the Trotters for years, and I want to thank those who graciously shared their knowledge with me, including: Lyle K. Wilson, Gerald Gems, John Carroll, Susan Rayl, and Robert Pruter (who, in addition to writing about basketball at Wendell Phillips High School, also sent me a copy of Michael Strauss's interview with Tommy Brookins on the origins of the Globetrotters). The Web site of the Association of Professional Basketball Research proved to be a gold mine of information about the Globetrotters, and I want to thank APBR members John Grasso, James B. Rasco, Dan Quinn, Bijan C. Bayne, and Robert Bradley for their help. Two noted Chicagoans, Timuel Black and Larry Hawkins, provided valuable insights on the Trotters' identity in Chicago's black community.

I want to give special thanks to Michael Strauss, for his detailed recollections of his interview with Tommy Brookins; Jay Smith, from WTTW in Chicago, the producer of an award-winning documentary on the Globetrotters, who shared his interview notes and contact list, which became guideposts for my own research; John Christgau, author of the recently published *Tricksters in the Madhouse,* on the 1948 Lakers-Trotters game, who recommended important works on the history of minstrelsy and shared an incredible sixteen-minute archival film of the 1949 Lakers-Trotters game. One of the most helpful, and enthusiastic, supporters of this project has been Bill Hoover, the resident expert on Globetrotters from Detroit, who hooked me up with J Michael Kenyon, shared his own biographical sketches of Detroit Trotters, and took me on a wonderful driving tour of famous sites in the history of Detroit basketball.

Many others assisted me along the way, including: Karen Siciliano, Sandi Frost, Carolyn Pendergrass, Robin Jonathan Deutsch, Jeff Sauve, Tom Frederick, and Josh Wetterhahn.

It was the personal recollections of actual participants in the Globetrotters' saga that brought this story to life. I want to thank Abe Saperstein's siblings, Leah Raemer Saperstein, Fay Saperstein, and Harry Saperstein (who passed away in May 2004, at age ninety-one), for sharing insights about their family and Abe's upbringing. I also appreciate the interest and support of Abe's grandson, Lanier Saperstein. Napoleon Oliver, the brother of one of the original Globetrotters, was a delightful resource for understanding the players and the world in which they grew up. Wyonella Smith, who worked for the Globetrotters for over twenty years, helped me understand the inner workings of the front office. I also deeply appreciate Nita Anzivino and Katherine Linehan for steering me to a treasure trove of untapped Globetrotter materials at the University of Texas. And I thank Ray Meyer, longtime DePaul University basketball coach, for sharing his memories of the College All-Star tours.

One of my biggest challenges was bringing Goose Tatum to life, and I appreciate the assistance of Darren Ivy, Jim "Newt" Ellis, Elvie Walker, Marzell Smith, and Jimmie Armstead in doing that. I also want to thank Goose's family—Shirley McDaniel, Bill Powell, Marjorie Tatum Byrd, and a late surprise, Reece Tatum III—for helping me portray the man as he was.

Ultimately, the richest source of information about the Harlem Globetrotters came from Globetrotters themselves, and I greatly appreciate the willingness of so many former Trotters to share their memories. I only wish there had been space to include more of their stories, and more of their names, in the book. I want to thank Rob Ashton, Geese Ausbie, Don Barnette, Nate Branch, Hallie Bryant, Alvin Clinkscales, Kara Coates, Mel Davis, J. C. Gibson, Chuck Holton, Bobby Hunter, John Isaacs, Bob Karstens, Dr. Johnny Kline, Elzie Lewis, Curly Neal, Charlie Primus, George Smith, Frank Stephens, Harry Sykes, Frank Washington, Jim "Nugie" Watkins, Bob Williams, and Vertes Zeigler. I had brief conversations with other former players, including Bob "Showboat" Hall, Mike Jackson, Max Jameson, Dedrick Reffigee, Larry "Gator" Rivers, Ernie Wagner, and Lynette Woodard. One of the nicest things that happened to me while working on the book was spending many hours on the phone with Marques Haynes, who provided invaluable details about the team. I am also extremely thankful for the input of current Globetrotter players and coaches, including "Sweet Lou" Dunbar, Paul "Showtime" Gaffney, Curley "Boo" Johnson, Clyde Sinclair, Wun Versher, Michael Wilson, and longtime coach Tex Harrison.

Finally, I want to thank two men who were absolutely essential to this project. Mannie Jackson, the owner and chairman of the Harlem Globetrotters, gave me unlimited access to the team's archives and went out of his way to encourage all former players to talk to me. I appreciate Mannie's trust that I would tell the story truthfully and fairly. And on a personal level, I have enjoyed the intellectual stimulation of talking to someone who has thought so deeply about the Trotters' legacy.

Without J Michael Kenyon, I could have written a book of some kind, but I never could have written *this* book. After nearly thirty years of research, he is the greatest storehouse of knowledge about the Trotters in the world. And in an incredibly generous act of professional courtesy, he shared all of that with me. He sent me hundreds of pages of material, answered dozens of late-night queries, fact-checked and critiqued the entire manuscript, and was undoubtedly the most valuable resource for getting this story right. J Michael, I can never express how much I value your help and, more important, your friendship.

Last, but not least, I want to thank my family—my wife, Tracie, and my daughters, Emmy and Eliza—for tolerating my living in a cave for the past six months, trying to finish the manuscript. I barely came out of my office, except for food and water. Girls, I owe you big-time, and am looking forward to returning to a normal life.

Index